pp. 26-28
on technology use in _____
useful conceptual critique explaining
why adopted ≠ant evidence.

Useful organization sociology paper
summary on institutional pressure:
pp. 31-32
& on how institutional forces constrain
everyday practice: p 71.

The Business of Birth

Malpractice and Maternity Care in the United States

Louise Marie Roth

NEW YORK UNIVERSITY PRESS
New York

NEW YORK UNIVERSITY PRESS
New York
www.nyupress.org
© 2021 by New York University

References to Internet websites (URLs) were accurate at the time of writing. Neither the author nor New York University Press is responsible for URLs that may have expired or changed since the manuscript was prepared.

Library of Congress Cataloging-in-Publication Data
Names: Roth, Louise Marie, 1970–   author.
Title: The business of birth : malpractice and maternity care in the United States / Louise Marie Roth.
Description: New York : New York University Press, [2021] |
Includes bibliographical references and index.
Identifiers: LCCN 2020015024 (print) | LCCN 2020015025 (ebook) | ISBN 9781479812257 (cloth ; alk. paper) | ISBN 9781479877089 (paperback ; alk. paper) | ISBN 9781479809097 (ebook) | ISBN 9781479826117 (ebook)
Subjects: LCSH: Maternal health services—United States. | Maternal health services—Economic aspects—United States. | Obstetricians—Malpractice—United States.
Classification: LCC RG960 .R66 2021 (print) | LCC RG960 (ebook) | DDC 362.1982—dc23
LC record available at https://lccn.loc.gov/2020015024
LC ebook record available at https://lccn.loc.gov/2020015025

New York University Press books are printed on acid-free paper, and their binding materials are chosen for strength and durability. We strive to use environmentally responsible suppliers and materials to the greatest extent possible in publishing our books.

Manufactured in the United States of America

10 9 8 7 6 5 4 3 2 1

Also available as an ebook

CONTENTS

To access the Technical Appendix, go to nyupress.org, navigate to the book page by searching for Roth or *The Business of Birth*, and click on the Links tab.

LIST OF ABBREVIATIONS

ACA Affordable Care Act ("Obamacare")
ACOG American College of Obstetricians and Gynecologists
AJOG *American Journal of Obstetrics and Gynecology*
CDMR cesarean delivery on maternal request
CMS Centers for Medicare & Medicaid Services
CNM certified nurse midwife
CPC crisis pregnancy center
CSR collateral source rule
D&C dilation and curettage
D&E dilation and evacuation
D&X dilation and extraction ("partial-birth abortion")
EBM evidence-based medicine
EC emergency contraception
EDD expected date of delivery ("due date")
EFM electronic fetal monitoring
FTCA Federal Tort Claims Act
HBAC homebirth after cesarean
HMS Harvard Malpractice Study
HR human resources
ICC intra-class correlation
IHS Indian Health Service
JSL joint and several liability
MFM maternal-fetal medicine
MLM multilevel model
NAPW National Advocates for Pregnant Women
NE non-economic
NICU neonatal intensive care unit
NPDB National Practitioner Data Bank
OB/GYN obstetrician/gynecologist
OR odds-ratio

PC   perinatal care
PL   proportionate liability
RHEA   Reproductive Health Equity Act
RJ   reproductive justice
SNAP   Supplemental Nutrition Assistance Programs
SOC   standard of care
TOLAC   trial of labor after cesarean
TRAP   targeted regulations of abortion providers
USDHHS   US Department of Health and Human Services
VBAC   vaginal birth after cesarean
WHO   World Health Organization

Introduction

The decision whether or not to bear a child is central to a
woman's life, to her wellbeing and dignity. It is a decision she
must make for herself. When Government controls that decision for her, she is being treated as less than a fully adult
human responsible for her own choices.
—Ruth Bader Ginsburg, from the Senate hearing on her
Supreme Court nomination

This book tells the story of how medical malpractice and reproductive
rights laws influence maternity care practices in the United States. It is
about how laws shape the decisions and experiences that are central to
a woman's life. Birth in the US is usually a high-tech medical event—it
happens in hospitals, where pregnant women are dressed in a hospital
gown, strapped to machines that flash and beep, and often isolated with
a partner who has no idea what to do while a nurse monitors their labor
from a nursing station down the hall. Maternity care providers artificially induce labor in over one fifth of births to women without a previous
cesarean. Almost one third of pregnancies end in major abdominal
surgery. Nearly 90% of women with a previous cesarean will have a
cesarean in all subsequent pregnancies, regardless of their preferences.
Most people believe that medical technology can only help them and
makes birth safer, but they are unaware that some technologies have
negative side effects. As one of my friends said when she was pregnant,
"I don't want them to use that technology, but I want it to be there just
in case." Few women really ask about the pros and cons, like the fact
that their maternity care providers are likely to use the technology if
it's there, just because it's there. Meanwhile, in spite of having advanced
technology, the US has the highest infant and maternal mortality rates
in the developed world. Obstetric technologies have not improved outcomes and they have propelled an epidemic of cesarean deliveries.[1]

Of course, over 90% of pregnant women in the United States give birth in a hospital with an obstetrician, and many contemporary women welcome technological advances in labor, especially epidural analgesia. But what happens to pregnant women during labor and childbirth is not purely a matter of choice—organizational and legal concerns constrain obstetricians and are the primary driver of obstetric practices. Women are often unaware of how legal and organizational considerations constrain their *maternity care providers*, which I define broadly to include birth attendants (obstetricians and specialists in maternal-fetal medicine, midwives, and some family physicians) and birth facilities (hospitals and birth centers). The *maternity care field*, an organizational field that includes obstetricians, midwives, hospitals, birth centers, legal risk managers, liability insurance companies, medical malpractice attorneys, and health insurers, institutionalizes these considerations. In this field, maternity care providers face cultural and legal pressures that influence their approaches to care during pregnancy, labor, and birth. These pressures emerge in a medical-legal environment that influences some of women's and families' most intimate, important, and life-changing moments.

One fact that many contemporary pregnant women do not understand is that the *hospital* (or birth center, or the decision to give birth at home) is much more important for their birth experience than the individual *doctor* (or midwife).[2] Women often choose an obstetrician based on recommendations in their social networks, without thinking about the characteristics of the hospital where that provider admits patients. If you tell pregnant women that the hospital where they plan to give birth has a high induction or cesarean rate, they invariably say that they love their doctor. Many women do not realize how little time their obstetrician will spend in the labor and delivery room when they are in labor, or how much the organization matters. Often pregnant women do not ask about the hospital's practices, and they rarely shop around for a provider or a hospital.

My own pregnancy and birth experiences with both midwives and high-risk obstetricians offered me a comparative perspective on birth settings. Coupled with my standpoint as a (white, cisgender, heterosexual) sociologist of gender, organizations, and law (and one who grew up in Canada with single-payer healthcare), I developed a growing interest in maternity care practices in the US. My first two pregnancies led me to a birth center–based midwifery practice, and my third to a high-risk obstetrician (and then back to the birth center). As I moved through these different settings, I observed the intrusion of organizational concerns into the type of care that I received and the variation in non-medical considerations across organizations.

It all started a couple of months after I got married. I was very good at using contraception and had never been pregnant before, so I didn't know how easy it would be to conceive. I had heard stories about other people's fertility challenges and I expected it to take a while to get pregnant, so I stopped taking birth control. A few weeks later, I was pregnant. Who knew that it could happen that fast? I felt tired, dizzy, and terribly nauseated. Then I had a miscarriage about three weeks after I found out that I was pregnant. It was the kind of run-of-the-mill miscarriage that happens in about 15% of pregnancies, even though few people realize how common they are and most people don't talk about them. My body completed the miscarriage without any medical interventions, like a D&C (dilation and curettage), but I had to go back and forth to my gynecologist's office for repeated blood tests. One of the nurses at my gynecologist's office was a certified nurse midwife (CNM) and one of the founders of the local freestanding birth center. Another nurse in the practice had also worked there, and my gynecologist herself had given birth there. Somehow I had stumbled on an extremely pro-midwifery gynecologist's office. I was interested in midwifery care and my best friend from high school, Janet, was very pro-midwife and had just had her first baby (by emergency cesarean after an attempted homebirth, but that's her story to tell). I had knowledgeable people to talk to about midwifery care and I knew that I wanted, at the very least, to look into the birth center as a potential option.

After the early miscarriage, I went back on birth control for about six months. I got pregnant again a couple of weeks after I stopped using it. The circumstances seemed ideal for an academic control freak like me: I got pregnant at the end of the summer, so I was not tired and sick during my most productive writing time. My due date was in the middle of May, right after the end of the semester. Aside from the fact that the first trimester felt like the worst hangover of my life without the party the night before, everything seemed to go according to plan. I decided to see the midwives at the birth center. I was unsure about having a completely unmedicated birth-center birth because an epidural definitely sounded good, but I knew that I could decide to give birth with the midwives at the hospital if I really wanted an epidural.

Everything went sideways in the second trimester. We went to the 20-week ultrasound and were super-excited to see the baby. We were not going to find out the sex/gender, but we thought for sure that it was a girl. Our nickname for her was "Nutmeg." As soon as the ultrasound technician started the probe, she said, "I have bad news for you." There was no heartbeat, and it looked like Nutmeg had died about three weeks earlier—which happened to coincide with a very intense virus that I had for several days. A high-risk obstetrician came in to talk to us about inducing labor to terminate the pregnancy. I was in shock. We went to the birth center, crying all the way, to consult with the midwives. They supported us and were there through the whole terrible induction in the hospital over the next two days. Nutmeg was, indeed, a girl, and that goofy nickname ended up on the death certificate. We had an autopsy and took a whole variety of tests, but they never found anything conclusive—no chromosomal or structural abnormalities.

After those two pregnancy losses, and one in the second trimester, I was "high-risk." I found the designation of risk in pregnancy fascinating. One can be "low-risk," but there is no such thing as "no-risk." Low-risk means that there is "no indicated risk," but risks can arise at any time and the concept of risk is ever-present. The obstetric profession redefines all uncertainty as risk, which means that it has a known, nonzero probability. Maternity care providers weigh different types of risk when they make decisions, and the philosophies of obstetricians and midwives differ in this respect.[3] The definition of normal pregnancy becomes increasingly narrow, as obstetricians have designated a growing number of pregnancies as "high-risk." The definition of some pregnancies as "high-risk" can also be strategic: the doctors who reviewed our case said that defining me as "high-risk" would make me eligible for extra tests and services through my health insurance. I was not enthusiastic about the "high-risk" label, but I understood that it might give me access to resources. Despite my profound grief, the sociologist in me took notice.

Less than two months later, I got pregnant again, so it turned out that it was a really good thing that I was good at using contraception before.

This time I was less sick but much more terrified. With my "high-risk" status, I sought out a "high-risk" physician: a specialist in maternal-fetal medicine (MFM). Her office was in a hospital, and was much less welcoming than the birth center. Artificial fluorescent light filled the sparsely decorated, sterile white waiting room with its standard medical office chairs. Sometimes the waits to see her were long because she was an attending physician and had to be available if something interesting was happening in the Labor and Delivery department. The birth center, on the other hand, had lots of natural light and comfortable couches in warm colors, with shelves full of interesting books that you could sign out. The midwives would take their time to explain things and were often very intuitive. For example, a midwife will feel where the uterus is and might notice that you have a lot of pressure on your bladder, and then ask about how you are managing with needing to use the bathroom all the time. An obstetrician will just ask if anything else is bothering you. But the MFM doctor was very understanding that we had "been through the wringer," and she was willing to give us extra office visits and a sonogram at almost every visit to reassure us that the baby was still alive. We liked her and thought that she was an excellent doctor.

In the meantime, I had kept in touch with one of the midwives from the birth center. Over lunch one day, she told me that MFM specialists are "very quick to section because their malpractice insurance is so high." This statement again piqued my sociological imagination—as well as my sense that I didn't want to have unnecessary surgery to alleviate a provider's liability fears. Even though the MFM specialist that I was seeing, and the hospital where she worked, did not have high cesarean rates, I wondered how much legal and organizational considerations affected what happens to women when they give birth, and how much they prevailed over what is best for the mother and baby.

Once I was in the second trimester and we had all survived the 20-week ultrasound, I asked the MFM specialist about what it would be like to give birth in the hospital. Emotionally, the pregnancy was still hard, but I could feel the baby moving so I didn't need as much external reassurance that he was still alive. She said that they would want me on an electronic fetal monitor the whole time. I knew enough about the medicalization of childbirth at that point to know that I didn't want to be strapped to a monitor and stuck lying in bed during labor. I told the doctor that I didn't love that idea and that the nurses would probably think that I was "a pain in the ass." I wanted to go back to the birth center. She laughed, but she acknowledged that the midwives at the birth center were good providers, and gave me her blessing. I went back to the birth center for the third trimester for a strikingly different organizational culture and philosophy of maternity care.

For my first live birth, I went into spontaneous labor two days before my expected date of delivery (EDD, more commonly called the "due date"). That took me a bit by surprise, since my mother's and grandmother's babies were all late. After I called the midwife, I managed a few contractions at home. Once we figured that it was the real thing, we called the doula that we had hired and we headed to the birth center.[4] I was already dilated 6 cm when we got there, so if I wanted an epidural I had to get back in the car and go the hospital. The drive over had been so unpleasant in the throes of labor that I decided that I would just try to do without it. I labored in a large Jacuzzi bathtub, and my doula massaged my back and offered me moral support the whole time. My partner was very thankful for the doula because he did not know what to do and hated seeing me in pain. The midwife used a handheld Doppler ultrasound to check the fetal heart rate every 10 to 15 minutes, and could do that even when I was in the tub. Not long after my water broke, I reached full dilation and was ready to push. I remember thinking, "This hurts more than anything that I have ever felt, and the only way for it to stop is to get this baby out!" I got out of the bathtub and sat on a birthing stool with my partner behind me, and I did a 200-pound squat that lifted him off the floor as I pushed the baby out. After two and half hours at the birth center, and a total of about five hours of labor, Troy was born.

Once he was born, I forgot all of the pain that I had experienced just minutes before (although no one tells you about the shaking that your body does after you give birth, and that freaked me out). The midwife put Troy on my chest and I fell immediately in love with my perfect little son. The birth was not without complications—my blood pressure was too high so we ended up going to the hospital—but I felt totally supported the whole time. (When we ended up in the hospital, I complained about needing to have an IV, and my partner remarked that I had just pushed a whole human being out of my body and now I was complaining about the IV.) Unlike so many women that I know, I had a positive birth experience. Positive enough to have three more unmedicated births, including a water birth with Axel at the birth center, another birth-center birth with Dash, and a hospital birth with the midwives with Cameron (where I wanted an epidural but my labor was too fast to get one).

When Troy was born, I was just beginning my intellectual journal into the maternity care field. My history of pregnancy loss, my experience seeing a high-risk obstetric specialist, and my births at the birth center with midwives had attracted my interest in the sociological and socio-legal aspects of the American maternity care field. The difference between the high-risk obstetric setting and the out-of-hospital birth-center setting, and between obstetricians and midwives, led me to think about the relationships between law, culture, and medicine in maternity care. Research has shown that midwifery-based care like I received at the birth center is optimal for managing most pregnancies, and that midwives are less likely to be sued than obstetricians, and yet midwives are not untouched by medical-legal concerns. Of course, medical-legal and organizational efficiency issues are larger influences in obstetric settings, where hospitals must develop protocols to coordinate multiple physicians, nurses, and other staff. Under these conditions, what is the effect of the legal environment on obstetric practices that are, and are not, common? How do professional norms interact with the legal environment to encourage certain obstetric practices and discourage others? Obstetricians and public health experts often point to medical malpractice risk as an important driver of practices like high cesarean rates, but how are tort laws that govern medical malpractice related to maternity care practices? How and why might this relationship change over time?

At a broad level, these are questions about how the legal environment contributes to a well-known outcome: the medicalization of childbirth. They are also questions with implications for women's ability to make reproductive choices on behalf of both themselves and their fetuses—which is, at the moment that I write this, very much under siege. In fact, reproductive rights are such a moving target at this time that my facts would be out of date immediately if I tried to enumerate current state-level laws. And while most debates about reproductive rights laws focus on abortion and contraception, they are also important for women's right to choose where, how, and with whom to give birth.

Reproductive Regimes

I began to conceptualize the legal environment that influences maternity care practices as *reproductive regimes*. A *regime* is an established system that shapes the way that things are done, especially when imposed by government or law. Scholars have analyzed gender regimes, policy regimes, jurisprudential regimes, factory regimes, crime regimes, knowledge regimes and, most famously, welfare regimes.[5] I define a *reproductive regime* as the set of beliefs, customs, laws and institutions that establishes the rights and responsibilities of fetuses, mothers, and healthcare providers in pregnancy and birth. A reproductive regime establishes norms and expectations about the role of government, the obligations of birth attendants, and the civil rights of women. Tort laws and reproductive health laws jointly influence a state's overall reproductive regime.

This book aims to address at least two interrelated sets of questions about reproductive regimes. First, how does the malpractice environment influence birth in the US? I began this research wanting to know how *tort regimes* (medical malpractice laws and lawsuits) influenced maternity care in the United States. Many healthcare industry insiders view the desire to defend against malpractice liability as a primary cause of continuous electronic fetal monitoring (EFM), unnecessarily high cesarean rates, and lack of access to vaginal birth after cesarean (VBAC). But I argue that the relationship between malpractice liability and these practices is not as simple as it seems: tort laws that regulate medical malpractice are intertwined with professional norms in obstetrics, so they influence each other in a reciprocal or even recursive fashion. More specifically, the obstetric profession both understands *and defines* the kinds of practices that increase or decrease the risks of litigation. Medical malpractice attorneys adopt the profession's definition of the situation because they must interpret the law within the medical standard of care (SOC). This represents a prime example of what Edelman calls "the endogeneity of law"—a point to which I will return in chapters 2 through 6.[6]

Many unintended consequences of tort laws are enshrined in the SOC that both clinicians and attorneys use as a guideline for non-negligent care. What determines the SOC is not scientific evidence, but rather organizational rituals and habits within a culture of medicine that emphasizes technological solutions to problems. Often providers frame these "problems" as medico-legal, in the sense that hospitals as organizations and the medical profession seek to defend against claims that their practices are harmful or negligent. In obstetrics, this emphasis combines with difficulties accurately estimating the likelihood of low-probability risks and encourages active intervention into labor and birth even when scientific evidence recommends against it. As a result, the risk of malpractice liability develops an oversized role that often contradicts the spirit of tort law, which aims to deter practices that are against the best interest of the patient. At the same time, tort laws are necessary to discourage risk-taking among providers. All else being equal, I find that pregnant women are more likely to receive evidence-based maternity care in *patient-friendly tort regimes* that hold providers accountable than in *provider-friendly tort regimes* that reduce their liability risk.

A second set of questions that I address in this book focuses on the connections between maternity care practices and reproductive health laws. As I learned more about reproductive justice (RJ) theory, my focus expanded beyond medical malpractice to include reproductive health laws and the potential effects of *reproductive health regimes* for women when they give birth. Reproductive health regimes consist of laws that govern contraception, abortion, and midwifery in ways that emphasize fetal rights or support women's autonomy. RJ theory argues that pregnant women's rights to informed consent and bodily integrity, and their ability to choose where and how to give birth, connect to regulations governing other aspects of reproduction like abortion laws. RJ theory also emphasizes the particular vulnerability of women of color and low-income women to reproductive injustice when laws restrict reproductive rights and access to care. Scholars have used RJ theory to analyze the unequal impact of reproductive health laws and policies on marginalized women, and to analyze *extreme cases* like court-ordered cesareans. But up to this point, no one has tested the predictions of RJ theory for maternity care practices in *typical cases*. Using a random sample of births, this book analyzes the relationships between laws regulating reproductive autonomy and practices like EFM, VBAC, and out-of-hospital or midwife-attended births. All else being equal, I find that pregnant women have more choices in childbirth when they give birth in states that protect abortion choice and prioritize women's rights over fetal life. More specifically, *fetus-centered reproductive health regimes* protect fetuses as separate from pregnant women, with negative effects on women's autonomy to make decisions about their own births. *Woman-centered reproductive health regimes*, on the other hand, protect women's rights to bodily integrity and informed consent in birth as well as their right to make decisions about when they should terminate a pregnancy.

Reproductive health regimes differentially affect pregnant women due to inequalities of race, class, and gender, and *not* because affluent women are choosing scheduled inductions and cesareans without labor. In fact, women of all races and classes may embrace medicalization and technologically intensive birth practices, but non-Hispanic white women of middle- or upper-middle-class status are more likely to convince healthcare providers to honor their preferences—and they are *less likely* to have cesareans without medical indications and *more likely* to have VBAC. Restrictions on contraception and abortion access also have their strongest effects on low-income women. Extreme cases involving violations of pregnant women's civil rights illustrate that poor women, especially poor women of color, are the most likely to face prosecution for feticide or substance use while pregnant. Women of color also have much higher maternal and infant mortality rates than non-Hispanic white women—regardless of social class—and are more likely to have cesarean deliveries in low-risk pregnancies. *The Business of Birth* considers the special vulnerability of women of color and low-income women for a variety of obstetric practices that are not evidence based.

The Study

To understand how the legal environment affects maternity care, I used data from multiple sources. I combined vital statistics data on over 8 million births from 1995 to 2015 (a 10% random sample of all births) with publicly available legal data on tort laws and reproductive health laws that were in effect, passed, or were repealed during this period. I used these data to analyze the effects of the legal environment on the odds of obstetric practices (early-term induction, electronic fetal monitoring, cesarean delivery, VBAC, homebirth), especially in pregnancies without medical complications. Throughout this book, I use quantitative data on births over time to demonstrate the impact of the legal environment and changes in the professional SOC on actual obstetric practices. Of course, analyses of large-scale birth data can only show broad patterns and are quite distant from the actions of individual maternity care providers. For this reason, I also conducted 26 in-depth interviews with key informants in the maternity care field: obstetricians, certified nurse midwives (CNMs), hospital administrators, and medical negligence attorneys. I use these data to understand how workers involved in the maternity care field understand medicine, law, and the relationship between them and to reveal different standpoints within the field. The interviews offer insights into how birth professionals describe their relationships to the law and how legal professionals understand obstetric medicine. The interview data also provide texture to the findings and they shed light on some mechanisms through which key players develop their legal and medical interpretations of medical malpractice liability and, to a lesser extent, reproductive rights. I detail the methods, data, and quantitative results in appendices A through C and an online technical appendix.

The Organization of the Book

In the first part of the book, I explore the cultural and legal environments that surround the maternity care field in the United States. Chapter 1 situates birth as an important rite of passage in a mother's and family's life and describes changes in hospital birth since the late 20th century. The medicalization of childbirth is the dominant institutionalized *schema* that organizes beliefs in American maternity care. The *medicalization schema* defines pregnancy and birth as pathological medical conditions that require technological intervention. Three principles guide the medicalization schema: pathologization, scienciness, and technology fetishism. In chapter 2, I discuss the theory of legal endogeneity and RJ theory, and I elaborate the relationship between law and medicine. I describe tort laws and arguments for and against tort reform and, based on relative liability risk, I define patient- and provider-friendly tort regimes. I also analyze the effects of provider-friendly tort laws on the rate of obstetric malpractice suits per 100,000 births, opening up a new puzzle: accounting for changes over time, laws that reduce providers' liability risk are associated with a *higher* rate of obstetric malpractice lawsuits. This chapter also defines fetus-centered reproductive health regimes as those that prioritize fetal life over women's rights by restricting access to abortion, criminalizing pregnancy among substance-addicted women, and prohibiting non-nurse midwifery. In contrast, woman-centered reproductive health regimes affirm the right to terminate a pregnancy and protect women's health clinics.

The next part of the book focuses primarily on the effects of tort laws and malpractice liability risk. In chapter 3, I use interviews with key informants to tease out some of the tensions and contradictions between law, culture, and medicine. I describe the culture of liability fear among maternity care providers, and I juxtapose their fear with medical injury attorneys' understanding of the risk of malpractice lawsuits. According to malpractice lawyers, medical malpractice suits have declined over time because of the cost of hiring experts, and *not* because defensive practices have reduced errors or negative outcomes due to negligence. Also, since the medical SOC defines what constitutes negligence, the obstetric profession holds the power to define what practices count as negligent, even though many obstetricians view malpractice liability as external to themselves and outside of their control. In chapter 4, I focus on whether tort laws have deterrence effects on risky maternity care practices like elective early-term deliveries. I find that maternity care providers know that inductions and scheduled repeat cesareans before 39 weeks' gestation violate the SOC and pose risks of late prematurity. The birth data illustrate that the odds of taking these risks are higher when providers face less liability risk, which means that tort liability deters risky medical practice—as it intends to do.

Chapter 5 analyzes the effects of tort regimes and reproductive health regimes on EFM in low-risk births between 1995 and 2003.[7] EFM provides an example of technology fetishism because hospitals adopted this technology before any research scientifically tested it—and they continue to use it even though scientific research has not supported it as effective. Most maternity care providers and medical negligence attorneys view EFM as an important tool for reducing liability risk, but I find that the odds of reporting EFM in low-risk births are higher when tort liability is *lower*. This contradicts what providers and attorneys believe, and suggests that something else actually motivates EFM use. I also find that the odds of EFM use are *higher* when reproductive health laws are more fetus-centered. I argue that EFM primarily serves important non-legal purposes like organizational efficiency, and women are more able to opt out of this non-evidence-based practice in patient-friendly tort regimes and/or woman-centered reproductive health regimes.

Chapters 6 and 7 address the dramatic rise in cesarean deliveries from 1995 to 2015. In chapter 6, I analyze the effects of tort laws on primary cesareans in low-risk births and repeat cesareans in VBAC-eligible births. While many obstetricians claim that cesareans are a legally defensive response to high liability risk, I find that tort reforms that reduce providers' liability risk have very little impact on the odds of a primary or repeat cesarean without medical indications. Professional guidelines, on the other hand, exert strong normative pressure on obstetricians and dramatically change the odds of both primary and repeat cesareans in pregnancies without medical complications over time. In chapter 7, I analyze the effects of reproductive health regimes on the odds of VBAC in women with a previous cesarean but no other pregnancy-related risks. While there are some contradictory effects of reproductive health laws, the overall trend is toward higher odds of VBAC in woman-centered reproductive health regimes and lower odds in fetus-centered reproductive health regimes, as RJ theory would predict. Finally, chapter 8 concludes with implications for theories of RJ and medical malpractice, reflects on the state of American maternity care, and considers possible policy implications of the findings.

1

Birth Matters

The Importance of Birth and the Logic of American Maternity Care

Birth is not only about making babies. Birth is about making mothers—strong, competent, capable mothers who trust themselves and know their inner strength.
—Barbara Katz Rothman

One way or another, every human being is the result of procreation—it takes an egg, a sperm, and a uterus to make a baby. Giving birth is a physiological process that billions of women have shared throughout human history, and that most women experience at some point in their lives.[1] Pregnancy and birth are life-changing experiences and represent an important rite of passage in a mother's and family's life. Women remember their births for their whole lives, and can remember if their care providers supported them and treated them with respect and compassion during labor and birth, or if they experienced abuse or trauma.[2] While giving birth feels profoundly *personal*, the ways that women experience labor and birth are also social and cultural.[3] On a social level, women's social status, gender inequality, and family structure all influence pregnancy and birth. For all of these reasons, birth matters.

Another meaning of "birth matters" is in terms of matters of birth. Since the 1970s, anthropologists and sociologists have uncovered striking differences in *birth systems* across cultures, highlighting the social and cultural aspects of pregnancy, birth, and the postpartum period. Birth systems are the socially patterned ways that different cultures organize and ritualize childbirth. They establish who should attend labor and birth, how they should treat pregnant and laboring women and new mothers, where women should give birth, what rituals surround birth, and how much birth attendants should intervene. Cross-cultural studies have illustrated that cultural rituals and routines are part of all birth systems, including indigenous systems, midwife-attended birth systems in developed countries like Sweden and the Netherlands, and the medical model that dominates obstetrician-attended hospital birth.[4] Feminist scholars have also critically examined high-tech obstetrician-dominated birth systems in Europe and North America. Their analyses of the *medical model* of birth have documented historical changes in childbirth through history, from a woman-centered process attended by midwives into a medical event managed by physicians.[5]

The Medical and Midwifery Models of Birth: A Brief History

I am an organizational sociologist, so my experience with nurse midwives at a freestanding birth center and with a high-risk obstetrician at a tertiary hospital suggested to me that there was an important organizational story to tell about American maternity care as an *institution* that is larger than the conscious intentions of individual physicians and hospitals. I also knew *enough* about medicalization to understand that the philosophy guiding midwifery care was very different from the one guiding obstetrics. I felt confident that I would only have a cesarean delivery under the care of the midwives if it were truly necessary, but I could have an unnecessary one in a hospital with an obstetrician. In her groundbreaking book, Barbara Katz Rothman defined the *medical model* of childbirth and its contrast with the *midwifery model*.[6] The medical model dominates childbirth in countries where obstetricians attend most births, like the contemporary United States.[7]

Midwives have assisted women giving birth throughout human history, while physicians' involvement in childbirth is more recent.[8] The midwifery model is based on holistic approaches and treats birth as a social event and a normal part of a woman's life.[9] In the midwifery model, giving birth is the work of the woman and her family. Midwives tend to wait for labor and birth to unfold and to intervene only when evidence suggests that it is appropriate or necessary. The obstetric profession calls this approach *expectant management*. The midwifery model emphasizes emotional support and awareness of the spiritual significance of birth for most women. Birth is a holistic, life-transforming process that takes place in the home or other familiar surroundings, and there is shared decision-making between the birthing woman and her caregivers. In the midwifery model, women in labor can walk, move, bathe, and eat and drink during labor—often giving birth in a squatting position or on all fours. Scientific evidence supports a low-intervention midwifery model of care as optimal for pregnant women without obstetric complications, and many contemporary midwives proudly say that they practice *evidence-based medicine.*[10]

On the other hand, in the medical model of childbirth, physicians manage labor and childbirth in hospitals, where they attempt to fit all labors into a standard timetable and to control the birth process using technology.[11] The medical profession calls this approach *active management.* In the medical model, doctors "deliver" babies rather than women giving birth. When physicians and hospitals control the birthing process, women in labor are typically immobilized in a hospital bed, attached to machines, and required to give birth while lying on their backs in order to give the physician easier access to the baby. Birth often involves surgical interventions like episiotomy and cesarean delivery.[12] The medical model is more technology- and medication-intensive than the midwifery model, but it is not always evidence based.[13] Many normal labors do not fit within standard timetables, and women find it easier to give birth in positions where their pelvis can open and gravity can assist them (in other words, not on their backs).

The medical model of childbirth began to take over European and North American birth systems in the 18th century, as male physicians competed with midwives for authority over pregnancy and birth. When doctors first started to attend women during labor and birth, their practices were not associated with better outcomes for mothers or babies than midwifery care. In the 17th and 18th centuries, male physicians were only involved in difficult deliveries and they used destructive instruments to remove obstructed fetuses—which led to a very high incidence of maternal death. Until the 1930s, midwives had much better outcomes than physicians, but physicians aimed to develop credibility as a profession and, in the long run, they succeeded.[14]

Physicians *professionalized* by limiting entrance into the medical profession: they engaged in *professional closure* strategies to set boundaries around medicine's professional jurisdiction and to establish the right to regulate themselves with limited legal interference.[15] Professional closure strategies include the development of medical school curricula and accreditation standards, entrance examinations, and licensing standards within the profession. Until the late 20th century, professional closure strategies ensured that white, affluent men dominated the medical profession. With the establishment of medicine as an exclusive profession, physicians gained status and distinguished themselves as the most prestigious attendants for childbirth. They also stifled competition from midwives by excluding them from training in technologies like forceps, and discrediting them as unenlightened, unscientific, and guided by superstition.[16]

The medical profession's goal was to raise the prestige of physician-attended birth, starting with affluent women, by claiming to offer a more modern and "safer" birth. At the same time, the medical takeover of the maternity care business was complete before the development of asepsis, anesthesia, surgical techniques, or antibiotics. Maternal and infant mortality both increased when birth first moved from the home to the hospital. In the 19th century, many physicians spread infection because they used unsterilized instruments (like forceps) and they often went from attending the dying and performing autopsies to attending women in labor without washing their hands. This led to many maternal deaths from puerperal fever (fever caused by uterine infection after giving birth).[17] Important innovations in the late 19th century lowered maternal and infant mortality in the 20th: the germ theory of disease, the discovery of penicillin, the development of vaccines, and improvements in public health and sanitation. The medical profession gladly took credit for these improvements.

As physicians professionalized and developed a strong power base, they successfully defined birth as a medical event and pregnant and laboring women as patients. Once they had attained dominance in the maternity care field, the vast majority of births occurred in hospitals. By the 20th century, the medical takeover of the birth system in the United States was complete: physicians attended births for the majority of women, including the poor and immigrants, whether they were normal or complicated. The institutionalization of the medical model changed the focus of labor and birth from the pregnant woman and her family to the medical staff. Obstetric medicine's scripts, rules, classifications, and rituals for childbirth came to be taken for granted as the right way to do things. In the language of organizational theory, the medical model of childbirth was *institutionalized*: it became a blueprint for what should happen during labor and birth, where and how it should happen, and who should be there.[18]

Institutionalization of the medical model gave obstetricians a monopoly on *authoritative knowledge* about childbirth.[19] Authoritative knowledge is the most culturally legitimate knowledge system within a field. According to Brigitte Jordan:

> For any particular domain several knowledge systems exist, some of which, by consensus, come to carry more weight than others, either because they explain the state of the world better for the purposes at hand (efficacy) or because they are associated with a stronger power base (structural superiority), and usually both.[20]

Obstetricians have authoritative knowledge over pregnancy and birth in most developed countries, where medical authority and control over pregnancy, labor, and birth grew stronger throughout the 20th century.[21]

Since childbirth is fully medicalized in American society, it requires medical evaluation, diagnosis, prevention, and, above all, treatment.[22] This leads obstetricians and hospitals to try to control the birthing process with medical procedures and protocols. Under active management, obstetricians require that every labor conform to statistical averages for dilation and progression (labor curves, or the "Friedman curve"). They place time limits on the length of each stage of labor and actively interfere when labors do not follow their timetable, leading to an "assembly line" model of birth. Each effort to control the physiological process of labor also leads successively to other procedures in a *cascade of interventions*. To fit most labors into the labor curve, obstetricians routinely use synthetic oxytocin (Pitocin) to artificially stimulate and speed up labor, even though Pitocin is a high-risk medication that can cause fetal distress. Artificial induction and stimulation of labor, continuous electronic fetal monitoring, the requirement that women give birth while lying on their backs, the artificial rupture of membranes (breaking the water), episiotomies, assisted vaginal deliveries with forceps and vacuum, and cesarean sections are all part of a well-known cascade of interventions. Most of these interventions into labor increase the likelihood of a cesarean delivery, contributing to an epidemic of cesareans.[23] Susan Dixon,[24] a CNM who attended births at both a freestanding birth center and a hospital, said,

> It's such a classic thing, to watch that whole cascade. It seems like from the minute an epidural is chosen, you have to be willing to accept that labor is probably going to slow down, that they may need the help of vacuum or forceps, or they may not ever get completely dilated . . . I think that overall it leads to an increased C-section rate.

The cascade of interventions in the medical model contrasts with expectant management in the midwifery model, which involves watching, waiting, and intervening only when necessary—and which scientific evidence supports as a "best practice" for optimal maternity care.[25] But the institutionalization of the medical model of childbirth has led to the persistence of many arbitrary, ritualistic, and unscientific maternity care practices.[26]

The Medicalization of Childbirth

The medical model of birth gained cultural authority when a majority of people viewed childbirth as a *medical* event. This occurred after the medicalization of normal bodily processes like pregnancy and childbirth: the medical profession redefined them in medical terms, using medical language.[27] As physicians expanded their jurisdiction to include procreative events that were previously the domain of women, they successfully defined every birth as a potentially pathological event. The remaining midwives in most developed countries had to follow medicine's professionalization model and develop credentialing guidelines and licensure requirements in order to survive.[28]

The medicalization of childbirth is complete in countries like the United States: most people view birth as a potentially dangerous medical event that requires hospitalization and medical care.[29] Medicalization is the dominant schema that organizes beliefs about pregnancy and birth for both physicians and lay people in the United States. In cognitive psychology, a *schema* is a deep, largely unconscious, conceptual framework that runs in the background of our minds to help us to understand the world around us. Cognitive schemas affect the kinds of information that people notice or ignore, leading them to *automatically* organize and remember information that is schema-consistent and to forget what is schema-inconsistent.[30] In institutional fields like the maternity care field, repeated and routine exposure to a schema like the medicalization schema gives it a habitual, taken-for-granted quality, leading individuals to view its principles as objective facts.[31] The medicalization schema is the dominant framework for understanding pregnancy and birth under the medical model—both physicians and laypeople in countries where most births occur in hospitals have automatic and unconscious understandings of birth as a medical issue with a high potential for problems. The medicalization schema views bodily processes as "treatable" with medical interventions and limits people's ability to view them in non-medical terms.[32]

Physicians internalize the medicalization schema during their medical training, where it is part of the "hidden curriculum" that teaches students informal lessons about how to do medical work, what kind of person they are when they do it, and the place of physicians in the division of medical labor.[33] Professional associations and hospital protocols reinforce the medicalization schema, which permeates the everyday behavior and routines of physicians and hospitals.[34] The medicalization schema provides the dominant cultural *strategy of action* in medicine.[35] In her classic article, Ann Swidler argued that culture influences action by "shaping a repertoire or 'tool kit' of habits, skills and styles from which people construct 'strategies of action.'"[36] For obstetricians, the primary tools in the toolkit are swift and successive interventions into labor and birth using advanced technologies. I argue that the medicalization schema is a toolkit that contains three key components: pathologization, scienciness, and technology fetishism.

Pathologization

Pathologization is the treatment of a health or behavioral condition as medically or psychologically abnormal. When physicians took over the maternity care field, they redefined women's reproductive systems as pathological and women as victims of their hormones and reproductive functions.[37] They also convinced the public that pregnancy and birth were dangerous. The first issue of the *American Journal of Obstetrics and Gynecology* (*AJOG*) described childbirth explicitly as "a pathologic process" from which "only a small minority of women escape damage."[38] Pathologization is also obvious when one hears obstetric terms like "incompetent cervix," as though body parts can have (or lack) skills. The medicalization schema transforms the normal occurrence of pregnancy and childbirth into an illness, with a narrow range for what is acceptable and normal. In this schema, everything outside that range requires medical treatment, which means that most pregnancies entail medical monitoring, management, and treatment. The medicalization schema reframes childbirth as a medical condition that calls for hospitalization and treatment with pain medications, intravenous drugs and fluids, high-tech monitoring, and frequently surgery. This reframing is essential for the dominance of the medical model, since active management of labor is only possible when physicians and women alike believe that birthing women are patients who need medical treatment in a hospital setting.

Scienciness

One might assume that intervening into labor is necessary to make birth safer, and that scientific evidence is behind typical obstetric practices, but many medical practices are pseudoscientific—claims that support them seem plausible, but have faulty or nonexistent evidence. The well-known cascade of interventions into labor is based on the *appearance* of being scientific, or "scienciness." *Scienciness* refers to anything that *seems* scientific but is not actually based on science, and is similar to the concept of "truthiness" that Stephen Colbert popularized in 2005: the quality of seeming or being felt to be true, even if not necessarily true.[39]

Why is scienciness important for maintaining the medicalization schema in the maternity care field? The medical model of childbirth needs to maintain an appearance of being scientific in order to persuade the public that physician-attended hospital birth is the safest way to give birth. Scienciness gives the illusion of scientific credibility and validity, and provides authority to unsubstantiated ideas. It underpins much of modern obstetric medicine, because it provides the *appearance* of rationality behind ritualistic habits and practices in the least evidence-based specialization in medicine.[40] Theoretically, medical technology and procedures are subject to rigorous scientific testing and the medical profession adopts them after medical research demonstrates their effectiveness. Practically, the obstetric profession has adopted many untested technologies and practices without scientific support.

This has occurred partly because pregnant women are a protected group of human subjects when it comes to medical research. That makes it difficult to do research that follows the *gold standard* for medical science: the double-blind, randomized control trial. Dr. Alec Yoder, a medical director for a health insurer, said,

> There are a lot of things we do in maternity care that don't have evidence because you can't do double-blind, randomized control studies on pregnant women. But we do it because we think it might be beneficial. So a lot of the testing we do prior to a woman having a baby, a lot of the testing that we cover, is basically done to try to ensure that there's not something wrong. But it isn't based in fact that it needs to be done.

As Dr. Yoder notes, an enormous amount of obstetric testing is based on theories and cultural beliefs rather than on science. These cultural beliefs encourage active, technological management of birth and the well-known cascade of interventions that is the hallmark of the medicalization schema.

Many routine obstetric practices are, at best, pseudoscientific: they are based on theories, beliefs, and rituals that developed in the absence of appropriate scientific testing, but the fact that they seem scientific gives them an aura of legitimacy. Pseudoscientific obstetric practices include routine pubic shaving, enemas, and episiotomies.[41] Until at least the 1980s, most hospitals subjected pregnant women to pubic shaving and enemas upon admission, often when they were in active labor. The theory behind shaving women's pubic hair was that it would reduce the likelihood of infection, but there was no research to support this theory.[42] It just sounded logical enough to have the appearance of being scientific. The lack of actual scientific evidence behind this practice led anthropologist Robbie Davis-Floyd to argue that pubic shaving primarily served ritual purposes: it marked the laboring woman as belonging to the hospital, separated the upper and lower parts of her body, and de-sexualized her genitals by returning them to a childhood state.[43] Scientific evidence later suggested that pubic shaving made infection *more likely* by abrading the skin and leaving small cuts that can help bacteria to multiply. Eventually, most hospitals abandoned the practice. (Now, of course, many women remove their pubic hair themselves, but that's a different story.)

Enemas were also typically part of the hospital prep for childbirth in the 20th century, with the goal of making it less likely that the woman would have a bowel movement during labor. The rationale was that this would reduce the risk of infection for the newborn. Once again, the argument in favor of enemas was based on pseudoscience. Some healthcare providers claimed that enemas shortened labor, but the real reason for them was that hospital staff disliked cleaning up fecal matter. This, of course, should surprise no one (especially if one has seen how hard hospitals work to avoid dealing with a little bit of vomit, which is something that I still find amazing for an institution that is supposed to deal with sick people). Davis-Floyd argued that the most important purpose of enemas is ritual cleansing for birth as a rite of passage: they signify the dirtiness and impurity of the woman's body and the ability of the hospital to make her clean.[44] By the 1980s, research found that enemas neither reduced the likelihood that women will have bowel movements during labor nor shortened labor. The risk of newborn infection also turned out to be very low, and enemas did not improve it.[45] Since enemas caused many women considerable pain and discomfort and research discredited the theory behind them, most hospitals have stopped subjecting women to them during labor.

Other sciency practices within the medical model have also gradually fallen out of use. In the mid- to late 20th century, most American hospitals separated labor and delivery into different rooms, and forced women onto a gurney to move to the "delivery room" during the most difficult and painful stage of labor—transition from the first stage of cervical dilation to the second stage of pushing. If the staff's timing was off or the second stage of labor was fast, women would give birth in the hallway. There was no scientific or safety-related basis for this practice. By the end of the 20th century, most hospitals had abandoned it in one of several changes that aimed to humanize birth in response to the natural childbirth movement. Most contemporary American women labor and give birth in the same room.

Other obsolete practices have gradually become less common over time. For much of the 20th century, obstetricians routinely cut an episiotomy during the "pushing" phase of labor: a surgical incision in the muscular area between the vagina and the anus (the perineum) to enlarge the vaginal opening and speed up the birth. The medical profession believed that a straight "clean" incision from medical scissors would heal more easily than a spontaneous tear and might prevent complications like incontinence. Once again, it sounded like a plausible theory and many women believed it, until someone did some actual research and found out that the opposite was true: spontaneous tears heal as well as or better than episiotomies and cause fewer complications and infections.[46] In fact, episiotomies not only fail to improve healing compared to natural tears, they actually hinder healing by causing more perineal pain, requiring a longer recovery period, and leading to more third- or fourth-degree lacerations. The rationale for routine episiotomy turned out to be a perfect example of scienciness. While episiotomy can help in cases where the baby is larger than expected or needs to be born quickly, the routine episiotomies of mid-20th-century obstetrics weakened millions of women's pelvic floor muscles and contributed to the very problems of incontinence that they were supposed to prevent. By 2012, 12% of vaginal births in the United States involved an episiotomy, which is a significant decrease from 31% in 1997 or 56% in 1979.

The obstetric profession adopted and routinized all of these practices without careful clinical research or peer review, based on theories about their benefits that later turned out to be false. The cultural rituals and routines of medicalized childbirth reinforce their scienciness: the whole basis for active management of labor is that it *seems* to be scientific. Rather than being based on science, these standard obstetric procedures were rituals that lacked a scientific basis and did more harm than good.[47] In fact, the contemporary medical management of labor and birth is not based on evidence, which has shown that typical obstetric practices like continuous EFM, induction with misoprostol,[48] the overuse of Pitocin[49] to induce and augment labor, and the use of a supine position for labor and birth are all potentially harmful. Along with the obsolete practices of pubic shaving, enemas, and episiotomy, these practices became routine because they supported the medicalization schema—which depends on the appearance of scienciness rather than actual scientific evidence.

When it comes to medicine, some medical scholars have criticized alternative or integrative medicine as "sciency," but few have scrutinized the scienciness of mainstream medical practices. In reality, physicians and hospitals often adopt medical technologies and use them routinely without scientific support because of their scienciness: physicians, patients, and administrators tend to view advanced technology in itself as signal of quality, sophistication, and state-of-the-art care.[50] Since most laypeople do not understand science and technology or are unsure about them, their scienciness is often their primary source of their legitimacy. Of course, some areas of medicine have had genuine scientific breakthroughs, like the use of angiogram and laparoscopic techniques to conduct surgeries, but obstetrics is a medical specialization that has often adopted technologies and procedures that have no scientific support.

Technology Fetishism

One important outgrowth of medicalization's reliance on scienciness is *technology fetishism*.[51] In the medicalization schema, advanced medical technology symbolizes quality and the scientific approach, and thus is inherently beneficial and better than nature. The medicalization schema encourages hospitals to adopt medical technologies before the medical community understands their risks, effectiveness, and costs. Frequently, hospitals and the obstetric profession lack evidence that new technologies are effective, or even safe, before they adopt them for routine use and integrate them into hospital protocols. For this reason, Barbara Katz Rothman has described the medical model as having a *technological imperative* and Robbie Davis-Floyd calls it "technocratic."[52]

Volumes of scientific research have found that some obstetric technologies are harmful and that using fewer technological interventions produces better birth outcomes. A prime example is EFM, which hospitals adopted in the 1980s before it was tested (I discuss this in detail in chapter 5). A high percentage of hospitals adopted EFM for routine use, imitating other hospitals in the field and integrating EFM into standard protocols. Then research found that continuous EFM did not improve on intermittent monitoring methods, interfered with the progress of labor, and increased the cesarean delivery rate.[53] The vast majority of providers still use it for hospital births.

One reason for this is that technology has a veneer of scientific legitimacy, even when it is untested, and it is such an intrinsic part of the medicalization schema that few observers (or patients) question its legitimacy. Technology can also be a tool that healthcare organizations use to signal compliance with legal and professional regulations and thus a tool of *defensive medicine* (medical practices designed to avert the future possibility of malpractice suits, rather than to benefit the patient).[54] In the medicalization schema, scientific support for technology is less important than its other benefits. The use of medical technology supports institutional needs like economic efficiency, price competition, and managerial strategies that have penetrated American healthcare since the mid-1980s.[55] An emphasis on organizational efficiency and competition encourages hospitals to adopt new medical technologies to satisfy organizational needs rather than medical ones. In fact, some obstetric technologies remain common after scientific research has definitively proven that they are harmful because they serve the interests of "scientific management," which emphasizes control over the process and organizational efficiency rather than medical effectiveness.[56] It encourages the use of medical technology, control over the physiological process of labor, and an "assembly line" model of birth. Once hospitals adopt technology, it also influences the training of personnel so that many newer staff members are only familiar with new technologies and are untrained in how to perform procedures with other techniques. Sunk investments in technology and the training of staff justify its continued use, so that it becomes routine after hospitals adopt it.[57]

The technological imperative or technocratic approach is also based on more than organizational efficiency: the medical model of birth *fetishizes* technology. In anthropology, a fetish is an inanimate object that people worship for its supposed supernatural influence, power, or ability, or because they believe that a spirit inhabits it. People imbue fetish objects with imaginary powers. In sociology, Durkheim described fetishization as an important social process: social groups animate certain objects by collectively projecting supernatural or special properties onto them. The resulting fetish (or totem) becomes sacred: it provokes qualitatively different feelings within the social group than typical, physical things. Marx also used the concept of fetishism to describe a particular relationship between humans and commodities under capitalism. According to Marx, people fetishize commodities when they view objects that they exchange in the market as having intrinsic value, rather than obtaining their value through social relationships. What all conceptualizations of fetishism share is the observation that people attribute special properties to fetishized objects and, in doing so, overestimate their social value.[58] It is in this respect that the medicalization schema fetishizes technology: medical technology has symbolic value and seemingly magical powers.

Technology fetishism in the medical model of birth occurs when obstetricians and hospitals ritualize technological interventions and turn them into taken-for-granted routines. Then obstetricians, hospitals, and birthing women can see no alternative. Many contemporary parents can hardly imagine experiencing labor without an electronic fetal monitor beeping in the background and acting as the primary focus of attention in the labor and delivery suite. Likewise, most women of my mother's generation believed that episiotomy was a good practice because it made sense that "a nice straight cut is better than a jagged tear." It was only later that research showed that it made their recovery worse, healed worse than a tear, and increased the likelihood of incontinence.

Challenges to the Medicalization Schema

What is wrong with scienciness and technology fetishism if the medical model produces healthy mothers and healthy babies? For one thing, the "healthy mother, healthy baby" metric ignores the importance of the birth experience for mothers and for mother-infant bonding. The United States also has a very poor record on infant and maternal mortality and morbidity, so it is not succeeding even by the "healthy mother, healthy baby" standard. The United States ranks 37th in the world for infant mortality, and has the second worst infant mortality rate in the developed world. The US also ranks 50th among 59 developed countries for maternal mortality. Given the lack of consistency in reporting of maternal mortality across states, it is also likely to be underreported. What is clear is that some developing countries provide better healthcare to women during pregnancy and childbirth. The American maternity care system is also rife with inequality: maternal and infant mortality and severe morbidity rates are much higher in Hispanic, Native American, and especially black populations, and low-income women of all ethnicities often receive inadequate care in the United States. While the Affordable Care Act (ACA), also known as Obamacare, expanded maternity care coverage as a required benefit in private insurance and through the Medicaid expansion, it is clear that the American medical model of maternity care has failed to produce optimal outcomes even by the very blunt "healthy mother, healthy baby" yardstick.[59]

Additionally, while most women view a healthy mother and a healthy baby as *necessary* outcomes of childbirth, many do not believe that they are *sufficient*.[60] The quality of the birth experience and a healthy outcome are not mutually exclusive: often what promotes a positive experience also produces healthy outcomes, even if it is less efficient for the hospital or is inconvenient for the physician. Optimal care in childbirth is supportive, evidence-based care that honors the importance of every birth in a family's life.[61] The women's health movement of the 1960s and 1970s encouraged women to learn about their own bodies and reject the medicalization of pregnancy, birth, and menopause.[62] By the 1970s, there was a resurgence of midwifery and out-of-hospital birth. Childbirth advocates encouraged women to take back their own birth experiences and avoid the unnecessary interventions that characterize the medical model of birth. The "natural childbirth" movement aimed to humanize birth, get women more involved in their pregnancies and births, and encourage breastfeeding. Hospitals and the obstetric profession subsequently incorporated some aspects of "natural childbirth" into hospital birth by eliminating some unnecessary procedures (enemas, pubic shaving), reducing the use of others (episiotomy), offering childbirth education, and permitting labor and birth to occur in the same suite rather than artificially separating them in different rooms. At the same time, critics like Barbara Katz Rothman have described these kinds of changes within hospitals as akin to "changing the wallpaper" because they leave the underlying medicalization schema intact.[63] In her view, the only way to escape medicalization is to move birth out of the hospital, where 99% of births in the United States currently occur.

Even as the maternity care field made some changes in response to women's health movements, other actions by hospitals, physician practices, and medical-legal risk managers have intensified some medical interventions. Nearly all hospitals routinely use continuous EFM for all births, even though research does not support this technology. Rates of artificial induction of labor are extremely high, despite evidence that they make labor longer and more painful, increase the need for pain medication, and increase the likelihood of an otherwise unnecessary cesarean delivery. Cesarean delivery rates have risen from 4.5% of births in the United States in 1965 to approximately one third today. Many hospitals stick to the adage "Once a cesarean, always a cesarean" and do not permit women with a previous cesarean to attempt to have a vaginal birth after cesarean (VBAC). Contemporary women have also developed intense fears about giving birth, leading many women to seek medical interventions like cesarean deliveries out of fear for their own well-being or that of their babies. The medicalization schema appears to be here to stay.

Given the pervasiveness of this schema, this book examines how much medicalized practices vary and, more importantly, how reproductive regimes across states in the US influence these practices. How do state laws and policies influence early elective delivery, EFM, cesarean delivery, VBAC, and out-of-hospital birth? How do state laws encourage or discourage quality of care over physician convenience or hospital efficiency? When states reduce healthcare providers' malpractice liability, what effect does it have on maternity care? To what extent do state laws protect pregnant women's civil rights to bodily integrity and informed consent over the separate interests of their fetuses, and how does that affect birth practices? What is the impact of the legal environment on racial-ethnic and class disparities in maternity care? The legal environment is an important backdrop for maternity care.

2

Law Matters

Tort Regimes and Reproductive Health Regimes

To understand how laws influence maternity care practices, I draw on neo-institutional theories and analyze the maternity care field.[1] *Organizational fields* are the community of organizations that interact with each other and "constitute a recognized area of institutional life: key suppliers, resource and product consumers, regulatory agencies, and other organizations that produce similar services or products."[2] *Neo-institutional* theories argue that technical efficiency is only one of many criteria that inform common practices in organizational fields, and another important goal is gaining and maintaining legitimacy.[3] Laws that govern organizational fields play an important role in shaping action, and fields' responses to the law often transform the fields themselves. As a result, laws matter.

In one of the most highly cited journal articles in sociology, DiMaggio and Powell described three types of institutional pressure that cause some behavior to be typical in organizational fields: normative, mimetic, and coercive pressures.[4] *Normative pressures* are values, beliefs, and informal rules that shape expectations within an organizational field. In the maternity care field, normative pressure is an outgrowth of medicine's professional dominance and professional autonomy.[5] The obstetric profession has a dominant position in the maternity care field. Obstetric professional associations, like the American College of Obstetricians and Gynecologists (ACOG) in the US, protect it from external competition, intervention, and oversight.[6] Professional associations like ACOG establish licensing and educational criteria, issue clinical guidelines, and maintain peer-reviewed journals like *Obstetrics & Gynecology* that define the SOC.

Mimetic pressure refers to the tendency of organizations within a field to imitate each other when they face uncertainty, under the assumption that they can't go wrong by doing what everyone else does. Common practices have a de facto legitimacy, uncertainty is risky, and no one wants to be the first to deviate from the norm.[7] In American maternity care, obstetricians and hospitals have responded to shifts in healthcare by mimicking each other.[8] This produces what neo-institutional theories of organizations describe as *mimetic isomorphism*, as organizations in a field tend to look and act the same. Pressures to follow the crowd can explain medicine's resistance to change in response to evidence-based medicine (EBM), and the diffusion of technologies like electronic fetal monitors across the field (see chapter 5).[9] When providers copy each other, their practices are not necessarily the most technically efficient or scientifically valid, but they follow the *institutional logic* of the maternity care field.[10] As I discussed in chapter 1, the dominant institutional logic in American maternity care is the medicalization schema, which defines pregnancy and birth as pathological, encourages technological intervention, and establishes the obstetric profession as the primary authority over pregnancy and birth.

DiMaggio and Powell describe the third type of institutional pressure that affects organizational fields as *coercive*, because its primary sources are laws and regulations that restrict some types of action within a field.[11] In DiMaggio and Powell's theory, law acts as a largely *external* force that governs behavior and inhibits opportunism in organizational fields. But more recent socio-legal theory argues that interpretations of the law arise *within* the organizational fields that the law affects, which Lauren Edelman refers to as the *endogeneity of law*.[12] Using the example of civil rights law, Edelman's *theory of legal endogeneity* argues that extra-legal actors, like human resources professionals, actively interpret laws that are often ambiguous, and they do so with their organizations' interests and cultural understandings in mind. They then create law-like policies to manage claims and avoid litigation and, over time, the courts come to view the policies that organizations have developed *internally* as benchmarks for what is legally appropriate. The result is legal endogeneity: "the meaning of law is shaped by widely accepted ideas within the social arena that the law seeks to regulate."[13] Because organizations interpret laws that affect them based on their own values, interests, and priorities, the policies that they develop protect them while signaling legal compliance in largely symbolic ways.

Tort Law

Tort law governs professional malpractice, and the tort system is based on the British system of common law. In the United States, tort law is a matter of state-level civil law. It has three main goals: (1) to promote justice, (2) to deter potentially harmful activities, and (3) to compensate victims for injuries caused by others' harmful activities.[14] Under tort law, healthcare providers owe a certain SOC to their patients, and tort laws aim to protect the public from gross negligence if providers breach the SOC and cause injury. Litigation for malpractice is often the only way to make healthcare providers accountable for unsafe or harmful practices and to compensate victims for their injuries. Tort laws provide a clear example of legal endogeneity because, by definition, malpractice only occurs when there is a violation of the SOC, and the medical profession defines the SOC. Since the SOC distinguishes between professionally appropriate and negligent behavior, the definition of medical malpractice is *internal* to medicine, rather than *externally* imposed by the law.

Under tort law, courts can award *economic damages* to reimburse injured patients for out-of-pocket costs associated with medical bills, legal fees, or lost wages if a medical professional is at fault. They can also award *non-economic damages* to compensate victims of malpractice for harms like permanent disability, disfigurement, blindness, loss of limb, paralysis, trauma, or physical pain and suffering. Because these awards are often the only compensation that injured individuals and/or their families receive for their loss of quality of life, they are also called *compensatory damages. Punitive damages*, on the other hand, intend to punish a defendant who knowingly engaged in harmful action and to deter others from engaging in similar conduct. Courts award punitive damages in only in 2% of civil cases that go to trial, typically after they compensate victims for their injuries with non-economic damage awards and in amounts that are strongly related to non-economic damage awards.[15] As a result, caps on non-economic damages should reduce liability risk substantially more than caps on punitive damages and should have stronger effects on provider behavior.[16]

There is evidence that medical negligence is very common in the United States. Using a population-based sample, the Harvard Malpractice Study (HMS) found that approximately 1% of all patients in

American hospitals experience an injury due to negligence, leading to an estimated 44,000 to 440,000 preventable deaths from medical errors each year.[17] Fewer than 1% of these injuries lead to payments, so most victims never receive compensation and providers are rarely accountable for substandard care. Even when victims do receive compensation, most receive less than they deserve and almost two dollars is spent in the tort system for every dollar that an injured victim receives. One study found that approximately 12% of the medical-legal expenses of a major hospital went to victims of malpractice, while the rest paid for attorney fees and administrative costs.[18] In short, the medical liability system is inefficient for delivering justice, compensating victims, or encouraging quality care because it compensates too few patients and does so in a way that has many additional costs.[19]

Tort Reform

To reduce the cost of the medical liability system, which is an estimated $55.6 billion per year or 2.4% of all healthcare spending, many states have reformed their tort laws.[20] In the 1980s and 1990s, insurance companies and corporations demonized lawsuits and lobbied pro-business legislators to enact tort reform legislation. The purpose of *tort reform* is to repeal legal protections for victims of negligence under the common law and to reduce the amount that victims can receive through litigation.[21] Arguments for tort reform claim that medical liability inflates the costs of care by encouraging providers to overuse tests and procedures in order to protect themselves from lawsuits (i.e., "defensive medicine"). They also claim that many medical malpractice claims are frivolous (lacking evidence of medical error or patient injury) and that malpractice lawsuits create an undue and costly burden for healthcare providers.[22] Tort reform advocates focus primarily on the costs of the tort system rather than on problems with quality or medical errors. At best, arguments for tort reform imply that the availability of legal remedies through the tort system is *unnecessary* to deter harmful practices. Since the mid-1980s, many states have implemented three common types of tort reform laws: caps on damage awards, reform of the joint and several liability (JSL) rule, and expert requirements.

Caps on Damage Awards

Caps on non-economic (NE) and/or punitive damage awards are common tort reforms that reduce providers' legal risk by decreasing the cost of losing a malpractice suit. From 1995 to 2015, the number of states with caps on punitive and/or non-economic damages rose from 31 in 1995 to 40 in 2015. Figure 2.1 illustrates the trend in caps on damages over time. Some states, including Texas, Georgia, and California, require the losing party to pay the court costs of the opposing party. Texas has particularly aggressive tort reform laws, creating $600 million in savings for insurance companies during the 1990s alone.[23] California, Indiana, and Michigan have very low caps on non-economic damages ($250,000), although Michigan raises the cap for plaintiffs who are hemiplegic, paraplegic, or quadriplegic due to physician negligence. The dollar amount of caps in states like Maryland, West Virginia, and Wisconsin are considerably higher. Five states have a single "umbrella limit" on total damages that ranges from $250,000 (Indiana) to $2,500,000 (Nebraska). Others have implemented legislative changes to tort laws, only to have them overturned by the courts.[24] For example, the Illinois legislature enacted caps on non-economic damages, but the state appellate court struck them down as unconstitutional in *Best v. Taylor Machine Works*, 689 N.E.2d. They ruled that a $500,000 cap on damage awards was a "legislative remittitur" that violated the separate powers of the judiciary, and that it made an arbitrary distinction between plaintiffs who sustained varying degrees of injury.[25]

While many states have adopted caps on damages, most socio-legal scholars oppose them because the tort system already does too little to deter negligent or risky medical practices and it under-compensates victims of malpractice.[26] Caps on damage awards reduce providers' liability risk regardless of whether or not they make any effort to improve care, so they do nothing to encourage caution on the part of providers.[27]

Joint and Several Liability (JSL) versus Proportionate Liability (PL)

The common-law JSL rule states that if two or more persons are liable in a case, they may be *jointly and severally liable*: claimants can file charges against any and all parties that share responsibility for the injury,

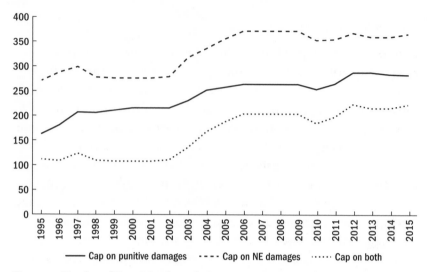

Figure 2.1. Number of State-Months with Caps on Damage Awards, 1995–2015.
Source: American Tort Reform Association, Senate Judiciary Committee and compiled legal data from Nexis Uni.

including those that played a very minor role.[28] The JSL rule is often called the "deep pockets" rule, because the defendant with the most ability to pay (the "deepest pockets") can be liable for the full award if other defendants are unable to pay. Because of the JSL rule, most medical malpractice cases involve multiple defendants, some of whom bear little or no direct responsibility for the injury. Defendants in a birth-related case can include the obstetricians who provided prenatal care and/or were at the birth, anesthesiologists, labor and delivery nurses, ultrasound technicians, and/or the hospital. JSL protects victims of negligence by ensuring that they receive compensation from some party involved in their injury, but it also means that individuals or organizations with little direct involvement are financially vulnerable. Dr. McDonald, an obstetrician and perinatal specialist, described the emotional impact of JSL on providers:

When one gets sued, my husband, my father, my sisters, my brothers, basically, everybody gets named. In a successful suit, that's what you do. You name anybody who might have some resources in case the individual doesn't have enough, you can go to these other people . . . That doesn't make sense to me. I didn't like the outcome, but I don't think that I did something that made that happen. But, it really awakened the idea that I'm vulnerable and not only am I vulnerable, but people around me are vulnerable for my actions and my choices in specialty. I like to do obstetrics. Who's going to pay for my liking to do it?

For Dr. McDonald, JSL contributed to her anxiety about liability because she worried about putting other people in her life at risk.

The elimination of the JSL rule and its replacement with proportionate liability (PL), whereby codefendants are liable in proportion to their direct responsibility, is a common tort reform. PL should reduce *unpredictable* sources of liability risk, which often cause providers to have the most anxiety, even if it does not change the risk of patients suing them. Some available research suggests that a change from JSL to PL reduces the number of malpractice suits, possibly because negligent providers do not always have deep pockets.[29] PL also makes individual healthcare providers more directly liable if they are responsible for harm, which could encourage them to be more cautious about the quality of care that they provide.[30] Figure 2.2 shows state-months with PL from 1995 to 2015, when there was a strong trend away from JSL. In 1995, 29 states had PL, and that rose to 38 by 2015.[31]

EXPERT REQUIREMENTS

Figure 2.2 also illustrates the trend in expert requirements over time, showing that 24 states had expert requirements in 1995 and this rose to 38 states by 2015. While caps on damage awards are the most well-known type of tort reform, expert requirements may be the most consequential. These laws establish minimum qualifications for expert witnesses and/or require that that an expert certify the merit of a tort claim before a lawsuit can proceed. Especially since 2002, a growing number of states have imposed expert requirements in medical malpractice cases. As I discuss in detail in chapter 3, expert requirements have dramatically increased the cost of pursuing a malpractice claim, leading to a large reduction in claims.

MALPRACTICE LITIGATION

Medical malpractice lawsuits are part of the malpractice environment. Physicians often follow court rulings in malpractice cases, and hospital

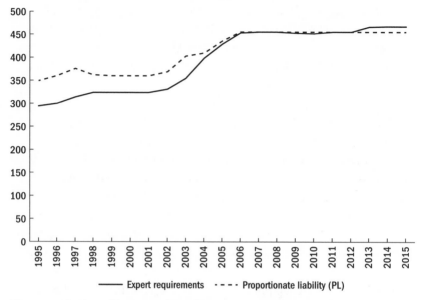

Figure 2.2. Number of State-Months with Expert Requirements and Proportionate Liability, 1995–2015. Source: Compiled legal data from Nexis Uni.

obstetric departments routinely discuss medical negligence rulings as well as medical errors, so high rates of malpractice suits in a state should heighten providers' awareness of liability risk. The impact of malpractice litigation could also be cumulative, although recent activity appears to have a stronger effect than more distant events.[32]

All malpractice claims in the United States are reported to the National Practitioner Data Bank (NPDB). I used the publicly available NPDB to calculate the number of obstetric malpractice claims from 1995 to 2015 and the rate of obstetric malpractice suits per 100,000 births for each state and year.[33] I also combined NPDB data on the total number of claims by year with census data to calculate the total rate of malpractice suits per 100,000 population for each state and year.[34] Figure 2.3 shows the national trend from 1995 to 2015, revealing a declining rate of malpractice suits in general and a steep decline in obstetric malpractice suits. As figure 2.3 reveals, the rate of obstetric lawsuits was higher than the overall rate of medical malpractice lawsuits, which confirms that maternity care providers have a higher liability risk than the average

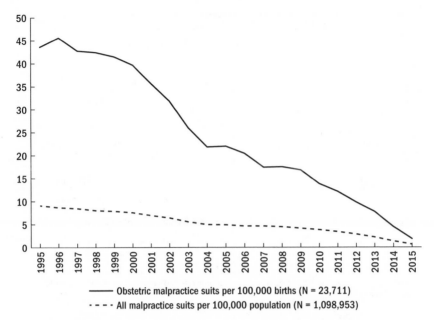

Figure 2.3. Rate of Malpractice Suits by Year, 1995–2015. Source: National Practitioner Data Bank, Public Use Data File.

specialty. In figure 2.3, the difference is especially large in the earlier part of the 1995–2015 period, and these rates appear to converge by 2015.

In sum, I have several measures of the malpractice environment in each state over time: the presence of caps on punitive and non-economic damages and expert requirements, replacement of the JSL with PL, and the rate of malpractice lawsuits per 100,000 births. In other chapters, I use these measures to analyze how the malpractice environment is related to common maternity care practices, with the expectation that maternity care providers in states with less liability risk should be less motivated to protect themselves legally. This could reduce wasteful defensive medicine, as tort reform advocates claim, but it may also make providers less careful—leading to more actual negligence.[35] Table 2.1 summarizes the expected effects of different tort laws on providers' liability risk.

I define states with caps on punitive and non-economic damages for most or all of the 1995–2015 period as provider-friendly tort regimes, because healthcare providers in those states have a relatively low risk of

TABLE 2.1. Expected Effects of Tort Laws on Liability Risk for Providers

Tort law	Expected effect on liability risk
No caps on damage awards (common law)	Higher risk (+)
Caps on punitive damage awards only	Lower risk compared to no caps (−)
Caps on non-economic damage awards (with or without caps on punitive damages)	➤Lower risk compared to punitive damages alone (−) ➤Much lower risk compared to no caps (−)
JSL (common law)	➤Higher risk liability for those with indirect responsibility (because of sharing of risk) (+) ➤Lower liability risk for those with direct responsibility (because of sharing of risk) (−)
PL	➤Lower liability risk for those with indirect responsibility (no sharing of risk) (−) ➤Higher liability for those with direct responsibility (+)
Expert requirements	Lower liability risk compared to no expert requirements (−)
Rate of obstetric malpractice suits per 100,000 births	Higher rate indicates higher liability risk (+)

TABLE 2.2. Tort Regimes

Regime type	States
Patient-friendly	Arizona, Connecticut, Delaware, Iowa, Kentucky, Maine, Minnesota, New Hampshire, New York, Rhode Island, Tennessee, Vermont, Washington, Wyoming
Provider-friendly	Alaska, Colorado, Florida, Idaho, Indiana, Kansas, Louisiana, Nebraska, Nevada, North Dakota, Oklahoma, Texas, Virginia

malpractice liability. The most provider-friendly states were Colorado, Florida, and Kansas because they had all tort reforms during the entire 1995–2015 period (see table 2.2). I define states without caps on damages as patient-friendly tort regimes, because these states make it easier for victims of negligence to sue their providers and to receive significant awards.

Figure 2.4 illustrates patient-friendly and provider-friendly tort regimes on a map. Patient-friendly tort regimes are somewhat concentrated in the north Atlantic states, while provider-friendly tort regimes dominate the central states.

An important question is whether tort reform laws reduce malpractice suits, as they intend to do. Medical liability insurance premiums

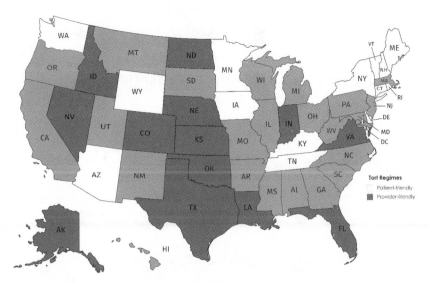

Figure 2.4. Tort Regimes. Source: Compiled legal data from Nexis Uni.

typically respond to caps on damages with the assumption that they reduce the cost of liability, and are consequently lower in tort reform states. I analyzed the relationship between tort laws and the rate of obstetric malpractice suits across states and over time, and I found that states with caps on damages had significantly *higher* rates of obstetric malpractice suits, all else being equal.[36] After I accounted for the general trend of declining lawsuits over time, there were about 11 *more* obstetric malpractice suits per 100,000 births in states with caps on punitive damages alone.[37] States with caps on non-economic damages (or caps on both non-economic and punitive damages) had approximately one additional lawsuit per 100,000 births than states without caps. States with expert requirements had an average of 1.0–1.2 more obstetric lawsuits per 100,000 births than states without them. States with PL had an average of 1.5–1.7 more lawsuits than states with JSL. All of these legal reforms should *reduce* providers' liability risk, but the rate of obstetric malpractice suits is *higher* when they are in effect. So tort reform laws do not appear to do what they intend to do, namely to reduce the number of malpractice claims. In short, the rate of obstetric malpractice lawsuits declined more in non–tort reform states than in tort reform states, so tort reform laws were *not* responsible for their decline from 1995 to 2015.

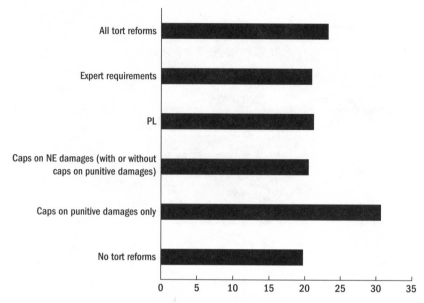

Figure 2.5. Predicted Rate of Obstetric Malpractice Suits per 100,000 Births by Tort Reform Laws. Source: National Practitioner Data Bank, Public Use Data File, and compiled legal data from Nexis Uni.

Figure 2.5 presents the predicted rate of obstetric malpractice suits per 100,000 births under different tort laws. This figure shows that states with *no* tort reforms have the lowest predicted rate of malpractice suits (19.8 per 100,000 births), versus 23.2 lawsuits per 100,000 births in states with *all* tort reforms.

These effects were surprising, so I dug deeper. Perhaps legislatures implement tort reforms only in states that already have a high rate of malpractice lawsuits or high malpractice awards in order to relieve a "malpractice crisis." To test for this, I examined whether suit rates and average payments were higher in the year before state legislatures implemented caps on damages, and then declined or remained stable afterwards—which would indicate that tort reforms were a response to high malpractice lawsuit activity.[38] For states that enacted caps on punitive damages, the first part bore out: they had slightly higher rates of malpractice suits (2.5 more suits per 100,000 births) during the year before they enacted these caps compared to other states without caps. The second part did not: obstetric suit rates were *even higher after* they capped punitive damages—by 9.2 lawsuits per 100,000 in the first year and 11.2 lawsuits per 100,000 in later years. In other words, states with somewhat higher rates of malpractice lawsuits may be more likely to cap punitive damages, but afterwards their rate of malpractice lawsuits increases further compared to states without any caps on damages.

There is even less support for the idea that states enact caps on non-economic damage awards in response to a medical malpractice crisis. In the year before enacting caps on non-economic damages, states that enacted these caps had *lower* average rates of obstetric lawsuits than similar states without caps on damages (3.2 fewer lawsuits per 100,000 births). Once non-economic damage caps were in place, they had an average of 1.1 more obstetric lawsuits in the first year, and 0.8 more in subsequent years, compared with states with no caps. This is the opposite of what tort reform laws intend. In short, tort reforms do not influence malpractice lawsuits in the ways that their advocates anticipated. Caps on damages do not reduce liability risk and are not the cause of declining lawsuits. Reform of the JSL rule also does not reduce the rate of obstetric malpractice claims. The only tort reform that appears to reduce providers' liability risk somewhat is expert requirements. This suggests that the objective legal reality that obstetricians face is not the source of obstetricians' fear of liability. Rather, this fear is based on *cultural myths* about liability risk.

Reproductive Justice and Reproductive Health Law

Reproductive health laws are the second set of laws that shape beliefs about the role of government, the obligations of birth attendants, and the rights of women and families in pregnancy and birth. Reproductive rights activists have focused largely on removing legal barriers to contraception and abortion so that women can choose when and if to bear children, but contraception and abortion are intimately connected to all issues surrounding fertility and birth: laws that support or undermine pregnant women's rights to abortion can affect the full spectrum of reproductive and parenting experiences.[39] These laws include abortion restrictions, fetal rights laws, targeted regulations of abortion provider (TRAP) laws, midwifery laws, and protections for women's health services, Many states have enacted increasingly restrictive laws over time.

While abortion is an issue that continually gets public attention, it is not isolated from the nature of pregnancy. Abortion rights are part of a broader spectrum of reproductive issues, with implications for inequalities of race, class, and gender.[40] From a reproductive justice (RJ) perspective, the *choice* frame of the abortion rights movement is too simplistic because it implies that all pregnant women are empowered patients, with status- and class-based resources that allow them to negotiate their care on relatively equal footing with their care providers.[41] This might fit with the experiences of white, heterosexual, middle-class women with access to healthcare, but it does not match the historical or contemporary experiences of marginalized women in the United States.[42] Historically, medical researchers have engaged in unethical practices toward people of color, including using African Americans as test subjects without informed consent.[43] For example, J. Marion Sims, often called the "father of modern gynecology," conducted experimental surgeries on enslaved black women in the nineteenth century without their consent and without anesthesia.[44] Throughout the twentieth century, the US federal government funded programs that involuntarily sterilized African Americans, Latinos, the poor, and the disabled.[45] Even after involuntary sterilization practices ended and research that violated the rights of human subjects was exposed, biases and stereotyping among providers has contributed to well-known racial-ethnic and class inequalities in health and healthcare.[46]

Low-income women of all race-ethnicities also experience a lack of *choice* and worse maternal and infant health outcomes because of financial barriers to contraception, abortion, and infertility treatment. Restrictions on abortion have their strongest effects on poor women, since 75% of abortion recipients in 2014 were low-income (below 200% of the poverty level) and 49% lived below the federal poverty line.[47] Since 1977, the Hyde Amendment has forbidden the use of federal funds to pay for abortions, except in cases of rape or incest or to save the life of the pregnant woman. This forces low-income women with government insurance through Medicaid, Medicare, the Indian Health Service (IHS), or the Veterans Health Administration to pay out of pocket for abortions. The result is more illegal abortions, more delays in obtaining an abortion as women obtain adequate funds to pay for the procedure, and more unwanted births that increase the risk of long-term poverty, food insecurity, and child abuse and neglect.[48] The economic hardships that low-income women face in obtaining abortion care and the availability of Medicaid- and IHS-funded sterilization also lead some low-income women to seek sterilization when they might otherwise choose a less permanent method of contraception.[49]

Meanwhile, infant and maternal mortality statistics put the United States to shame, and their details reveal a pervasive inequality. It is well known that maternal and infant mortality and morbidity are highly correlated with race, ethnicity, and income. Negative maternal outcomes are concentrated among low-income women, who tend to have less prenatal care, more discontinuity of care, and more medical risk factors.[50] While no credible contemporary scientist believes that race has any biological or genetic basis, there are profound racial-ethnic disparities in maternity care outcomes, independent of socioeconomic status, that are rooted in a white supremacist and genocidal colonial history.[51] Native Americans, Hispanic Americans, and especially African Americans have higher infant and maternal mortality rates than non-Hispanic whites, providing a striking marker for exposure to structural racism.[52] African American women tend to begin prenatal care after the first trimester, are less likely to receive adequate care or continuity of care, and die from pregnancy-related causes four times as often as other racial-ethnic groups.[53] Racial-ethnic minority women are also more likely to have pregnancy complications, and some research has argued that differences in clinical profiles are the cause of racial-ethnic disparities in outcomes (i.e., African American women are more likely to have pregnancy-related health risks).[54] At the same time, women of color are more likely to experience pressure from providers to accept unwanted procedures during labor and to have cesarean deliveries when they have no pregnancy complications or preexisting health risks.[55] Both medical and non-medical hospital staff engage in much more surveillance of pregnant women of color and immigrant women, especially those who receive public assistance through Medicaid and Supplemental Nutrition Assistance Programs (SNAP), and this added surveillance often continues after they give birth.[56] As a result, many women of color have been understandably skeptical of reproductive health movements that emphasize women's *choices* around pregnancy and reproduction.

In short, instead of focusing narrowly on abortion rights, the RJ movement aims to link access to safe and legal abortion to other reproductive health issues that particularly affect poor women and women of color in the United States.[57] RJ issues include food security, economic security, freedom from violence, paid maternity and sick leave, supportive welfare policies, and environmental justice. In the RJ framework, genuine reproductive *justice* can only exist when *all* individuals have the right to *have* children and to *parent with dignity* as well as the right to *not* have children.[58]

What does an orientation toward RJ mean for reproductive regimes and their effects on common maternity care practices? Maternity care providers may not think much about laws governing contraception, abortion, and midwifery when they provide prenatal care or attend births. But it is useful to conceptualize *choice* in both abortion and childbirth as issues of pregnant women's rights to bodily integrity and informed consent.[59] The non-profit legal organization National Advocates for Pregnant Women (NAPW) first recognized the links between abortion and birth in the legal arena. Under the direction of Lynn Paltrow, NAPW has legally represented many of the legal cases involving forced cesareans, punitive treatment of pregnant women with addiction to substances, and the use of feticide laws to punish pregnant women for terminating a pregnancy or suffering a stillbirth. When others dealt with abortion and birth-related issues as separate, NAPW advocated for women facing legal threats to their constitutional and human rights because of the outcomes of their pregnancies, regardless of whether those pregnancies ended in abortion, miscarriage, stillbirth, or live birth.[60] Following their lead, I argue that reproductive health laws provide a legal backdrop that can subtly tip the balance from pregnant women's rights to fetal rights, or vice versa, when women give birth.

Because approaches to abortion and views about the nature of pregnancy are intertwined, laws that prioritize fetal rights over pregnant women's rights can have seemingly unintended effects—undermining pregnant women's right to informed consent or permitting disrespectful care. These restrictions are associated with worse health and well-being for women and children, even though many abortion opponents argue that they support birth when they try to protect fetuses from mothers who want (or need) abortions. Laws that grant rights to fertilized eggs, embryos, and fetuses take rights away from pregnant women, and states with more abortion restrictions have less affordable healthcare and higher maternal and infant mortality.[61] As a result, I define states that restrict access to contraception, abortion, and midwifery, and that define fetuses as having rights separate from the pregnant women who carry them, as *fetus-centered reproductive health regimes*. I define states that protect access to contraception, abortion, and midwifery as *woman-centered reproductive health regimes*. The laws that define reproductive health regimes include abortion bans at particular gestational ages, procedure bans, mandatory counseling and waiting periods, feticide laws, and laws that criminalize pregnant women with substance abuse problems instead of treating their problems as health issues.

Feticide Laws

Prosecutions of pregnant women are especially common in states with feticide laws that protect fetuses as separate from their mothers. Many state legislatures passed feticide laws with the intention of increasing the punishment for intimate violence against pregnant women, but these laws divert resources away from promoting health and offering preventive care in favor of punitive action against pregnant women, especially low-income women.[62] Some high-profile cases illustrate this, including two cases in Indiana that NAPW represented and won. In March 2011, the state of Indiana charged Bei Bei Shuai with murder and attempted feticide after she attempted to commit suicide by ingesting rat poison when she 32 weeks pregnant. She was a Chinese immigrant to the United States who suffered from severe depression. She survived, but her daughter died two days after an emergency cesarean in January 2011. The Supreme Court of Indiana declined to dismiss the state's murder charges against her, even though her intention was to kill herself and not specifically her fetus.[63] Bei Bei Shuai clearly needed psychiatric help and emotional support, but instead the state prosecuted her for harming herself while she was pregnant because Indiana's fetus-centered reproductive health regime emphasized protecting fetuses and not women. In 2013, Ms. Shuai pled guilty to a lesser charge of criminal recklessness and was released after serving 435 days in prison.

Also in Indiana, Purvi Patel was an Indian American woman who had a self-induced second-trimester abortion in July 2014. She went to a hospital emergency department with profuse bleeding and told the doctors that she had a miscarriage. They investigated the circumstances of the miscarriage and found out that she had ordered a drug that would induce an abortion (misoprostol) from a pharmacy in Hong Kong. Because she did not have a prescription for the drug, the court did not view her pregnancy loss as a legal abortion and prosecuted her under the Indiana feticide law. A jury convicted Patel for felony child neglect and feticide in February 2015, and the court sentenced her to 20 years in prison. In September 2016, the Indiana Court of Appeals overturned her conviction and released her after she had served 18 months. This was the first case where a state used a feticide law to punish a woman for attempting to have an abortion.

Feticide laws can undermine pregnant women's rights even when they plan to carry their pregnancies to term.[64] In 2010, Christine Taylor was a mother of two who faced charges in Iowa for attempted feticide after she fell down the stairs during the second trimester of pregnancy. When she went to the emergency department at her local hospital, she told a nurse that she had considered abortion before deciding to carry her pregnancy to term. The nurse then reported her to law enforcement for attempting to self-abort by falling down the stairs and they arrested her under Iowa's feticide law. After two days in jail, the court released her because Iowa's feticide laws only apply in the third trimester, but it did not suggest that the feticide law should exempt pregnant women who have accidents, miscarriages, or stillbirths.

The contrast with woman-centered reproductive health regimes is very clear. In New York State in 2015, an appellate court reinforced a pregnant woman's right to autonomy in a case involving a car accident. In 2008, Jennifer Jorgensen of Sound Beach, NY, crashed head-on into another car when she was eight months pregnant. Six days after an emergency cesarean, her infant daughter died. She was not wearing a seatbelt, and there was an allegation that she was under the influence of prescription drugs and alcohol. The New York district court prosecuted and convicted Ms. Jorgensen of manslaughter for causing the reckless endangerment and death of her unborn child, but the New York Court of Appeals overturned this decision.[65] The appeals court argued that it set a precedent that would allow the criminal prosecution of pregnant women for a wide range of behaviors that others may define as risky, but that are within the rights of a competent adult. In short, New York's court granted full citizenship to pregnant women and prioritized women's rights over fetal rights, exemplifying a woman-centered reproductive health regime.

Punitive Laws for Prenatal Substance Abuse

States with restrictive reproductive health regimes have also used fetal protection and child abuse laws to take punitive actions against pregnant women who are addicted to drugs or alcohol by prosecuting them for prenatal harm.[66] More than one third of states consider pregnant women's substance abuse to be a form of child abuse, and the worst violations of pregnant women's rights under these laws have targeted low-income women of color. Once again, NAPW has offered legal representation in these cases, with a goal of treating addiction during pregnancy as a health issue rather than a crime.[67] For example, Regina McKnight was a homeless, 22-year-old African American woman with an addiction to crack cocaine who gave birth to a stillborn baby. Prosecutors argued that she murdered her fetus by using crack cocaine when she was pregnant, and the court sentenced her to 12 years in prison for committing "homicide by child abuse." The South Carolina Supreme Court rejected her case on appeal in 2003. Similarly, in 2006, a low-income African American teenager in Mississippi named Rennie Gibbs gave birth to a stillborn daughter whose umbilical cord was wrapped around her neck. Mississippi's medical examiner found traces of a cocaine *byproduct*— not cocaine—in the infant's blood and charged Gibbs with homicide due to "cocaine toxicity." At 16 years old, Gibbs was sentenced by the court to life in prison for murder. After seven years of legal battles, the Lowndes County Circuit Court dismissed the case.[68] Mississippi has the worst status in the nation on infant and maternal mortality, with huge racial-ethnic disparities, but it put years of public resources into prosecuting a poor African American teenager who suffered an unpreventable stillbirth.

Another stillbirth case that used fetal protection arguments in the criminal prosecution of a mother involved Melissa Rowland, a low-income white woman in Utah who had used cocaine and alcohol while pregnant. In 2004, Ms. Rowland was pregnant with twins when her obstetrician recommended an immediate cesarean delivery. She rejected the doctor's advice and left the hospital. She returned 11 days later for a cesarean delivery of one daughter and a stillborn male fetus. Rowland had previous felony convictions and a history of substance abuse, making her an easy target for prosecution. The Salt Lake County District Attorney's Office used a state statute that defines a fetus as a person for the purpose of criminal prosecution to file a murder charge against her *for refusing to have an immediate cesarean.* This emphasis on "following doctor's orders," as though physicians are infallible, is a hallmark of restrictive reproductive health regimes.[69] Notably, courts cannot legally require individuals to undergo any other medical procedure, like donating a kidney, for another person's benefit, even if the other person might die as a result. Ms. Rowland pleaded guilty to a lesser charge of child endangerment based on her substance use during her pregnancy, and not her refusal of a cesarean. But the state of Utah's willingness to nullify the right to informed consent and bodily integrity *for pregnant women only* suggests that pregnant women are subject to different standards than other citizens.

Disrespectful Care/Obstetric Violence

When reproductive health regimes take away pregnant women's right to informed consent, they institutionalize the treatment of pregnant women as less than full citizens—which makes disrespectful care during labor and delivery more likely in ways that can amount to *obstetric violence.*[70] Obstetric violence is a form of institutional gender-based violence: a human rights violation caused by an institution's daily activities that perpetrates physical and/or emotional harm against a person's will and expresses power inequalities based on gender.[71] There are intersectional effects of institutional violence like obstetric violence: victims are especially likely to be individuals who are vulnerable due to race-ethnicity, class, gender identity, and disability as well as gender.

There have been well-publicized instances of disrespectful care in which healthcare providers violated pregnant women's rights, and the mistreatment of women during childbirth is a sufficiently large problem that the World Health Organization (WHO) has launched a campaign against "disrespectful, abusive, or neglectful treatment during childbirth" around the world. A recent article in the *Annals of Internal Medicine* described two shocking incidents of disrespectful care, with an accompanying editorial that described them as clear instances of misogyny and disrespect with some "heavy overtones of sexual assault and racism."[72] Journalists have also documented obstetricians taking selfies next to naked patients who were either giving birth or unconscious after a cesarean section, and then posting these photos on social media alongside sexually objectifying remarks.[73] Many women experience trauma after being subject to verbal humiliation or harassment or physical violence. Others feel coerced into agreeing to obstetric procedures that they later discover to be unnecessary.[74] A grassroots movement, ImprovingBirth.org, has emerged as a visible social media presence through the #BreakTheSilence campaign, which highlights the stories of individual women who felt traumatized or victimized by poor-quality or insensitive treatment.[75]

Three recent lawsuits in the United States have highlighted the kind of disrespectful care that occurs when physicians and hospitals override pregnant women's right to refuse treatment. In a legal case that led to a $16 million jury verdict in August 2016, Caroline Malatesta sued an Alabama hospital where she gave birth in 2012.[76] The hospital had aggressively advertised its willingness to honor women's birth plans if they preferred a low-intervention birth. But when Malatesta was ready to give birth on her hands and knees, the hospital nursing staff physically forced her onto her back and pushed her baby's head back in for six minutes because the doctor was not in the room. As a result, Malatesta suffered from pudendal neuralgia, a permanent debilitating nerve injury that has interfered with her ability to engage in normal daily activities, and has caused her considerable psychological trauma. The jury found that the hospital had violated the standard of care and had engaged in false advertising. The jury in the case determined that the hospital's advertising was a "reckless misinterpretation of fact."

In a California case that settled in March 2017, Kimberly Turbin sued the obstetrician who attended her 2013 birth for assault and battery after he gave her an episiotomy against her will.[77] She verbally refused an episiotomy, telling the attending physician, Dr. Alex Abbassi, "No, don't cut me. No!" "No! Why? Why can't I try?" He defied her wishes and cut her perineum twelve times without consent, saying, "What do you mean,

'Why?' I am the expert here, okay?" Turbin was a sexual assault survivor and had specifically asked the hospital staff to be gentle and get her permission before touching her, to avoid triggering traumatic memories, only to be violated and re-traumatized by her obstetrician when she gave birth. Ms. Turbin's mother captured the incident on video, which garnered international attention after she posted it on YouTube and used it as a primary source of evidence for the case.[78] These legal cases illustrate that hospital labor and delivery settings sometimes violate pregnant women's rights in ways that share features with other types of gender-based violence.[79]

Court-Ordered Cesareans

Cases involving forced cesareans also highlight the violation of pregnant women's rights under fetus-centered reproductive health regimes. The courts usually uphold the rights of pregnant women to bodily integrity and informed consent, at least in principle, but some states have legally permitted forced medical interventions into labor in the name of fetal protection.[80] Forced and court-ordered cesareans are rare but extreme cases that illustrate the effects of prioritizing fetuses over pregnant women's rights. At least a dozen states have obtained court orders to force unwilling pregnant women to undergo cesarean deliveries, even though it is *not legal* to force a woman to undergo surgery.

In the notorious 1987 case of Angela Carder, hospital administrators and liability risk managers at George Washington University Hospital in Washington, DC, obtained a court order to force Angela Carder to have an emergency cesarean delivery when she was 26 weeks pregnant.[81] Carder was a 27-year-old cancer survivor, and her cancer recurred during the 25th week of her pregnancy. She had an inoperable lung tumor and agreed to palliative care to prolong her life until she was 28 weeks pregnant, with the goal of staying alive long enough to hold her baby. The hospital insisted instead that she needed an immediate cesarean delivery to preserve the life of her fetus, even though Angela Carder, her husband, her parents, her obstetricians, and her cancer specialist all opposed it because they believed that neither she nor the fetus would survive the surgery. The hospital obtained a court order to perform a cesarean without Ms. Carder's consent based on the argument that they had a compelling interest in preserving fetal life, and Angela Carder's attorney was unable to convince the court to block the court order. Angela Carder and her baby both died within 48 hours of the surgery. Ms. Carder's parents, Daniel and Nettie Stoner, sued the hospital for malpractice, deprivation of human rights, discrimination, and wrongful death of their daughter and granddaughter, and won a settlement in November 1990 with the goal of protecting future patients like Angela Carder.[82]

An appellate court later concluded that it is *not* appropriate to sacrifice a dying woman for her fetus, and that women should make medical decisions for both themselves and their fetuses.[83] In the same year, a United States Supreme Court decision in a "right to die" case, *Cruzan v. Director, Missouri Dept. of Health*, affirmed that "a competent person has the right to refuse medical treatment."[84] If pregnant women are full citizens, then these principles of informed consent and refusal must apply to them. In 1994, the Appellate Court of Illinois reaffirmed the rights of a competent pregnant woman to refuse medical advice to undergo a cesarean delivery in *In Re Baby Boy Doe*.[85] In that case, the court held that a mentally competent pregnant woman can refuse a cesarean, even if it might harm her fetus, because the state's interest in protecting the potential life of a fetus does not override the individual's right to refuse treatment. Put simply, a mentally competent person has a right to bodily integrity and informed consent and does not lose that right because she is pregnant.

While this seems clear as a matter of law, reproductive health regimes that prioritize fetuses over women's rights have used a logic of fetal protection that is similar to the one in the case of Angela Carder in more recent court-ordered cesarean cases. For example, in an attempt to force a woman to have a cesarean delivery, doctors at Wilkes-Barre General Hospital in Pennsylvania told Amber Marlowe in January 2004 that her baby was too large and that she needed a cesarean.[86] She was pregnant with her seventh baby and had given birth to other large babies, so she refused to consent to the surgery and left the hospital. Her obstetricians then consulted the hospital's attorneys to obtain legal guardianship of her fetus, and to obtain a court order for a cesarean delivery if she returned to the hospital. They said that a vaginal delivery could lead to the infant's death, and cited the hospital's interest in preserving and protecting *the rights of the fetus* (not the rights of the mother). The

Luzerne County Court approved the request but, in the meantime, Marlowe had a healthy vaginal birth at Moses Taylor Hospital in Scranton and proved that her doctors were wrong. The actions of obstetricians at Wilkes-Barre hospital undermined 50 years of case law that grants mentally competent individuals the right to refuse medical treatment, even if they are pregnant. Amber Marlowe and her husband turned to the NAPW to contest the judge's ruling, in an effort to protect other women who gave birth at Wilkes-Barre General Hospital.

Cases like Marlowe's illustrate that obstetricians do not necessarily know whether a cesarean delivery will lead to a better outcome than a vaginal birth—and the high overall cesarean rate in the United States suggests that they are quick to recommend surgery when it may not be necessary.[87] The willingness of the court to issue an order that granted guardianship of the fetus to the hospital underscores a widespread belief that fetal interests are opposed to women's rights.[88] Treating pregnant women as hostile to the interests of their fetuses obscures the reality that should be obvious: the strongest advocate for the health and safety of a fetus is its mother. The rhetoric of fetus-centered reproductive health regimes pits mothers and fetuses against each other and clouds common sense.

A view of medical professionals as the protectors of fetuses from their mothers is also a way to reaffirm the power of the medical profession and the doctrine of "doctor knows best." Even without a court order, women can lose their rights when they do not cooperate with medical staff. This was a significant part of what happened in Caroline Malatesta's and Kimberly Turbin's cases, where physicians and nurses used their power and position within the hospital to force women to do it their way—whether they consented or not. In another case, a New Jersey couple lost custody of their infant daughter because the mother, "V.M.," failed to cooperate with medical personnel, behaved erratically during labor, and refused to consent to a cesarean delivery.[89] An obstetrician tried to convince her to consent to a cesarean, and concluded that she had the mental capacity to give informed consent with regard to the surgery. V.M. refused, and then she gave birth vaginally *without incident* and the baby was "in good medical condition." Even though a cesarean was clearly medically unnecessary, the New Jersey district court relied on V.M.'s refusal to consent to a cesarean as a basis for finding child neglect.[90] The court then terminated her parental rights because she had been under psychiatric care for 12 years before the birth, was not completely truthful about her psychiatric history, and failed to take her prescribed psychiatric medication. In this case, what precipitated the separation of an infant from her parents from the moment of her otherwise uneventful birth was the mother's refusal to consent to a cesarean that was demonstrably unnecessary.

These case studies, most of which received legal assistance from NAPW, reveal how laws and policies that aim to protect fetuses as separate from their mothers also provide justifications for denying basic civil and human rights to pregnant women who carry their pregnancies to term.[91] When reproductive health regimes grant rights to fertilized eggs, embryos, and fetuses, they deny pregnant women the fundamental rights that all persons normally have: the right to life, physical liberty, bodily integrity, due process of law, and equal protection. Of course, cases involving court-ordered cesareans and criminal prosecutions of pregnant women for allegedly harming their unborn children are relatively rare, and there has been no empirical research to examine how reproductive health laws influence what happens in more typical cases.

Reproductive Health Laws by State

Since abortion became legal in 1973, most states have passed laws to restrict reproductive rights. These laws include gestational limits for abortion, bans on the dilation and extraction (D&X) procedure for abortion (which abortion opponents describe using the non-medical term "partial-birth abortion"), laws requiring parental involvement in minors' abortion decisions, and mandatory waiting periods, ultrasounds, or counseling before an abortion.[92] Some laws, like "partial-birth abortion" bans and mandatory ultrasound laws, did not exist in 1995, but many states had these laws by 2015. To examine the effects of state-level reproductive health laws, I collected information about state laws and when the states passed or repealed them.[93]

There has been a flurry of legal activity to restrict abortion rights at the state level, especially since 2010.[94] State-level abortion restrictions include outright abortion bans and second-trimester abortion bans. Twelve states never repealed their pre-*Roe* bans on all abortions.[95] Between 1995 and 2015, three others legislated unconstitutional total abortion bans that will go into effect immediately if *Roe v. Wade* is over-turned.[96] After 2007, a growing number of states implemented unconstitutional bans on second-trimester abortions at specific gestational ages between 18 and 24 weeks, often with titles like the "Pain-Capable Fetus Protection Act" (based on the scientifically unproven assertion that fetuses can feel pain in the second trimester). Six states had these bans in 1995, and that rose to 23 states by 2015.[97]

Other laws attempt to persuade women not to have abortions by requiring parental involvement for minors or mandating biased counseling and waiting periods before women can undergo the procedure. In 1995, 28 states had parental notification or consent laws for abortions involving minors. That figure rose to 39 states by 2015. In 2015, over half of states had waiting periods between meeting with an abortion provider and the time of the abortion, and some had lengthened their waiting period from 24 to 48 or 72 hours. Mandatory waiting periods impose an especially large burden on low-income women and women who live far away from abortion providers, who may struggle to get consecutive days off from work, to find childcare for the children that they already have, and/or to travel to an abortion provider.

In 25 states, abortion providers also must provide biased counseling that sometimes includes required language that states a link between abortion and breast cancer, describes fetal pain, or warns about negative psychological effects of abortion—which scientific evidence does not support. Some biased counseling laws require that abortion providers refer women who are seeking an abortion to crisis pregnancy centers (CPCs) that give out misinformation in an effort to convince pregnant women to continue their pregnancies. Additionally, a growing number of states mandate that providers must perform an ultrasound and show it to the woman seeking an abortion before every abortion procedure. No states required an ultrasound in 1995, and Louisiana was the first in 2000. By 2015, 16 states had mandatory ultrasound laws.[98]

State governments also regulate insurance and restrict providers in ways that reduce abortion access, especially for low-income women who rely on government-funded programs to obtain contraception and other reproductive healthcare. Twenty states have gag rules that prohibit public employees and/or providers who receive any Title X funding or Medicaid payments from discussing abortion options.[99]

After 2010, many states passed TRAP laws that imposed medically un-necessary restrictions on facilities and providers that offer abortion ser-vices. TRAP laws include onerous licensing requirements for abortion providers, restrictions on the facilities where a woman can obtain a medication abortion, reporting requirements that force abortion pro-viders to give private medical information to state regulatory agencies, requirements that abortion providers have hospital admitting privileges or be within close proximity of a hospital, and requirements that abor-tion facilities meet standards for ambulatory surgery centers, including detailed, medically unnecessary specifications for the size of procedure rooms and corridors. These laws forced many reproductive health clin-ics to close, leading to a shortage of abortion providers in many states and forcing many women to go long distances to obtain an abortion.[100]

Before the state of Texas passed TRAP laws in 2013, there were 44 abortion clinics in Texas. After the TRAP laws went into effect, over half of them closed. Only two reopened after the Supreme Court struck down the law in *Whole Woman's Health v. Hellerstedt* (2016). In her con-curring opinion in *Whole Woman's Health*, Justice Ruth Bader Ginsburg wrote that abortions are very safe relative to other medical procedures, including childbirth, so claims that TRAP laws protected women's safety were patently false.[101] The real aim of these laws is to force clinics to close and to make it difficult for women to obtain abortions, which has its strongest impact on low-income women and women in remote areas, who may be unable to travel to obtain an abortion. Many states also at-tempt to reduce abortion access by prohibiting insurance coverage of abortion for public employees and/or in private insurance plans. Since the passage of the ACA in 2010, 27 states prohibit insurance plans on the health insurance exchanges from covering abortions. This means that women seeking abortions must pay out of pocket, regardless of their financial means or insurance status.

States have adopted other laws that criminalize pregnant women who have abortions, suffer from pregnancy loss, or have addictions to controlled substances. Thirty-five states have "fetal homicide" or *feticide* laws that protect fetuses as separate from their mothers. Their stated goal is to treat murders of pregnant women as aggravated offenses be-cause they involve two deaths rather than one, not to prosecute pregnant women for seeking an abortion. Yet some states have used feticide laws to prosecute pregnant women for ending a pregnancy, attempting to end a pregnancy, or suffering an unintentional pregnancy loss. Another growing trend has been the prosecution of substance-addicted pregnant women by defining prenatal substance use as child abuse. These laws criminalize pregnant women with substance addiction instead of offering them treatment, and the worst violations of pregnant women's rights under these laws have targeted low-income women of color.[102] In 1995, three states defined prenatal substance abuse as child abuse. By 2015, 21 had adopted this definition.

State laws can also support or restrict other aspects of reproductive healthcare. Sixteen states permit pharmacists to refuse to dispense prescriptions if they object to them for moral reasons, which gives pharmacists discretion over access to contraception.[103] Eleven states legally prohibit direct-entry (non-nurse) midwifery, which reduces pregnant women's choices about where to give birth. On the other hand, some states directly support reproductive choice by requiring pharmacists to dispense contraceptive prescriptions, regulating non-nurse midwives as licensed practitioners, and protecting women's health clinics from violence. In 1995, 17 states licensed direct-entry midwives. That figure increased to 28 by 2015. Twelve states legally protected women's health clinics from violence in 1995, and that rose to 17 states by 2015. These laws and policies affirm pregnant women's rights to make decisions about their medical care.

Reproductive Health Regimes

While a few states increased protections for women's health clinics and direct-entry midwives over time, the overall trend between 1995 and 2015 was toward increasing reproductive health restrictions. Figure 2.6 shows the change in the average number of state-level reproductive health restrictions over time.

Based on the data in figure 2.6, I defined states with less than four reproductive health restrictions as *woman-centered* and those with more than eight reproductive health restrictions as *fetus-centered* (see table 2.3). The most woman-centered state was Oregon, with no abortion restrictions, licensing for direct-entry midwives, and protections against violence for reproductive health clinics for the whole 1995–2015 period. In contrast, Mississippi was the most fetus-centered state: it never repealed its pre-

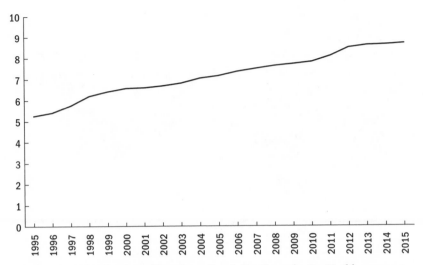

Figure 2.6. Average Number of State Laws Restricting Reproductive Health, 1995–2015. Based on a count from 0 to 16 of the following laws: a ban on first- or second-trimester abortions, a "partial-birth abortion" procedure ban, misleading counseling requirements, mandatory waiting periods before an abortion, parental notification or consent laws, feticide laws, the definition of prenatal substance use as child abuse, a law that permits pharmacists to refuse to fill contraceptive prescriptions, special licensing requirements for abortion clinics, requirements for abortion clinics to meet ambulatory surgery center specifications, requirements that abortion providers have hospital admitting privileges or operate within 30 miles of a hospital, mandatory ultrasound laws, a lack of licensing for direct-entry midwives, and a lack of protection against violence for reproductive health clinics. Source: Compiled legal data from Nexis Uni.

TABLE 2.3: Reproductive Health Regimes

Regime type	States
Woman-centered (most to least)	Oregon, Washington, California, New York, Colorado, Vermont, Montana, New Hampshire, Nevada, New Mexico, New Jersey, Delaware, Connecticut, Hawaii, Maine, Wyoming
Fetus-centered (most to least)	Mississippi, Indiana, South Dakota, Missouri, Kentucky, Louisiana, North Dakota, Alabama, Arkansas, Michigan, South Carolina, Georgia, Ohio, Arizona, Nebraska, Oklahoma, Pennsylvania

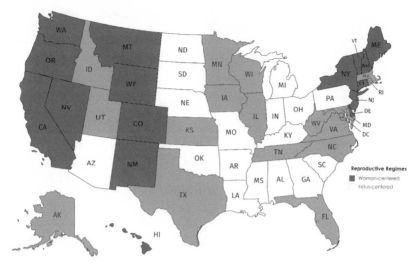

Figure 2.7. Reproductive Regimes. Source: Compiled legal data from Nexis Uni.

Roe abortion ban, and it imposed a growing number of restrictions over time. These included a "partial-birth" abortion ban and biased counseling laws in 1997, a pharmacist refusal provision in 1998, a feticide law in 2004, one of the first mandatory ultrasound laws in 2007, and a requirement that abortion providers have hospital admitting privileges in 2012. From 1995 to 2015, Mississippi maintained parental consent laws, a mandatory waiting period for abortions, special licensing requirements for abortion providers, requirements that abortion clinics meet the standards of ambulatory surgery centers, and a gag rule prohibiting counseling about abortion. Currently, Mississippi has only one remaining abortion clinic.

Figure 2.7 illustrates the states that are most woman- or fetus-centered, with woman-centered reproductive health regimes concentrated in the Northeast and the West, and fetus-centered reproductive health regimes concentrated in the South and the Midwest. Other states had more mixed reproductive health regimes, although most of them enacted increasing reproductive health restrictions over time.

Reproductive health regimes are products of the overall political environment of a state, and woman-centered states had more liberal state legislatures, on average, while fetus-centered states had more conservative legislatures.[104] Of course, terms like *conservative, moderate,* and *liberal,* or *Democrat, Independent,* and *Republican,* often mean different things to different people and they do not fully capture the variation in reproductive health regimes. While some conservatives and some Republican state legislatures focus on social issues in ways that lead to restrictive reproductive health laws, others care more about protecting business interests or individual rights. Similar differences exist among liberal voters and Democratic state governments, which can lean in more or less libertarian directions. Of course, some legislatures are more divided, and the electorate in some states swings between liberal and conservative views, leading legislators to juggle the needs and preferences of more than one master. Others exhibit consistent political views and party power over time. But while public opinion about tort reforms and reproductive health laws can change, most laws remain in place for a long time after they pass. This legislative inertia, combined with changing citizen views, can make state laws somewhat independent from the political leanings of the electorate. Courts also play an important role in reproductive health regimes: they can overturn state laws as unconstitutional, defying the political will of state legislators and/or the voters that elected them. This happens occasionally with tort laws and more often with reproductive health laws.

RJ theory argues that woman-centered versus fetus-centered laws affect birth as well as contraception and abortion, with their greatest impact on vulnerable women. But there has been no empirical research to examine how reproductive health laws influence typical practices surrounding birth in the United States. This book attempts to fill that gap. I argue that state laws that restrict or enable reproductive choice in the area of contraception and abortion are an important aspect of the reproductive health regimes that influence common maternity care practices like elective induction, EFM, cesarean delivery, and VBAC.

Throughout this book, I will return to the ideas of patient- and provider-friendly tort regimes and woman- or fetus-centered reproductive health regimes to understand the role of the legal environment in maternity care outcomes. But first, a key argument of neo-institutional theories is that fields like the maternity care field respond to the law by intensifying their existing cultural scripts and routine practices. In the next chapter, I explore beliefs about medical malpractice risk in the American maternity care field.

3

Myths of Malpractice

Liability Risk in American Maternity Care

The *institutional culture* in maternity care includes symbols, values, goals, and understandings that maternity care providers internalize and take for granted.[1] This institutional culture helps maternity care providers to maintain certainty and stability by drawing on the underlying vocabulary of the medical profession to create order, coordinate communication, and develop cultural *strategies of action* (skills, habits, routines, classifications, and scripts).[2] The culture of medicine includes beliefs about the tort system that define it as an arbitrary, unpredictable, and irrational threat to the medical profession. Tort regimes matter because American medicine defines malpractice liability risk as a problem that creates unacceptable uncertainty and ambiguity.

In an effort to maintain certainty and stability, medical schools have both formal and informal curricula that emphasize the likelihood of facing malpractice lawsuits and the need for physicians to protect themselves from them.[3] Clinical rotations and residencies in hospitals reinforce this fear of liability risk. The tort reform movement of the 1980s and 1990s launched an aggressive and successful public relations campaign that helped to fuel a culture of fear in medicine. Liability insurers and hospital legal counsel also heighten awareness of liability risk in medicine by forcefully reminding healthcare providers that they are vulnerable to malpractice lawsuits.[4] Liability insurance companies require physicians to take approved continuing education courses that exaggerate the risk of lawsuits and encourage legally defensive practices. Risk managers in hospitals develop strategies and design protocols for avoiding liability. These front-line legal workers play a unique role in *constructing risk* by focusing providers' attention on liability risk and institutionalizing a culture of fear in American healthcare. They are analogous to the HR professionals and compliance officers who interpret civil rights laws and develop policies and procedures for the workplace.[5]

At the same time that there is a strong, institutionalized culture of malpractice liability fear in the American healthcare field, medical malpractice suits have been declining over time (see figure 2.3). One might argue that this decline was caused by more defensive medicine (the use of unnecessary extra tests and procedures to reduce malpractice liability risk), but medical malpractice attorneys said that these cases declined because the cost of litigating increased. In other words, the belief that there is a high risk of malpractice lawsuits and that many malpractice suits are frivolous is at least partly a cultural myth—albeit one that is powerful for shaping obstetric and organizational behavior in the maternity care field.

A Culture of Fear

Even though medical malpractice claims have declined since the first decade of the millennium, a fear of liability is deeply rooted in the culture of the medical profession. The two major journals of the American obstetric profession, *Obstetrics & Gynecology* and the *American Journal of Obstetrics and Gynecology* (*AJOG*), published over 75 articles and editorials on malpractice risk and "the professional liability crisis" between 1995 and 2015.[6] Obstetricians worry about liability more than most medical specialists do because of the higher average rate and cost of obstetric lawsuits. A 2005 study found that OB/GYNs experience a professional liability claim an average of once every 11 years, and a 2009 ACOG survey revealed that ACOG members had an average of 2.7 malpractice claims and 90.5% had experienced at least one claim.[7]

The risk of malpractice liability is higher in obstetrics than in most other medical specializations for at least three reasons. First, many families that experience a birth injury need resources to care for a child that needs lifelong care. Dr. Ribeiro, an obstetrician who worked in a rural area, said,

> The real issue is that if you have a damaged child, it costs a fortune to raise that child and there should be some mechanism by which you have

the money to take care of that child but we don't have to pay lawyers and others a tremendous amount too. Bad physicians should be prosecuted and should lose their licenses, but so many of these things are just unavoidable. Like cerebral palsy occurs in utero, and there's nothing you can do about it. If you have a child with cerebral palsy, how are you going to get the money, other than by suing me, to raise that child?

As obstetricians know, families that experience a bad birth outcome often seek compensation through the tort system to help them to care for a child with special needs, which costs much more than an infant death. As a result, the worst possible birth outcome in terms of liability risk is a damaged baby. Dr. Brooks, who worked at a teaching hospital, said, "A dead baby doesn't pay as much as a damaged baby, so they don't want a damaged baby because that pays out the most." When a birth injury occurs due to medical negligence, the use of tort litigation to obtain compensation fulfills one of the goals of tort law: to compensate victims for injuries caused by others' harmful activities. Because the United States has few publicly funded resources to assist citizens with significant disabilities, many families can only obtain these resources by suing the healthcare provider. This is one reason that the United States has 50% higher rates of malpractice claims than the United Kingdom or Australia, and 350% more than Canada, even though all of these countries follow British-style tort law.[8] Medical malpractice lawsuits would be less necessary if the US provided universal healthcare and other services that reduce the cost of disabilities for individual families.

Second, juries are often sympathetic to plaintiffs in cases involving babies. Dr. Judy Hart, a hospital administrator, said,

It's a very high-risk area because, for the jury, nobody likes to see a baby that's expected to be born healthy, to not be born healthy for whatever reason. Even bad outcomes that could not have been avoided can draw some sort of opinion.

Lisa Cheung, another hospital administrator, said, "I think that the juries seem to be more sympathetic when you have a baby involved, versus for example, a knee surgery case." Jury sympathy increases the likelihood of a judgment for the plaintiff and the typical amount of the damage award, although very few cases go to trial and defendants win most cases that do.[9]

A third reason was that liability insurance premiums are very high in obstetrics, which means that liability risk has material consequences for maternity care providers.[10] Most maternity care providers maintain liability insurance to protect themselves from direct financial loss if someone sues them for malpractice, but liability insurance costs do not affect all providers equally. Some hospitals underwrite group insurance for their physician-employees, which means that they assume the financial risk of liability and cover employees up to standard coverage limits. Dr. Hart said,

> We do have some physicians who are employed and are insured by us. By "us," I mean that the hospital has a group liability plan and they insure themselves and insure a handful of physicians. The claims attorney gets involved in helping those physicians know where their risk is, and whether risk management needs to occur. Any employed physicians are expected to attend close-claim reviews. And they would also advise us with regard to medical staff privileges and credentialing.

These kinds of in-house group insurance plans meant that eligible providers in hospital-based practices did not need to purchase individual liability coverage and they were less susceptible to fluctuating premiums, although they were subject to oversight by hospital legal counsel and risk management. Four of the obstetricians that I interviewed worked for a hospital or practice group that covered their malpractice insurance. Dr. McGinley, who worked at an academic hospital, said,

> Because I'm at an academic center, I'm pretty well protected in that we have a group insurance plan. I don't pay my own premiums, so I couldn't tell you what they are. Now, certainly, I don't want to get sued and we have an in-house legal department.

Working at a self-insured hospital limited providers' personal financial burden, so that they did not have to think about the cost of liability insurance on a daily basis.

Other providers worked at federally qualified health centers that are covered by the Federal Tort Claims Act (FTCA). They pay no out-of-pocket liability insurance premiums because the FTCA protects government healthcare employees from individual liability. Dr. Bennett, who worked for a community health center, said:

> We are covered by the Federal Torts Claims Act. . . . And that's actually a nice coverage to have because if you want to sue us, you have to sue the federal government. So I think there is less frivolity involved with this coverage.

Anyone who wants to file a malpractice claim against a provider who works at a federally qualified health center has to sue the government—which is much more daunting and expensive than suing a private healthcare provider. The FTCA and self-insurance by hospitals meant that some maternity care providers did not need to think about liability insurance costs. Partly as a result, the smaller pool of providers in need of private insurance paid more, because fewer providers had to share the risk of all providers in the pool. That is how insurance risk pools work—but it means that obstetricians who have to purchase liability insurance have a larger financial burden.

Providers with private liability insurance often work several months out of the year simply to cover their premiums, and every claim leads to higher premium rates. When I asked him what affects individual's premium costs, Sam Durand, who worked in risk management, said:

> If you have a physician that has had more claims or lawsuits against them, from an insurance perspective, they'll be considered higher risk. All of those cases could be completely defensible, which sometimes frustrates physicians, because you'll find that a particular physician may have been sued three times and then has a colleague who has never been sued. The one that's been sued three times is the one that's considered the high-quality provider by everybody else, but just happens to have gotten into these situations that were perhaps completely defensible. But because they've been sued three times, on paper, they are going to be charged more.

In short, providers with a history of malpractice claims cost much more to insure, even if they were not at fault.

At the same time, liability risk is only one of many influences on liability insurance premiums. These premiums also respond to returns on investments from liability insurance companies' investment portfolios and mergers of liability insurance companies that reduce market competition.[11] Malpractice insurance markets go through "soft" cycles with stable premium rates, broad coverage, and strong competition among insurers, and "hard" cycles that are driven by weaker competition, a higher number of malpractice claims, rapidly rising premiums, narrower coverage options, and fewer insurers. During the last "hard" market cycle from 1993 to 2000, net investment income grew at a lower rate, leading to higher premiums for reasons unrelated to liability risk. Dr. Garcia, an obstetrician with 20 years of experience, said,

> Premiums are a huge part of the overhead. They have come down recently, but we pay the highest overhead of any subspecialty, especially when you compare our overhead to what our income is. It's huge, especially when compared to any other specialty because we don't make salaries like general surgeons or cardiovascular or neurosurgeons. Most of us are doing just a little bit better than country practice doctors.

It is well known that obstetricians pay higher liability insurance premiums than other medical specialties, so it is unsurprising that their premiums are burdensome compared to their incomes.[12] When I asked her how medical liability premiums affected the way that she practiced, Dr. Murray, an obstetrician at a hospital with a birth center, said, "It takes a lot of the joy out of what I do. I think I work three to four months of the year just to pay malpractice insurance."

The high cost of liability insurance led some providers to stop practicing obstetrics altogether. Dr. Carlson, who now worked exclusively in gynecology, described how she decided to exclude obstetrics from her practice:

> I wanted my own little practice, and I really thought, "Do I want to deliver babies?" I really did like delivering babies, but I was getting a little older at that point and I thought, "I don't know if I want to deliver babies

and being on call 24/7." Then I thought, "How much would this cost in malpractice premiums?" . . . For OB, it was around $65,000 a year. What I did is I figured out how many babies I would have to deliver to pay for the $65,000 per year minimum malpractice insurance. I figured that I would have to deliver at least twelve babies a month for six months just to pay for the malpractice insurance and so I decided that wouldn't work for me.

At the time that she opened a solo practice, the cost of insurance to practice obstetrics was prohibitive. It has only increased since then.

One reason for very high liability insurance premiums in obstetrics is that the statute of limitations for birth injuries is very long in most states, often extending two to three years after a minor reaches 18 years of age.[13] Providers are vulnerable for this long because the statute of limitations on birth-related cases does not begin until the child reaches the age of majority, 18 years. This means that liability insurance needs to cover maternity care providers for births up to 21 years in the past. When maternity care providers terminate their insurance plan in order to change jobs or retire, they need "tail" insurance to cover their liability exposure until the statute of limitations runs out.

A Bitter Pill to Swallow: Experience with Malpractice Litigation

I interviewed five obstetricians who had experienced litigation firsthand, although only three were named in birth-related suits. Dr. McDonald was an experienced high-risk specialist who had been practicing obstetrics for over thirty years and had been sued more than once:

> My first suit I had when I was a resident. I remember how disturbing it is to be sued. Most of us try to do the right thing. Not everybody agrees on what the right thing is. . . . The first time I got sued, I thought I had done things as well as could be. . . . Then, for a while, I looked at every patient like, "Are you going to sue me?" because there is a personal level of it. It sounds like it's all about me, but I never wanted this woman to have this outcome. On the other hand, it really seems sort of absurd that somehow, because this happened, it would somehow be my fault, or I should pay. In my not-so-humble approach, nature has a lot of possibilities that can happen, and not everything is above average.

Dr. McDonald was anxious about liability risk because she believed that patients could sue her for any bad birth outcome, even when it was beyond her control.

The complexity of pregnancy, labor, and birth make it impossible to guarantee perfect outcomes in every pregnancy, but cultural expectations around birth changed with modernization—along with improvements in public health and sanitation, declines in maternal and infant mortality, and the medicalization of childbirth. These changes led to unrealistic expectations about uncertain, random, and uncontrollable events.[14] Because most families expect good outcomes, some will sue the doctor or hospital when they have an unavoidable tragedy. Dr. Alec Yoder was a medical director for a health insurance plan and had experience in obstetrics, and he said,

> Everybody wants a happy, healthy baby, so the minute your baby's not happy, healthy, and completely normal, it has to be somebody's fault. So OBs get sued all the time for babies that may have a bad outcome, and oftentimes it just happened. There is no rhyme or reason to it. But the doctor is held responsible for it because, if you don't have a happy healthy baby, it has to be somebody's fault. . . . I had a patient who wasn't my patient, but was in my practice, who had a completely normal pregnancy. Two days before she was scheduled to deliver, the baby stopped moving. She came in and had a fetal demise. It was because there was a knot in the cord. There was nothing you could do to diagnose it, and nothing you could do to prevent it. She actually sued everybody and their grandmother, and ended up with about $4 million. Even though there was no reason, you get a sympathetic jury and a mom with pictures of a dead baby, and they say, "Well, somebody had to be at fault."

In this case, a patient successfully sued her care providers even though medical errors or negligence did not cause the tragic outcome. This provides an example of the kind of lawsuit that escalates maternity care providers' fear of liability, because the tragedy was real but a provider's negligence did not cause it. Cases like this increase providers' uncertainty and make them worry about the possible legal ramifications of an unpredictable bad outcome in every birth.

Theories of risk can help to explain the persistence of a culture of fear in maternity care, despite the declining rate of litigation. Contemporary developed societies have used scientific analysis and technology to reclassify *uncertainty* into *risk*. *Uncertainty* is an unknown, whereas *risk* reframes unfavorable outcomes as statistically predictable events.[15] In this context, childbirth is no longer a physiological process with inevitable uncertainties because there is a statistical probability of an unexpected bad birth outcome.[16] At the same time, it is difficult to understand and evaluate *very rare probabilities*, like the likelihood of a catastrophic birth outcome in a normal pregnancy. In response, individuals and organizations tend to either ignore or exaggerate the odds of highly unlikely events.

When it comes to liability, maternity care providers usually exaggerate the threat and overestimate the risk of a bad birth outcome because the downside of a birth injury or death is much larger than the upside of a normal birth. For providers, malpractice litigation leads to serious financial and reputational losses and can affect their ability to obtain hospital privileges and liability insurance coverage. Dr. Judy Hart was a hospital administrator who made decisions about physicians' admitting privileges, and she said,

> As an administrator, and the responsible party for credentialing and privileging, I had to make sure that we were fully informed through the application and reappointment processes, and that we knew what the history was for each applicant . . . For a new application of a physician, the malpractice history is reviewed from the very beginning of the license. The reappointment we do every two years. We review what has been decided or what has occurred during the previous two years. In the new applications, we have a right to turn down privileges based on the fact that we don't think the application represents someone that we want to have on staff. Generally, rather than saying, "No," we tell the applicant that it doesn't look good for privileges, and they can voluntarily withdraw. In that case there's no black mark against them that they have to answer for the rest of their lives. They can just withdraw their application.

As Dr. Hart noted, physicians' malpractice histories influenced their ability to obtain hospital privileges, so claims could threaten their livelihood even if they won the case or the plaintiff dropped it.

A history of malpractice claims could also affect a provider's ability to obtain liability insurance, especially if they lost a case. Julie Connolly, a malpractice attorney, said:

> OB/GYNs pay close to the highest premiums, and if you have one "bad baby," you're almost uninsurable. There aren't many carriers who will come in and say, "You've been tagged for X-million ten years ago, but we'll be happy to write you another policy." It just forces the OBs to make very conservative decisions even if it's not medically correct.

In her view, the risk of becoming uninsurable encouraged defensive medicine, even if that meant deviating from evidence-based practices. Even for those who did not lose their insurance, high liability premiums could elevate the importance of legal risk in obstetricians' minds, leading to a strong preference for *risk avoidance*.[17] This preference has encouraged overcautious policies and practices and has narrowed the definition of normality in pregnancy and childbirth.

Just What the Doctor Ordered: Defending against Liability Risk

For maternity care providers, defense against liability risk involved unreflective and taken-for-granted actions that fit with the culture and cognitive schemas of the maternity care field. As Powell and Colyvas argued, institutional forces frame the possibilities for action in ways that individuals can apply in everyday practice.[18] The culture of the maternity care field offered two paths for maternity care providers to defend themselves against liability risk.

The first path was to follow an evidence-based SOC. This strategy was particularly common among CNMs and among obstetricians who practiced in academic hospitals that emphasized EBM. When I asked her how malpractice suits influenced the way that she practiced, Dr. Brooks said:

> You don't like to think about covering your butt in medicine, but you always are. You keep thinking, "Down the road, how would this look, if this went to court?" Does one argue that you're making better decisions then? *Is this the standard of care?* Because the thought is, with someone

in a community similar to mine, would they consider this an appropriate decision? That's what you're being measured against. *That's a good question to think about:* "Am I practicing within an acceptable boundary that colleagues in another community, similar to mine, would find my actions appropriate?"

Liability risk motivated Dr. Brooks to be especially diligent about following accepted practices. This response to legal risk followed an evidence-based principle for reducing litigation, which meant that tort laws met one of their intended goals: to deter risky practices. In fact, research has demonstrated that physicians who aim to offer the best patient care, rather than to defend themselves against litigation, are less likely to be sued.[19]

Following accepted evidence-based practices should defend maternity providers against lawsuits most of the time, because an estimated 70% of obstetric malpractice lawsuits are a result of substandard care that has injured a patient. The other 30% are an unpredictable threat. Rob Thompson, a defense attorney, said,

> Typically, if you do a procedure, there are risks involved in the procedure. If you did a C-section and it was unwarranted, and you got a bad result, then you can get sued. If you do a forceps delivery, and not a vacuum extraction, or something else, that creates a risk. I think the bottom line is that, as a physician, if you do anything at all and there is a bad result, you have the risk of being sued.

With some medical injuries, there is ambiguity about whether a provider was negligent, so providers can be vulnerable to lawsuits even if they follow "best practices."

Most obstetricians shared Rob Thompson's assessment and believed that bad outcomes could lead to legal action even if they provided excellent care. When I asked her what kind of things increase or decrease the likelihood of being sued, Dr. Garcia said:

> Bad outcomes increase it, no matter what, even if the doctor does everything they are supposed to do. We just know, particularly in OB, even if

you did everything right, if something comes out wrong, you just know
that you are probably going to be sued.

Most obstetricians believed that patients would sue them for unavoidable bad outcomes. This increased their anxiety and fueled the culture of
fear because they felt like liability risk was beyond their control.

Some physicians felt victimized by the tort system because they offered the best care that they could, but faced lawsuits anyway. Dr. Murray said,

> It doesn't matter how well we do stuff, you are still just a lottery ticket
> for somebody to sue you. You can do everything perfectly and counsel
> somebody perfectly, but if the outcome of the baby isn't perfect, it doesn't
> really matter if you did everything right. You're just a lottery ticket. It's
> not always some person's fault, and that's what's really frustrating. I think
> the social contract as a physician is to "above all, do no harm." I took
> an oath to do that. Above all, I will do no harm. I will do everything I
> can to try to do the right thing. Of course, if somebody makes a mistake
> there should be compensation, but when you've done everything right, it
> doesn't even matter.

She believed that offering good care did not protect her from liability,
with all of its emotional and financial costs.

In fact, Dr. Murray was the only informant who described a frivolous
claim against her, when a patient filed a claim after apparently having a
good outcome:

> I had a patient who was very happy with the procedure, until she got the
> bill, and then she decided that she wanted to make a claim against the
> hospital. She never had a lawyer look at the case. She never even hired a
> lawyer. She just made a personal claim to the hospital that she was un-
> happy with the bill, so they settled the bill, and my name went into the
> National Data Bank. It was a claim, but it wasn't a formal suit. It was a
> request for money, and because it was a claim against the hospital, I still
> got reported to the National Data Bank. . . . It was so threatening, and
> then I had to go through hiring a lawyer, going through [the liability in-

surance company], and hiring somebody else of expert opinion to look at the case. It was totally groundless. I can't counter-sue her, saying this was ridiculous. I had to go through all the threats and it doesn't matter that I did everything right anyway.

Cases like this fueled obstetricians' beliefs that malpractice lawsuits were frivolous, unpredictable, and often unrelated to the quality of care.

The uncertainty and unpredictability of lawsuits magnified obstetricians' liability fear and shifted their attention toward the second path of *self-protection*, for both financial and emotional reasons. For some, legal claims amplified the emotional distress that they already felt after births with tragic outcomes. Dr. Carlson said,

> If you're in a situation where something bad happens, then the malpractice threat is on top of all of the other difficult stuff that you have to deal with. All of the emotional difficulties of dealing with a death, or the sorrow that you feel, the sadness for the family. And the malpractice threat is just another threat on top of that, so it's kind of like insult to injury.

Most obstetricians enter the medical profession to help people, and specialize in obstetrics because they want to work with women and infants. They try to offer the best care that they can, so malpractice litigation is not only a financial threat, it is also an emotional one.

The stress of dealing with malpractice lawsuits led some maternity care providers to stop practicing. Dr. Ribeiro worked at a rural hospital where one of the few other obstetricians in his practice left after he faced a malpractice suit:

> One of the physicians [in my hospital] quit doing obstetrics. . . . A large part of that had to do with a malpractice case against him. He did nothing wrong but he was sued, and his whole attitude toward the practice of medicine changed. He was controlling before, but now it drives him crazy. He wants to know everything that is going on in the labor and delivery room, and that's just not a way you can live because you have to trust the nurses to let you know if something is going wrong. You can't be there all the time. So he quit. . . . Being sued, even though people tell

you it is not personal, is incredibly personal. People are saying not only that you did something wrong, but that you knew about it. For most of us, that's a direct attack on who we believe we are.

Most maternity care providers dedicate themselves to a career of service to women and families, and medical malpractice lawsuits challenged their beliefs about their purpose as physicians. This could encourage maternity care providers to leave the field, especially if they felt like they had been sued in spite of doing their best.

In short, offering high-quality, evidence-based care was one strategy for reducing medical liability, but it was not always enough. Facing malpractice suits after doing their best to listen to patients and meet their needs could be traumatic, so obstetricians often attempted to protect themselves from medical malpractice lawsuits by intensifying their dominant cultural *strategy of action*: the medicalization schema.[20] For example, Dr. Nelson, a perinatal specialist, described her experience with a malpractice suit for shoulder dystocia, which lowered her threshold for intervening into labor and delivering babies by cesarean:[21]

> I was sued once for shoulder dystocia. After that, I was more inclined to do C-sections on big babies. I took on a patient who was a midwifery patient, who was obese, and she had diabetes, and I took on her care at the end of her pregnancy. . . . [After that lawsuit], I would not have taken a patient who was in that condition. She would not have had the option of the natural birth plan. I would be much less inclined to honor her desire to labor.

Dr. Nelson's experience with a malpractice suit made her less willing to take chances with patients who wanted fewer interventions or had birth plans that deviated from typical care. After that, she became much quicker to override her patients' preferences and to intervene with a cesarean than she was before. She said,

> She didn't want a C-section. She wanted to be induced. It was a recipe for disaster. She was three hundred pounds. She had gestational diabetes. It's a bad combination. That baby, unfortunately, died also because I couldn't get the baby out for the life of me so I had to push the baby back in and

take her to the operating room. . . . After that I was just a little more gun-shy with things. I probably documented better. It changed how I docu-mented. I began to document more defensively in advance, especially when it came to those types of patients. . . . It was an unfortunate loss, but in the end, I grew from it. It made me a better doctor.

As Dr. Nelson learned from her experience, she also took a more inter-ventionist approach and did not take chances that she might have taken before. When I asked her if she had advised the patient who sued her not to labor, she said:

No. I think I was just a cowgirl and I scanned the baby and it didn't seem big. I used the ultrasound, but the estimated fetal weight was off, and I was off. You can't really assess, in a three-hundred-pound woman, how big her baby is. You really don't know. . . . Now I am more seasoned so now I am really looking at everything. Is it a boy baby? Did she get Pi-tocin? Did we induce her labor? Did she go into labor spontaneously? What's her labor curve? I go down the ACOG list. I never did anything wrong, but they call up the ACOG technical bulletin, and they say, "Dr. Nelson, did you know it was a male fetus?" for example. I'm not clairvoy-ant, but now all of those things register with me so I think twice about allowing people to labor.

As Dr. Nelson said, she was more risk-avoidant after she experienced this malpractice lawsuit, which meant that she relied more on the medi-cal model of birth and was quicker to override her patients' preferences and intervene with a cesarean. As this example illustrates, obstetricians' strategies for managing malpractice liability risk follow professional guidelines that reinforce strategies of action from the medicalization schema: more technology, more interventions, and more cesarean deliveries.[22]

This approach to managing ambiguity reinforced the obstetric pro-fession's definition of high-tech solutions as the most appropriate way to cope with uncertainty. It may have been medically appropriate in extreme cases like the one that Dr. Nelson described, but it is not an optimal approach for managing the average case. It is also impossible to predict shoulder dystocia, so attempts to do so tend to cast a wide net—and a wide net inevitably catches a lot of false positives.[23] Obstetricians tend to cast this wide net when they believe, first, that there is a significant legal threat and, second, that the medical model will protect them. As Dr. Nelson noted above, ACOG's professional recommendations encourage providers to view the medical model of birth as legally defensive and they offer institutional legitimacy to medicalized practices. Cultural scripts based on the medicalization schema help maternity care providers to maintain professional legitimacy while managing legal risk.[24]

To summarize, most obstetricians share a culture of liability fear and a majority have some experience with malpractice claims. They often believe that providing evidence-based care reduces the risk, but does not eliminate it. As a result, most obstetricians feel vulnerable to lawsuits and view liability risk as outside of their control. This produces a culture of anxiety and risk avoidance. A common strategy for managing risk is to fall back on the medicalization schema: ordering more diagnostic tests and intervening more into labor and birth. This raises the question of whether these approaches to managing legal risk reflect the legal reality that obstetricians face. The answer is both yes and no.

The Burden of Proof

While obstetricians and hospitals worried about the threat of medical malpractice suits and engaged in risk avoidance behavior, the NPDB revealed that malpractice lawsuits have declined over time—and all of the malpractice lawyers that I interviewed knew this. Rob Thompson said,

> The largest insurer in Arizona insures physicians. Over the last three years, it has seen a drop of 35–40% in the usual caseload. In the early 2000s, the number of malpractice cases filed around the state was about 600. About three years ago, in 2007 or 2008, they dropped significantly. The numbers went down about 30%. The next year they went down about 30% more than the year before. They are starting to come up a little now, but they were down into the 300s and 400s. It's been at least 30–40% less cases being filed than there used to be. That's true nationally as well.

Similarly, Josh Shaffer, a highly experienced plaintiff's attorney, said, "If you go to the Clerk of Courts, and you ask for medical malpractice filings over the last ten years—and they keep these statistics—you will see that they have fallen by about 75–80%." Both of these highly experienced medical malpractice attorneys had seen a substantial drop in the number of cases over time (even if they disagreed in their estimates of how much these cases had declined).

Some might argue that the rate of medical malpractice lawsuits has declined because a growing number of states adopted tort reform laws during the same period (see figures 2.1–2.3). After all, tort reforms should reduce the rate of malpractice lawsuits by making it harder to file frivolous lawsuits and limiting the amount that victims of negligence receive in those lawsuits. I interviewed attorneys in a state that had no caps on damage awards, which is what most people think of when they think about tort reform, and all of them said that lawsuits were declining.[25] When I asked Jane Hart-Thompson, a defense attorney, why the number of medical malpractice cases had decreased, she said, "There's a faction of people who say that it's tort reform but we don't have tort reform in Arizona, and Arizona's caseload has gone down the same as California's or Texas's." Attorneys with a lot of experience in the field were unanimous in their observation that the number of birth-related malpractice cases had declined along with all other types of malpractice suits, even without caps on damages. Given that state legislatures did not enact caps on damages in response to high liability risk, and these caps did not reduce liability risk, why did the rate of malpractice lawsuits decline?

It Costs an Arm and a Leg

One reason for the decline in malpractice lawsuits was that the tort reform movement waged a successful public relations campaign against trial lawyers that affected juries' attitudes toward medical negligence cases. Josh Shaffer firmly believed that they had effectively *miseducated* the public in ways that made medical malpractice cases harder for plaintiffs to win:

> Over the last 15 years or so, there has been a profound effort and plan
> by the insurance industry to inculcate the public with the notion that

lawsuits are wrong, that medical malpractice lawsuits in particular are a scam, and that it is the reason that health costs have gone up. That doctors practice defensive medicine, and that all of this is because of—and this is so important the way that they framed it—this is not because of injuries to people, but because of the greedy plaintiff lawyer. . . . It is very simple for someone to look at a plaintiff's lawyer who gets a million dollar verdict, who makes a million bucks in a case, and say, "You greedy fucking lawyers." The reality is that the person is first hurt, the person seeks out a lawyer, and then the lawyer processes the case for them. But they have completely changed that characterization around.

In his view, lobbyists for the medical and insurance industries had successfully turned public opinion against plaintiffs in medical malpractice cases, to the point where over half of all states capped damage awards. Also, over 90% of verdicts favor the defendant (provider), whether they settle in arbitration or (more rarely) go to trial.[26]

While public relations efforts in favor of tort reform may have swayed public opinion and affected potential jurors, all of the attorneys said that one of the biggest changes in the previous decade was a dramatic increase in the cost of litigating malpractice lawsuits. Sam Durand, a hospital administrator involved in risk management, said,

I attribute part of it to the type of cases that they are. They are actually very complex to litigate and they are very expensive to litigate, from a plaintiff perspective. Most good plaintiff attorneys will not take cases that are not good. At one time, and this was a long time ago—I've been doing this for about 25 years now—it was easier to sue and not as expensive to sue. I think they've become more sophisticated and more expensive.

In this respect, Mr. Durand agreed with most attorneys.

Only one attorney that I interviewed suggested that it had anything to do with reductions in negligence. Mark Wagner said, "I think it's because medical malpractice cases have resulted in doctors and hospitals developing checklists and being more careful and giving better care." None of the other attorneys believed that lawsuits had declined because physicians and hospitals had become more cautious or quality had improved. Instead, there was a clear consensus that the number of cases declined primarily because they were expensive to litigate, and even Mark Wagner said that plaintiff's attorneys could only pursue cases with a high dollar value because of the cost of litigating medical malpractice claims. When I asked him how he decides whether to take a case, he said,

> The gist of it is that we have to conclude that the negligence is very clear and very easy to prove, and the injury has to be profound. We don't take medical malpractice cases that are a judged to be a value of less than seven or eight hundred thousand dollars because they are too expensive to process. We learned the hard way that, even when we take a clear liability case of medical negligence but our case has a value on it of two or three hundred thousand dollars, by the end of the day, when we get a settlement, after we pay the costs and attorney's fees, the clients are getting hardly anything and we aren't getting that much for the time we put into it. It really doesn't do anybody any good. There are a lot of cases out there that never get dealt with anymore because plaintiff attorneys, by and large, will not take them. And there aren't very many of us anymore who do plaintiffs' negligence cases because they are so expensive.

Like all of the plaintiff's lawyers that I talked to, he said that the cost of litigating was a deterrent to practicing medical malpractice law, leading to fewer lawyers who represented plaintiffs in these cases. Attorneys who did represent plaintiffs could only serve victims with injuries that were dramatic enough to command large damage awards.

Why were medical malpractice claims so expensive to pursue? The big contributor, according to attorneys, was expert requirements that set standards for expert testimony and/or required an expert to certify that a malpractice claim represents genuine medical negligence. Josh Shaffer said,

> When you look at the process that the med mal crisis has led to, it has led to much more rigorous requirements. Before you file a suit, you have to file an affidavit by a physician in that specialty, that he has reviewed it and that there is medical negligence. It's right up front. So you have to have it reviewed by someone, and that ensures that the claim is not frivolous. Then you have to, at the time of disclosure, have a more extensive statement of what the negligence was and what the causation is. Then, during

a designated time, you have to reveal your experts and you have to give a very detailed explanation of what they think the negligence is.

In short, experts must certify the merit of the claim and provide testimony, which dramatically increases the cost of lawsuits and forces plaintiff's attorneys to review cases more carefully before they file them.

Most expert requirements mandate that expert witnesses in malpractice cases share the same medical specialty as the primary defendants.[27] If the lawsuit names defendants from more than one specialty, such as obstetrics and anesthesiology, then both an obstetrician and an anesthesiologist must provide expert testimony. Most experts write a report that describes the SOC, how the providers involved did or did not follow the SOC, and how violations of the SOC caused injury or death to the patient. Medical experts ensure that malpractice cases have merit and, in cases that go to trial, they explain the technical details of what went wrong to the jury.

Expert requirements have dramatically increased the cost of pursuing a malpractice claim, even if it does not go to trial. Most experts charge very high hourly rates and it takes a lot of time to review documents, analyze the case, and write a report. Every attorney that I interviewed said that the number of medical malpractice suits had declined over time and that the main reason for the decline was the high cost of hiring experts. Jane Hart-Thompson said,

> Physicians, to some extent, have gotten back at plaintiff's attorneys by the fact that a case cannot go forward without a standard-of-care expert and a causation expert. Those people have to be physicians. When I first started practice 15 years ago, everybody charged $250 an hour, and now the numbers are more like $500 to $750 an hour. That raises the cost not just for the defense, but for the plaintiffs as well.

Even without caps on damage awards, the requirement that both sides hire experts in the same specialties as the defendants, coupled with the rising rates charged by expert witnesses, had increased the cost of litigating malpractice cases for both sides. Expert requirements may be the unsung triumph of the tort reform movement because they achieve one of its stated purposes—to eliminate frivolous lawsuits.

The high cost of expert witnesses meant that attorneys could only pursue claims when there were catastrophic injuries. When I asked Peter Connolly, whose practice represented both plaintiffs and defendants in medical malpractice cases, how he determines whether to take a malpractice case, he said,

> Get expert reviews. That's where I start, but it has to be a catastrophic or serious injury. If you're talking on the plaintiff side, you definitely don't want to pursue something that's weak because the cost of prosecuting a plaintiff case when you hire as many experts as are required is so high. Sometimes, there can be as many as eight or nine experts, and at their hourly rate, it's cost-prohibitive if it's not a good case.

He took all of the defense cases that the liability insurance companies brought to him because they guaranteed payment. He was less likely to take plaintiff cases because they cost a lot to litigate and they pay on contingency, so the attorney only earns money if the plaintiff wins. They had to have both catastrophic injuries and clear violation of the SOC.

The high cost of expert testimony has changed plaintiff's lawyers' calculations about which malpractice cases are worth pursuing, because they make many legitimate claims too expensive to pursue. Jeff Nolan, a plaintiff's attorney, said,

> The reason that there aren't any frivolous cases in this area is because they cost so much money and so much time and you have to have multiple experts involved. You have to have an OB/GYN, a perinatologist, a neonatalogist, somebody who does the court analysis, and then somebody who takes the information from the court analysis and does another analysis. You have to have all of these incredibly specialized experts on a case on either side to prove it. I think the cost of a case that I resolved a few years back was $50,000. That's not unusual. It can be higher than that. The statutes that they have passed make it very difficult for someone who has a mild to moderate injury—that being an injury worth less than a quarter of a million dollars—to bring a malpractice case.

There was a strong consensus among attorneys that the high cost of pursuing a malpractice case meant that many genuine victims of negligence could not find representation. This is why expert requirements are a primary mechanism for attaining the goals of the tort reform movement: they increase the cost of suing.

The whole point of the tort reform movement was to make it harder for medical malpractice plaintiffs to win large awards. In this respect, expert requirements were successful. Josh Shaffer said that changes to tort law specifically intended to protect the power of physicians and hospitals:

> There are just a lot of little things that have been thrown into the law that make it more difficult to process a malpractice case. First of all, the defendants defend the cases heavily, and they do that so that it is expensive. Most plaintiff's lawyers can't afford to handle it. Secondly, the doctors who participate in a malpractice case, even on the plaintiff side, they charge $600 or $700 an hour for their time. Third, if you get a judgment in a case, the defendants will often appeal. . . . The lobby for the medical profession is so strong that they go to the legislature and throw in every little thing they can to make it more difficult to take the case and give these guys protection.

In his view, medicine's professional dominance is alive and well. Its lobbyists successfully promote tort reforms that impose barriers to malpractice lawsuits, so that most victims of medical negligence cannot find legal representation to help them to pursue compensation through the courts. Rob Thompson also said,

> In order for plaintiff lawyers to take a case, they're going to have to be assured that, number one, there are significant damages. So I'm convinced that nowadays the public is severely underserved with regard to recoveries in all malpractice cases. Unless the extent of the injury reaches a certain threshold, it's not economically feasible for anyone to take the case. I deal with the same dozen plaintiff's lawyers every week, every year, and probably for the last 20 years. They're not going to take a case unless it has at least a half million dollars in potential recovery because they will have invested $50,000 to $100,000 and a year or two of time in the case.

Like many plaintiff's lawyers, Thompson believed that many victims of medical malpractice could not obtain justice through the tort system because of the high cost of litigating.

Jeff Nolan was the only plaintiff's attorney I spoke to who would consider cases with a lower potential value:

> I handle a lot of cases that settle for between $250,000 and $500,000, which a lot of malpractice lawyers won't take because they don't consider them to be cost-effective. You can work within the rules and still help people who have been victims of bad care. And there is bad care. Some of these statistics show people dying because of hospital mistakes. Eighty thousand people a year die from hospital mistakes. That's just hospital mistakes—that's not doctor mistakes, that's not pharmacy mistakes. It's probably three to four times that, which is really horrifying. If there were that many people dying in plane crashes, or anything, people would be up in arms. But people look at it like the number of deaths in automobile accidents as that's just what happens. You die when you go to the hospital. That's just what happens. They might kill you there, and that's part of the deal. But there's not the public outrage, and there wasn't when those statistics came out. I was really surprised. There is an underlying acceptance that that's just part of what happens.

As Jeff Nolan notes, the rate of negligent medical injuries is high and many people die every year because of preventable errors in medical care, but victims of medical negligence often cannot find legal representation to sue for malpractice.

This is the opposite of "frivolous lawsuits." Because of the high cost of pursuing a malpractice claim, attorneys could not afford to take cases with anything less than catastrophic damages and clear negligence. Jeff Nolan said,

> There are no fluffy medical malpractice cases because you can't afford to file frivolous medical malpractice cases. We spend tens or hundreds of thousands of dollars every year having these cases evaluated. There are cases that we don't even take. We do a tremendous service to the medical community and we don't get any thank-you notes. But we have hundreds of cases evaluated a year by medical experts who tell us that there isn't a case, and then we explain that to the people who are wanting to bring the case.

Contrary to the claims of tort reform advocates that frivolous lawsuits contribute to out-of-control health care costs, there was a strong consensus among attorneys that there were *no* frivolous malpractice cases.

By demonizing "frivolous lawsuits," the tort reform movement had set up a straw person. Rob Thompson said,

> I've been doing this over 30 years, and I haven't paid out anything for a frivolous lawsuit. I pay out millions when we debate the esophagus of a six-year-old having an appendectomy instead of a tracheotomy, and they have brain damage for life. Or for the death of a mother of three children. That's where the cost comes from. It's not frivolous lawsuits.

Like the plaintiff's attorneys, he agreed that frivolous malpractice claims would not find legal representation. The medical and insurance lobbies promote the idea that many medical malpractice claims are frivolous, but this has little basis in reality.

The example of my brother-in-law, who broke his arm in a motorcycle accident while visiting from Canada, illustrates how hard it is for victims of malpractice to obtain legal representation. The emergency department at a local hospital surgically repaired the break but the hospital released him immediately when the billing department found out that he did not have supplemental insurance beyond the provincial health insurance plan. They did not prescribe him antibiotics, and he returned to Canada within 48 hours with a raging staph infection. To clear up the resulting gangrene, doctors in Canada gave him IV antibiotics several times a day for six months, and he faced a very real risk of amputation. In an effort to address the negligence on the part of the hospital, he called several malpractice attorneys in Arizona. One of them said bluntly, "Call me back when you lose your arm." If he recovered, the case was not worth pursuing. Even though there was clear negligence, the injury simply was not catastrophic enough to justify the cost of litigating it.

Another myth of malpractice is the claim that liability risk has caused a shortage of doctors, especially in high-risk specialties like obstetrics. The lawyers that I interviewed said instead that changes to the conditions of practicing medical injury law had caused a shortage of *malpractice lawyers*, especially on the plaintiff side. Rob Thompson noted that fewer and fewer lawyers entered the malpractice litigation field compared to a couple of decades earlier:

> The cost has also limited the number of players. Twenty years ago, it would cost less to prosecute a case, and less-affluent lawyers could take a case. . . . The lawyers have become far more selective. The lawyers are older. Most of the people I deal with have been lawyers for 30-plus years. . . . When I started out, there were plaintiff law firms that had a number of lawyers. The senior lawyers tried large medical malpractice cases. The younger lawyers, the 30-year-old lawyers, would try the car accident cases, not the dead mother cases. They would try the whiplash cases and the broken arm cases, the slip-and-fall cases at the grocery store. The $20,000, $30,000 cases . . . I tried dozens of cases where I started at under $50,000 in value back then, and that was how you learned how to try lawsuits and become comfortable in being a trial lawyer. . . . But then we got mandatory arbitration, which started out at $25,000 and is now $50,000. Any case that has a potential value of $50,000 or less goes to arbitration, and the statutes and the legislature have passed things that make it very difficult for people to appeal. . . . There aren't any more 30- and 40-year-old lawyers coming along and learning how to try cases and feeling comfortable with regard to it. The pool of lawyers on both sides has diminished.

Medical malpractice attorneys generally agreed that their field had narrowed over time as the cost of litigating pushed out younger and less experienced lawyers. Only the highly experienced attorneys survived, leading to an aging population in the field.

So, rather than decreasing the number of obstetricians, the "malpractice crisis" appears to have weeded out the less selective, inexperienced plaintiff's lawyers. Josh Shaffer also said that expert testimony requirements and increases in the cost of litigating eliminated the number of opportunistic "ambulance chasers" pursuing medical malpractice cases:

> In the olden days, when a malpractice case came in, there were indeed a lot of guys who didn't know what they were doing who would hear that a baby

died or a mom died. Before they even consulted with a doctor, they would go ahead and file the suit and then hope for the best and, in the middle of the case, find out that they didn't have a case. Especially when the reality is that 100% of med mal suits are defended by excellent lawyers, but 100% of plaintiffs' cases are not. There's probably 15–20% of lawyers who handle plaintiffs' med mal cases who know what they're doing. The rest think it's easy. They don't know what the medicine is, and they're under-funded.

As the medical profession obtained new legal protections, only the most effective attorneys survived, and they survived by being selective about taking cases that offered enough potential awards to be worth the cost of their time.

In addition to weeding out less-experienced lawyers, changing conditions of practicing malpractice law squeezed out small law firms and pushed more cases toward arbitration and settlements for the limits of liability insurance coverage. This occurred because the insurance industry changed the ways that malpractice defendants obtained legal counsel and, around the same time, some larger plaintiff firms began advertising their services. Those who advertised came gradually to command a larger share of the market and squeezed out the smaller law firms. Rob Thompson, a defense attorney, said,

As a result of lawyer advertising, you don't have as many cases. They go to the advertising lawyers, who rarely try any cases. I bet they don't try 1% of the cases that they get, but they get massive numbers of them. They mainly get settlements out of insurance companies. That volume of cases is no longer going to smaller law firms, or even larger law firms. From a defense side, when I grew up as a defense lawyer in a large insurance defense firm, we used to represent 15 insurance companies. That volume has shrunk significantly. The insurance companies also started going to in-house counsel about 20 years ago. [The big insurance companies], instead of hiring a law firm in town, like my old law firm, to defend them in those cases, they have their own employees who look like a law firm, but they are really in-house lawyers. As a result, they don't try those cases. They all get arbitrated or settled.

In short, two changes since the 1990s have restructured medical negligence law and increased the likelihood that malpractice cases would settle for the limits of the provider's insurance. First, personal injury lawyers who engage in direct marketing have increased their share of the market, and they have incentives to process cases efficiently by settling for the limits of the defendant's insurance. Second, insurance companies brought many of their legal services in-house. Both of these trends had the effect of decreasing the number of medical malpractice cases and, especially, the number that moved past the initial stage and through the legal system.

The common practice of settling malpractice cases for the limits of a provider's liability insurance coverage also limited the size of the awards that victims of negligence could obtain through the law. While obstetricians who bought private liability insurance coverage complained that it cost too much, plaintiff's attorneys complained that physicians had too little coverage to adequately compensate victims of medical negligence. Josh Shaffer said that it was hard to get negligent parties to pay after a legal judgement against them:

> A new problem that we have in all of these cases is that they are underinsured and they don't give a shit. We find that these doctors routinely carry one million. It's not enough, but they don't care, because they will hide their assets. Because they have a year and a half (between the claim and the judgment) to do it. They will move assets, or they'll simply declare bankruptcy after they have moved all of their assets. . . . You don't get the money, and they know that.

As his remarks highlight, the liability insurance system may not prevent claims against physicians or hospitals, but the tendency for providers to settle cases for the limits of their liability insurance policies limits awards—no tort reforms are necessary. Most physicians carry liability insurance and any malpractice claims against them settle for the limits of their policy, even if that means that they do not fully compensate victims of malpractice.

In sum, lawyers said that the malpractice legal field had changed over time in ways that produced a declining rate of malpractice lawsuits and a shrinking pool of attorneys who practiced medical injury law. None of the reasons for that change were based on improvements in the quality of care or a reduction in medical errors. Obstetricians' culture of fear about liability might have been a lingering response to a battle that ended in an earlier era, or it might just have been a bogeyman lurking "out there" and causing providers unnecessary anxiety. It also seemed to be based on a perception that legal risk was external to the obstetric profession, when really obstetricians' professional dominance over the maternity care field was alive and well and embedded in tort law as the SOC.

Medical Dominance and the Standard of Care (SOC)

Medical malpractice attorneys' insights about trends over time revealed how the maternity care field protects obstetricians. The medical profession has used its power, with the help of insurance companies, to reshape tort laws in ways that limit physicians' liability. Even without tort reforms, the medical profession has the power to define what constitutes negligence under the law because it establishes the SOC. In the US, ACOG issues practice guidelines that establish the legal SOC, which highlights the continued dominance of the medical profession in defining the appropriate management of pregnancy and childbirth. Medical malpractice lawyers like Julie Connolly, who represented both plaintiffs and defendants, deferred to ACOG when asked what physicians could do to reduce their odds of losing a medical negligence case:

> First and foremost is to follow the ACOG practice guidelines. They should be familiar with those and reread those on an annual basis. Some of the insurance companies require their physicians to do just that. It's amazing what you can forget. That's first and foremost because when you use an ACOG-approved form, it's a tri-fold that has, by trimester, all of the key points that need to be discussed and obtained. . . . When there is an indication of an aberration from the prenatal course, seek consultation, preferably from a perinatology high-risk OB group that is uninvolved.

Because tort law exists to punish professionals who violate the community SOC, the definition of legal compliance is completely *endogenous* to the medical profession.[28] In maternity care, the medical profession defines the SOC based on its *typical* practices, so the standard for negligence is internal to the profession. Whether or not that SOC is optimal or evidence-based, legal actors like attorneys and the courts use that standard as the benchmark for legally appropriate, non-negligent care.

Because the medical profession defines the SOC, plaintiff's attorneys had to use two criteria to determine whether it was worthwhile to take a medical malpractice case: *negligence* (a violation of the SOC) and *causation* (that negligence was the cause of the injury, rather than something else). The fundamental question in malpractice suits is whether healthcare providers could have prevented or reduced harm, but there is often ambiguity about whether substandard care caused harm and about whether medical staff provided substandard care. Attorneys knew that a clear violation of the SOC was a minimum requirement to meet the definition of medical negligence under tort law and to convince experts to testify on the plaintiffs' side against their colleagues within the professional community. Since most physicians feel threatened by malpractice lawsuits, few are willing to testify as experts against their colleagues unless the defendant made egregious mistakes that clearly violated community standards. Michelle Morales, a plaintiff's attorney, said, "I think that if there was no breach in the standard of care, we're not going to find an expert. It's as simple as that." In short, while obstetricians said that they felt vulnerable to malpractice claims even when they followed the SOC, malpractice attorneys said that they would only represent plaintiffs if there was a clear violation of the SOC.

Malpractice attorneys also understood the medical SOC well enough to make that judgment. When I asked him how he determined whether to represent a plaintiff in a birth-related malpractice case, Peter Connolly said,

> My criteria for taking a bad baby case would be, first and foremost, there has to be a clear violation of the standard of care. What I mean by that is that there is an abundance of literature out there that talks about basic principles in terms of management of expectant mothers as well as management of delivery. You look to ACOG. They publish all kinds of practice bulletins which are readily available. The medical text that's the bible in OB/GYN practice is called *William's Obstetrics*, and then of course consultation with a quality expert. First and foremost is the standard of care.

Since the medical profession defines the SOC and malpractice attorneys follow professional medical guidelines as the basis for the SOC, the medical profession retains its professional jurisdiction, authority, and autonomy.[29] In fact, it is impossible for tort laws or malpractice lawsuits to undermine medical authority *from the outside* because the principles underlying tort law define malpractice *from the inside*. Hospitals, physician groups, liability insurers, and professional associations like ACOG interpret what malpractice is and what is an appropriate defense against malpractice claims.

Because the SOC is the benchmark for medical malpractice, the lawyers that I interviewed all had some understanding of medical standards. When I asked Barbara Collins, a plaintiff's attorney, how she decides to take a birth-related malpractice case, she said,

> I do an investigation, which means first I get all of the relevant medical records. I read them myself. I am not a trained healthcare provider in any way, but I can recognize problems in the theory of what went wrong. People usually come to me with a particular concern. Then I expand it based on my knowledge. So sometimes I don't even go further than that, but if I see it as a potential case, then I have the case reviewed by a medical expert, and that may be an obstetric nurse.

She believed that she could do the initial review and then bring in experts to identify whether the case involved a violation of the SOC. Similarly, Josh Shaffer said,

> The reality is that I've been doing this for 35 years, so I have an extensive library and I know medicine. . . . The primary way you determine whether or not to take the case is predicated on what care was given. The way that you determine substandard care is by careful review of the medical records, which is much more comprehensive than most people think. Most people think that you look at the chart and the consults and the reports, but that's not really the way you make a decision. After review of the charts, we do consultation with experts. That's what determines whether you have negligence and causation.

Like Josh Shaffer and Barbara Collins, all of the medical malpractice attorneys had some knowledge of how to read medical records and all of them consulted with medical professionals. Sometimes they had nurses on their law firm staff and then consulted with physician specialists if they believed that there was a clear breach of the SOC.

Myths of Malpractice

Clearly, the medical profession has maintained dominance over definitions of medical malpractice. In the maternity care field, the *obstetric profession* interprets the laws that regulate the field and defines what practices comply with the law.[30] That does not mean that individual providers had complete discretion over how to practice obstetrics. They had to follow common standards within the field, even when they knew that scientific evidence did not support some of those standards, and they had to document everything. Instead of focusing on their relationships with patients and the time that they could spend with them, obstetricians used technological and medical interventions to signify "doing everything that could be done" and they copied other providers in the field so that their actions would make sense to their peers.

Also, while the obstetric profession as a whole maintains its dominance over the maternity care field, intermediate internal actors like liability insurers and hospital legal counsel are front-line workers who translate the law into organizational routines and enforce those routines using inspections, reviews, and rules.[31] The medicalization schema informs legally defensive practices in American maternity care, and these front-line legal workers codify those practices into formal policies. They insist on a clear definition of the SOC, ensure that providers are aware of the SOC, and demand careful documentation. They institutionalize a set of typical practices, policies, and protocols across the maternity care field, which the courts and other legal institutions use as a reference for what is legally appropriate behavior.

Comparing obstetricians and malpractice attorneys, it is clear that a culture of liability fear coexists with a decline in actual liability risk in the maternity care field. I initially believed that many common obstetric practices were defensive responses to legal risk that is external to maternity care, but the reality is far more complicated. Obstetricians have high levels of fear in spite of declining liability risk, because medical training and front-line legal workers in medical organizations actively construct a fear of liability. They institutionalize standards and requirements for documentation that intensify the definition of pregnancy and birth as pathological. The significant financial and emotional impact of medical malpractice lawsuits, along with a huge emphasis on liability risk during medical training, in professional obstetric literature, and through risk management efforts, elevates the importance of liability risk and encourages defensive medicine. In the medicalization schema, defensive medicine means more technological interventions so that providers can demonstrate that they have done everything that can be done. But the emphasis on legal risk avoidance obscures the reality: malpractice lawsuits are declining, and they are declining more in states where providers face greater liability risk (non–tort reform states) than in states with less (tort reform states). The myth that malpractice lawsuits are an ever-present and immanent threat only persists because that is how the obstetric profession talks about it. The obstetric profession emphasizes defense against lawsuits without understanding their actual frequency or what is necessary for a victim of negligence to pursue a lawsuit.

The prominence of risk management in the field also prevents obstetricians from fully recognizing the extent to which lawyers, juries, and judges defer to the medical profession's definition of the SOC. Community standards within the medical profession define malpractice, which ensures the representation of its perspectives, solutions, strategies, and interests. In this respect, professional associations, hospital legal counsel, and the medical liability insurance companies are the front-line legal workers: they interpret and enforce medical liability laws when they license providers, offer or revoke hospital privileges and liability insurance coverage, require careful documentation in medical records, and review medical negligence cases. Hospital legal counsel and medical liability insurers also encourage the adoption and use of technology to protect providers from malpractice lawsuits, with the view that advanced technology provides a symbol of high-quality care and a strategy for generating documentation. Courts defer to definitions of legal compliance from inside the medical field partly because they lack an insider's knowledge and understanding of the field and partly because the medical SOC defines the boundary of legality. Even if the SOC reinforces obsolete practices, maternity care providers who follow it should not be vulnerable to malpractice lawsuits.

4

What's the Rush?

Tort Laws and Elective Early-Term Births

I'm not opposed to social inductions, but if the cervix isn't ripe,
then you're looking at potentially many days of induction and
nobody's patient with that. So there's social expectations about
outcomes, some of which are for the physician, and some of
which are for the patient.
—Dr. Marie McDonald

Dr. McDonald was an obstetrician and perinatal specialist with over
30 years of experience, and she worked in a hospital that emphasized
research-based practices. She was not morally opposed to *social* or *elective*
inductions of labor for non-medical reasons, but she recognized that they
could cause problems because labor and birth are not completely control-
lable events.[1] Elective inductions occur when maternity care providers use
medications to ripen the cervix (an *unripe* cervix is one that has not yet
dilated and effaced) and stimulate contractions to artificially start labor
for the convenience of the provider, hospital, or pregnant woman.[2] Dr.
McDonald said that pregnant women sometimes request an induction in
order to manage their birth experience: "In our society, they may feel they
should be able to control this." Some media accounts, citing prominent
obstetrician-researchers, say that women ask to be induced for *convenience*,
implying that they request induction for selfish, consumer-driven reasons.[3]
Those selfish mothers—bearing the next generation just for their own convenience, and trying to schedule it as though it were a hair appointment.

Patient Choice and Elective Deliveries

Popular accounts about women requesting induction of labor suggest
that pregnant women are driving the trend toward elective deliveries.

Dr. Garcia, an obstetrician with 20 years of experience, supported this idea, saying, "Usually it's the patients begging for it." Some pregnant women ask their providers to induce their labor early, usually with the belief that it will do no harm. Of course, most women feel huge, uncomfortable, and tired in late pregnancy, and it is appealing to no longer be pregnant. Susan Dixon, a CNM who attended births at both a freestanding birth center and a hospital, observed that a combination of discomfort in late pregnancy and a lack of information about the risks sometimes leads women to request an induction:

> I think it's more of a pressure on women not to be pregnant anymore, and that's why they become induced. Or at the end of their pregnancy they are really big and bulky . . . and they are really uncomfortable and don't want to be pregnant anymore. They don't have anyone to point out the risks of an induction and all they can think of is the benefit of not being pregnant anymore.

It is easy to understand why women in late pregnancy want their pregnancies to end—it's uncomfortable, it's hard to sleep, and swollen ankles, heartburn, and bladder incontinence are enough to make anyone cranky.

There are other reasons why some women try to schedule an induction. Sometimes they want "their" doctor to deliver their baby, rather than another doctor in the same hospital or practice—not realizing that nurses provide most of the care during and after labor and that most obstetricians only show up for a few minutes to catch the baby. Some women want to schedule their birth around the time that they have leave from work or their family members are available to help them with infant care or to care for their other children.[4] Dr. Alex Yoder, a medical director for a health insurer with experience in obstetrics, said,

> I can tell you that there are women out there who want the convenience . . . this was the mindset: let's make it convenient. That's like scheduled [repeat] C-sections, after the primary. A lot of our patients really liked it, because you could say, "I'll stop work on the 20th, plan on delivering on the 25th, and I'll be home on the 29th. My other kid's birthday party is on the 4th." It makes it convenient.

There is some irony in using the word "convenient" to describe having a newborn, no matter what the timing, but planning an induction or a scheduled repeat cesarean offers women opportunities to time their births around the logistics of their lives. Since most women with a previous cesarean have a scheduled repeat cesarean in later pregnancies, they often try to arrange their births around their other commitments just like any other surgery.

Elective deliveries include induction of labor in low-risk pregnancies and scheduled repeat cesareans in otherwise low-risk pregnancies to mothers with a previous cesarean.[5] Some families in the United States request elective deliveries for health insurance and taxation purposes, especially in late December when they can claim a dependent tax deduction for the year and avoid paying an annual insurance deductible for a birth in January.[6] For this reason, the most common birthdate is now the last Friday in December, rather than the traditional mid-September date that falls nine months after the holiday season.[7] Elective deliveries are especially attractive for military families, who may have limited opportunities for an active-duty non-birthing parent to be at the birth. Dr. Ribeiro, who served many military families, said,

> It's a little bit different than some places. Thirty percent of my patients have TriCare [VA insurance]. A lot of times, your husband's in Afghanistan, and he can come home for a week, but what if you don't have the baby? I think that there are medical reasons for labor induction. There are also social reasons that I think are fine, if the patient is inducible.

In his view, the availability of the deployed parent to attend the birth was a good reason to induce.

Some women request labor induction because they live far away from the facility where they plan to give birth. They view induction as much less frightening than the possibility of enduring a long drive while in labor or giving birth on the way to the hospital. Dr. Garcia said,

> It has to be really extenuating circumstances, and a lot of times I see a lot of people who will say, "My husband's going out of town, or he's going to Afghanistan, and he wants to be there for the delivery." So we have people

who beg us for inductions for that. Or, "I live two hours away, so I can't get here fast." Sometimes we'll be willing to do it if there are really extenuating circumstances.

While she usually discouraged elective induction in her practice, some of her patients requested it for logistical reasons. Thinking through all of the possible circumstances that can make a planned birth desirable to pregnant women and their families, women don't look as selfish and silly as some popular accounts of "deliveries on demand" suggest.

Importantly, claims that pregnant women's requests are driving increases in elective deliveries implies that patients have enough *cultural health capital* to negotiate their care.[8] Empowered patients are likely to have race and class privileges that offer them healthcare advantages, including an ability to effectively advocate for their preferences in ways that physicians will honor.[9] It is also important to remember that elective deliveries are only partly patient-driven. The maternity care *provider* is always an important part of the equation because, no matter how much pregnant women might beg for an induction or request a particular date for a repeat cesarean, they have to find a *willing provider*. It is up to providers to explain the risks as well as the benefits of any medical procedure and to refuse to do things that are medically risky. Some maternity care providers do not induce labor unless there are good medical reasons to do so, while others offer elective induction without giving a lot of information about its risks, and even encourage elective deliveries. They do this because scheduled deliveries offer quality-of-life benefits *to the provider*, who can schedule births on weekdays, during the day shift, or while on call. (A physician's golf game is sometimes described, tongue in cheek, as a medical indication for induction.) Dr. Alex Yoder, a medical director for a health insurer, said that one provider under his plan's coverage tended to do elective deliveries:

This provider always gives it as an option, and to me, I find that a little difficult to swallow. . . . The doctor would say, "You're going to be 38 weeks on Thursday. You know, I'm on call Friday. Do you want to have a baby?" And he'll bring them in and induce them at 38 and 1. They don't do that anymore because insurance has clamped down, but this was the mindset: let's make it convenient.

Whether or not women ask for a scheduled early delivery, they are more convenient *for providers* because they allow them to manage their work-load and to plan their patients' births around their schedules.[10]

As a result, some providers agree to women's requests for elective deliveries and others actively encourage women to schedule their births without explaining the potential downside. Barbara Collins, a plaintiff's attorney, described a birth-injury case that she represented where an induction that was not medically indicated contributed to a catastrophic outcome:

> In this case, part of the problem is that she didn't go into labor. . . . [The obstetrician] induced her for reasons that aren't clear to me. After all was said and done, he said he induced her because she had high blood pressure, but she didn't. She said he induced her because it was time to have the baby. She was never going to deliver that kid safely. . . . But it didn't help that when he started, she wasn't ready. She wasn't even close to fully dilated or effaced, so he had to do all of that with drugs. . . . The nightmare labor and delivery went on for three days.

In this case, the physician decided to artificially induce labor when the mother's body was not ready, and it led to an extremely long labor and efforts to pull the baby out with a vacuum extractor and then with forceps—causing serious neurological damage.

One question with cases like this is why the maternity care provider induced labor on a pregnant woman whose body was not ready. But from an organizational perspective, hospitals and OB/GYN practices benefit enormously from scheduling births. For hospitals, inductions and scheduled repeat cesareans make it easier to manage their space and their staffing, so that they can avoid having too many or too few available beds or nurses on duty. For OB/GYN practices, the benefits of scheduled births depend on the practice model. In many group practices and in hospitals with obstetricians that are hospital employees, it makes no difference which doctor is there for the birth. But in some private practices, physicians must maintain a full clinical schedule and "deliver" their own patients to receive their full reimbursement. This practice model overwhelmingly favors scheduled deliveries.[11] Dr. Garcia, who worked in a group practice, said this about scheduled inductions:

In my group, we share out income equally and we're not assigned to any one patient, so we pool the income and then it is evenly distributed. So there is no incentive to induce. But some of the people who are in private practice, who do get incentives to do it, do more inductions.

In short, obstetricians in private practices often have a huge motivation to induce labor or schedule cesareans. There is one hospital in the city where I conducted my research where the obstetricians have this practice model—and they have the highest induction and cesarean rates in town. On the other hand, some hospitals have residents-in-training or employ hospitalists who can manage labor around the clock.[12] When there are physicians in the hospital who can attend births at any time of the day or night and it has no impact on other physicians' income, obstetricians have less motivation to schedule elective deliveries.

Induction of Labor

Induction rates have risen over time at a much faster rate than medical indications can justify, and many experts speculate that at least half of inductions are elective.[13] Figure 4.1 illustrates these overall trends in the rate of induction from 1995 to 2015.[14] Labor was induced in 16.0% of all live births in 1995, rising to a peak of 23.6% in 2015. In low-risk births, the induction rate rose from 14.8% in 1995 to a high of 26.4% in 2008.

If women want to schedule an induction and providers want to schedule their patients' births, then what's the big deal? The answer is that it may seem convenient to schedule an induction, but there is no free ride. Artificial induction of labor is a tool of active management of labor and is not risk-free.[15] When I asked her about induction, Susan Dixon said,

I think it should be very carefully saved for only specific medical indications, and in the case that there is good medical evidence that it improves the outcome. I think a lot of times it is way overused and that even physicians are aware that they're playing a game if they think it's easier to just do an induction. . . . I think it increases deception and reliance on other interventions like the use of vacuums or forceps. The increase of pain medications and epidurals is all related to the induction and the woman not being able to tolerate the pain of an induction, whereas she might

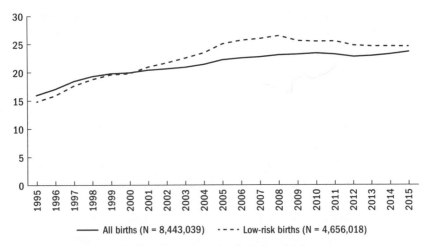

Figure 4.1. Percentage of All Births with Medically Induced Labor, 1995–2015.
Source: Natality Detail Files.

have been able to tolerate natural labor. . . . So it also then leads down that path of induction, Pitocin, epidural, and C-section.

She was critical of medically unnecessary induction, which poses risks to mothers and babies and often initiates the well-known cascade of interventions.[16] If a woman's cervix is unripe, induction often does not work, and the medications that obstetricians use to induce labor can cause hyperstimulation of the uterus and fetal distress.[17] Fetal distress and failed induction are major causes of unnecessary (or questionable) cesarean deliveries.

All of the maternity care providers that I interviewed knew that induction doubled the likelihood of a cesarean delivery when the cervix was not ready, especially for first-time mothers.[18] Dr. Murray observed that "Without a favorable cervix, it increases the risk of C-section two to three times." This is partly because, as Dr. McDonald observed at the very beginning of this chapter, patients, physicians, and hospitals all have expectations about how long labor should take. Induced labor is usually longer and more intense than spontaneous labor, so elective inductions often do not meet those expectations. Neither pregnant women nor providers are patient with long, drawn-out inductions, which waste valuable hospital resources and encourage obstetricians to further intervene in order to move things along. As Dr. Bennett said, "If you keep patients in the bed for three days, it's not fun." Induction also increases the risk of shoulder dystocia, when the baby's shoulders get stuck behind the mother's pubic bone during birth—which is one of the most terrifying complications of labor and delivery.[19] For mothers, it increases the risk of third- and fourth-degree perineal tears, blood loss, and pelvic floor injuries.

Because induction has these known risks, all but one of the providers that I interviewed said that they avoided inducing labor unless there was a clear medical reason for it.[20] Dr. Ribeiro was the exception:

> There is a school of thought that you should just say to these people, "No. You just need to go on." But if you can induce them, I feel paternalistic to say, "No, what you want doesn't count. Your baby is mature and your cervix is ripe and you just want to have your baby, but no." I think it's controversial. A lot of people would disagree with me and say no, you shouldn't do these social inductions and just let nature take its course.

Dr. Ribeiro's positive view of elective induction was somewhat unusual, but he worked with many military families and had a strong commitment to allowing women to make their own reproductive decisions—as long as the conditions were right for it to be successful. But he also knew that elective delivery before 39 weeks posed unnecessary medical risks:

> They have to be 39 weeks. I think that's pretty much across the board for everyone. Below that, you have an increased risk of respiratory distress and babies being placed in NICUs.

In fact, *all* of the maternity care providers that spoke to me knew that deliveries for non-medical reasons before 39 weeks were risky.

Medical research and professional guidelines discourage obstetricians from scheduling elective deliveries before 39 weeks because early deliveries increase the risk of bad outcomes without offering medical benefits. For this reason, elective delivery before 39 weeks is the kind of practice that tort laws aim to prevent, by punishing healthcare providers for bad outcomes that occur after they knowingly take unnecessary risks. And yet, labor induction and repeat cesareans in births before 39 weeks rose dramatically after 1995.

Early-Term Births

The average pregnancy lasts 40 weeks, and ACOG defines a term pregnancy as between 37 and 42 weeks.[21] ACOG has recommended against scheduling deliveries before 39 weeks for non-medical reasons since 1982.[22] In its 2013 Committee Opinions, ACOG even changed the definition of a *term* pregnancy to redefine the period from 37 to 39 weeks (37 weeks and 0 days to 38 weeks and 6 days) as *early-term*, 39 to 41 weeks (39 weeks and 0 days to 40 weeks and 6 days) as *full-term*, 41–42 weeks (41 weeks and 0 days to 41 weeks and 6 days) as *late-term*.[23] ACOG's intention was to recognize that early-term births can pose unnecessary *iatrogenic risks* to newborns (risks induced by medical treatment or diagnostic procedures), including respiratory and digestive problems, intraventricular hemorrhage (bleeding into the fluid-filled ventricles inside the brain), hypoglycemia (low blood sugar), and preventable disabilities or death due to late prematurity. Babies born before 39 weeks are more likely to require care in a neonatal intensive care unit (NICU) and to have low five-minute Apgar scores than full-term newborns, even when there were no medical risks before delivery. Infant brain development also benefits enormously from the last few weeks of gestation.[24]

While some births before 39 weeks are spontaneous, the percentage of births between 37 and 39 weeks increased too dramatically from 1995 to 2015 for changes in the timing of spontaneous labor to be the cause. Figure 4.2 illustrates the percentage of low-risk early-term births (37–39 weeks) and the percentage of all low-risk births (37–42 weeks) that involved artificial induction of labor between 37 and 39 weeks. It also shows the percentage of VBAC-eligible births that occurred via early-term repeat cesarean.

As figure 4.2 shows, labor was artificially induced in over 19% of all low-risk early-term births from 1995 to 2015, suggesting that nearly one fifth of these births were intentionally early. Early-term inductions occurred in 3.1% of all low-risk births to mothers without a previous cesarean in 1995, but that more than doubled to reach a high of 7.3% in 2006 and 2009.[25] In VBAC-eligible births, 33.6% involved an early-term repeat cesarean, with a low of 22.3% in 1996 and a high of 42.6% in 2006. While some of these births may have had undocumented medical

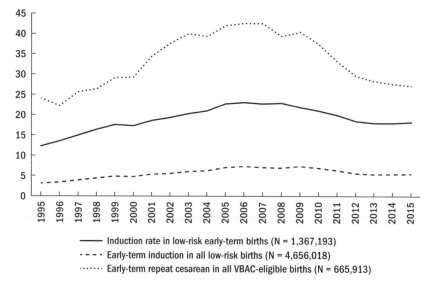

Figure 4.2. Percentage Induction and Repeat Cesarean between 37 and 39 Weeks in Births without Medical Indications for Early Delivery, 1995–2015. Source: Natality Detail Files.

reasons for early delivery, the overall trend in figure 4.2 is clear: the percentage of early-term deliveries rose substantially until 2005 and then leveled off before declining somewhat around 2009.

The rising rates of elective early-term births suggest that the normative pressure of ACOG's professional guidelines eroded over time. This might have occurred partly because medical research in the 1980s found a higher risk of stillbirth in pregnancies that last *more than 42 weeks*. In 1989, ACOG issued a practice bulletin that recommended induction by 42 weeks gestation because of the hazards of *post-maturity*: the placenta can stop providing adequate oxygen and the amount of amniotic fluid can decline.[26] The debate over the risks of post-maturity changed the clinical consensus about how long a pregnancy should last, as the obstetric community focused on how early was early enough to reduce the likelihood of the rare, but devastating, event of a stillbirth.[27] Most contemporary obstetricians induce labor by 41 weeks and schedule repeat cesareans before 40 weeks. But while clinical researchers debated the need to deliver babies by 41 or 42 weeks, the percentage of births before

39 weeks skyrocketed. The more that some providers offered elective early deliveries, the more that the obstetric community viewed any birth between 37 and 42 weeks as acceptable. The problem is that, when early births are *elective*, they put more newborns at risk for negative outcomes without a medical justification.[28]

For this reason, ACOG issued a practice bulletin in August 2009 to clearly restate the SOC: labor induction for logistic reasons or psychosocial indications should establish a gestational age of at least 39 weeks.[29] Also in 2009, The Joint Commission, a US healthcare accreditation organization, issued a set of four evidence-based measures for perinatal care (PC measures).[30] One of them required hospitals to report their rate of delivery before 39 weeks and to make efforts to decrease that rate. Hospitals began to collect data on the PC measures in April 2010, right after President Obama signed the ACA into law. The ACA was another institutional force encouraging providers to offer evidence-based care by establishing health quality and performance measures for hospitals, although some quality metrics did not take effect until 2014–16.

The rate of early-term induction declined after ACOG reinstated its guidelines and a growing number of hospitals adopted policies that strictly prohibited elective induction of labor before 39 weeks.[31] Dr. McGinley, who worked at an academic hospital, said,

> [The hospital] is really big on clinical consensus groups. . . . There's been a big push among specialty organizations about no induction before 39 weeks. As a department, we really try to hold to that. We're all about academics and it's all evidence based, and we try to not do inductions.

While hospitals vary somewhat in their specific policies, many have a clear policy against elective induction before 39 weeks.

Dr. Murray, who worked at another local hospital, said that her hospital prohibited elective induction of labor before 39 weeks and required a favorable cervix:

> We are pretty strict at [my hospital] about induction of labor and I think currently, about 29% do it. You can have an elective induction at 39 weeks if your cervix is dilated two to three centimeters, and at least halfway

thinned out, so there's a Bishop score that has to be favorable.... There's a hospital policy that you cannot do an elective induction at 39 to 41 weeks unless they're ready.

Hospital policies can reduce early-term births by restricting the conditions under which maternity care providers can offer elective inductions.

This is one way that hospitals comply with clinical guidelines and manage uncertainty: by creating formal structures that ensure that providers observe professional recommendations. Rosemary MacLeod, a CNM with privileges at a different hospital, said that her hospital discouraged elective induction by restricting the medications that providers could use before 41 weeks:

> In the hospital that I work at, if a woman is under 41 weeks and there is no medical reason for induction, you are limited in the types of methods that you can use.... The thing about induction is that if the cervix is not ripe, then you would use a ripening agent, like something called a dilator to soften and ripen the cervix. So the [hospital] guidelines are, if there is not a medical reason for induction and she is not 41 weeks, you cannot use cervical ripening agents. That is a guideline that was developed by the clinical practice team, which is physicians and nurses and administrators. What it does is, if you've got a patient that is 40 weeks and wants to be induced because she wants to go away in a month, but her cervix is not ripe, then you've got to sit down and say to her, "This is not right. We can only use this. This is going to put you at risk for a C-section." So that's a system limit. If you're inducing someone at 41 weeks because she's got hypertension and her cervix isn't ripe, you've got all of the options available to you. But it also stops practices from booking all of their patients for inductions just because that's the day they're on call.

In this instance, the hospital policy prohibited cervical ripening agents before 41 weeks, and any effort to provide informed consent should inform pregnant women of the high risk of a failed induction, which is likely to outweigh any benefits of a planned induction. Hospitals also adopted policies prohibiting maternity care providers from scheduling repeat cesareans before 39 weeks unless there is a compelling medical need. After 2009, some Medicaid programs began to deny payment for early deliveries without medical indications. The normative, organizational, and economic pressures in the maternity care field pushed for lower early-term birth rates.

Tort Regimes and Elective Early-Term Births

How did tort regimes and liability risk affect trends in early-term births during this period? Clearly, elective deliveries before 39 weeks violate the professional SOC, which is the benchmark for medical malpractice, and they have since at least 1982. This means that fear of liability should discourage elective early births, especially in patient-friendly states, where providers face more malpractice liability risk. Elective early-term births should be more common in provider-friendly states with tort reforms that reduce providers' liability risk. But do tort regimes have these effects?

To test this, I analyzed the odds of early-term induction in low-risk births, compared with induction after 39 weeks or spontaneous labor between 37 and 42 weeks.[32] Notably, the odds of an elective early-term induction were higher for non-Hispanic white women than for Hispanic, black, or Asian women.[33] The odds also increased with higher levels of maternal education. These racial-ethnic and class-related effects may support the argument that patient requests drive these inductions, because non-Hispanic white women and more educated women tend to have more *cultural health capital* that they can mobilize to negotiate their care with providers. Providers are also more likely to honor the requests of patients that they view as having higher social status.[34] This is one instance where empowered patients seem to be less likely to receive evidence-based care.

In terms of the legal environment, caps on damages should reduce providers' liability risk more than JSL reform or expert requirements, and caps on non-economic damages should have larger effects than caps on punitive damages. Indeed, I found that caps on punitive damages alone had no significant effect, but the odds of an early-term induction in a low-risk birth were 9.5% higher in states with caps on non-economic damages (with or without caps on punitive damages) than in states with no caps on damages. This supports the idea that caps on non-economic damages reduce providers' liability risk and weaken the deterrent effect of tort laws. It also suggests that liability risk deters risky medical prac-

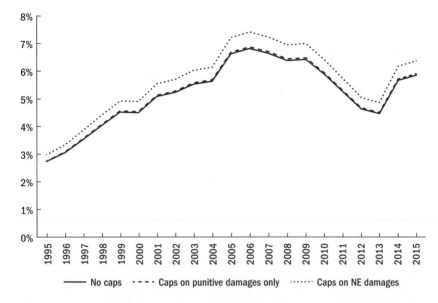

Figure 4.3. Predicted Probability of Early-Term Induction (37–38 Weeks) in Low-Risk Births by Caps on Damages, 1995–2015. Source: Low-risk births (37–42 weeks) in the Natality Detail Files (N = 4,641,161).

tices like early-term induction and that reducing liability risk emboldens risky practices. Figure 4.3 shows the predicted probability of early-term induction for low-risk births by caps on damages from 1995 to 2015.[35]

Other tort laws that can influence liability risk include joint and several liability (JSL) (the "deep pockets rule") versus proportionate liability (PL).[36] As I discussed in chapter 2, malpractice liability for defendants like hospitals that have significant assets ("deep pockets") is higher under JSL, so hospitals should enforce stricter policies against early-term births in states with JSL. On the other hand, PL can make individual healthcare providers more cautious because they are accountable for their individual responsibility for negligence.[37] I find that the odds of early-term induction were 11.2% higher in low-risk births under JSL than PL, which suggests that PL encourages clinicians to take fewer risks with labor induction. Expert requirements, which also reduce providers' liability risk, had negligible effects on early-term induction in low-risk births. The effect of obstetric malpractice suits per 100,000 births was negative but extremely small.[38]

For early-term repeat cesareans in VBAC-eligible births, the results were similar, although black women were more likely than non-Hispanic white women to have an early-term repeat cesarean, especially after the 2009 restatement of guidelines.[39] This confirms findings from other research that preterm and early-term cesarean rates are higher for non-Hispanic black women with singleton pregnancies, and that African American women are more often subject to substandard medical care. Most women with a previous cesarean have a planned repeat cesarean in subsequent births, so the question for most of these women is not *if*, but *when*. When I analyzed the odds of an early-term repeat cesarean compared to a VBAC or a repeat cesarean after 39 weeks, caps on punitive damages alone had no significant effects but the odds were 5.6% higher in states with caps on non-economic damages (with or without punitive damages) than in states without caps on damages.[40] The effects of JSL reform on the odds of an early-term repeat cesarean were the opposite of its effects on early-term induction: they were 6.1% higher under PL than under JSL. Expert requirements were associated with 17% higher odds of an early-term repeat cesarean in VBAC-eligible births.

In figure 4.3, there is a sharp drop in early-term induction rates after 2009, although the odds began to creep up again by 2014–2015.[41] To examine the effects of liability risk before and after the reinforcement of professional guidelines in 2009, I analyzed the 1995–2009 and 2010–2015 periods separately. As I discussed in chapter 2, coercive pressures from the legal environment are most important when normative pressures from the profession are weak, so liability risk should be especially important for guiding behavior when providers are uncertain about what courses of action are professionally acceptable.[42] While ACOG guidelines have recommended against induction for non-medical reasons before 39 weeks since 1982, the normative pressure of those guidelines appears to have eroded between 1982 and 2009. As more births occurred in the early-term period, induction of labor and scheduled repeat cesareans between 37 and 39 weeks became the new normal—at least until ACOG and the Joint Commission increased normative pressures to reduce early-term deliveries in 2009.

This suggests differences between two periods, 1995–2009 and 2010–2015. Tort regimes should matter more in the earlier period because of weaker normative pressure from the profession to avoid elective early deliveries. The erosion of professional norms and informal rules before 2010 should have made the legal environment more important for guiding behavior in the maternity care field. During this period, maternity care providers should have known that elective early-term induction was medically risky, but they may have dismissed the likelihood of causing harm to their low-risk (i.e. healthy) patients and been willing to take the risk of scheduling elective early-term deliveries, especially if they worked in provider-friendly tort regimes. After all, many women wanted to end their pregnancies a bit earlier and providers could benefit from scheduling their births.

Sure enough, I analyzed low-risk early-term induction from 1995–2009 and found that tort regimes did affect their odds more during this period.[43] All else being equal, the odds of early-term induction in low-risk births were 13.7% higher when there were caps on punitive damages alone, and 24.5% higher when there were caps on non-economic damages, than when there were no caps on damage awards, suggesting that liability risk did reduce risk-taking behavior during this period.[44] Figure 4.4 shows the predicted probabilities based on caps on damages from 1995 to 2009. This figure suggests that liability risk was important to motivate providers to engage in more cautious practices from 1995 to 2009.

The odds of early-term induction in low-risk births were also 16.5% higher in states with JSL, and 8.6% higher in states with expert requirements. Since both PL and expert requirements reduce liability risk, this suggests that maternity care providers were more likely to induce early-term labor without medical reasons when they faced less liability risk.

The findings were similar for early-term repeat cesareans in VBAC-eligible births from 1995 to 2009. The odds of an early-term repeat cesarean compared to a VBAC or a repeat cesarean after 39 weeks were 17.6% higher when there were caps on punitive damages alone, and 25.5% higher when there were caps on non-economic damages, than when there were no caps on damage awards.[45] These are larger effects for 1995–2009 than for the whole 1995–2015 period.[46]

All of these effects are in the expected direction: from 1995 to 2009, induction and repeat cesareans between 37 and 39 weeks without medical indications were more likely when maternity care providers faced a lower risk of liability. In other words, malpractice liability risk deterred risky practices, exactly as tort laws intend. After 2009, ACOG Practice

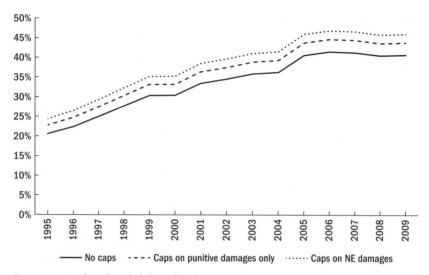

Figure 4.4. Predicted Probability of Early-Term Induction (37–38 Weeks) in Low-Risk Births by Caps on Damages, 1995–2009. Source: Low-risk births (37–42 weeks) in the Natality Detail Files (N = 3,506,639).

Bulletin 107 reestablished professional limits on elective early-term births and The Joint Commission required hospitals to report (and reduce) their early-term induction rate. These normative pressures on the maternity care field should have reduced the need for tort laws to act as a deterrent because many hospitals responded by implementing formal policies to limit early-term births. With this change in normative pressure, the effects of tort laws on low-risk early-term induction also changed after 2009: from 2010 to 2015, the odds of early-term induction in low-risk births were 11.9% *lower* in states with caps on punitive damages alone. Caps on non-economic damages, with or without caps on punitive damages, had no significant effect. This suggests that early-term inductions declined more in states with caps on damages after 2009 than in states without them. Figure 4.5 shows the effects of caps on damages on early-term induction from 2010 to 2015.

Caps on damages had no effects on the odds of early-term repeat cesareans from 2010 to 2015, in contrast with the strong positive effects that they had from 1995 to 2009. Reform of the JSL rule, expert requirements, and the rate of obstetric malpractice suits had no significant effects in the period from 2010 to 2015. The change in the effects of caps

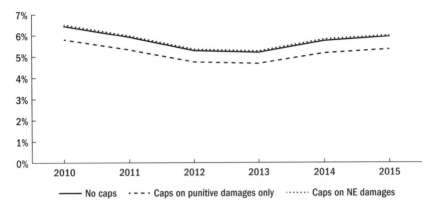

Figure 4.5. Predicted Probability of Low-Risk Early-Term Induction (37–38 Weeks) by Caps on Damages, 2010–2015. Source: Low-risk births (37–42 weeks) in the Natality Detail Files (N = 1,134,522).

on damages after 2009 suggests that liability risk was an important deterrent against early-term births *as long as* there was weak normative pressure from professional associations.

Taken together, I find that liability risk became less important after ACOG and The Joint Commission issued firm statements against elective induction before 39 weeks. When these professional associations clearly reinforced and circulated their clinical guidelines, pressure from the legal environment became much less important. The sharp change in the rate of low-risk early-term induction after 2009 (figure 4.3), and in the effects of tort liability (figures 4.3 and 4.4), suggests that professional guidelines have the power to deter physicians and hospitals from medically risky practices. But while professional norms can make legal enforcement under the tort system largely unnecessary, liability risk is an important deterrent against risky behavior when normative pressures erode, as was the case before 2009.

Medical Liability Risk: An Effective Deterrent

In summary, elective early-term deliveries are risky for mothers and babies, but they also offer organizational efficiencies to hospitals and physician practices as well as quality-of-life benefits for individual providers. For this reason, elective early-term births pit evidence-based medicine and quality of care against organizational interests. Changes over time in elective early-term births highlight these tensions in American maternity care, and the effects of tort regimes reveal the mediating role of liability risk. While previous research has argued that tort laws have a weak deterrent effect, most existing studies have focused on adverse events that have already occurred.[47] What is different about this study is that I analyzed the effects of tort reform laws on practices that increase the risk of injury but do not cause injury in every instance: early-term deliveries for non-medical reasons. The evidence for neonatal and maternal risks due to early-term birth has been clear for many decades, but some providers have been willing to induce labor or schedule repeat cesareans before 39 weeks for non-medical reasons, under the assumption that they will not produce bad outcomes most of the time. As a result, the odds of a non–medically indicated early-term induction or repeat cesarean were higher, all else being equal, when providers faced less liability risk. In other words, tort liability is an effective deterrent against this risky obstetric practice, especially in the absence of strong professional pressures to do the right thing. By weakening this deterrent effect, tort reforms that reduce providers' liability risk encourage risky behavior.

In particular, caps on damages undermine the tort system's ability to protect patients from preventable injuries by reducing the pressure on healthcare providers to "do no harm." Liability deters risky practices, exactly as tort laws intend, especially when there are no *recent* professional statements to reinforce normative pressures on maternity care providers. In the case of non–medically indicated early-term births, the effects of professional guidelines eroded over time, making tort laws important for discouraging risky, opportunistic, or harmful practices that benefit providers over patients.

Since risky practices like early-term induction without medical indications do not cause harm in every case, legal regulations, organizational policies, and professional guidelines are all necessary to tip the balance in favor of evidence-based medicine (EBM). EBM uses scientific evidence about the "best practices" for managing a health condition to develop practice guidelines that are based on well-designed, clinically relevant scientific research. EBM can improve the quality and consistency of clinical decisions, decrease the probability of medical errors, and improve patient outcomes.[48] But many physicians do not understand the evidence, or they believe that their clinical judgement is superior to guidelines that are based on what is effective for the average patient because of the professional principle of *clinical autonomy*, which assumes that "doctor knows best."[49] Physicians and hospitals can also benefit from ignoring evidence-based guidelines in terms of scheduling, staffing, and reimbursement, which cloud their clinical judgement and undermine patient safety—especially if they view the risks as small and they see everyone else doing it.[50] State-level tort regimes can intervene by emphasizing patient safety or, alternatively, permitting profit and organizational efficiency to override it. In the next chapter, I will further investigate the effects of liability risk on a common obstetric practice that lacks the support of scientific evidence for most births: continuous electronic fetal monitoring.

5

The Machine That Goes Ping!

Technology Fetishism and the Electronic Fetal Monitor

> Obstetrician 1: More apparatus, please, nurse.
> Obstetrician 2: The EEG, the BP monitor, and the ABV.
> Obstetrician 1: And get the machine that goes 'ping!'
> Obstetrician 2: And get the most expensive machine—in case the
>   Administrator comes.
>   . . .
> Patient: What do I do?
> Obstetrician 1: Nothing, dear, you're not qualified.
> Obstetrician 2: Leave it to us.
> Patient: What's that for?
> Obstetrician 2: That's the machine that goes 'ping!'
>   [*Obstetrician 1 presses a button and the machine goes 'ping!'*]
> Obstetrician 2: You see? That means your baby is still alive!
>   . . .
> Hospital Administrator: Ah, I see you have the machine that goes 'ping!'
>   This is my favourite. You see, we lease this back from the company
>   we sold it to, and that way it comes under the monthly current
>   budget and not the capital account.
>   [*The doctors and onlookers applaud.*]
> Hospital Administrator: Thank you, thank you. We try to do our best.
>   Well, do carry on.
>   (*Monty Python's The Meaning of Life*, Part I: The Miracle of Birth, 1983)

In *Monty Python's The Meaning of Life*, the machine that goes "ping!" is a very important piece of technology. It is an expensive machine, and its "ping!" tells the doctor that the baby is still alive. It also delights the hospital administrator, who can pat himself on the back for his clever accounting and feel impressed by the technological sophistication of his hospital. Does the machine serve any medical purposes? Not in this sketch on "The Miracle of Birth," where the doctors are posturing for each other and the administrator, and the pregnant woman is "not qualified" to participate in the birth. At the end of the sketch, the doctor hands her a prescription for "lots of happy pills," presumably to help her to cope with the way that the hospital ignored and belittled her during the birth. But the machine clearly serves some very important extra-medical needs. In maternity care, the electronic fetal monitor is the machine that goes "ping!"—it has questionable medical value for most births and distracts attention away from the woman in labor. It has a seven-inch screen that mesmerizes everyone in the room, including the nurses, the pregnant woman's partner, and often the pregnant woman herself. It hums and beeps, while it emits a continuous stream of paper with line graphs of the fetal heart rate and uterine contractions. Hospital staff call these paper graphs EFM tracings or simply a "strip." Figure 5.1 shows a sample of EFM output.

The use of EFM offers a prime example of technology fetishism (see chapter 1). In the 1960s, obstetricians introduced continuous EFM to manage high-risk labors. Though its effectiveness was untested, continuous EFM became routine for all labors in the 1970s. The EFM machine has two round, flat, hard-plastic transducers that are about three inches in diameter. They use ultrasound and pressure sensors to convert uterine contractions and the baby's heart rate into electric signals that the machine can store, display on a computer screen, and print out on paper as a written record. The nurse or other provider puts clear ultrasound jelly on the transducers and attaches them to wide elastic belts that wrap around the pregnant woman's belly and hold them in place. Most EFM machines have wires that connect the transducers to the machine and require the pregnant woman to stay close by.[1] So unlike using a handheld Doppler ultrasound to intermittently monitor the fetal heart rate by moving the device around the pregnant belly, EFM requires the laboring woman to stay in place to accommodate the machine.[2] Figure 5.2 shows the EFM machine.

Taking its materiality into account, EFM became a routine aspect of American maternity care partly because its physical and technological properties made it a symbol of high-quality, high-tech care.[3] Most EFM machines report the baseline heart rate (e.g., 140 beats per minute) and the length of the uterine contractions. Many also report variability in the

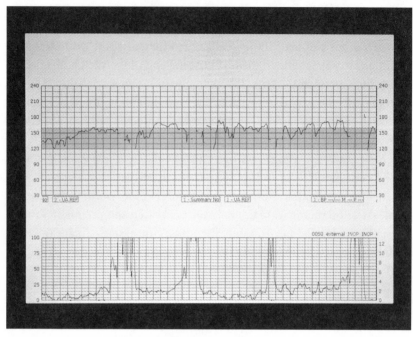

Figure 5.1. EFM Output Strip. Photo by Carolina K. Smith MD.

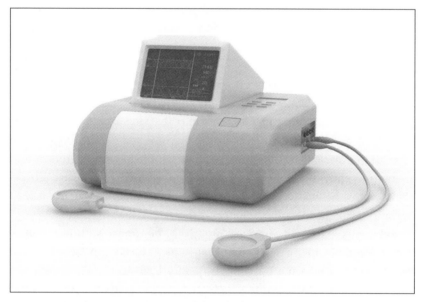

Figure 5.2. An Electronic Fetal Monitor. Photo by rendeep kumar r.

fetal heart rate (e.g., minimal, moderate, or marked variability) and an analysis of the fetal heart pattern (e.g., episodic accelerations, episodic variable decelerations, early decelerations, late decelerations). They have alarms that alert the staff with loud beeping noises if the heart rate is abnormal or the machine is not picking up the fetal heart rate. These beeping sounds distract everyone in the room and can cause anxiety for pregnant women and their families. The temptation to watch the computer screen often takes attention away from the laboring woman, although many pregnant women welcome the technology and view it as a symbol of their status as patients.

EFM machines typically have a built-in interface to the central nursing station so that nurses can watch the heart rate from outside the room and can monitor multiple laboring women simultaneously, which leads to less hands-on physical and emotional support for women in labor. This aspect of EFM technology changes the work-flow of obstetric nurses and Labor and Delivery departments by enabling them to take a hands-off approach to monitoring labor.[4] Some nurses might even prefer that distance from patient care, especially if they have negative attitudes towards their patients, as Khiara Bridges found for nurses who worked with low-income pregnant women on Medicaid.[5] But research has found that hands-on labor support is an optimal practice in maternity care and it leads to shorter labors, fewer cesarean deliveries, increased breastfeeding, and higher maternal satisfaction.[6] This type of supportive care is uncommon when EFM is routine.

With continuous EFM, the transducer can lose the baby's heart rate if the pregnant woman moves around or changes position during labor. If the nursing staff is monitoring the labor from outside the room when this happens, a nurse will often rush into the room to reposition both the monitor and the woman to ensure that the transducer gives a clear signal. In this way, the EFM machine emphasizes the smooth functioning of the *machine* over the mobility and comfort of the pregnant woman.

The Electronic Fetal Monitor's (In)Effectiveness

One might argue that the loss of attention from the hospital staff and the lack of mobility for the pregnant woman is worthwhile if EFM improves outcomes, but this technology lacks the support of scientific evidence. North American hospitals widely adopted EFM for routine use before medical research could test its effectiveness. It had all of the hallmarks of *scienciness*: it seemed scientific and technologically sophisticated, but it primarily served organizational and ritual purposes. After EFM use spread, medical research revealed that it is no more effective for identifying fetal distress than "intermittent auscultation" (listening to the fetal heartbeat every 10 to 15 minutes during active labor). Rates of cerebral palsy and intrapartum hypoxia (oxygen deficiency during labor) have remained steady despite widespread use of EFM, which has an extremely high (greater than 99%) false-positive rate. False positives occur when the EFM suggests that the fetus is in distress when it is not. Partly because of its high false-positive rate, EFM is associated with increases in the rate of operative vaginal delivery (with forceps or vacuum) and cesarean delivery.[7] Medical science has shown for more than 30 years that the benefits of EFM do not outweigh its risks, especially in low-risk births.

The obstetricians and CNMs that I interviewed *all* knew that using EFM was not evidence-based for most pregnancies. Dr. Carlson, a gynecologist who had stopped practicing obstetrics, said,

> I know, from studies, that it hasn't changed the incidence of cerebral palsy. . . . The rates of prematurity have not improved, and the rates of cerebral palsy have not improved. Over all these years, with fetal monitoring, those things are the same. Despite all the monitoring, all the C-sections, we still have the same rate of prematurity and the same rate of cerebral palsy that we did 30 years ago.

Dr. Carlson recognized that EFM, and the medicalization of childbirth more generally, have failed to improve birth outcomes.

Maternity care providers knew that intermittent auscultation was equally effective for monitoring the fetal heart rate during labor. Dr. Brooks, who worked at a teaching hospital and emphasized evidence-based practices, said that EFM was no more effective than intermittent monitoring:

> Our literature tells us that electronic fetal monitoring does not improve outcomes. Intermittent monitoring is the same as continuous monitoring

in that outcomes are not improved by continuous monitoring. It just leads to more C-sections.

As she notes, EFM does not offer medical benefits, but it does increase the likelihood of a cesarean. In this respect, EFM worsens outcomes because cesareans pose health risks to infants and especially to mothers.

Dr. Murray, an obstetrician at a hospital with a birth center, was similarly skeptical of EFM:

> I don't think that any continuous electronic fetal monitoring has been shown to improve outcomes. It's so hard to show that impact. Either doing intermittent monitoring—listening in active labor with a contraction to see how the baby is doing—or doing continuous can show you if the baby is having a hard time with the contractions. And certainly it's frustrating (to have continuous monitoring), because you can have a tracing that looks really dire . . . and you've got a [fetal] scalp pH that tells you it looks good, and you got a nice healthy baby out of it. It helped me realize that that tracing isn't always as accurate as they like to believe. I think it gives us false reassurance as well.

Dr. Murray's experience showed her that EFM was an unreliable technology, and she said that she used intermittent auscultation—but only if women asked for it.

The only obstetrician who thought that EFM was effective was Dr. McDonald, who specialized in high-risk pregnancies and viewed it is as useful for some complex cases: "We use monitoring for the contractions. Technology helps in the high-risk pregnancies and there's data for that. But most people aren't high-risk." In other words, continuous EFM was evidence-based for complicated pregnancies. But her hospital also used it routinely for low-risk pregnancies even though the evidence did not support it.

In addition to the research showing that continuous EFM offers no benefits, it also introduces iatrogenic risks.[8] All of the maternity care providers that I interviewed knew that EFM reduced women's mobility in labor, increased the need for pain medication, and contributed to unnecessary cesareans, with all of their potential complications (see chapter 6). EFM leads to preventable cesareans because it often produces false alarms, where the hospital staff interpret the heart rate reading as an indication of fetal distress when the fetus is actually doing well (a *false positive*). This led most obstetricians to say that the primary effect of EFM has been to increase the cesarean delivery rate. Dr. Ribeiro said, "I trained at a place with one of the first electronic fetal monitors. That is a thing that you can look at and say that all it has done is increase our C-section rate." Dr. McGinley also said, "Continuous monitoring increases the C-section rate because you can watch everything. . . . When you have too much information you can't just sit and watch the bad heart rate." With continuous EFM, more information is not necessarily accurate information, but EFM's known false-positive rate does not stop obstetricians from acting on monitor output that suggests a "bad heart rate."

Even in academic hospitals that emphasize evidence-based medicine and try to reduce their cesarean delivery rate, EFM causes unnecessary cesarean deliveries. Dr. McDonald, who specialized in high-risk pregnancies, said,

> I do think that, depending on people's level of interpretation of the fetal monitoring strips, it can result in too many C-sections. I think they're over-reading them. It is labor-intensive and there's a responsibility there. I feel comfortable that I can read it without overreacting to it, but it has its own price as well. It makes me feel better, but the patients have to have the straps on them, which decreases their mobility, and that results in less activity during labor, and that affects pure vaginal births.

Dr. McDonald underlines the costs of using continuous EFM: less mobility for laboring women and less ability to have an uncomplicated vaginal birth.

Even when EFM strips do not trigger immediate concerns about fetal distress, EFM often makes other interventions into labor and delivery necessary. As I mentioned above, the material properties of the external EFM typically require hospital staff to restrict laboring women's movement and immobilize them in a hospital bed in order to obtain accurate readings. Dr. Carlson described how staff would have to position laboring women so that the monitor could find the fetal heart rate, and avoid position changes that caused the monitor to lose the fetal heart rate:

Sometimes with the belt (external fetal monitor), you couldn't get the tracing of the contraction, so you'd go put on the internal monitors and put a clip on the baby's head, and it was much easier. You didn't have to keep fiddling around with this thing (the belt for the external monitor). I think I did that a lot (used the internal monitor with scalp clips) so that I wouldn't have to be bothered with the nurse constantly calling me, saying, "Where's the baby? I can't find the heart rate."

Dr. Carlson preferred to use the more invasive internal monitor that clipped into the fetal scalp. But screwing clips into their babies' scalps was not a big hit with mothers, and it required breaking the amniotic sac and introducing the risk of infection. So obstetricians usually relied on the external EFM, despite its inaccuracy and the challenges with positioning it correctly. Then, because hospital staff emphasized the functioning of the machine, EFM usually immobilized laboring women in a hospital bed (figure 5.3). Notably, positioning women for effective *monitoring* does not necessarily help to position women for effective *labor*, and efforts to position laboring women on the monitor reduces them to objects that a machine acts on, rather than active participants in the process of giving birth. Like *Monty Python's* machine that goes "ping!" the machine becomes more important for the labor and birthing process than the pregnant woman.

Since most pregnant women have continuous EFM throughout labor, this emphasis on the technology over the woman immobilizes laboring women in ways that interfere with the normal progression of labor. Scientific research has shown that being able to move around shortens labor and assists with non-medical pain management by giving women opportunities to reposition themselves in ways that make labor contractions bearable. With mobility, the force of gravity can assist with labor progression. When a laboring woman is flat on her back in a hospital bed and hooked up to an EFM, gravity cannot work the baby down. The lack of mobility can also make it impossible for women to reposition themselves in ways that help them to manage the pain. I had some firsthand experience with this, even though I gave birth at a freestanding birth center where the midwives primarily used intermittent monitoring. When I was in labor with my second son, I remember a short amount of time on the EFM as more unbearable than the rest

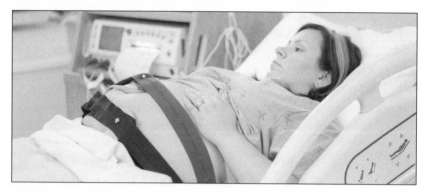

Figure 5.3. A Laboring Woman Attached to an Electronic Fetal Monitor. Photo by Tyler Olson.

of my labor. I arrived at the birth center in hard labor and Gina, the midwife, wanted a "strip" of heart-rate tracings to see how the baby was doing. She strapped the two elastic belts around my belly, and I had to lie in one position. I don't remember how long I was in that position, but I was having hard contractions, one after another, and it was *excruciating*. It might have been 20 minutes. At one point, I moaned, "That epidural looks pretty great right now." I could not manage the pain without being able to move around. Gina wanted to help me to avoid unnecessary interventions so she took me off the monitor and helped me into a big whirlpool bathtub. There I could move around and the warm water was soothing. As I labored in the tub, my doula massaged my back and encouraged me through each contraction. Gina monitored the baby's heart rate with a Doppler that allowed me to stay in the water and to move around until I was ready to push. It hurt like only childbirth can, but I don't know if I could have managed it if I had had to lie still for the monitor.

Because EFM makes it harder to manage the pain of labor, it leads to a greater need for pain medication like epidural analgesia. Epidurals are the most popular form of pain relief during labor, and they have the amazing ability to numb the mother's lower body so that she does not feel the pain of labor and birth. But many women do not investigate the downside of epidural analgesia: it causes low blood pressure, which can affect the baby's blood supply and interfere with the hormones that cause uterine contractions, leading to a longer labor, a much higher risk of severe perineal tearing, and a higher risk that the baby's head will be face up when it enters the birth canal.[9] Babies should be facing back for the birth, so this can lead to a cesarean. Epidurals can also cause fever, shivering, sedation, nausea, and vomiting, and they increase the need for other interventions, like intravenous Pitocin to artificially stimulate contractions. Pitocin can cause fetal distress and lead to a cesarean.[10] Susan Dixon, a CNM, noted this effect:

> If you are on the monitor continuously, you are at risk for everything else. I've seen other methods for pain control such as getting up, taking a shower, and trying other things that you can't do if you are on a monitor and have to watch a baby's heartbeat. I've walked into situations where a woman is watching the monitor and then she looks at me with this fear in her eyes and says, "I don't think I can do this." Then the minute I take them off of the monitor and suggest that this person get up and take a shower or walk or get on her hands and knees, it seems possible to give birth without an epidural, whereas it didn't five minutes before that.

The material nature of the EFM machine makes it hard to manage labor pain. It requires that the woman lie still and it draws attention to the monitor with its screen and sounds. This is one reason that EFM often triggers a *cascade* of interventions into labor and birth, including epidural analgesia, artificial stimulation of labor, episiotomy, and cesarean delivery.

Another significant problem with EFM is the fact that maternity care providers have varying interpretations of fetal heart-rate tracings. Obstetricians and midwives knew that interpretations of EFM readings varied significantly, and that this could influence birth outcomes. While most maternity care providers would agree about what constitutes a perfectly good or perfectly bad heart-rate tracing, they often disagreed about how to interpret the vast majority of strips that fall in between.[11] Dr. McDonald, who saw valid uses for EFM in high-risk cases, said,

> I do think that it has resulted in more C-sections. Our C-section rate is only 23%, which is still too high. We're a little more tolerant of strips

that are different than normal. We are a little more tolerant of labors that take longer than average, because we're really pleased to have a successful vaginal delivery.

Dr. McDonald highlighted the importance of the provider and the hospital for interpreting EFM output. Providers who interpret fetal heart-rate tracings with a view toward the worst-case scenario will perform a lot of unnecessary cesarean deliveries.

Hospital staff also sometimes disagreed about their interpretation of the EFM tracing, which could contribute to the cascade of interventions. Dr. Garcia had clinical experience in unconventional settings that made her confident about her own interpretation of the EFM tracings. But others who were involved in the birth could overreact to the strip and encourage her to intervene:

> Sometimes if you have a strip that you know in your heart is fine, but it has concerning issues, you feel a lot of pressure not just from the nurses, but from the patients themselves. Some patients get very anxious, even though you know in your heart that it's fine. Nurses will push us to get the baby out because they worry. It's really pretty rare that a tracing that looks worrisome to me, but that I know in my heart is fine, ever comes back with a real problem. A lot of patients get so worried and they themselves perceive that it's worse than it is. And they don't want to continue laboring on. So sometimes it's not just us. It's the whole team. I then get pressured to do a cesarean.

As in this case, most maternity care providers recognized that interpretation of the strips is subjective and that sometimes EFM strips suggested that there might be a problem even though a baby was tolerating labor well. But EFM, with its loud alarms and attention-drawing screen, could cause anxiety among patients and staff. Disagreements about interpretations of EFM output tended to encourage more intervention, and were often resolved with a cesarean delivery.

Because of the known problems of interpreting EFM and its high rate of false positives, some maternity care providers, like midwives, avoided routinely using this technology. Rosemary MacLeod, a CNM, said,

Over time, we have become increasingly reliant on medical technologies, and some of them came into place without really good studies to look at their impact. As a midwife, I want to use as few of those technologies as possible, and in out-of-hospital births, we are listening to that baby. If I'm in the hospital, I am there for different reasons, and I will use more of those technologies as I need them. If I have a well and healthy laboring woman who is there by her own choice, then I don't have to use the technologies they have there. And I think that sometimes when you're in the hospital, you're the one that's swimming against the flow because the nurses expect to use everything that's there. So it's a little different when you say, "No, I'm not going to do this. I'm not going to do that." You always get questions. But we have many more technologies than we need for a normal, healthy labor and birth.

Rejection of the routine use of technology was common for CNMs, even when they had hospital privileges, in accordance with a midwifery philosophy of birth. Midwives have different professional norms and emphasize hands-on supportive care with fewer interventions.

Some obstetricians were also comfortable using intermittent monitoring and having more mobile patients. Dr. Garcia said,

When I was in medical school, I remember there was a lot more stuff than we do now. I remember that routinely we put in scalp monitors, and decompressions. I don't do that now. If everything is going well, and the patient is motivated, I let them walk around. I let them use the shower. I let them use the Jacuzzi.

To permit laboring women to have this mobility, Dr. Garcia had to use intermittent monitoring instead of continuous EFM. At least four of the obstetricians that I interviewed were willing to use intermittent monitoring rather than continuous EFM for uncomplicated labors. But continuous EFM was their default monitoring strategy, unless women specifically requested intermittent auscultation. They also said that they were going against the tide because continuous EFM is routine in American hospital protocols and staff are used to using it.

Electronic Fetal Monitoring as Defensive Medicine

Given that continuous EFM is not evidence based and has negative effects, why do most maternity care providers use it routinely? As I discussed in chapter 2, technical efficiency is only one criterion that organizations use to inform their practices. Hospitals and the obstetric profession must consider competitive, legal, and professional pressures in order to maintain both cultural legitimacy within the maternity care field and organizational performance. Organizational uncertainty, needs for efficiency, and competition with other hospitals encourage the adoption of new obstetric technologies. *Technology fetishism* is also one of the pillars of the medicalization schema (chapter 1). As the Monty Python scene illustrates, technology provides a symbol of medical excellence even when it does not improve outcomes and detracts from the patient's experience. In fact, both patients and doctors view advanced technology as signal of quality, modernity, and advanced care.[12] Since quality is hard to measure and consumers often lack full information, this perception is enough to give cultural legitimacy to technologies like EFM, even when they lack scientific support.

Also, hospitals follow overall trends in the healthcare field, through a process that neo-institutional theories of organizations describe as *mimetic isomorphism* (see chapter 2): hospitals imitate each other in the services, technologies, and amenities that they offer.[13] One way that obstetrics departments have mimicked one another is by adopting EFM technology, which diffused across North American hospitals in the 1980s.[14] It gained cultural legitimacy because of its scienciness: it has the *appearance* of being scientific and it creates a paper trail. Once a significant number of hospitals adopted electronic monitors, they became a symbol of quality and efficiency and, by most accounts, of legally responsible obstetric practice in hospital obstetric departments.

Theories of law and organizations emphasize the power of governments, laws, courts, and professional regulatory bodies to standardize practices within organizational fields by establishing and enforcing rules that organizations must follow. Then organizations and professions find ways to comply visibly with legal and professional regulations and guidelines and to signal a good-faith effort to comply with the law. One way to do this is to adopt technology that seems scientific, even if scientific research has not supported its use, to protect themselves from liability. Illustrating this, Dr. Brooks remarked that she was more likely to use technology to intervene when she worried about legally defending herself:

> I think certainly if you have a labor that is not going the way that you want and you are concerned about a bad outcome, you tend to use all the technologies that are available to prove to yourself that you've done everything you can for this baby and mom and that everything is going okay. That's where the "cover your butt" medicine comes in. If you really start to think that this is going to be a bad outcome, you start to throw everything that you have at it to prove that the baby is doing okay. So I would say that the thought of sitting in court and defending what I'm doing, I would much rather have more technology assuring me that the baby is okay on my side if I'm trying to defend a bad outcome that happened.

While she viewed technology as legally defensive, she took a medically conservative approach to using it, reserving it for cases where she worried about a bad outcome rather than using it routinely.

But most obstetricians used technology like EFM routinely, and legal defensiveness was an important justification for it. In fact, all maternity care providers knew that the evidence did not support continuous EFM, but they had a lot to say about its legally defensive purposes. Dr. Nelson, a perinatal specialist, said that obstetric technology was a tool for protecting against liability risk:

> We use more tests with the hope that we can document that we have done the right thing and that basically, babies were OK up until point X, so that we can be off the hook. So when the baby comes and the heart rate doesn't look good, or it's dead, we can demonstrate that we did everything. Basically, the technology allows us to protect ourselves. That's how we use it. We use it to protect ourselves more than to actually impact care.

Dr. Nelson said that the technology that she used most often was ultrasound but, like all obstetricians, she also used continuous EFM. As neo-institutional theories would predict, and as Theresa Morris found in *Cut It Out*, obstetricians' most common explanation for using medical technology during pregnancy and birth was their belief that it is necessary to protect them against medical malpractice suits—not that it improved outcomes.[15] Their basic claim was, "We're stuck and we have to protect ourselves from lawsuits, even though we know that the technology is flawed and causes harmful interventions into labor. It's not our fault. It's because of the lawyers and insurance companies."

Obstetricians, CNMs, medical malpractice attorneys, and, to a lesser extent, health insurers all shared a cultural narrative about legal risk being a primary reason for the routine use of EFM. They claimed that the risk of malpractice litigation and the requirements of liability insurance companies demanded it. Dr. Ribeiro said,

> This is one place where litigation and insurance have just meshed. You cannot *not* monitor these people electronically because of the malpractice risk. Yet, from a clinical point of view, you're not doing anything better than by just listening to the baby's heart rate every 15 minutes. So I think it interferes a lot with the birth and the mother on that level. . . . I think the technology is, like anything else, it's a double-edged sword. But the real technology that we think about is fetal monitoring. We all do it. Everyone has to do it, but it is just being forced on us because of medical-legal considerations.

Obstetricians all claimed that the legal system and their liability insurance carriers imposed a norm of continuous EFM, even though they knew that it was not beneficial in most births. In this respect, they took on a kind of victim status that is unusual in the powerful medical profession—although perhaps not when doctors talk about malpractice liability. Despite having authoritative knowledge over contemporary labor and childbirth (see chapter 1), they described themselves as powerless in the face of lawyers and juries and claimed that they had to use EFM to avoid liability, even though they knew that it did not improve the quality of care.

Even midwives, who typically avoided using technology unless it was clearly beneficial, viewed EFM as a technology that offered legal protection. Rosemary MacLeod, who attended births both in a hospital where continuous EFM is routine and in an out-of-hospital birth center where it is not, said,

I suspect that if there was a poor outcome, and there was a trial, then each side gets experts, and an expert from their side and an expert from our side review everything that went on. Say that you had a patient that was not being monitored and had thick meconium, and you had a poor outcome. I think that both sides would say that this was not practice according to the standard of care. . . . I think there is an understood standard of care out there, and if you don't adhere to the standard of care, then it could affect your practice.

Monitoring is a key component of the standard of care, and continuous EFM is the default method of monitoring.

The definition of EFM as legally defensive could also increase obstetricians' level of anxiety about liability. Dr. Carlson said that using EFM for legal reasons was necessary to protect against malpractice suits, but that it negatively affected everyone's peace of mind because it made them more nervous about liability risk (and its hard-to-position, beeping and flashing material qualities did not help):

I think that fetal monitoring is a good example of a technology that causes us to do things to protect ourselves legally because there is some evidence there in the form of the fetal monitor and, if the outcome is bad, we'll go back and retrace. [Plaintiffs and their lawyers] can possibly say that [something] happened, when you didn't do anything and it's your fault. So that definitely is a technology that I think is not a good technology overall. I think it's caused a lot of stress and distress among physicians and patients. . . . The use of these fetal monitors, even though we know that cerebral palsy incidents do not change with the use of them, you use them now because if you didn't use them and something happened, you could be confronted as trying to conceal something.

Evidence or no evidence, obstetricians believed that they needed to use continuous EFM to legally protect themselves, and it still caused stress about liability risk. This stress, and the high cost of liability insurance to practice obstetrics, was one of the reasons that Dr. Carlson stopped attending births and only practiced gynecology.

While most maternity care providers viewed EFM as legally protective, if anxiety-provoking and inaccurate, one CNM suggested that the emphasis on technology could create unrealistic expectations that actually increased the likelihood of litigation. When I asked Laura Pierce, a CNM, about the use of medical technologies during labor, she said,

> I think they increase the likelihood of lawsuits. I think it gives people these expectations that are not realistic in general. That we have all of this power over birth and death, but really, we have a limited sway over those things. I just went through this with somebody who was going to have a baby that died, and they really thought that we were going to be able to save this baby. There was nothing we could do. It's so hard for people to understand that there's nothing you can do sometimes.

While Laura Pierce was the only maternity care provider who explicitly claimed that technology increased the odds of a lawsuit, she was far from alone in believing that modern medical technology could create unrealistic expectations about perfect outcomes in every birth. Most maternity care providers believed that these expectations contributed to medical malpractice suits in obstetrics, an area of medicine where unfortunate events were sometimes unavoidable. This reinforced their beliefs that they had to routinely use EFM to legally protect themselves when bad things happened.

The Standard of Care and The Endogeneity of Law

What makes EFM legally defensive? Obviously it is not that scientific evidence supports it, because it does not, so it is important to think about how law influences medicine (and how medicine influences law). As I discussed in chapters 2 and 3, tort laws aim to remedy violations of standards of care that individuals owe to one another as members of society, including healthcare providers' duties of care to their patients. The primary goal of medical malpractice lawsuits is to make clinicians accountable for *negligence*: unsafe, harmful, and substandard healthcare practices. So how did routine EFM become a marker of non-negligent care?

Recall from chapter 3 that definitions of medical negligence are based on the standards set by the medical profession. Lawyers and the courts lack specialized and intimate knowledge about the practice of medicine, so tort laws follow community-based and professional standards as the benchmark for whether negligence has occurred. Sam Durand, a corporate insurance manager who was responsible for risk oversight in a hospital network, noted that providers were accountable for following standard practices in their professional community:

> I think the impact is that, if you don't do it, and something happens, you are at far greater risk. I also think that if you don't do it, but someone else is doing it in the community, you may be held to a community standard that you should do it.

Community standards mean that conformity is more important than science or clinical judgement. By definition, standard practices are the benchmark for malpractice, not adherence to evidence-based guidelines or efforts to individualize care. Lawyers and the courts look to the field of medicine for guidance on appropriate practices, and adopt the standards that are set within medicine.

In many ways, this represents a perfect example of *legal endogeneity* because the definition of legal compliance comes from within medicine, rather than the law imposing it from the outside. The medical profession defines the SOC that is the legal benchmark for whether malpractice occurred, and it legally binds both lawyers and individual physicians. EFM is a prime example: hospitals adopted it and the obstetric profession embraced its routine use. It became the SOC and all obstetricians believed that they had to use it despite the lack of evidence for its effectiveness. Dr. McGinley said,

> There's no good data to show that it's any better than intermittent monitoring but, for malpractice reasons, it's the standard of care so it has to be used. It's hard for them to go back. When something becomes a standard, it's hard to say, "We were wrong."

Once EFM was part of the SOC and integrated into hospital protocols, doctors believed that they were stuck with it, even though the medical profession establishes the SOC and has the power to change it. In 1997, ACOG overturned a longstanding policy that favored EFM because of its known risks and lack of benefits.[16] ACOG reiterated the problems with

EFM in its most recent practice bulletin on intrapartum fetal heart-rate monitoring.[17] But most obstetricians continued to use EFM routinely and ACOG did not explicitly recommend against it. The American Academy of Nursing actually advised against the routine use of EFM in 2015, but most nurses lack the authority to reject hospital protocols that require routine EFM.[18]

Why was it hard to abandon EFM after reputable journals published clear evidence that it had a high false-positive rate, increased the cesarean rate, and did not reduce the incidence of cerebral palsy? Once EFM was in place, it had a stickiness to it. Other stakeholders such as hospital administrators, risk managers, and liability insurers had vested interests in maintaining it as the SOC. Standard practices have also continued to include the routine use of EFM because the courts have treated EFM tracings as a valid source of evidence in medical malpractice cases. Medical malpractice attorneys and the courts fully embraced EFM as a legal tool because it provides documentation in the form of a paper "strip" of heart-rate tracings. Both attorneys and providers fetishized EFM strips as important forms of evidence for medical malpractice cases. Susan Dixon, a CNM who attended births at a hospital and a freestanding birth center, noted that the physical existence of a paper strip made EFM more legitimate than intermittent monitoring, even though science has shown that intermittent monitoring is equally effective: "Things like that do have greater validity in malpractice cases. A nurse who says she came in every 15 minutes is not given the same validity in court as a piece of paper with scribbles on it." Her description of the strip as paper with "scribbles on it" clearly suggests that she thought that courts placed too much faith in these heart-rate tracings.

Jane Hart-Thompson, a defense attorney who was also skeptical about the value of EFM tracings, agreed that malpractice attorneys often fetishized EFM strips as evidence. When I asked her if birth-related malpractice suits had increased or decreased over time, she said, "In the beginning of my practice, they were going up because of fetal heart tracings. For the first time, the plaintiff's counsel had something seemingly concrete to look at and to be able to point to." Even though these two individuals rejected EFM as a flawed technology, they knew that court cases treated EFM strips as legitimate evidence. Since lawyers, judges, and juries rarely had specialized medical knowledge and were unaware of the problems with EFM technology, they were more likely to believe that these pieces of paper provided valid evidence. After all, it seemed scientific, and a high-tech machine produced the paper strip.

In fact, EFM strips provided one of the only forms of written documentation available in birth-related malpractice cases, so most disputes over medical malpractice focused on these strips. When I asked him to describe a typical birth-related malpractice suit, Rob Thompson, a defense attorney, said,

> The main cases involve allegations of failure to properly read an external fetal heart-rate monitor. That's where the fight always occurs. . . . The plaintiff's expert will always testify "There's clearly a pattern of late decelerations, the baby was clearly in trouble, and should have been delivered and if the baby had been delivered at this moment, the baby would have been a Rhodes Scholar. However, the baby is now brain-damaged." The defense expert will say that "No, this is not a pattern of late decelerations, and there have been plenty of babies born that have this type of pattern."

Once routine EFM became common, the heart-rate tracings that it produced offered attorneys a written record to dispute in medical malpractice cases, even though reinterpretation of the fetal heart-rate tracing is often unreliable. Rob Thompson described a case in which opposing experts offered different interpretations of the same EFM strip:

> In that particular case, the plaintiff's expert, who was a highly qualified physician, said that the external monitor was equivocal, and that it was also difficult to tell at times whether it was monitoring the fetus or the mother's heart rate. [He argued that] as the labor progressed, they should have placed scalp electrodes, or checked the mother's heart rate manually vis-à-vis what was being said on the monitor in order to see that what was being read on the monitor was recording the baby's heart rate. Our expert said it was not particularly alarming and it didn't look that atypical. And it didn't look that atypical. This was not the typical case, where there really are patterns of late decelerations. But this plaintiff's expert was pretty forthright and said, "No, you can't tell. And since you can't tell, you should have done something else."

This type of dispute contributed to the fetishization of the EFM strip by defining the machine output as a valid measure of what happened.

The EFM then becomes a replacement for care providers who pay close attention to a woman in labor and what is happening over time. Illustrating this, Josh Shaffer also described a particular case that involved disputes over the EFM strip:

> The labor was not monitored properly and the fetal strips showed fetal distress and the nurse didn't catch it. The doctor came in, and what the doctor is supposed to do is to review the whole strip and compare it, but as you know, a labor can be seven hours, eight hours, so what they may do is they may come in and go back ten minutes. Their presumption is that if they go back ten minutes and the baby is fine, then the baby has been fine. There are times when the strip can show some fetal distress, but then it will resolve. It can resolve by repositioning the baby and all kinds of different things. The problem with that approach is, you have to know what the baselines are. A baseline that may have been established during the first, second, third hour, where a heart rate is 135 beats per minute. If all of a sudden you are looking at 150, and you look for ten minutes and all of the variables are good, then you may think everything is okay, but when you leave the room it goes down to 120 and it doesn't recover properly. Then you are missing some of the subtleties.

Catching the "subtleties" has less to do with the EFM strip and more to do with watching and intervening if and when something changes—which requires an attentive and experienced birth attendant, not a machine that spits out a stream of paper.

But plaintiff's attorneys fetishized the EFM strips as a form of concrete evidence. The simple fact that the technology printed out a heart-rate tracing on paper appealed to attorneys' desire to have documentation. Michelle Morales, a plaintiff's attorney, said,

> If there is a concern about the strip, there are other ways to confirm heart rates of babies versus mothers, and there's that you can do it by manual if there is a problem. But if you are monitoring the wrong heart rate, or you don't catch when there's a deceleration of the baby's heart rate, and then not properly following up, I think that that is something that is

routinely seen by us and probably a lot of other people. That's because it's right there. It's on a record. Usually, they keep the patient on the heart-rate monitor the entire time, so you're going to have five to ten hours of strips. So that's something where it's evidence. You have what the patient says, but when you have evidence that's right in front of you, that's always stronger.

Plaintiffs' attorneys viewed EFM heart-rate tracings as valid evidence primarily because they were *on paper*. Never mind that interpretation of the output is variable and reinterpretation of the tracings is unreliable. This is a clear statement of fetishism of EFM technology and the output that it produces, in the sense that Michelle Morales revered an inanimate object (the paper output from the EFM machine) for its supposed magical powers.

She was not alone—most plaintiff's attorneys that I interviewed were true believers in EFM technology and viewed it as infallible. It's important to remember that most medical malpractice attorneys lack clinical experience and do not read the scientific research behind typical practices, although they often know what constitutes the SOC. Because plaintiff's attorneys had never used EFM in a clinical setting, they had no experience with the problems that providers had with obtaining accurate readings and false alarms. All of the plaintiff's attorneys that I interviewed believed that EFM provided accurate and objective data, and they were largely unaware of medical research that demonstrated low efficacy and high false-positive rates. They also only represented birth-related cases with tragic outcomes, not the large numbers of births where EFM led to unnecessary cesareans or non-catastrophic maternal morbidity. As a result, plaintiff's attorneys often viewed EFM as a foolproof tool for uncovering fetal distress, and attributed errors to the operators of the technology.

From a plaintiff's attorney's perspective, negligent birth injuries occur when clinicians fail to pay attention to the EFM output, or do not have the training or expertise to read it correctly. Jeff Nolan, a plaintiff's attorney, had a very high level of faith in EFM. He said,

The cases that I see are birth asphyxia cases. They are usually related to someone not reading the fetal monitoring records. They are either not reading them or they aren't reading them properly.

In his view, there were no flaws with the technology, and challenges with obtaining accurate EFM readings amounted to operator errors. Jeff Nolan also expressed an extreme version of technology fetishism: he claimed that the problem was with the *users* of the technology, not with the technology itself, and that more systematic and accurate reading of the EFM tracings would eliminate birth asphyxia cases:

> The best thing to do would be to come up with a computer program that looks at the fetal monitoring machine. I think it would help a lot to analyze the late decelerations and if there's a couple of those, then an alarm goes off, and you can do a number of things.

In his view, the technology is infallible but the humans who use it are not. He was adamant that EFM machines were accurate, and that the solution to human fallibility is more technology. When I asked him if it was possible for two people to read an EFM strip differently, he said:

> If they are reading it differently, then one is reading it wrong. There are some very definite parameters. There are late decelerations that show up on fetal monitoring strips for certain lengths of time and it's really pretty cut and dry. If you see this on the monitor strip, the baby is in distress, but I think that the problem is that maybe people aren't properly trained to read them.

His belief in the accuracy of EFM meant that he was unaware of variability and subjectivity in interpretations of EFM output. He believed that the problem must lie with the training or expertise of the provider reading the strip and not with the heart-rate tracings themselves. Then, the only possible improvement can come from more monitoring machines to monitor the bad monitoring machines that we already have (but which he fetishizes as infallible). A problem with this view, and one of the reasons that scientific research fails to support EFM, is that interpretations of fetal heart-rate tracings are far from clear.

Taking the perspectives of maternity care providers and attorneys together, the consensus was that the obstetric profession adopted EFM as the SOC without testing it, and it became essential for legal defense in birth-related malpractice suits. For many maternity care providers, it looked like the legal system imposed EFM on them, although the practice of routinely using EFM originated in medicine, not in law. While others, like Theresa Morris, have also found that obstetricians say that they must use EFM because of liability risk, it is important to remember that the *medical* SOC is the legal benchmark: it was the medical profession, not the legal profession, that defined EFM as legally defensive. Once hospitals had adopted EFM, the tort system wholeheartedly validated the EFM strip as evidence in medical malpractice lawsuits, especially because it produced tracings *on paper*. This is a primary way that the materiality of EFM contributed to its fetishism among legal practitioners. Then, once EFM was part of the SOC, it became difficult for providers to reject it.

In this way, definitions of legal compliance in American medicine have a recursive nature, and law and medicine weave together in complex ways. Medicine adopts technology before science can evaluate it, it enters routine practice and becomes the SOC, legal actors accept and embrace it as a signal of non-negligence, and providers then believe that they must use it for legal reasons. In many ways, this is a perfect example of legal endogeneity: hospitals, the medical profession, risk managers, and liability insurers define a technology as meeting legal compliance needs, and their definition traps both medical and legal actors in an iron cage of technology fetishism and unscientific practices. As a result, maternity care providers use EFM, at least in part, to reduce their liability risk, even though they recognize it as a flawed technology. They believe that they *must* use it to produce paper evidence in the event of a medical malpractice suit, and they feel legally vulnerable if they do not.

EFM and Tort Laws in Action

This story about the interaction between law and medicine suggests that EFM should be more common when there is more litigation risk. But how is liability risk related to EFM use? Does EFM use rise and fall as liability risk rises and falls? Taking the accounts of obstetricians and attorneys at face value, the odds of reporting EFM use on birth certificates should be *lower* in provider-friendly tort regimes with less malpractice liability risk.[19] Because rates of malpractice suits fluctuate over time and across states, the odds of reporting EFM should be *higher* in states with more recent obstetric malpractice suits. To test this, I used the same strategy as in chapter 4 to examine the effects of state laws on the odds of reporting EFM use in low-risk births from 1995 to 2003 (2,100,376 births).[20] (I could not analyze these effects after 2003 because many states had adopted a revised birth certificate form that stopped collecting information about monitoring.) Among all low-risk births, reported EFM use increased from 81.6% in 1995 to 85.8% in 2003. But when I analyzed the effects of tort laws and accounted for maternal and state characteristics, the results were *the opposite* of what I expected. Instead of higher odds of EFM use when there was more liability risk, which might indicate that maternity care providers use EFM for legally defensive purposes, the odds were substantially *lower* in states with more liability risk. Caps on punitive damages alone had no significant effect, but the odds of reporting EFM use in low-risk pregnancies were 21.2% *higher* in states with caps on non-economic damages than in states without caps on damages.[21] This is the opposite of what providers' and lawyers' accounts about legal defensiveness would predict. Figure 5.4 illustrates the predicted probability of EFM from 1995 to 2003 for states with no caps on damages, caps on punitive damages only, and caps on non-economic damages (with or without caps on punitive damages). In figure 5.4, the predicted probability of EFM is *higher* in states that limit providers' legal risk by capping non-economic damage awards.

The odds of EFM use are also *higher* in states with expert requirements, which reduce liability risk by imposing barriers to suing for malpractice.[22] While expert requirements should reduce malpractice lawsuits, this is easier to understand than the positive effects of caps on non-economic damages because experts tend to use EFM strips as a primary source of evidence in birth-injury cases. So expert requirements could increase the emphasis on EFM as a legal tool at the same time as they reduce the number of lawsuits. A higher rate of obstetric malpractice suits has a negligible, but negative, relationship with EFM, so a greater volume of recent lawsuit activity *does not increase* the odds of EFM. In fact, the only legal effect that was in the expected direction was the effect of JSL versus PL: PL is associated with *lower* odds of EFM than JSL, which is what one would expect if hospital protocols require routine EFM to avoid liability under JSL.[23] Figure 5.5 shows the predicted probability of EFM use in states with expert requirements, without expert requirements, with JSL, and with PL.

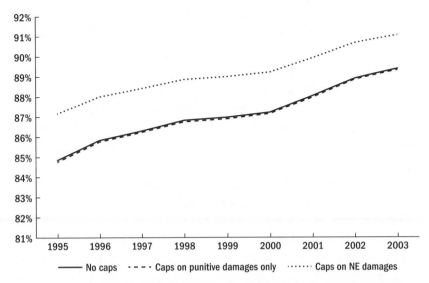

Figure 5.4. Predicted Probability of EFM in Low-Risk Births by Caps on Damages, 1995–2003. Source: Natality Detail Files (N = 2,100,376).

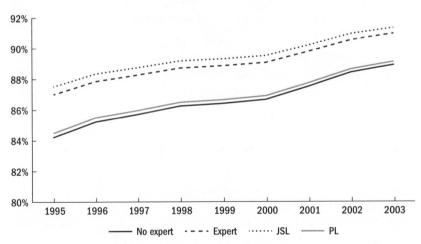

Figure 5.5. Predicted Probability of EFM in Low-Risk Births by JSL versus PL and by Expert Requirements, 1995–2003. Source: Natality Detail Files (N = 2,100,376).

Why would the odds of EFM be higher when tort reforms reduce liability risk? One possibility is that states only enact caps on damages *after* they have a particularly serious or visible "malpractice crisis." Then legally defensive behavior like EFM use should be more common before a state enacts reforms like caps on damages, and it should remain steady or decline after reforms take effect. I examined the odds for births in the year before and the year after tort reform legislation, as well the effects of having damage caps in place.[24] Accounting for these effects, there is still no support for the theory that EFM use is a defensive response to the legal environment. For caps on punitive damages alone, the odds of EFM are *lower* in the year leading up to caps on punitive damages than in other years without caps, and they *increase* after caps are enacted—which is the opposite of what should happen if tort reform legislation responded to a malpractice crisis.[25] When it comes to caps on non-economic damages, the odds of EFM were higher in births during the year prior to the enactment of caps on non-economic damages, but they were *even higher* during the year after a state enacted these tort reforms.[26] If liability risk was a significant driver of EFM use then the odds should have decreased or remained stable rather than increasing after tort reforms reduced liability risk.

In short, objective legal risk is *not* a significant contributor to EFM use in American maternity care. The odds of EFM are *higher* when providers' liability risk is *lower*, which is the opposite of what one would expect if EFM were a response to legal risk. This undermines the legal basis of many obstetricians' explanations for routine EFM use. So then why do maternity care providers routinely use EFM in hospital births?

Institutional Motivations for EFM Use

Considering the analysis of the legal and birth certificate data and the accounts of maternity care providers and attorneys together, it is clear that the culture of medicine has a ready-made account that explains seemingly irrational (or, at least, unscientific) behavior: protection against legal risk justifies non–evidence-based practices. But this account is just an account, because legal risk may *justify* EFM use but it does not actually motivate it. The obstetric profession justifies its practices based on fear of liability, and most obstetricians probably genuinely believe their shared cultural account that they must use EFM because of legal risk: the lawyers make us do it this way, and there is too much legal risk to do otherwise. In reality, there are other institutional motivations that promote routine EFM use. This implies a "dual process" of understanding in the maternity care field.

Dual process theory argues that conscious accounts about behavior, like the justification of EFM as legally defensive, are based on shared cultural scripts that do not necessarily correspond to people's underlying motivations.[27] In the maternity care field, deeply internalized values based on the medicalization schema (see chapter 1) and pressures to mimic other organizations in the field (see chapter 2) motivate maternity care providers' behavior in ways that diverge from their conscious explanations based on legal risk. Obstetricians learn a shared cultural account of liability fear during their training, and they also internalize the medicalization schema and adapt to organizational routines in ways that unconsciously motivate their behavior independently of what is happening in the legal environment. The medicalization schema guides obstetricians' medical training and is the foundation of most hospital protocols. It is built on a *technological imperative* that emphasizes using technology like EFM to intervene in bodily processes, based on the assumption that technology is inherently "scientific" and superior to nature. Technology fetishism encourages the premature adoption and routine use of medical technologies like EFM before their risks, effectiveness, and costs are understood.[28] Once hospitals have adopted a technology, it becomes ritualized and physicians and nurses use it habitually because it is there.

In maternity care, market pressures also encourage organizations like hospitals to mimic the practices of others in their field in ways that reinforce routine EFM use.[29] If other hospitals have EFM, then only those who adopt it can compete. How else can they claim to offer high-quality, state-of-the-art care? And once they have bought the EFM machines, which cost about $2,000 to $3,500 each, hospitals want to cover the cost of that equipment by using it regularly and charging payers for its use. Insurance companies collude in this, because they pay for routine EFM as part of a standard package of maternity care benefits. Dr. Alex Yoder, who was a medical director at a health insurance plan and had experience in obstetrics, said, "In a low-risk pregnancy it doesn't show that it adds anything, but we'll cover it." Even the medical directors at the insurance plans knew that EFM was not evidence based, but their plans paid for it. Health insurers, including Medicaid, pay for services that fit within the SOC, including continuous EFM, and this contributes to EFM's universal use by paying for hospitals' investment in the technology.

While insurance coverage is important, there is an even larger economic gain to hospitals from using EFM: it reduces obstetric nursing workloads by permitting nurses to monitor multiple laboring women from a nursing station outside their rooms. This reduces nursing costs by allowing Labor and Delivery departments to operate with lower nurse-patient ratios.[30] Having fewer nurses on each shift cuts hospitals' labor costs, but it also jeopardizes safety and depersonalizes care—which might explain why EFM use is especially common in tort regimes that reduce providers' liability risk with tort reforms that do not encourage improvements in quality of care. Hospitals in states with less liability risk might be more willing to permit low nurse-to-patient ratios, and several obstetricians remarked that low nurse-to-patient ratios make intermittent monitoring more challenging. Dr. McDonald said, "It's tougher on the nurses. We have lots of worn-out nurses who are not used to labor. It takes a lot of focus and a lot of energy." Dr. Murray similarly said that nurses' preference for continuous EFM, and their higher workload without it, deterred her from offering intermittent monitoring more frequently:

> To me, it's intermittent or continuous. The nurses really push back here about intermittent. Some of it is just this particular hospital that I work at, the culture here. Most of the patients have epidurals, most patients have continuous fetal monitoring, so the nurses have to work a little bit more when it is unmedicated. They have to really be there, they have to be willing to doctor the bedside—it's a different type of nursing care.

These obstetricians suggested that typical obstetric nurses were more comfortable with routine EFM and that intermittent monitoring was more labor intensive for the nursing staff. They also seemed to blame the nurses, and did not directly criticize the hospital for having too few nurses because of the machines. There were important structural reasons that hospital-based nurses had difficulty with the added workload of intermittent monitoring—hospitals adjusted their staffing plans to assume continuously monitored and medicated patients. As a result, most Labor and Delivery departments did not have enough nurses on staff during any given shift to use intermittent monitoring on most laboring women.

In short, the routine use of continuous EFM serves hospitals' managerial and administrative goals by reducing staffing costs and improving cost efficiency. At the same time, providers and even some attorneys recognized that hospitals' emphasis on technology over personal contact between patients and care providers could undermine the quality of care. Josh Shaffer, a plaintiff's lawyer, said,

> Here's what happens: one, the physician is busy, because he is handling all of the group's deliveries, so he or she relies more upon the nurse who is in the labor room. And the physician is physically involved in delivering these babies, so there is less time for him or her to check and go in and read the strips. Two, they don't know the patient. When you establish care and you see this person for nine months, they are aware of any unique problems that you may have been having. But under this system, what happens is they may rely on the rule, not the exception. Then they usually deal with any exception in an acute situation. So, it has become a lot more of a routinized, mechanized, efficient system of delivering healthcare, where the individual gets lost. The most frequent things that I see are improper interpretation of fetal strips, which involves the nurses, followed by inadequate monitoring by the physician, who is relying upon the nurse because he or she is busy doing other things.

As he observed, EFM did not necessarily reduce negligence, because reliance on technology to reduce staffing could *create* the kinds of problems that he witnessed in birth-related malpractice cases. EFM was part of the problem, not the solution: this technology provided hospitals with opportunities to cut their costs, at the expense of quality and individualized care.

But once hospitals integrated EFM into their staff training, organizational protocols, and scheduling plans, all hospital staff expected to use it and that made it difficult for individual providers *not* to use it. Dr. Bennett remarked,

Continuous monitoring—I think it's more the normal practice here. I don't necessarily feel that I always have to use it. But it's kind of what's done here so if you have an area where the nurses are comfortable using it, then for the providers that's probably the better way to go. For that reason, I'd say that my patients are almost always continuously monitored. If somebody specifically does not want it and everything is fine, I'll agree to it if everything is progressing okay. . . . But it's the common practice so if you ask people to do that which they're less comfortable with, it's probably not the best way to practice.

In her view, using continuous EFM was part of being a good team player because it was important to follow hospital protocols and standardize the experience of the nursing staff. There was some sense to this, since many newer Labor and Delivery staff only have training on how to monitor labor with EFM and have limited experience with intermittent auscultation. This was also part of the cycle of technology adoption: once hospitals invested in EFM and trained their staff to use it, it became part of the standard protocol of hospital birth.[31] Capital investments in technological equipment and the training of staff to use it justified its continued and routine use, even when scientific evidence did not support it.

The real alternative for women who wanted to avoid continuous EFM was to give birth outside a hospital—either at a freestanding birth center or at home. Rosemary MacLeod, a CNM, remarked,

A midwifery practice is different than an obstetric practice because we tend to labor with our women, while other situations are doing office hours or they're in the hospital all of the time and that definitely changes how they do things. They are more likely to rely on a monitoring strip.

Hands-on, time-intensive labor support meant that midwives could avoid using unnecessary technology in out-of-hospital births. Intermittent monitoring was the standard for births in the birth center. EFM was the common practice in hospital births because intermittent monitoring is more labor intensive and therefore more expensive, and not because of legal risk. CNMs could also attend births in the hospital but, once in the hospital, they experienced pressures to use EFM because it was part of organizational protocols.

Revisiting Tort Laws and Deterrence

A few things now seem clear. EFM meets legal needs for documentation, and obstetricians and attorneys that I interviewed shared a cultural account about EFM as legally defensive. Obstetricians claimed that they had to use continuous EFM for legal reasons, but an analysis of the effects of liability risk on EFM reporting does not support that claim. EFM also satisfies organizational needs of hospitals, regardless of liability risk. But the fact that the odds of reporting EFM actually *increase* as liability risk *decreases* presents a puzzle. What can explain this?

One possible explanation relates to the findings on elective early-term induction in chapter 4. Chapter 4 revealed that reductions in liability risk were associated with higher odds of medically risky behavior, while greater risk of medical malpractice litigation encourages maternity care providers to be more careful. Tort laws enforce providers' responsibilities to patients, and patient-friendly tort regimes (those without tort reforms) lean in the direction of protecting patients' rights. An environment that emphasizes patient's rights and providers' responsibilities encourages higher-quality, more individualized care and the protection of principles such as informed consent. When states enact tort reforms such as caps on damages that reduce providers' liability risk without improving the quality of care, they tip the balance away from patients' rights. This encourages providers to prioritize organizational and operational efficiencies, and reduces their motivation to offer individualized care in order to better serve their patients.

How does this apply to EFM? EFM is part of the obstetric SOC, not a contraindicated practice like elective early-term induction, but obstetricians know that EFM is not an evidence-based "best practice." It is a typical obstetric practice that meets efficiency needs for hospitals. If caps on damage awards reduce providers' liability risk, they can encourage them to prioritize efficiency needs over the quality of care (as chapter 4 illustrated with elective early-term births). This could encourage them to use EFM routinely without offering women other options or ensuring that women give their fully informed consent to use this technology.[32] All of the providers that I interviewed worked in a state without tort reforms, and a majority were willing to individualize care by using intermittent monitoring for women who asked for it. While I have no interviews with providers in tort reform states, it is possible that providers might be less willing to offer women choices that conflict with organizational efficiency when they face less liability risk.

It is, of course, difficult to establish that a legal environment with less liability risk motivates more "assembly-line" approaches to maternity care. For example, lower liability risk could reduce providers' motivation to offer genuine informed consent, but informed consent laws do not vary much and patients rarely sue for lack of informed consent (less than 1% of obstetric cases). As a result, actual informed consent *laws* are unlikely to influence informed consent *practices*. Even if I had interview data from tort reform states as well as a non-reform state, it is unlikely that obstetricians would openly reject a deeply held ethical principle like informed consent. But informed consent is part of patient-centered care, and tort reforms that limit liability risk might signal to providers that it is less important.

EFM and Reproductive Health Regimes

Another aspect of the legal environment that can influence women's access to choices in childbirth and, therefore, providers' motivation to individualize care is the regulation of reproductive health. As I discussed in chapter 2, reproductive health regimes can influence the full spectrum of reproductive health by emphasizing women's rights or fetal rights. When the legal environment places a higher priority on women's rights by giving women more autonomy over their pregnancy decisions, then women should have more choices in childbirth—including the choice of intermittent monitoring. The opposite is also true: when the legal environment prioritizes fetuses over women, women may have less influence over their care when they give birth and provider preferences may take on more weight.[33] As a result, laws that govern reproductive choice could establish a context that influences providers' willingness to put women's needs and preferences above institutional priorities.

I tested this proposition by analyzing the effects of state laws that restrict reproductive autonomy or affirm access to reproductive services on the odds of reporting EFM use.[34] I found that restrictions on reproductive rights are, in fact, associated with increased odds of routine EFM use: the odds of EFM are 6.4% higher in states with bans on abortions during the first or second trimester, 3.7% higher in states with waiting periods for abortion, 8.1% higher in states with parental notification or consent laws, 17.9% higher in states that define prenatal substance use as child abuse, 18.6% higher in states that require abortion clinics to meet the standards of ambulatory surgery centers, and 27.3% higher in states where direct-entry midwifery is illegal by statute. The odds of EFM were also 15.5% lower in states that protected women's reproductive rights by explicitly protecting women's health clinics.[35]

There were contradictory effects for "partial-birth abortion" procedure bans, which were associated with 3.3% lower odds of EFM. The odds of EFM were also 7.9% lower in states with feticide laws, but many states originally passed feticide laws as a strategy to increase punishment for domestic violence offenders and only began to use them to prosecute pregnant women beginning around 2010. The odds of EFM were 24.6% lower in states with requirements that abortion providers have hospital admitting privileges or be located within 30 miles of a hospital, which I cannot explain. But overall, the results suggest that EFM use is more common in fetus-centered reproductive health regimes, possibly because these regimes emphasize fetal life and reduce maternity care providers' motivation to individualize pregnant women's care. Figure 5.6 illustrates the predicted probabilities of EFM in fetus-centered and woman-centered reproductive regimes.[36]

The odds of EFM in a hypothetical *fetus-centered* state that restricts reproduction with an abortion ban in the first or second trimester, a mandatory waiting period for abortion, parental notification or consent laws, feticide laws, a law defining prenatal substance use as child abuse, and a prohibition of direct-entry midwifery by statute, are approximately 4.4% higher than in a *woman-centered* state that prohibits clinic violence and does not restrict abortion access. In short, when the legal environment restricts women's rights to make decisions about their pregnancies, there is more use of EFM—suggesting that women are more likely to receive one-size-fits-all obstetric care. In contrast, when the legal environment affirms women's access to reproductive services, there is less EFM—possibly because support for reproductive access includes access to more individualized care and stronger rights to refuse typical procedures that improve organizational efficiency but do not enhance care.

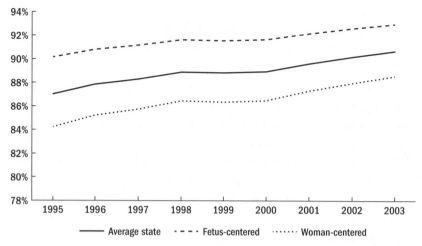

Figure 5.6. Predicted Probability of EFM in Low-Risk Births by Reproductive Health Regimes, 1995–2003. Source: Natality Detail Files (N = 2,100,376).

Amplify the "Ping" Machine

In short, many accounts of the routine use of EFM suggest that clinicians use this technology because of fear of litigation, even though it does not meet evidence-based standards for most births. My interviews confirmed these cultural accounts: obstetricians recognize that EFM use is not supported by science, and they justify using it anyway for legally defensive purposes. But there was a problem with this shared justification: testing the effects of the liability environment, I found that the odds of EFM were actually *higher* in states that reduced liability risk with caps on damage awards. Instead of exhibiting the characteristics that one would expect from legally defensive practices, it seems that EFM serves extra-legal institutional needs in the maternity care field. It creates economic efficiencies by standardizing and automating care and reducing the need for nursing staff. It satisfies a technological imperative in modern medicine that assumes that more technology is a symbol of superior care. It fits within the medical model of childbirth, with an emphasis on active intervention into bodily processes and technology for its own sake. It is particularly common in states that permit providers to emphasize organizational priorities over patient needs, especially those of pregnant women. As a result, EFM is likely to remain ubiquitous even if the courts decide to follow the research and reject it as "junk science," which is unlikely given that the legal field fetishizes any form of documentation on paper.

Overall, it is clear that common justifications for EFM based on legal risk are decoupled from providers' primary motivations for using this technology, which emerge from the medicalization schema. Market pressures to follow other organizations in the field and to reduce costs are also important when the legal environment shifts the focus away from patients' rights and, especially, pregnant women's rights, and reduces providers' motivation to offer individualized care. The findings regarding laws governing reproductive choice also support this argument.

In the next chapter, I will examine another obstetric practice that is widely perceived to be a marker of defensive medicine: cesarean delivery.

6

If in Doubt, Cut It Out

Malpractice and Cesareans

Cesareans are usually the first thing that people think about when they think about defensive medicine in maternity care. Many experts believe that obstetricians do unnecessary cesareans because they want to avoid malpractice litigation, and there is some evidence to support this belief.[1] Cesareans were the primary outcome that interested me when I started this research, even though I never had a cesarean myself. When I gave birth to my first son in 2003, cesarean rates were rising dramatically in the United States. That was one reason that I insisted on midwifery care for my own births, even after two pregnancy losses that led me to an excellent maternal-fetal medicine specialist: I knew that I would only have a cesarean if it were medically necessary, and I did not believe that all cesareans were medically necessary. I also knew that the rise in cesarean deliveries was part of a long-term trend that had nothing to do with the physiology of birth, and I wanted a provider who was more interested in serving my family's needs than the needs of an organization. I often ask women about their birth stories, and I have heard about many cesareans. About half of them sound like they had sound medical reasons, but the other half do not. If I did end up with a cesarean, I didn't want to wonder which group I was in.

Cesarean Rates in the United States

The historical trend in cesarean deliveries is clear: only 4.5% of US births occurred via cesarean in 1965 but that figure rose to a high of 32.9% in 2009. Since then, it has remained close to one third of all births. Figure 6.1 shows the trends for 1995–2015, when cesarean deliveries increased for all births, low-risk births to women without a previous cesarean, and VBAC-eligible births to mothers with a previous cesarean but no other

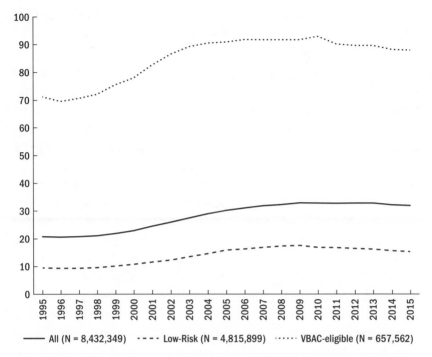

Figure 6.1. Cesarean Rates in the United States, 1995–2015. Source: Natality Detail Files. (See table 6.1 in the online Technical Appendix for the raw percentages.)

medical indications for a repeat cesarean.[2] As figure 6.1 shows, the rate of primary cesareans in low-risk births increased from a low of 9.4% in 1996 to a high of 17.6% in 2009. For women with a previous cesarean but no other risk factors, repeat cesarean rates were lower in the 1990s but increased after 1999, when ACOG issued recommendations that changed the SOC for VBAC.[3]

The WHO recommends a cesarean rate of 10–15%, based on scientific evidence that cesarean rates below 10% are too low to safeguard against maternal and infant death at the population level, but that maternal deaths increase when the rate exceeds 15%.[4] Since 1984, the primary cesarean rate in the United States exceeded 15% every year except 1995–1997 and the total cesarean rate has exceeded 15% since 1979.[5] Some recent research has found that maternal and infant outcomes can improve up to a total cesarean rate of 19%, but no one argues that rates close to one third of births are beneficial.[6] On the other hand, some physicians and hospitals have argued that the 15% WHO threshold is arbitrary, that cesarean deliveries are safe, and that many women prefer a cesarean over a vaginal birth.[7]

Why worry about nearly one third of all births occurring via cesarean if the surgery has become safer over time and has saved many babies? Despite popular beliefs that cesareans are an equal alternative to vaginal births and that surgery is not a big deal, cesarean deliveries are associated with a risk of maternal death more than three times as high as for vaginal deliveries—a rate of about 13 per 100,000 women, versus 4 per 100,000 for vaginal births.[8] The United States has a higher maternal mortality rate than any other developed country, with an estimated 14.0 deaths for every 100,000 live births in 2015. It is one of few countries where maternal mortality has increased in the past two decades.[9] Figure 6.2 illustrates the trend in maternal mortality in the US, the European Union, Australia, Canada, and Sweden from 1995 to 2015. As figure 6.2 clearly shows, US maternal mortality rates were increasing at the same time as cesarean rates were rising. Maternal mortality rates were decreasing in other developed countries during the same period.

The overall maternal mortality figures hide significant racial-ethnic inequality in the United States, where black women have a rate of maternal mortality 3.4 times as high as non-Hispanic white women.[10] Black women are also at higher risk for primary cesarean deliveries without clear medical indications, which mirrors the trends in maternal mortality. In contrast to some research that has argued that cesareans are more common among affluent women who receive too much care, the odds of a low-risk primary cesarean were 35% higher for black mothers and 10% higher for Hispanic mothers than for non-Hispanic white mothers from 1995 to 2015.[11] They were 6.6% lower for Asian mothers. Figure 6.3 illustrates the racial-ethnic differences in the predicted probability of a primary cesarean in a low-risk birth, clearly showing that the odds are much higher for black women and substantially lower for Asian women than for other racial-ethnic groups.[12] Given that figure 6.3 only includes low-risk pregnancies without complications, race-ethnicity should be unrelated to the odds of a cesarean. Of course, the United States' history of racial discrimination coupled with its for-profit healthcare industry mean that race-ethnicity is re-

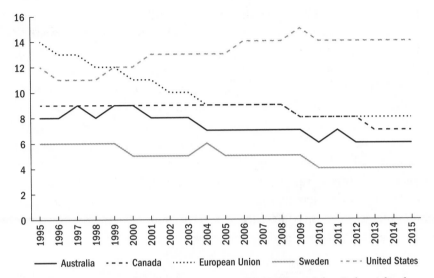

Figure 6.2. Maternal Mortality Rates per 100,000 Live Births in Select Industrialized Countries, 1995–2015. Source: The World Bank DataBank, 2019.

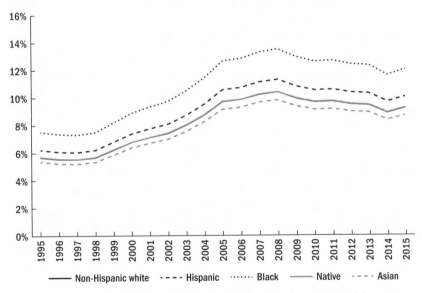

Figure 6.3. Predicted Probability of a Primary Cesarean in a Low-Risk Birth by Race-Ethnicity. Source: Natality Detail Files 1995–2015.

lated to health insurance status, cultural health capital, and discrimination by healthcare providers—all of which points to non-medical influences on cesareans.[13]

Other variation among women with low-risk pregnancies also suggests that evidence-based medical judgments cannot inform all decisions about cesarean deliveries. The odds of a low-risk primary cesarean are 17% higher, and the odds of a repeat cesarean in VBAC-eligible pregnancies are 15.5% higher, for unmarried women than for otherwise similar married women. Since many adults with private insurance or Veterans Administration insurance gain eligibility through a spouse, and many unmarried pregnant women qualify for Medicaid, insurance may play a role in this difference by marital status.[14] Figure 6.4 illustrates the effects of marital status on the odds of a primary cesarean in a low-risk pregnancy.

Each additional level of education is associated with 7% lower odds of a primary cesarean delivery in low-risk births to women without a previous cesarean and 8% lower odds for a repeat cesarean in VBAC-eligible pregnancies. Education is an important marker of class status and cultural health capital, as well as a person's ability to obtain employment with benefits like private health insurance coverage.[15]

In short, patterns of cesareans based on non-medical characteristics reveal that evidence-based medical judgments are not the only reason for decisions to deliver by cesarean and that some cesarean deliveries are unrelated to medical need for a cesarean. If they were related, cesarean rates would be consistent across hospitals and regions, but there is wide variation across hospitals, counties, states, and countries, as well as over time. Some research has found that the characteristics of the hospital where a woman gives birth—including the distance between delivery rooms and delivery-to-room ratios—influence the likelihood of having a low-risk primary cesarean.[16] All of this suggests that many women in the United States have cesarean deliveries that they could safely avoid.

Do Choosy Mothers Choose Cesareans?

As with elective induction, some popular accounts have attributed the rise to women's requests for a quick delivery that they can schedule. Some

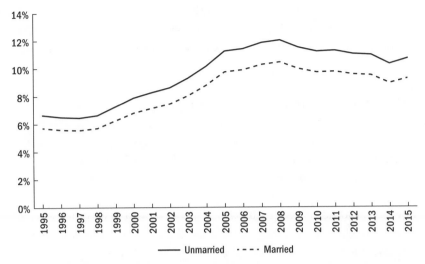

Figure 6.4. Predicted Probability of a Primary Cesarean in a Low-Risk Birth by Marital Status. Source: Natality Detail Files 1995–2015.

media accounts of celebrity mothers who schedule cesarean sections—perhaps with a tummy tuck at the same time—have described them as "too posh to push."[17] They suggest that affluent women have increasingly demanded elective cesarean sections without medical indication in order to fit delivery into their busy schedules and to avoid the pain of childbirth, viewing a cesarean as low-risk and "the easy way out." Susan Dixon, a CNM who attended births at both a freestanding birth center and a hospital, said, "There is this belief, not only among physicians, but among consumers, that there is relatively little risk in C-sections to either the mom or the baby, so why not have a C-section and get out of labor?" This belief fits with a Hollywood culture of cosmetic surgery that views surgery as no big deal, exemplified by the late Joan Rivers's joke about her 77-year-old figure in a 2011 GoDaddy Superbowl commercial: all you need is "a shake for breakfast, a shake for lunch, and extensive surgery for dinner!"[18]

But most researchers are skeptical of the idea that women are choosing cesarean deliveries.[19] Is this a real trend? Some providers said that there has been an increase in requests from patients for primary cesareans, and that it was a reason that cesareans had increased. Dr. Judy

Hart, who was a hospital administrator and not an obstetrician, said that cesarean rates had hovered around 25% for a long time but a recent shift to rates over 30% was due to cesarean delivery on maternal request (CDMR):

> People started saying, "I would like to have a C-section. I do not want to have a vaginal birth." Vaginal births are associated with loss of pelvic floor stability, sick babies, anoxic babies, all kinds of things. "I want a controlled birth. I want an elective C-section." And doctors are doing it. That's why they're going up.

Since she did not practice obstetrics, it was clear that a cultural narrative shaped her perceptions, rather than interactions with patients who requested a cesarean without labor. But she touched on a rationale for CDMR about pelvic preservation that came out of the clinical research literature.

From the mid-1990s until about 2012, some highly cited clinical articles found that pelvic floor disorders were more likely with vaginal birth than with cesareans, especially cesarean delivery without labor.[20] Dr. Brooks said that the mass media had publicized that research and it led to increases in requests for cesarean deliveries for a period of time:

> Maybe three years ago was when it really hit the media and we had a smidge or a bump, but we're not seeing that anymore. I'm not seeing women coming in asking for an elective primary. . . . The media blitz talked a lot about protecting against urinary incontinence later on, and how much more manageable it was to just schedule, show up, have your baby, and you can time it. . . . Maybe it's the population that I have, but we're not seeing that, "I must plan my life out." It's probably more of a media blitz thing. It hit all of the Glamour and Vogue and Cosmo about the elective C-section.

Dr. McGinley also said, "Women have become more knowledgeable and some research came out about preserving the pelvic floor. Then doctors became more willing to do primary elective C-sections." While she specialized in gynecological procedures, including procedures to address pelvic floor damage, she was not in favor of this trend: "I think it's unfortunate. There are risks to the mother involved with C-sections. Then if you are going to have more than one or two babies, your risks with each pregnancy go up significantly."

From obstetricians' accounts, it seemed like many of those requesting cesareans without labor were obstetricians and/or gynecologists themselves. Dr. Murray had not received a lot of requests for planned cesareans, but those she knew of came from women who were physicians and knew about the research on pelvic floor damage:

> There are certainly people who don't want the impact of a delivery on their bottom and there's research on that. It definitely disrupts the integrity of the perineum. A lot of docs that I know opted to have a C-section rather than a vaginal delivery. I remember a couple of GYNs that I knew from [another state] who would not labor.

Dr. Carlson also said, "I've known of some GYN doctors that wanted a C-section on their primary delivery because they wanted to save their pelvis. They wanted to avoid prolapse and leaking, so they did a primary C-section." Both of these physicians observed that it was physicians who knew about the clinical research who requested primary cesarean deliveries. One of the obstetricians that I interviewed also admitted to me at the end of the interview that she had planned cesarean deliveries with both of her children, even though she counseled her patients against them, because her own mother had experienced a uterine prolapse and she viewed the benefits of a planned cesarean as worth the risks. At the same time, the evidence in favor of a cesarean delivery for the purpose of pelvic preservation is hardly iron-clad. Other causes of pelvic floor damage include obesity, aging, and pregnancy itself. Dr. Brooks, who worked at an academic hospital, said, "I think that we've kind of disproven that a C-section protects you from urinary incontinence. It's the pregnancy itself that puts you more prone to any pelvic floor injury."

The 2007 ACOG Committee Opinion on Cesarean Delivery on Maternal Request defined CDMR as ethically acceptable. This affected some providers' willingness to offer it.[21] For example, when I asked him why cesarean rates had risen, Dr. Ribeiro said,

I think that they are slowly climbing for a number of reasons. One of them is patients. The question is, what if a patient asks for a C-section and has no reason to have one? We've had about three ask. Thirty years ago, I would have said, "Tough. I'm not doing it." Now, if you really want it, I don't know. ACOG is saying that a woman should be able to do that, because women can't have paternalistic decisions put on them. Even if you think it's a bad decision, it's their decision. . . . I will tell them that I don't think it's a good idea, but if they're for it, they can make a lousy decision.

He interpreted the ACOG Committee Opinion to mean that he had a professional obligation to agree to a medically unnecessary cesarean delivery if a pregnant woman asked for it. Notably, the ACOG Committee Opinion cautiously suggests that CDMR is *acceptable*, but it recommends against it for women who desire several children.

One important effect of the 2007 ACOG guideline was that insurance directors had to respond to it. Dr. Alex Yoder, a medical director for an insurance plan who had experience in obstetrics, said:

This has gotten to be a point of contention. The American College of Obstetrics and Gynecology says that if a woman does not want to go through a trial of labor, she should not have to. I actually do not see this very often. We have one provider who tends to do this, and I have gone around and around with him. We avoid covering primary C-sections unless there is a medical need.

Notably, he implicated a *provider*, whose patients were presumably similar to the patients of other providers in his health plan. This suggests *provider-initiated*, not *patient-initiated*, cesareans. But the ACOG Committee Opinion offered maternity care providers new justifications for doing cesareans without a compelling medical need: they could blame them on women.

Still, insurers only wanted to pay for cesarean deliveries if they were medically necessary, especially since they typically reimburse providers approximately 50% more for a cesarean than for a vaginal delivery.[22] But providers can come up with subjective medical rationales for doing cesareans if they want to. Dr. McGinley, who worked at a teaching hospital, said, "You have to have a medical reason, but you can often find one." Insurers also know that providers can fabricate a medical rationale. Brian Mitchell, a medical director for a health insurer, said,

> We did have a provider that we felt was being very generous with offering elective cesareans, and we had a discussion with them. It becomes challenging because often they come up with some subjective criteria like fetal movement, pelvis size, that kind of stuff.

Health insurance plans knew that providers could find ways to do more cesarean deliveries if they wanted to, and that normative permission from ACOG to permit CDMR further encouraged them to do so.

On the other hand, as with elective inductions, obstetricians did not have to honor patient requests for elective cesareans. Some did because cesareans benefit the provider in terms of time efficiency and quality of life as well as reimbursement rates. Dr. McGinley said,

> I think that the change in C-section rate has a lot to do with patient request and doctors being more willing to do it because of patient request with that little bit of data about preserving the pelvic floor. Then physicians who might prefer to do C-sections will offer them. I personally prefer to do C-sections because then you're done! You don't have to sit through labor for who knows how long. But with that little bit of data, doctors might say, "You want a C-section? Okay, great! Let's do it." And the insurance covers it, so they'll just do it.

She viewed cesareans as worse for mothers and would not counsel women to choose a cesarean delivery, but she was aware of the quality-of-life advantage of cesareans for obstetricians compared to waiting for labor to unfold.

This is one of several reasons to be skeptical of the idea that CDMR is driving the rise in cesarean deliveries. The notion that women are freely "choosing" cesareans obscures the ways that obstetricians and hospitals are their real beneficiaries. It co-opts the rhetoric of "choice" from the consumer choice and women's health movements, which view individuals as rational actors who can make active, informed choices about their health and healthcare, and blames women for a trend that puts their health at risk while increasing the cost of healthcare.[23] It also absolves providers from their duty to provide *informed consent*, which requires that they counsel their patients on the risks and benefits of every procedure in comparison to the alternatives, including doing nothing.

Another reason to be skeptical of the "choice" rhetoric is the fact that the groups of women who are likely to have the most accurate information, the best health insurance coverage, and the most choices in healthcare—non-Hispanic white, more educated, and married women—are *less* likely to have a primary cesarean in a low-risk pregnancy and *more* likely to have a VBAC after a previous cesarean. In contrast, African American women are more likely to receive unwanted interventions into childbirth, including cesareans with no indicated risk.[24] In fact, there are no racial-ethnic differences in cesarean deliveries when there are strong medical reasons for a cesarean, but black women are more likely to have a cesarean than non-Hispanic white women when medical indications are absent. This is not what one would expect if the reason for rising cesareans without medical indications is that women with healthcare choices and bargaining power with their providers are "too posh to push." The effects of marital status and education are also the opposite of what should happen if CDMR is driving trends in cesarean deliveries—more educated, married women who are likely to have better insurance and more bargaining power are choosing vaginal birth.

Recent surveys of mothers offer another reason to doubt that CDMR is the cause of high cesarean rates. Using a nationally representative sample of 1,573 mothers with hospital births in 2005, the *Listening to Mothers II* survey found that only one of 252 mothers with a primary cesarean (0.4% of all cesareans) had a planned cesarean without a medical reason based on her own request.[25] After the 2007 ACOG Committee Opinion on CDMR, the *Listening to Mothers III* survey of 2400 mothers with hospital births in 2011 and 2012 found that 1% of mothers with a primary cesarean requested a planned cesarean delivery for no medical reason.[26] At the same time, these surveys found that a substantial percentage of women who had a cesarean delivery felt pressured by their providers (9% of all mothers in *Listening to Mothers II* and 13% in *Listening to Mothers III*). Cases of CDMR exist, but they represent such a small percentage of cesarean deliveries that they cannot explain the dramatic change in cesarean rates over time.

Also, as with elective induction, patients can request risky procedures, but providers do not have to agree to them. Dr. Garcia said,

> I had someone ask the other day and I said, "I'm sorry, we don't really
> do that." Unless they've had a history. Like I had a patient who had some
> elaborate renal surgery and her urinary tract was completely redone, and
> her urologist didn't recommend that she have a normal delivery because
> she had so much scar tissue down there. Or someone who's had pelvic
> fractures, but generally, we don't do that.

Providers like Dr. Garcia knew that they were responsible for educating
their patients about the risks of cesarean deliveries, and were not obli-
gated to take medical risks in the service of consumer choice.

In fact, several providers said that requests for primary cesarean deliveries were uncommon, and that most pregnant women changed their
minds after they counseled them about the risks. Rosemary MacLeod, a
CNM, summed it up this way: "I'm thinking that maybe we've had one
of those in five years, when it first came up. I don't think that's a huge
factor in the rise, and most of us will counsel women against that." In
short, maternity care providers are not required to honor requests for
planned cesarean deliveries, but they sometimes have to take time to
educate the pregnant women who make those requests. As Jane Hart-
Thompson, a malpractice defense attorney, said, "I think that educated
patients would not choose elective C-sections."

Risk and Cesarean Delivery

While some have debated whether women are "too posh to push," the
WHO and accreditation organizations like The Joint Commission have
made efforts to reduce medically unnecessary cesareans. Like early-term
inductions (chapter 4), cesareans pose iatrogenic risks to both mothers
and infants. For mothers, these iatrogenic risks include uterine and/or
incision infection (40%), hemorrhage (1–6% require a blood transfusion),
injury to internal organs such as the bladder or bowel (2%), adhesions
of scar tissue inside the pelvic region (46% after one cesarean, 75% after
two), extended recovery time, secondary infertility, and ectopic pregnancy or potentially life-threatening placental abnormalities such as

placenta accreta and percreta in future pregnancies (where the placenta attaches abnormally to the uterine wall).[27] Women with cesarean births are also at a higher risk of requiring a hysterectomy, especially after repeated cesareans.[28] Psychologically, mothers with cesarean births are less satisfied with their births, take longer to bond with their infants, and are less likely to breastfeed than mothers with vaginal births.[29] Cesareans in low-risk pregnancies also have iatrogenic risks for infants, including a higher likelihood of respiratory problems, fetal injury during surgery (1–2%), and stillbirth or death in the first 28 days.[30] Newborns are at risk regardless of whether the surgery was necessary, but the risks are hard to justify when the procedure offers no medical benefit. Maternity care providers should balance these iatrogenic risks against the medical risk of a vaginal birth in each case, but maternity care providers often consider a third type of risk as well: their own liability risk.

Risk and uncertainty are central problems within organizational fields. They encourage individuals and organizations within fields to adopt similar practices to ensure stable, orderly, predictable behavior. Fields like maternity care can repress some types of risk-taking and can encourage others. In the maternity care field, no choice is completely risk-free—the issue is how the field prioritizes avoiding some types of risk and taking others. Which risks have the greatest potential gains and the lowest potential losses?

From a risk perspective, cesarean deliveries are a response to three types of risk: medical, iatrogenic, and legal.[31] As the WHO acknowledges, medical risk justifies cesarean delivery in 10–15% of births (WHO 1985). Medical risks include complications like preeclampsia (pregnancy-induced hypertension) that can necessitate an immediate delivery in order to prevent seizures, stroke, damage to the mother's liver, heart, or kidneys, and degradation of the placenta. Gestational or preexisting diabetes increases the risk of high blood pressure, pre-term birth, or a large baby if the pregnant woman is unable to control her blood sugar, so it increases the probability of a bad outcome from a vaginal birth. Some less common but very serious pregnancy complications like placenta previa (where the placenta attaches over the cervix) or cord prolapse (when the umbilical cord comes out of the cervix before the baby) are *absolute indications* for a cesarean delivery, because they make vaginal birth very dangerous. These and other complications help to explain why cesarean delivery rates are higher for all births than for low-risk births (figure 6.1).

Since the risks of cesarean surgery are the same, regardless of whether a cesarean is medically necessary, providers should weigh the medical risks against the second type of risk: iatrogenic risk to the mother and infant due to the surgery itself. All of the maternity care providers that I interviewed recognized iatrogenic risks associated with cesareans. For example, Dr. Garcia said,

> Sometimes the wound opens up and takes longer to heal. That's always unpleasant. They say that women bond less, but I don't see how, if the baby's in the NICU, you would bond less. Scar tissue problems later on are likely. And babies who are born by C-section tend to spend some time in the NICU, more commonly, because the fluids in their lungs don't get squeezed out, so they tend to have some problems.

She mentioned some well-known short-term problems due to cesarean deliveries, including higher likelihood of admission to the NICU due to newborn respiratory problems. Another that she did not mention directly is that mothers and infants are more likely to have problems breastfeeding after a cesarean than after a vaginal birth, because the mother has exposure to fewer hormones during labor and/or because the mother has more difficulty positioning the baby for breastfeeding while managing her own incision pain.

While wound infections were common short-term complications of cesarean deliveries, these surgeries could also cause long-term pain and discomfort. Laura Pierce, a CNM, said, "Adhesions are long-term injuries. Anemia, painful intercourse, damage to surrounding organs, uterine rupture in subsequent pregnancies." Five of the obstetricians and two of the midwives talked about serious iatrogenic risks from repeat cesareans. Dr. Brooks said,

> Short-term, especially with obesity, the complications include wound infections. Bad wound infections, where a couple of our morbidly obese women ended up with a tummy tuck by accident, and not a pretty-looking one by any means. Long-term, it's really not a good idea to have C-section after C-section after C-section, so if you are planning a large

family, multiple C-sections are really not a good idea. It makes each subsequent C-section harder and more risky for injury to the bowel and bladder, more risky for the placenta implanting in the wrong spot and growing into the wall of the uterus, and losing your uterus because the placenta has grown into the wall. It's not to be taken lightly.

When I asked her about complications from cesarean deliveries, Dr. Bennett said,

> You typically lose more blood with a C-section. Some of the complications that predispose someone to bleeding are much more common with C-sections, like your accretas, your previas, percretas. If you've had three to four C-sections and you've had a previa, you have a 50% chance of having an accreta. You'd better sign the blood transfusion consent forms right then and there, because there's a pretty high likelihood that you're going to have a hemorrhage.

Wound infections and life-threatening placental problems were serious complications of repeated cesarean deliveries. One of the most dangerous risks for mothers in future pregnancies is the higher chance of the placenta attaching abnormally by adhering too deeply and firmly to the muscular wall of the uterus (accreta or increta) or growing through the uterus and extending to nearby organs (percreta). When these placental abnormalities occur, the placenta does not separate completely from the uterus after birth, which can lead to life-threatening bleeding and an emergency hysterectomy.

As these obstetricians highlight, the biggest iatrogenic risks occur in subsequent pregnancies for women who have more than one cesarean. Dr. Bennett said, "I will say that to me, a maternal death after a C-section, especially after a third, it just makes me think to myself, 'I really hope that this person had a good reason for their first C-section.'" Providers knew that maternal deaths were more common after cesareans, especially when women had multiple cesareans. When I asked him about risks associated with cesarean surgery, Dr. Ribeiro said,

> Long-term, I think you can get adhesions that cause chronic pain. That's pretty rare, but when it occurs, it doesn't matter that it's rare. Certainly,

complications occur in subsequent pregnancies. I'm lucky enough to not have seen too many of those. You can get ruptures of the uterus that can occur. It's not without risk. People have injured bowels, and there's a urinary tube that goes from your kidney into your bladder, which can be damaged. And people die. I think that people don't fully realize that all this can happen from a regular pregnancy.

It is well known that cesareans, especially repeated cesareans, increase the risk of maternal death, largely because of the iatrogenic risks of the procedure itself.

It is medically and ethically acceptable to take the risks associated with a cesarean delivery when the procedure will protect the health of the mother and/or infant. But the ethical case is harder to make when cesareans are medically unnecessary, despite the 2007 ACOG Committee Opinion that defined CDMR as ethically permissible.[32] Providers also face the challenge of trying to predict which births will present rare but extreme complications. Most providers agree about the course of action when labor is unambiguously normal or there are clear complications that require intervention, but there is a huge grey area where they cannot make accurate predictions. In that grey area, providers use subjective clinical judgments to make decisions and their clinical judgements often cast a wide net to avoid low-probability catastrophic outcomes. As cesarean surgery has become safer, obstetricians have lowered the threshold for doing cesareans because they exaggerate the likelihood that a catastrophic event will occur.[33] The result is a growing number of cesarean-related complications, with no overall improvement in results. In fact, infant mortality was stable and maternal mortality and morbidity increased as the cesarean rate climbed.

Medical Liability Risk and Cesarean Deliveries

Most physicians and public health scholars attribute the declining threshold for performing a cesarean to the third type of risk: liability risk. Because there is a risk of patients suing them, obstetricians develop strategies to avoid litigation. Obstetricians' fears about malpractice claims encourage an epidemic of cesarean deliveries because they know that patients are more likely to sue them for *not doing* a cesarean than for doing an *unnecessary* one. In the NPDB, 9.4% of malpractice claims against obstetricians from 1995 to 2015 involved an allegation that the provider improperly performed vaginal delivery (i.e., should have performed a cesarean), while only 2.0% alleged that the provider improperly performed a cesarean.[34] Susan Dixon, a CNM, said,

> Physicians know that they are more likely to be sued for not having done a C-section than for having done an unnecessary one. . . . I think it's a fear of malpractice that makes physicians more ready to intervene. In this culture, I think they'd say it's better to do something than to do nothing. "Something" in a physician's mind is interpreted as a C-section, whereas doing nothing is not really doing nothing. It's observing. It's the skill of an observer to determine when something really truly is wrong.

From the midwifery model, Susan Dixon viewed watching and waiting (expectant management) as an active way to assist with birth. But obstetricians tend to intervene where midwives would watch and wait, and cesareans are their go-to intervention.

When I asked obstetricians why the cesarean rate in the United States was over 30%, many of them said bluntly that malpractice liability was the reason. Dr. Carlson said, "It's very much medical-legal . . . because nobody can fault you if you do a C-section. If the outcome is good, they're not going to fault you for doing an inappropriate C-section." Similarly, Dr. Garcia said, "You'll always be faulted for not doing a C-section if the outcome is not good." Dr. Ribeiro also said, "I think that is where you have a huge impact of medical-legal. I think it's very difficult for a physician to get sued for a healthy mother and a healthy baby." Since most cesareans result in a healthy baby, liability risk takes on much greater weight than iatrogenic risk.

Malpractice attorneys also viewed cesareans as legally defensive, even when they understood the iatrogenic risks of cesarean surgery. Peter Connolly, who represented both plaintiffs and defendants in medical malpractice cases, said,

> I've never seen a case where a suit has been brought because a cesarean was performed. The mentality of the obstetricians in their training is,

"When in doubt, cut. Don't take the chance, it's not worth it." The old-school doctors have long since moved on. They struggle because they grew up with the risk of cesarean. It's not a benign procedure. It increases the risk of mortality and morbidity eight-fold, but most women believe that it's no big deal. It's still a big deal. But that whole mentality has shifted because of the reality of knowing that if [physicians] get a bad outcome without intervening, they are going to get sued. They know that and they are trained that way.

Unlike most malpractice attorneys, who downplayed the risks of cesareans, Peter Connolly knew that they posed risk to mothers and he believed that doctors who practiced before cesareans became common were more aware of those risks. But he also saw a shift over time toward obstetricians embracing cesarean deliveries as defensive against malpractice. The culture of liability fear was now an integral part of medical training and experience in the obstetric profession.

Julie Connolly, his partner, added that patients also view cesareans as the solution to every problem that leads to a bad birth outcome:

> Plaintiffs use that also, saying, "We'll never know because you didn't do the C-section, which could have protected the baby from this insult." If you do the C-section, that eliminates that argument. There can't be the insult that they're claiming. I think that leads practitioners to say, "I'm not going to risk it."

Since the dominant view is that cesarean deliveries will prevent all birth injuries, and that injured patients and their lawyers will argue that a timely cesarean would have prevented an injury, obstetricians view cesareans as a procedure that reduces their legal exposure.

Many malpractice attorneys viewed rising cesareans as a sign of a cautious approach, often without acknowledging their risks. When I asked him about the rise in the cesarean rate over time, Mark Wagner said,

> I think that's a good thing. I think that demonstrates that doctors are taking less risks. There aren't really that many very serious downsides to doing a C-section. If there's a question, then that's the right thing to do, I think. . . . The babies seem to come out a lot better. . . . I can't think of any

case we've ever had where the decision to do the C-section was negligent, or where that was a bad decision to make.

Most malpractice attorneys, like Mark Wagner, did not seem concerned or, perhaps aware, of the public health case for reducing cesarean rates. Even attorneys who did not believe that liability risk motivated physicians' behavior most of the time viewed cesareans as a special case where defensive medicine was a reasonable approach. Michelle Morales said,

> All of the doctors blame the lawyers, and they say, "When in doubt, do a C-section." I don't buy into the theory of defensive medicine generally, but I think that if there is any validity to it at all, it would apply in an OB case. But I also think that OB cases are different because when you have a baby, you are always going to err on the side of caution of getting that baby out healthy and alive. . . . I also think that if there is any validity to defensive medicine, it would probably be an OB case because you have a live human being that you have to get out.

As these quotes illustrate, there was a general sentiment among malpractice attorneys that cesarean deliveries could prevent bad birth outcomes and ensure a healthy baby. From their point of view, it made sense to override concerns about iatrogenic risk in favor of a more liberal attitude toward surgery.

The clearest statement of this came from Jeff Dyer, a malpractice lawyer, when I asked him if the rise in cesarean rates was due to defensive medicine:

> There's possibly some degree of overreaction of physicians. They are afraid they are going to get sued. But I don't think that's a bad thing. I think that if there is an increase in C-sections that's caused by physician concern, that means they are concerned that what's going on on the monitor strips is going to lead to a bad result, and they don't want to be sued. I don't think that they should roll the dice and say, "Well, most of the time this isn't going to result in a catastrophic birth injury. Sometimes it is. Most of the time it isn't. Just go ahead and have that vaginal birth." I think that's a bad idea. If that is the reason why there is a rise in C-sections, or part of the reason, I think that's a legitimate reason. I think that doctors

should err on the side of caution. The idea is, "First, do no harm," and if one out of ten of the times that you see this particular profile on a fetal monitor strip it's going to result in a baby with a catastrophic injury, you do the C-section all ten times. The risks associated with a C-section are so much lower than what happens to that baby. . . . Hopefully, the rise in C-sections is also associated with a decrease in the number of catastrophic birth injuries.

Jeff Dyer's view illustrates an approach to risk that emphasizes avoiding a rare but catastrophic event by lowering the threshold for action. At the same time, higher cesarean rates have not reduced the incidence of cerebral palsy (CP), birth injury, or infant mortality. CP rates have remained around 1.8–1.9 per 1,000 births since the mid-1980s.[35] Birth injury rates dropped dramatically after 1960, but have been stable since 1975—long before the dramatic rise in cesarean rates. Infant mortality rates were largely flat, and maternal mortality and morbidity rates rose during this period—hitting women of color and low-income women the hardest. So concerns about liability risk appear to have lowered the threshold for intervening with a cesarean, but there is no evidence that this has produced better overall results.[36]

Still, most birth-related malpractice claims argue that a cesarean would have prevented a bad birth outcome. Rob Thompson, a defense attorney, said,

They always get sued for not doing it because the claim is that if they had done it, the baby wouldn't have been damaged. Generally, every case involving cerebral palsy or brain injury to a fetus, or the death of a fetus, every one of them is the claim that they should have done a C-section, and delivered this baby earlier.

In short, cesareans offered obstetricians a solution to liability risk and most attorneys endorsed that solution. If they performed a cesarean at the first sign of trouble, then the courts interpreted it as "doing everything that could be done" to improve the outcome.

The use of cesareans to do "everything that can be done" was an important way that obstetricians reduced uncertainty. Cesarean deliveries are attractive from a liability standpoint because they are *predictable.* Most cesarean deliveries lead to a healthy baby, and many of the most serious problems for mothers do not arise until future pregnancies. For this reason, liability insurance companies encouraged obstetricians to turn to cesareans before there was a real emergency. Dr. Murray said,

> If you look at current [liability insurance company] education, the idea of an easy vaginal delivery and an easy C-section came from that. They are really pushing that they don't want to have a complicated vaginal delivery or a complicated C-section.

As I discussed in chapter 3, liability insurance companies are important players who develop institutional responses to liability risk in the maternity care field. They emphasize predictability and view a quick decision to do a cesarean as a risk-reduction strategy.

Similarly, hospital risk managers like Sam Durand viewed cesarean deliveries as a means to reduce uncertainty:

> If you have a high-risk patient, and you are thinking, "I could do the C-section here, that normally goes very well. This patient may have some type of complications, but I'm just going to go with the C-section." C-sections can also have complications, so it's not like they are completely out of the woods as far as malpractice, but from a birth-injury perspective, it seems to be a little lower-risk. A "high-risk" patient may be a patient that has high blood pressure, for example, or a patient with no prenatal care. It could be a patient that is diabetic or has some other medical condition.

Mr. Durand emphasized the "high-risk" patient, but obstetricians' definitions of some patients as "high-risk," and their thresholds for doing a cesarean, varied depending on their tolerance for uncertainty. Their general consensus seemed to be that the perceived harm *to the provider* is greater from waiting for vaginal birth than from doing a cesarean. The maternity care field defines risk in a way that views both the benefit of vaginal birth and the risk of harm from a cesarean as low, and emphasizes avoiding legal risks to the provider above the best interests of the patient.

Tort Laws, Liability Risk, and Cesarean Deliveries

To analyze how legal risk influences the threshold for performing a cesarean, I examined the effects of tort regimes on primary cesareans in low-risk births and repeat cesareans in VBAC-eligible births. Given that the risk of malpractice litigation varies across states and over time, are cesareans without medical indications more likely when there is more liability risk? What is the connection between liability risk, on one hand, and the odds of a primary cesarean in a low-risk pregnancy or of a repeat cesarean in a VBAC-eligible pregnancy? I used a strategy similar to other chapters to examine how state-level tort regimes affect the odds of a cesarean in term pregnancies without medical complications.[37]

Cesarean delivery can become medically necessary during labor in low-risk births without preexisting clinical indications, so one should not expect the odds to be zero. But if providers are quicker to do a cesarean when they worry about protecting themselves from litigation, then the odds of a low-risk cesarean should be *higher* when providers face more liability risk—in patient-friendly tort regimes with no caps on damages, no expert requirements, JSL, and a higher rate of obstetric malpractice claims. It should be *lowest* in provider-friendly tort regimes with caps on damages and expert requirements, PL, and a low rate of obstetric claims.

First, I analyzed the effects of tort laws and obstetric malpractice claims on the odds of a primary cesarean in low-risk births between 1995 and 2015.[38] I found that the odds of a low-risk primary cesarean were 3.3% lower in states with caps on punitive damages only, and 3.5% lower in states with caps on non-economic damages, than in states without caps on damages. These effects are in the direction that I expected, but they are small. Figure 6.5 illustrates the predicted probability of a primary cesarean in low-risk births by caps on damages based on the statistical model.

Reform of the JSL rule in favor of PL and expert requirements should also reduce providers' liability risk, but they are both associated with *higher* odds of a primary cesarean in low-risk pregnancies. The rate of obstetric malpractice claims has no discernible effect. These results differ substantially from Currie and MacLeod's findings for earlier years, when caps on damages were associated with *higher* odds, and PL was associated with *lower* odds, of a primary cesarean.[39]

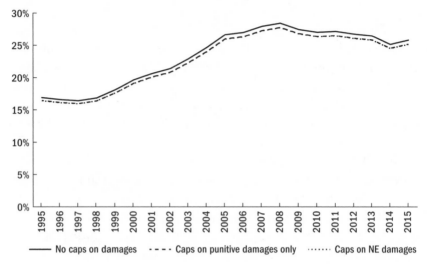

— No caps on damages   - - - Caps on punitive damages only   ······ Caps on NE damages

Figure 6.5. Predicted Probability of a Primary Cesarean in a Low-Risk Birth by Caps on Damages, Natality Detail Files 1995–2015.

In VBAC-eligible births to women with a previous cesarean, the effects of caps on damages were similar.[40] Caps on punitive damages alone had no effect, but the odds of a repeat cesarean were 5.8% lower in states that capped non-economic damages than in states with no caps on damages. The odds of a repeat cesarean were also 19.2% higher in states that reformed the JSL rule in favor of PL. This suggests that reductions in liability risk do encourage VBAC. The only effect that differed substantially for repeat cesareans was that VBAC-eligible births in states with expert requirements had 26.8% *lower* odds of a repeat cesarean, suggesting that expert requirements also may encourage VBAC. The rate of obstetric malpractice claims had no discernible effect.

As in chapter 4, I tested the effects of the period before and after enacting caps on damages to ensure that these effects were not a legislative response to a malpractice "crisis" that preceded the enactment of caps, and to see if reductions in liability risk reduced cesareans during the year after a state passed caps on damages. I found that the odds of a primary cesarean in low-risk births were 3.0% *lower* in states that enacted caps on punitive damages alone during the year prior to tort reform legislation than in other states without caps on damages, which is *the opposite* of what I would expect if these caps responded to a malpractice crisis. The odds of a low-risk primary cesarean also did not change during the first year after enacting these caps. For caps on non-economic damages, the year prior to legislation was not significantly different in states that enacted caps than in other states without caps on non-economic damages, but there was a 9.1% decline in the odds of a primary cesarean in low-risk births during the year after legislation to cap non-economic damages. This supports the idea that caps on non-economic damages reduce providers' motivations to do cesareans to protect themselves from legal risk, although the difference does not last beyond the first year after tort reform legislation.

For VBAC-eligible births, the odds of a repeat cesarean were 4.8% lower in states that enacted caps on punitive damages in the year before the legislation than in other states, and they increased to be 3.4% higher in the year after the legislation, which is the *opposite* of what I would expect if caps on damages reduced motivations to choose repeat cesarean over VBAC. States that enacted caps on non-economic damages had 6.8% higher odds of a repeat cesarean in VBAC-eligible births during the year before the tort reform legislation, which could indicate that a malpractice crisis precipitated the passage of caps on damages. After passing these caps, which should theoretically reduce repeat cesareans, the odds of a repeat cesarean in VBAC-eligible births were indeed 11.1% *lower* during the year after the legislation to cap damages. But more than one year after the legislation, the odds of a repeat cesarean were 5.7% *higher* in states with caps on non-economic damages than in states without caps on damages. In short, tort reforms have some modest effects on the odds of a cesarean delivery, but not all of those effects are in the direction that a theory of defensive medicine would predict.

Normative Pressure from the Obstetric Profession: Three Periods

Professional guidelines, public health mandates, insurance company policies, and accreditation organizations all exert normative pressures on the maternity care field, and the 1995–2015 period involved a lot of change in professional guidelines concerning cesarean deliveries. Cesarean rates increased dramatically between 1965 and 1987—from 4.5% to 25%. In the

1990s, the obstetric profession and public health authorities encouraged VBAC and put normative pressure on obstetricians to reduce cesarean rates. These normative pressures changed dramatically in July 1999, when ACOG issued a Practice Bulletin on Vaginal Birth after Previous Cesarean Delivery" that cautioned obstetricians against VBAC unless a surgical team was immediately available to perform an emergency cesarean in the event of a uterine rupture.[41] Studies of VBAC in the 1990s revealed a small but significant increase in the risk of uterine rupture during labor after a previous cesarean, especially in cases involving artificial induction of labor.[42] While one logical response would have been to ban *induction* of labor after a previous cesarean, many hospitals banned VBAC and returned to the adage of "once a cesarean, always a cesarean." Notably, repeat cesareans are not without risk and the risks increase with each subsequent pregnancy, but pregnant women with a previous cesarean often could not find a provider or hospital that would allow them to labor after July 1999. Efforts to reduce cesarean rates lost steam, and both the primary and the total cesarean rate skyrocketed. In short, professional guidelines aimed to reduce cesarean rates before August 1999, but became more favorable to cesareans in the 2000s. ACOG gave additional normative support to high primary cesarean rates in December 2007, when it issued a committee opinion saying that it is ethically acceptable for obstetricians to offer CDMR without medical indications.

Normative pressures changed again in 2010. President Obama signed the ACA into law in March 2010, and the ACA initiated new quality controls. At the same time, hospitals began to collect data on evidence-based measures for perinatal care (PC measures) in 2009, to maintain accreditation through The Joint Commission, a national healthcare accreditation organization. One of the PC measures defines quality of care in terms of decreasing the hospital-level rate of cesarean deliveries among low-risk first-time mothers.[43] In August 2010, ACOG also issued a new Practice Bulletin on Vaginal Birth after Previous Cesarean Delivery, which offered normative support for VBAC as an option for some women with a previous cesarean.[44] These institutional changes in the maternity care field led to a slight decline in the total cesarean rate beginning in 2010.

Following these changes in professional guidelines, I examined separate periods: before the July 1999 ACOG bulletin that restricted

VBAC (pre-ACOG), from August 1999 until March 2010, when President Obama signed the Affordable Care Act into law (post-ACOG/pre-ACA), and after March 2010 (post-ACA). I expected minimal effects of tort laws in the pre-ACOG period, because the obstetric profession supported efforts to reduce unnecessary cesareans. The findings supported these expectations: tort reforms had no significant effects on the odds of a low-risk primary cesarean in the pre-ACOG period. For VBAC-eligible births, caps on punitive damages alone were associated with 8.5% lower odds of a repeat cesarean and expert requirements were associated with 17.5% lower odds of a repeat cesarean, suggesting that liability risk encouraged repeat cesareans over VBAC to some extent, even before the July 1999 practice bulletin.[45]

The changes in normative pressure after July 1999 should have encouraged more legally defensive cesareans, but the effects of tort laws in the post-ACOG/pre-ACA period were weak. The odds of a primary cesarean in low-risk pregnancies were 5.1% lower in states with caps on punitive damages alone than in states without caps, but caps on non-economic damages had no effect. Reform of the JSL rule in favor of PL is associated with 3.5% higher odds of a cesarean in low-risk pregnancies. Expert requirements had no effect. For VBAC-eligible pregnancies during this period, the odds of a repeat cesarean were 10% lower in states with caps on non-economic damages, and were 40.8% lower in states with expert requirements. These effects support the idea that obstetricians do repeat cesareans for legally defensive reasons. The odds were also 30.1% higher in states with PL than in states with the JSL rule.

In the post-ACA period, normative pressures to reduce cesareans and offer VBAC increased again, but did they override liability risk as a motivation for primary cesarean deliveries? For primary cesareans in low-risk births, there were no effects of tort laws from 2010 to 2015. For VBAC-eligible births, the odds of a repeat cesarean were 29% higher when there were caps on punitive damages alone than when there were no caps on damages and were 29.8% higher when there were expert requirements. This is the opposite of what I would expect if liability risk were an important motivation for repeat cesareans because it suggests that providers are more likely to do repeat cesareans and discourage VBAC when they face less liability risk.

At the same time, the over-time changes in the odds of a cesarean were much larger than the effects of tort reform laws, and the cesarean rate changed much faster than the adoption of tort reforms. The odds of a low-risk primary cesarean were 1.7 times as high in 2015 than in 1995–1997, and 2.0 times as high at its peak in 2008 than at its low point in 1997. Rising cesarean rates between 1996 and 2008 also did *not* coincide with increasing legal risk. In fact, the rate of obstetric malpractice claims per 100,000 births declined from 1995 to 2003 and then flattened out (figure 2.3). During this period, a growing number of states passed tort reform laws that reduced healthcare providers' liability risk: caps on damages, expert requirements, and reform of the JSL rule (figures 2.1 and 2.2). Cesarean rates were rising the whole time, even though liability risk was theoretically stable or declining (figure 6.1).

Some might argue that obstetric malpractice claims declined because cesarean deliveries improved the quality of care, reduced medical errors, and lowered the incidence of bad birth outcomes. But it is well known in public health that too many cesarean deliveries cause significantly more harm than good, at least at the population level. For this reason, quality initiatives aim to *lower* the cesarean rate, especially the primary cesarean rate for low-risk pregnancies. Since cesarean surgery is associated with a fourfold increase in the odds of maternal death and causes an array of complications, some of the increase in maternal mortality and morbidity is likely to be an effect of the procedure itself. Altogether, this suggests that increases in cesareans have not *caused* the decrease in malpractice claims by reducing the incidence of bad outcomes. So why did cesarean rates rise so dramatically? While it is not possible to model other influences using the birth certificate data, the interviews pointed to several reasons for the increase that were unrelated to liability risk.

Benefits of Cesarean Deliveries for the Provider

Like inductions, cesareans offer a variety of benefits to obstetricians and hospitals. Even providers who encouraged vaginal births for their own patients recognized that cesareans are more convenient *for the obstetrician*. Dr. Carlson said,

I think there's a high C-section rate because when you section some-body, it's delivered. It's done. You can get out of there. . . . It's partly expedience, in that the doctor can get done and get home. You're not sitting there all night, long hours working and waiting. It's really hard to deliver a baby. Sometimes it's so much easier to do a C-section. To be the doctor sitting there, it gets fatiguing. I think the hardest work I ever did was working with women laboring and laboring. So C-sections do put an end to all of that.

As this comment highlights, the real issue is often that cesareans are more efficient and more convenient for the obstetrician, and not fear of malpractice liability. Of course, the culture of fear that I described in chapter 3 provided a useful narrative that obstetricians could use to jus-tify doing more cesareans, and claims that women requested cesareans were another useful narrative. These justifications cover up the fact that obstetricians could gain huge improvements in their quality of life by doing more cesareans. As Susan Dixon, a CNM, said,

It's an easier option than waiting through some tough moments and see-ing what happens. Just going to the operating room and having it over with. Practitioners aren't really there for the labor, per se. They are hu-man beings and they want to sleep and they have families, and they are overworked. . . . I think that although they won't admit it, sometimes the decision to do a C-section has to do with what time of day it is, and how they're feeling physically, emotionally, and how much they can take during the shift. Rather than reassure and wait and watch, they are much more willing to say, "You're right, we should just do a C-section." It's more scheduling than economic, but that's economic in a sense. It's efficient.

Convenience and efficiency for the provider sometimes encouraged labor induction first, and then cesarean delivery when induction failed. When I asked Laura Pierce, a CNM who attended births at a hospital, if labor induction increased the likelihood of a cesarean, she said, "I think so, because . . . the doctor wants to go home. Definitely I see that it'll be 5 and we started at 7 in the morning and the doctor wants to go, so let's move it along."

Josh Shaffer, a plaintiff's attorney, said that fear of liability offered an excuse for obstetricians to do cesareans for their own convenience:

> I know that doctors say that they are afraid of liability, so they do more. It's total bullshit. I think they do it because they can plan it. If you really were able to take a look at all of these things, I think that you would find that yes, there is some concern. I think it is a factor that they don't want to be exposed to liability. However, the medicine is that, for instance, they use [repeat] C-sections on VBACs. They don't want to do VBACs, and the reason they don't want to do VBACs is because it takes close monitoring. So when you have a woman in labor, and a VBAC situation, you can't just delegate to an RN to monitor it. You've got to be there because there is an increased complication rate that can occur. Also, when you do VBACs, there is an increased rate of emergency cesarean that would be required if a prior stitch or prior scar bursts. Then you have to be prepared, and it becomes a huge inconvenience to the physician.

In his view, the culture of malpractice fear provided a shield that allowed obstetricians to justify doing what was best for themselves, especially after the 1999 professional guidelines made it more labor intensive to manage VBAC in births to women with a previous cesarean.

Since cesareans are convenient for obstetricians and hospitals, some obstetricians did not go out of their way to educate pregnant women about the risks of cesarean deliveries or to dissuade pregnant women from planning a cesarean. As remarks from medical directors at health insurance plans suggested, there was often a pattern among specific *providers*, not a pattern among patients. Some providers performed a large number of medically questionable cesareans. At the same time, acknowledgement that cesareans were more convenient could merge together with the culture-of-fear narrative. Dr. Alec Yoder, a health insurance medical director, illustrated this point when I asked him why cesarean rates had increased so dramatically over time:

> I think a lot of it is malpractice, and I think a lot of it is for convenience. A scheduled C-section is a controlled event. You have good dates. The woman comes in at 39 and 2, you do the C-section, you have good heart tones. I always describe having a baby as hours of boredom punctuated

by points of terror, because until you have the baby out and the placenta out, a lot can go wrong. . . . When you can set up a controlled environment, everybody's happy. But is that really what we want? We actually had a C-section rate, when I was program director—and this was very high-risk inner city—at 14%. That was because they took the time to talk women through the pregnancy. During the labor process, we were able to get the baby out right away if need be, but we didn't always have to because we knew somebody was there and we could let the process take its course. We had very good outcomes. So I think it's a combination of convenience, and that you don't have to worry about the malpractice like you do when you have a vaginal delivery.

Dr. Yoder's comments highlight two issues. One is that pointing to a fear of malpractice liability can cover up the convenience motivation, or the two can become intertwined in the minds of maternity care providers. This occurs partly because, when the provider controls the birth by doing a cesarean, it is more convenient for the provider and it reduces the uncertainty that triggers malpractice fear.

The second point that Dr. Yoder makes is that the organizational culture and characteristics of the practice can increase or decrease the importance of expedience for the provider. As with elective induction (chapter 4), the importance of convenience depends on the practice model. Dr. Yoder described a practice model that discouraged decision-making based on physician schedules. He worked in an inner-city practice with a high-risk population in another state before he became a medical director for a health plan, and his practice was able to maintain a low cesarean rate because they developed good relationships with their patients, offered accurate information and informed consent, and had 24-hour physician coverage to handle emergencies if they arose. Other practice models encouraged providers to choose expedience instead, and insurance would cover their choices because insurers do not have resources to police subjective physician decisions.

When obstetricians work in groups that share patients and attend births in hospitals with around-the-clock coverage, their motivation to do what is expedient for the provider is quite low. But when obstetricians work in private practice with a full clinical schedule and they have disincentives to allow other physicians to attend their patients' births, providers' schedules can become very important. When I asked her why cesareans now occur in one third of births, Dr. Nelson said,

> I think it's for convenience. It's convenient mostly for the doctor. People can make a case for it more often than not. And the way that most practices are designed, it's not designed in a way that gives a physician the patience to sit and wait and go through the process, because they have to see all of those other patients. Economically, it's just not a good fit.

As Dr. Nelson points out, when practice patterns require an obstetrician to attend births and to provide prenatal care to all of their other patients during regular business hours, it makes it hard for them to wait through hours of labor on an unpredictable timetable. Their economic incentives encourage cesarean deliveries. She added,

> That's why this whole hospital has this model of having a doctor just devoted to labor and delivery. I think that the presence of a laborist would decrease your C-section rate, because when you have a laborist there 24/7, then there is no motivation to make the people hurry up. She's there regardless.

A laborist is an obstetric hospitalist—a physician who has no designated patients of their own but who can attend labor and delivery at any time of the day or night.

Hospital staffing issues could also push decision-making in favor of cesareans. For example, Dr. Ribeiro described how he decided to deliver a baby by cesarean sooner rather than later because of concerns about the availability of an anesthesiologist:

> Yesterday, I did a C-section on someone, which I probably would have done anyways because she had two dips that lasted into the thirties. All the time, you have to look at the strip. If you're working in a rural area, there are times when you say, "The strip doesn't look that great. It's not bad enough for me to do a C-section now, but the anesthesiologist is about to step into a three-and-a-half-hour case." So what do I do? These are staffing issues that can't be avoided.

In this case, concerns about the EFM heart-rate tracing coupled with staffing issues made decisions about additional interventions into labor more urgent. Given that there was no guarantee that an anesthesiologist would be available later, watching and waiting to decide if a cesarean was necessary was not feasible within the constraints of the hospital.

Another feature of many practices that contributed to cesareans for the sake of expedience was the erosion of the physician–patient relationship over time, which has occurred in all areas of medicine. Josh Shaffer had adult children and said,

> Back then, my wife saw the same physician all the way through. When we went to the hospital, he was the one that came for both of my kids' births. That's not the way it is anymore. Half the people who walk in here, the physician they have been receiving prenatal care from is not the physician who delivers, and they are astonished when a strange head pokes into the room.

The lack of a personal connection between the obstetrician and the patient, coupled with the fact that the obstetrician who attends the birth is only there for the last few minutes and most pregnant women primarily interact with nurses (and machines) during labor, makes it hard for obstetricians to care more about their patients' desires than their own. It also means that patients are less likely to like and trust the obstetrician who is at their birth, and more likely to sue if something goes wrong. When I asked her what kinds of things increase or decrease the likelihood of being sued for malpractice, Dr. Garcia said,

> Sometimes when you deliver patients that never meet you, sometimes if you're covering for somebody or you end up in a situation where you care for someone who you've never met before, and they didn't like the outcome, then I think you have a higher risk of being sued. I think if the patients think that you don't like them, and you've never bonded with them, that usually increases the risk.

In other words, the lack of a physician–patient relationship before many births is a contributor to liability risk.

Most obstetricians pointed to bad provider–patient communication as a contributor to liability risk. When I asked her what increases or decreases the likelihood that patients will sue, Dr. McDonald said,

> The decrease is having the best possible relationships with your patients that you can. Anticipating questions, asking questions, asking in a way that makes sense to people. If things are complicated, trying somehow to make sense and not to be defensive. If you make a mistake, let people know as quickly as you can. It's very anti-intellectual to do that, and a lot of doctors will make a mistake and not tell anybody, that's your first reaction. But I need to let people know this, and apologize. The things that don't work are the opposite of that—disregard of patients, or assuming a superior attitude. A lot of it is just around the relationships with people.

There was a strong consensus among obstetricians that poor communication with patients increased liability risk, while strong relationships decreased it. Dr. Brooks also said,

> The biggest one is lack of communication with the patient. Unfortunately, everyone has bad outcomes. But if you communicate with a patient, if you explain what has happened and why it has happened, and apologize for the bad outcome, because you can still be sorry about a bad outcome even if you didn't mean to do it. But I think that communication is important. I think [liability risk] decreases if you are upfront, if you offer an apology, be empathetic.

A better rapport between providers and patients reduced the likelihood of malpractice claims, and Dr. Murray noted that patient characteristics could affect this rapport:

> If the patients like me, that decreases the risk. If they have a relationship with me over time, I think it really helps. I think if I have documented very well and have explained things the best that I can, even though it doesn't protect me 100%, I think it's very helpful when you document clearly all of the risks and when you talk to the patients about all of the risks. . . . I have to feel like I'm dealing with someone

who is educated, who is normal, who doesn't have some sort of psychiatric problem, and who's followed all of the rules.

In her remarks, Dr. Murray highlights the need for both a good relationship with the patient and effective informed consent, but she also mentions her definition of a compliant patient: an educated person who follows rules. This remark suggests that providers' biases in favor of patients with higher socioeconomic status can influence the care that women receive.

Some practice models encouraged better relationships between providers and patients. Midwives are less likely than obstetricians to face malpractice lawsuits, and the midwives I interviewed typically pointed to the provider–patient relationship under the midwifery model of care as an important reason for their lower rates of claims. Rosemary MacLeod said,

> A midwifery practice is different than an obstetrician practice because we tend to labor with our women, while other situations are doing office hours or they're in the hospital all the time and that definitely changes how they do things. They are more likely to rely on a monitoring strip.

As the CNMs observed, the midwifery model of care was a practice model that reduced liability risk, both because midwives tended to be there with pregnant women during labor and because they involved women more in their own care. Susan Dixon, another CNM who attended births at a freestanding birth center and a hospital, said,

> For most people, part of their reason for choosing a midwife is that they want a low-intervention birth and they feel more, in general, empowered to make decisions than some other people do. That affects my approach to them. It's a symbiotic relationship because I'm not the kind of provider who wants to tell people what to do. But midwives attract people who wouldn't otherwise have choices given to them, and want to be given information about choices rather than just be told, "I'm the provider. I know what's best, so I'll make the decision for you." . . . It affects [malpractice risk] because clients who are willing to take responsibility for their own decisions are not likely to turn around when they have a bad

outcome and say, "You told me if I did this, everything would be fine, and it wasn't fine." They are more willing to accept that they made choices and that some of those choices may have affected the outcome. I think that lowers the malpractice cases.

By involving pregnant women in decision-making during pregnancy and labor, midwives developed stronger provider–patient relationships and those relationships reduced their liability risk.

Changes in Obstetric Training

Another contributor to rising cesarean rates that several maternity care providers mentioned was that many obstetricians have limited training or experience in other methods of dealing with problems during labor. At one time, cesareans were a last resort and physicians often used forceps to assist in vaginal deliveries. Dr. Carlson said,

> I do remember that one technology was pretty much abandoned because of health insurance and medical malpractice and that's forceps. I was trained and I learned how to use forceps and I did forceps deliveries all the time because they were really a useful tool and, I thought, very humane, safe, and I knew how to use them really well. And I liked them. I felt very comfortable with them. But apparently, not too long after I was trained, there were so many lawsuits involving forceps that I think that they were just abandoned, so that technology is just lost. That was one of the earliest technologies that we had, dating back to the 1600s, and it was really life-saving. I thought they were great, but I guess that a lot of OBs don't use them anymore . . . A lot of medical students don't learn. Forceps are now a dead art, or a lost art.

While policy and recommendations can change from year to year, the skillset of physicians who are practicing is less flexible because training at any given period is closely tied to recommendations that are currently in place.

Since forceps and vacuum deliveries are legally risky, learning to use them is no longer a standard part of medical school curricula. Susan Dixon, a CNM, said,

I think there is a decreased use of vacuums or forceps because there are fewer and fewer physicians who know how to use vacuums and forceps safely. So it is true that the younger physicians who don't have experience with them will do a C-section instead.

Without adequate experience, obstetricians turned to the solutions that they were more comfortable with, regardless of tort laws, because of the lack of alternative solutions. When faced with a "difficult" birth, doctors can only use the tools that are in their toolkit. Since incorrect use of forceps can cause harm to infants, forceps present a greater legal risk than cesareans, which have become the normative solution to every difficult birth. Dr. McGinley said,

> I think there have been so many good things like forceps. What I think happens is that people don't have enough experience with forceps, so they won't put on forceps because of concerns about malpractice, and if you can't put on forceps then it's a C-section.

Even if used correctly, forceps are associated with far more pelvic floor injuries than unassisted vaginal births.

Even physicians with training and experience with forceps were reluctant to use them now because they fell outside standard protocols. Dr. Murray said that she had trained with forceps, but no longer used them very often:

> I was trained with forceps. They did a lot of forceps in [another state]. It's a dying art. I just talked to one of our newer colleagues, who graduated from [a distinguished medical school], which has this great perinatal program, and they don't do forceps unless they have some sort of model to do it. If a baby is really in distress and you need to expedite a delivery, you need a forceps delivery with skilled hands. In terms of helping a baby get out, I think it's a very helpful thing to know how to do. . . . I think I'm much more inclined, rather than doing a forceps delivery, to do a C-section if I can. . . . If you really need to get a baby out, I can get a baby out by C-section as well. So sometimes I think rather than having a complicated forceps or vacuum delivery, which just increases the morbidity so much, I absolutely do more C-sections.

As in this example, cesareans became the go-to solution for most obstetricians to deal with challenging births, regardless of their training, once the obstetric profession abandoned assisted vaginal deliveries.

Another practice that the obstetric profession stopped teaching was vaginal breech birth, after research published in the late 1990s found that outcomes were better with cesarean than with vaginal birth when fetuses were in a breech position (head up).[46] After that, most obstetricians had either never seen a vaginal breech birth, or had not attended one for a very long time. Dr. Ribeiro said,

> I also think that the fact that we don't teach breech deliveries anymore, and I haven't done a breech delivery in 25 years. If your baby is breech, would you rather have me do a C-section, which I've done 1–2 a week for the last 30 years, versus a breech, which I haven't? It becomes about having the experience to do that.

As vaginal breech birth became less common after 1995, fewer maternity care providers had the necessary experience to ensure safe outcomes for breech babies without a cesarean delivery.

Reducing Unnecessareans

Clearly there were a variety of influences that contributed to rising cesarean rates. Malpractice liability was one that obstetricians mentioned, but it was not necessarily the dominant cause. In fact, the effects of tort reform laws were tiny and the rate of medical malpractice lawsuits had no effect at all. But there were few solutions for bringing down the high cesarean rate, and certainly no simple ones. Rosemary MacLeod, a CNM who worked at both a freestanding birth center and a hospital, said that the hospital's cesarean rate was about 30% even though the hospital culture did not encourage cesareans:

> I think it's a really high C-section rate. Some of that is related to things like not doing vaginal breech births. Some of it may be related to the technology in terms of seeing a risk when a risk may not be there. It is the medicalization of normal birth. There is really good literature out there that says that a woman who has labor support has a better chance of

vaginal birth than a woman who doesn't have labor support. But we put women by themselves, attached to a monitor, with only a partner there. As a practice, we are privileged to work at [the hospital where we have privileges], because I think that their C-section rate is about 30% but they definitely are not quick to jump at C-sections. . . . They are very willing to wait, and to give people time. So they are very generous in that area. I think that everyone agrees that 30% is too high, but how do we reduce that? No one can agree on how you can reduce it. . . . You can't look at one thing and say I'll fix this one thing and then everything else will fall into place.

These remarks touched upon several of the best solutions that the interviews and the existing research support. These include more labor support, often by doulas (non-medical maternity support workers who offer pregnant women support and non-medical pain relief during labor), hospital practice models with around-the-clock obstetrician coverage, opportunities to build stronger provider–patient relationships, making VBAC available for women with a previous cesarean, and a midwifery model of care. But the dominance of the medical model of birth, for-profit healthcare that limits face-to-face contact between providers and patients and restricts coverage for midwives and doulas, and VBAC bans are major obstacles to reducing cesarean rates in the United States.

These characteristics of the American maternity care field appear to be more important than medical liability, which has weak and/or contradictory effects. If limiting providers' liability risk would reduce unnecessary cesarean deliveries, then caps on damages should reduce the odds of a low-risk cesarean, but there were few conditions under which they did—and when they did, their effects were small. This is, perhaps, unsurprising given that malpractice risk is likely to play a very small role in each individual medical procedure and for each individual provider. Also, while the culture of fear that I discussed in chapter 3 makes it seem like liability risk is an important driver of obstetric practices, this culture is loosely coupled with the reality of liability risk.

What should be clear at this point is that cesarean rates rose dramatically after 1999 in the United States, and there were many reasons for this rise. The significant changes to obstetric professional guidelines in

1999 and 2010 helped to shape a strong over-time trend. Malpractice liability risk had no significant effects in the 1990s, when ACOG encouraged VBAC for mothers with a previous cesarean, even though the actual rate of obstetric malpractice claims was higher during this period. Tort laws only mattered when the obstetric profession had suspended normative pressures to reduce cesarean rates: after ACOG restricted the conditions for VBAC and reduced its efforts to limit cesarean deliveries. After the 1999 ACOG practice bulletin, tort regimes did influence the odds of low-risk primary cesareans a small amount. But the effects of liability risk disappeared again after President Obama signed the ACA, and ACOG and The Joint Commission encouraged providers to reduce the rate of primary cesarean deliveries. As with early-term elective induction, the changes in normative pressure in early 2010 had a stronger effect than medical malpractice liability risk. In fact, these normative pressures, in combination with convenience for the provider, changes in medical training, and shifts in the SOC, played a much larger role than liability risk. Professional norms, based on the undercurrent of medicalization as a solution to every problem, offered a nice, simple narrative about defending against liability risk, but this risk was less important than many providers claimed.

7

Choice Matters

Reproductive Health Regimes and VBAC

Laws embody cultural values, and political "culture wars" are often fought on legal terrain. This is nowhere more evident than in laws governing reproduction, which are common topics of political debates and an increasing focus of state-level legislation that aims to restrict reproductive rights.[1] Reproductive rights movements and counter-movements typically juxtapose the rights of fetuses against the rights of pregnant women and emphasize the sanctity of one or the other.[2] Those who emphasize fetal rights often valorize women who give birth, but some women's rights advocates argue that laws that restrict abortion in the name of fetal rights also jeopardize the rights of all pregnant women, including those who carry their pregnancies to term.[3] As I mentioned in chapter 2, this is one of the arguments of the National Advocates for Pregnant Women (NAPW), which has provided legal assistance in cases involving forced cesareans, parent-child separations, and criminalization of substance-addicted pregnant women. From a reproductive justice (RJ) perspective, a fetus-centered orientation that prioritizes fetal well-being over women's well-being limits women's birth choices as well as contraception and abortion.

Reproductive health advocates argue that efforts to restrict abortion are often more about controlling women's sexuality than they are about "the sanctity of life." For example, the best strategy known to reduce the number of abortions is to promote accurate contraceptive knowledge and improve access to effective contraception, yet many abortion opponents oppose access to contraception and comprehensive, medically accurate sex education. Of course, denying contraceptive coverage to women, especially low-income women, only increases the rate of unintended pregnancy—and therefore the need for abortion. When I asked her if Medicaid insurance restricted her ability to provide care in any way, Dr. McDonald said definitively,

Contraception. We have a state that is very anti-abortion, but they don't want to cover contraception. That might even work except, hmm, where do babies come from? I think it's sex. [Laugh.] Unless you are paying for some reproductive technologies, let's assume that most babies are the product of sex. . . . Is it the woman's responsibility to keep from becoming pregnant? If you have insurance and you can't get contraception covered, I don't get it. Where's the social responsibility here? "Hey, I don't want you to get pregnant, and I don't want you to have an abortion, but we're not going to help you not get pregnant. But we're going to let men have their way. We're not going to pull men in on this." What kind of message is that? Do you think that women don't get that?

As she pointed out, opposition to public funding for contraception shows a total lack of understanding of the circumstances of women's lives, the dynamics of heterosexual relationships, and men's role in family planning (or lack thereof). Of course, it is hardly cost-effective for Medicaid to cover prenatal care and birth for low-income pregnant women but not to help them to avoid getting pregnant in the first place. It is clear to maternity care providers how these attitudes (do not) fit together, especially since their work with women of childbearing age exposes them to the complexity of people's reproductive lives.

Reproductive Justice and VBAC

One of the central questions of this book is "How do reproductive health laws affect birth choices?" How do reproductive health regimes influence women's and families' abilities to make informed choices when they give birth? One example where reproductive health regimes can affect birth choices is in the availability of VBAC. As I discussed in chapter 6, VBAC is a birth option that maternity care providers have increasingly restricted since July 1999. Research shows that 60–80% of women who attempt a VBAC will have a successful vaginal birth, but many hospitals have formal policies that prohibit a trial of labor after cesarean (TOLAC). Others have de facto bans that informally produce the same result. When women request an opportunity to attempt a VBAC, hospitals and physicians can "fire" the patient, refuse to admit the patient, bully the pregnant woman with threats that her baby will die, or threaten to call Child Protective Services and report her for child endangerment.[4] Some research has found that about one third of women who want a VBAC in an urban area will change hospitals so that they can attempt a VBAC, but VBAC-friendly options are not available in many smaller cities and rural areas.[5] Approximately half of physicians and one third of hospitals across the United States have VBAC bans, and some regions have no VBAC options. This means that women with a previous cesarean delivery have limited access to an alternative that may be better for their health than a repeat cesarean.

VBAC is an RJ issue because, as chapter 2 discussed, RJ theory connects choices during pregnancy with choices about birth, including the right to choose a vaginal birth. Cases involving court-ordered cesareans and the lack of availability of VBAC for the many women who have had a previous cesarean have led some advocates, including NAPW, to take up the cause of VBAC as an RJ issue. They argue that forcing a woman to have major abdominal surgery (or any medical procedure) without her consent is a violation of her civil rights.[6] Connections between abortion restrictions and limits to women's birth choices are integral to a full-spectrum RJ perspective, which includes pregnant women's rights to respectful care, informed consent, and bodily integrity during labor and childbirth.

Legally, a pregnant woman's right to bodily integrity and informed consent is the basis for "choice" in both abortion and childbirth.[7] Bodily integrity is a fundamental human right protected under the Universal Declaration of Human Rights and the International Covenant on Civil and Political Rights.[8] This right emphasizes the inviolability of the physical body and the importance of individuals' self-determination over their own bodies. Because patients have a right to bodily integrity, their care providers do not have overriding authority over their medical decisions. In fact, tort laws define the performance of a medical procedure without consent as a form of assault.[9] Medical malpractice can take two forms: *negligence*, which arises when a medical professional fails to follow the SOC, or *battery*, when a medical professional consciously decides to perform a procedure that a competent patient has not authorized.[10] Battery is subject to more severe punishment, even when the healthcare provider believes that they have performed a procedure in the best interests of the patient, because it imposes treatment against a patient's will and violates patient autonomy. When it involves pregnant women, this type of battery is a form of obstetric violence.

To avoid claims of battery, care providers must ensure informed consent: they have to explain the risks and benefits of every procedure in comparison to the alternatives, including doing nothing. The doctrine of informed consent protects patients, who must voluntarily consent to any medical procedure. To give informed consent, patients must have evidence-based information and be involved in decision-making about their medical care. A competent individual has the right to refuse medical treatment, even if the treatment will benefit them, and the courts have upheld this right.[11] In practice, though, patients often lack access to research evidence and have less information about treatment options than they would like, so most patients rely heavily on the recommendations of their healthcare providers.[12]

Because of the doctrine of informed consent and the right to bodily integrity, court-ordered cesareans are legally precarious.[13] But in some noteworthy cases, obstetricians and/or courts have forced cesarean sections on women who attempted to have a VBAC.[14] For example, Laura Pemberton had a cesarean delivery with her second child due to placenta previa (a condition where the placenta partially or completely covers the cervix and a cesarean is medically necessary). In 1996, she wanted to attempt a VBAC with her third baby. She had a classical (vertical) incision, which increased the risk of uterine rupture from 1% to 2%, so the obstetricians at the hospital in Tallahassee, Florida, denied her request for a TOLAC and insisted that she must have a repeat cesarean. But Pemberton wanted a VBAC, so she decided to have a homebirth with a midwife. During labor, she felt dehydrated and went to the hospital for IV fluids. As soon as she arrived, the hospital staff insisted that she had to have a cesarean. She refused and fled the hospital. The hospital then obtained a court order and a sheriff and state's attorney went to her home, strapped her legs together, and forcibly took her to the hospital for surgery. The courts appointed a lawyer for *her fetus*, but not for her. During the surgery, she said repeatedly, "I do not consent." But when she sued the hospital for violating her right to bodily integrity, refusal of treatment, and family privacy, the court argued that the rights of a fetus at term overrode Laura Pemberton's right to make decisions about her medical care. She obtained legal assistance from NAPW but, in *Pemberton v. Tallahassee Memorial Regional Medical*, the court claimed that a state's interest in preserving the life of the fetus at term outweighed a pregnant woman's constitutional right to bodily integrity.[15] (You may recall from chapter 2 that *In Re A.C.* and *In Re Baby Boy Doe* affirmed that pregnant women have the right to make decisions on behalf of themselves and their fetuses, including the right to refuse recommended treatment.[16]) This ruling undermined the doctrine of informed consent *for pregnant women only*, so that pregnant women in Florida have fewer rights than everyone else. After her forced cesarean in 1996, Laura Pemberton had five VBACs without incident. Notably, she is a woman who fervently believes that abortion is murder and yet she has become an RJ advocate based on this experience.

In another case of forced repeat cesarean, Rinat Dray had two previous cesareans but wanted to attempt a VBAC with her third child. Her obstetrician at Staten Island University Hospital in New York attempted to persuade her to have a repeat cesarean instead but she did not consent. When she went to the hospital to give birth in 2011, she was already in labor but her obstetrician told her that her uterus was likely to rupture if she did not have a cesarean—also known in the maternity care field as "playing the dead baby card" to obtain patient compliance. The physician threatened to report her for child endangerment and to have her baby taken away. The medical team performed cesarean surgery despite Dray's protests, and the hospital's director of maternal medicine wrote in her medical records that she had decisional capacity but "I have decided to override her refusal to have a C-section."[17] This private hospital had a secret "Managing Maternal Refusals" policy that authorized physicians to subject competent pregnant women to surgery without a court order if they refused doctors' medical recommendations—even though it violates New York law to force patients to undergo medical procedures without consent. During the surgery that Dray did not consent to, the physician lacerated her bladder and it required extensive surgical repair. In 2014, Dray sued the hospital and two physicians for malpractice with legal assistance from NAPW. The New York District Court ruled in favor of the hospital, arguing that the state's interest in the well-being of a viable fetus overrides a mother's rights to informed consent and bodily integrity.[18] On

April 4, 2018, the New York appeals court also disregarded the logic of *In Re A.C.* and *In Re Baby Boy Doe*, and concluded that physicians can override their pregnant patients' decisions to refuse treatment because of the state's interest in the well-being of a viable fetus.[19]

One might argue that these are extreme cases, especially given that Laura Pemberton and Rinat Dray did not meet the conventional medical definition of a "good candidate" for VBAC—which usually refers to women with *only one previous cesarean*, no other complications, and a *low transverse* cesarean scar.[20] But these case studies reveal how laws and policies that aim to protect fetuses as separate from their mothers justify denying pregnant women's rights to bodily integrity and informed consent. When fetuses have legal rights, pregnant women lose the fundamental rights that all persons normally have: the right to life, physical liberty, bodily integrity, due process of law, and equal protection. The same fundamental rights are at issue in the more general case of VBAC in the United States: the doctrine of informed consent and the right to bodily integrity require that pregnant women with a previous cesarean be able to labor without surgical intervention *if they so choose*. But the trend of hospitals and physicians banning VBAC has undermined many women's rights to informed consent by forcing most women with a previous cesarean to have repeat cesareans in future pregnancies. Many maternity care providers never offer VBAC as an option, and they often accentuate the risks of VBAC while downplaying the risks of repeat cesareans.[21] In fact, obstetricians may prefer to take a chance that a woman will sue them for doing surgery against their will rather than take a risk with a VBAC. For this reason, restrictions on VBAC represent a form of *reproductive injustice*.

VBAC and the Standard of Care

Recall from chapter 6 that the SOC regarding VBAC changed over time. Before the 1980s, most cesareans involved a vertical incision, and physicians followed a principle of "once a cesarean, always a cesarean." In the 1980s, obstetricians began to use a low transverse (horizontal) incision and the National Institutes of Health determined that VBAC was a safe option for many women with a previous cesarean.[22] From 1985 to 1999, there was a significant push within the obstetric profession to encourage

VBAC because many women with a previous cesarean can later have a healthy vaginal birth, especially if the reason for the initial cesarean is absent in the subsequent pregnancy (e.g., breech presentation). In the 1990s, many providers encouraged women with a previous cesarean to attempt a VBAC, and this led to a substantial reduction in the overall cesarean delivery rate. Barbara Collins, a plaintiff's attorney, gave birth to her children during this period and had a negative experience with a VBAC attempt that her provider pushed:

> There was a short period of time where doctors were really excited about VBACs. I had two C-sections. . . . I had a cervix that wasn't going to dilate, so I went two weeks past my due date [in my first pregnancy], then went into labor, and it didn't progress. [My daughter] got into trouble. It was an emergency C-section, which was awful, but she was fine. And with my second, there was a lot of discussion about if that same thing would happen again. They said, "No, we're going to try a VBAC" and I said, "OK, but you have to promise that if I tell you that I want a C-section then you'll do it." The same thing happened. I went a week past my due date, and the same thing happened. I got to the point after 20 hours of labor where I said, "This isn't happening, and it's going to be the same thing. I'm not going to dilate. Take the baby." [My obstetrician] said no. She made me labor for another 12 hours. Then she took the baby by C-section. In the meantime, [my son] had a six minute episode of bradycardia, where they almost performed a C-section in the room without anesthesia. I wasn't happy.

In her case, the emphasis on attempting a VBAC meant a different lack of choice than many women currently experience, and she ultimately had a second emergency cesarean.

Barbara Collins's situation could also have been far less risky if her obstetrician did not have a full clinical schedule that interfered with her ability to monitor her labor:

> I loved my doctor, but where was she? She was working. It was no coincidence that she delivered me after her full day, and after the business meeting dinner she went to. After I spiked a fever! That could have been a train wreck.

This example highlights some problems when providers try to manage office appointments while also attending to patients in labor, especially VBAC patients. Labor is unpredictable for all vaginal births, not just VBACs, and a full schedule of office appointments makes it hard for obstetricians to effectively monitor them. This is a problem of contemporary medical practice models rather than a problem with VBAC or vaginal delivery in general.

Of course, the whole point of efforts to offer VBAC is that not all women who have had a previous cesarean will need another one. Among women with a previous cesarean who attempt a VBAC, the majority are successful. Dr. McDonald worked at a teaching hospital that continued to offer VBAC, and she said,

> The VBAC studies aren't very supportive of the reason that there was a prior section. "Failure to progress" is the most common reason. Our VBAC success rate is 80%. It's actually closer to 90%. I joke with the residents that you have a higher chance of having a vaginal delivery if you've had a C-section before. That's not quite accurate but our C-section rate is 23% and it's more like 10–15% with a prior C-section. We do a lot of VBACs here.

In other words, when hospitals and physicians encouraged VBAC and had staff available to pay attention to women in labor, VBAC success rates were very high. Successful VBACs are associated with a quicker recovery after giving birth and lower rates of infection, blood loss, blood clots, fever, and emergency hysterectomy compared to a repeat cesarean—whether the cesarean is planned or unplanned.[23] During the 1990s, some insurance plans even required that women with a previous cesarean attempt labor and VBAC. Dr. McDonald said, "There was a time when one of the military insurance plans insisted that any woman who'd had a prior C-section had to labor. They were requiring a trial of labor."

VBAC is often the safer choice for women with a previous cesarean, especially when you consider the risks of multiple cesareans, including an increased risk of hemorrhage, placental anomalies like placenta accreta and placenta percreta, emergency hysterectomy, and maternal and neonatal mortality. But while maternity care providers recognized the risks of repeated cesareans, some clinical studies in the 1990s found a heightened risk of uterine rupture in VBAC deliveries compared to a scheduled repeat cesarean. Attempting a VBAC is associated with a 3.2 per 1,000 risk of a uterine rupture (0.32%), which is slightly higher than the risk of uterine rupture in vaginal births without a previous cesarean.[24] Uterine rupture is potentially life threatening for both the mother and the baby, and leads to an intrapartum death rate of 2.9 per 10,000 (0.029%). The risk of uterine rupture is higher if the original surgery used single-layer rather than double-layer suturing or when the provider artificially induces labor, especially if they use cervical ripening agents.[25] Stimulation of labor with Pitocin (artificial oxytocin) also increases the risk. Dr. Bennett said, "You double the risk if you use oxytocin. . . . I just don't use it. If you deliver spontaneously, fine; otherwise, C-section." As Dr. Bennett mentioned, one of the problems with VBAC is that the risk of uterine rupture is much higher with induction or augmentation of labor with synthetic oxytocin (Pitocin) or other drugs.

In July 1999, ACOG issued the practice bulletin that recommended that obstetricians should not attend VBAC deliveries unless there was an immediately available surgical team to perform a cesarean in the event of a uterine rupture.[26] After that, the VBAC rate declined and the repeat cesarean rate increased dramatically, without any improvement in neonatal or maternal mortality rates. In fact, infant mortality and especially maternal mortality rates increased during the period from 2000 to 2010. The 1999 VBAC guidelines represented a significant change in the SOC, making repeat cesareans the most legally conservative approach to managing pregnancies after a previous cesarean. Susan Dixon, a CNM who attended births in a freestanding birth center and a hospital, said,

The story about the possibility of being sued had a huge impact on all of the midwives. When I joined the staff back in 1999, there was a huge discussion among all of the midwives about whether to continue to offer VBACs at the birth center, because when I got there they were doing VBACs at the birth center. And it was primarily a fear of lawsuits. It was right when that memo came out from ACOG. Then that prompted a discussion about whether we should continue to do it. There was a VBAC study being done at that time by the American

College of Nurse Midwives. There was a vote and the decision was made not to do VBACs at the birth center anymore. And that had to do with the ACOG statement, the liability, and the big discussion was that even if there was never any proof that being at the birth center contributed to a bad outcome, the fact that you were at the birth center would cook someone.

After July 1999, most maternity care providers, including midwives, worried about their liability risk if they attended VBAC deliveries.

Importantly, the view of repeat cesareans as the most legally cautious approach to managing pregnancies after a previous cesarean was not the only conclusion that the profession could have drawn from the VBAC studies. The science found that the probability of a uterine rupture during labor for a woman with a previous cesarean is less than 0.5%. It is lower than that for VBAC with spontaneous labor but it is higher with induced labor, especially if the provider uses cervical ripening agents like misoprostol.[27] The use of synthetic oxytocin (Pitocin) to induce and augment contractions also increases the risk. But instead of prohibiting induction and augmentation in VBAC attempts, ACOG's guidelines effectively restricted all VBACs.

Even providers who did attend VBACs after 1999 often restricted the conditions under which they were willing to consider it. There was a consensus that mothers with more than one previous cesarean were not good candidates for VBAC. Rosemary MacLeod, a CNM who attended births at a freestanding birth center and a hospital, said,

> The stats out there on women who have had two previous C-sections is almost universal in saying that the woman has to have a C-section. Again, we have to push the gates on showing that some women will have a successful vaginal birth after two C-sections. Then you go back to that standard of care and if she has a uterine rupture and a loss, then they go to court and someone is going say, "You never should've done this."

The change in the SOC for VBAC produced strong normative pressures that restricted the conditions under which providers were willing to permit women with a previous cesarean to go into labor. Dr. Bennett said,

We do VBACs, but it has become much more restrictive since that journal article in 1999. So I would say that we still do VBACs but definitely fewer than in the past. . . . We won't induce now, and it's very uncommon that we would do a VBAC on someone who's had two C-sections. When I trained from 1998 to 2002, we did all of those. We could induce a VBAC. If you'd had two C-sections, and you wanted to do a VBAC, we'd council you, but we'd still do it. Here, I pretty much don't do it. Recently, I had a patient who was from another country who'd done a VBAC after two C-sections there. I said, "She's had a successful VBAC, I'm going to let her do a VBAC." Because she had already done it successfully. It's hard to say no in that kind of situation. But generally no, not after two.

The increase in restrictions on VBAC after 1999 led many obstetricians to discourage women from attempting VBAC or to simply refuse to attend a trial of labor after a previous cesarean. As Susan Dixon, a CNM, said,

So many people are told "I don't do VBACs" by their provider, and that it's not an option. The primary C-section rate increases the risk of repeat C-sections because nobody's willing to do a VBAC. Hardly anybody is encouraged to think of VBAC as an option. Then even if they're going in to their provider and asking about VBAC, their provider is saying, "Sorry, I don't do that, for legal reasons." So they don't even have the option if they thought they did.

Because so few providers are willing to attend VBAC, many women with a previous cesarean have no real options other than a repeat cesarean.

The ACOG guidelines nearly eliminated VBAC options in part because they introduced *organizational* challenges. Dr. Ribeiro described how the restrictions made it hard for the rural hospital where he worked to offer VBAC at all, which forced women who wanted VBAC to drive one and a half hours to an urban hospital that would accommodate them. This contributed to rising overall cesarean rates:

We don't do vaginal births after cesareans anymore. They are done in [a nearby city], but in order to do it, as a physician, you have to be there in labor and delivery. There has to be an anesthesia crew there in labor and delivery. In most hospitals, unless they're a tertiary care center or have a teaching program, that's impossible. You just can't do it. Because of that, they don't allow people to VBAC.

The need for around-the-clock coverage with obstetricians and anesthesiologists created organizational obstacles for many hospitals, especially smaller hospitals in rural areas and smaller cities. Women who wanted a VBAC often had to fight for the option or travel to find a provider that would allow it—if they could find one that they could get to.

The dramatic drop in VBAC availability returned the obstetric profession to its previous adage of "Once a cesarean, always a cesarean." This influenced providers' willingness to offer VBAC and patients' willingness to try for a VBAC. Dr. Garcia said,

> A lot of patients will not do VBACs. We're just now starting to see people again be interested in them, but that's usually people who are educated, who are looking into it, and have actually done their own reading about it. But a lot of people don't. . . . Even if they are a great candidate—say a young girl who had a breech baby before and is now pregnant again— they will not entertain a vaginal birth. It's sad. That is kind of frustrating. There are some people who should be doing it, and then some people who shouldn't are giving it a try.

Many women with a previous cesarean assumed that a repeat cesarean was an equally safe or better alternative to VBAC, and they often did not want to take a chance on having an emergency cesarean instead of a scheduled one.

One thing that stops many women who are good candidates for VBAC from attempting it is the information that they receive about the risks of VBAC—often as part of the informed consent process. Dr. Bennett said,

> Then of course people have to want a VBAC. The informed consents that we have to use here are—I'm not saying that we shouldn't offer informed consent to our patients because we should—but it's got to be so detailed about all of these horrible things that can happen.

While the risks of repeat cesareans are often greater than the risks of VBAC, informed consent processes in American obstetrics since 1999 have tended to imply that VBAC is the riskier option.

Of course, many women with a primary cesarean are unhappy about the lack of VBAC availability, especially when many women had successful VBACs in the 1990s.[28] Sometimes they view their first cesareans as having been medically unnecessary and want a second chance to have a vaginal birth. Others examine the research and view the risk of uterine rupture in VBAC, especially without artificial induction of labor, as lower than the health risks associated with a repeat cesarean, which increase with each subsequent pregnancy. For women who want more than two children, VBAC after a primary cesarean is a much healthier option than repeated cesareans.[29] Some opt for homebirth after cesarean (HBAC), with or without a midwife.[30] Others travel long distances in order to find providers that will allow them to attempt a vaginal birth. But many women with a previous cesarean cannot find a provider who will attend a VBAC, so they end up with a repeat cesarean.

Reproductive Regimes and VBAC

The case of VBAC illustrates the fundamental tensions between legal liability and women's control over their bodies. I have argued that laws that reinforce the rights of pregnant women versus those that grant rights to fertilized eggs, embryos, and fetuses as separate from their mothers can have profound effects on the treatment of birthing women as well as access to abortion and contraception. But we currently know very little about how reproductive health regimes influence VBAC options for women with a previous cesarean. Cases involving court-ordered cesareans and criminal prosecutions of pregnant women for allegedly harming their unborn children are rare and extreme cases, and there has been no empirical research to examine how laws governing abortion, fetal personhood, criminalization of prenatal substance abuse, and regulations of abortion providers (TRAP laws) influence the majority of births in the United States. How do fetus-centered or woman-centered reproductive health regimes influence the availability of choices in childbirth? For women with a previous cesarean but no other indicated risks, how do reproductive health laws affect the odds of a VBAC?

I used a strategy similar to in other chapters to analyze how state-level reproductive health laws affected the odds of VBAC in VBAC-eligible pregnancies.[31] Accounting for trends over time, women with a previous cesarean had lower odds of vaginal birth in states with more fetus-centered reproductive health regimes, with a few exceptions. The odds of VBAC were 7.1% lower in states with abortion bans in or before the second trimester and were 9.5% lower in states with "partial-birth abortion" procedure bans—as I would expect if VBAC is a reproductive rights issue. In other words, women with a previous cesarean were less likely to have a vaginal birth in states that restrict legal abortion. The odds of VBAC were 4.1% lower in states that criminalized prenatal substance use, so women who are good candidates for VBAC were more likely to have repeat cesareans in states that punish pregnant addicts instead of offering them treatment. In terms of TRAP laws, the odds of VBAC were 15.6% lower in states with special reporting requirements for abortion clinics, but requirements that they meet ambulatory surgery center standards and that providers either have hospital admitting privileges or that clinics be located close to a hospital had no effect. The odds of VBAC were also 15.5% lower in states where direct-entry midwifery was illegal by statute, and 5.3% higher in states that provided legal protection against violence to women's health clinics.[32] Taken together, these results point in the same direction: fetus-centered reproductive health regimes constrain women's ability to make reproductive decisions about both abortion and birth, at least when it comes to VBAC. (The exceptions were that the odds of VBAC were 12.9% *higher* in states that required a waiting period before having an abortion and 3.8% *higher* in states with feticide laws.) Figure 7.1 shows the average predicted probability of VBAC in VBAC-eligible births from 1995 to 2015 for the average state, a hypothetical state with all fetus-centered laws,[33] and a hypothetical state with all woman-centered laws.[34] Figure 7.2 shows the predicted probability of VBAC over time in each of these reproductive health regimes.[35] As figures 7.1 and 7.2 illustrate, all else being equal, the probability of VBAC was highest in states with woman-centered reproductive health regimes and lowest in states with fetus-centered reproductive health regimes, independent of the strong over-time trend.

Since normative pressures from the obstetric profession differed dramatically before and after the 1999 ACOG Practice Bulletin, I also

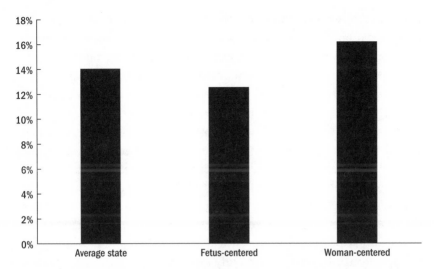

Figure 7.1. Average Probability of VBAC for Births that Are Good Candidates by Reproductive Health Regimes, 1995–2015. Source: Natality Detail Files and compiled legal data from Nexis Uni. (See the online Technical Appendix, table 7.2, for the model results.)

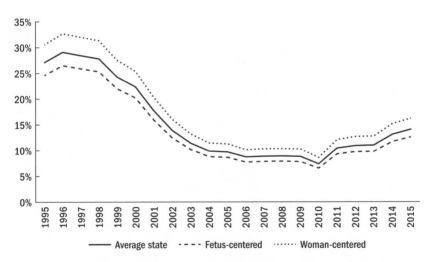

Figure 7.2. Predicted Probability of VBAC for Births that Are Good Candidates by Reproductive Health Regimes, 1995–2015. Source: Natality Detail Files and compiled legal data from Nexis Uni. (See the online Technical Appendix, table 7.2, for the model results.)

examined the effects of reproductive health laws separately before and after July 1999.[36] In the 1990s, most hospitals and obstetricians were more open to VBAC, and many encouraged it, but the odds were still higher when there were fewer reproductive health restrictions. From 1995 to July 1999 (pre-ACOG), the odds of VBAC were 22.1% lower in states that had abortion bans in the second trimester or earlier and 16% lower in states that required abortion clinics to meet the standards of ambulatory surgical centers. They were also 7.4% lower in states that defined prenatal substance use as child abuse, even though relatively few states had these laws in the pre-ACOG period. These effects are all in the direction that RJ theory would predict, with one main exception: women with a previous cesarean had 17.3% lower odds of vaginal birth in states that protected women's health clinics.[37] Figure 7.3 shows the average probability from 1995 to July 1999 of VBAC in the average state, a hypothetical state with all fetus-centered laws, and a hypothetical state with all woman-centered laws. What is noticeably different about figure 7.3 compared to figure 7.1 is that the average probability of VBAC is higher overall, but it is lower in woman-centered reproductive health regimes because of the effect of laws prohibiting violence at women's health clinics.

After the 1999 ACOG Bulletin (post-ACOG), normative pressures to restrict VBAC increased dramatically across the maternity care field, leading VBAC rates to drop rapidly. Interestingly, and disturbingly, the effects of a mother's race-ethnicity changed: black and Hispanic women had lower odds of VBAC than non-Hispanic white women before the July 1999 ACOG bulletin, when the obstetric profession *promoted* VBAC as a beneficial practice. After July 1999, when the obstetric profession *cautioned against* VBAC as a risky practice, the odds of VBAC were considerably higher for black, Hispanic, and Native American women than for non-Hispanic white women. In other words, providers were more likely to offer the accepted SOC to non-Hispanic white women and to deviate from the SOC with women of color in both periods. The effects of marital status and parity (a mother's number of live births) also changed after July 1999, creating a larger difference in the odds of VBAC between married and unmarried women and women with more previous births than in the earlier period (with VBAC more likely among married women and women with more live births).

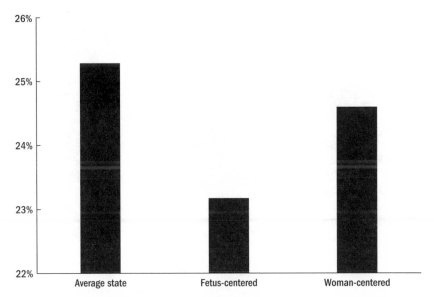

Figure 7.3. Average Probability of VBAC for Births that Are Good Candidates by Reproductive Health Regimes, Pre-ACOG (1995–July 1999). Source: Natality Detail Files and compiled legal data from Nexis Uni. (See the online Technical Appendix, table 7.3, for the model results.)

After July 1999, the effects of reproductive health regimes were also stronger, suggesting that VBAC became more of an issue of reproductive choice after ACOG restricted it. The odds of VBAC were 8.3% lower in states with a ban on abortion in or before the second trimester, and 19.6% lower in states with a "partial-birth abortion" procedure ban. They were also 4.1% lower in states with feticide laws, 2.6% lower in states that treat prenatal substance use as child abuse, 29.8% lower in states with laws that have special reporting requirements for abortion providers, and 22.5% lower in states where direct-entry midwifery is illegal by statute. The big exception was the effect of mandatory waiting periods before abortion, which had no relationship to VBAC before 1999 but were connected to 24.7% *higher* odds of VBAC after July 1999. Figure 7.4 illustrates the probability for the average state, a hypothetical state with all fetus-centered laws, and a hypothetical state with all woman-centered laws for the post-ACOG period. In this figure, the difference between woman-centered states and fetus-centered states is

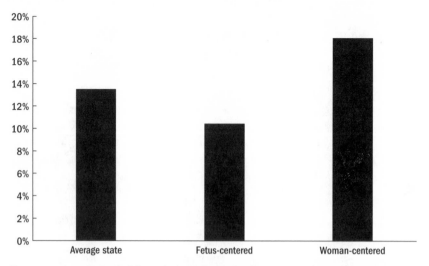

Figure 7.4. Average Probability of VBAC for Births that Are Good Candidates by Reproductive Health Regimes, Post-ACOG (August 1999–2015). Source: Natality Detail Files and compiled legal data from Nexis Uni.

much larger than in figure 7.3, suggesting that VBAC aligned with other reproductive "choice" issues after July 1999.

What stands out the most from these results is that reproductive health regimes create an environment that supports or restricts pregnant women's autonomy over their healthcare decisions, and this is evident in practices like VBAC. VBAC became a reproductive choice issue after July 1999 because the change in ACOG's professional guidelines restricted access to it. The odds of VBAC were already lower in the pre-ACOG period in states with abortion bans, prenatal substance abuse laws, and requirements that abortion clinics meet standards for ambulatory surgery centers, but VBAC followed reproductive rights trends even more after July 1999. It appears that the legal culture surrounding abortion choice has profound effects on birth choice, especially the right to reject obstetric norms.

VBAC as a Choice Issue

As a matter of practice, obstetricians know that it has become legally risky and organizationally inefficient to offer VBAC since ACOG stipulated that there should be an immediately available surgical team whenever a woman attempts a VBAC. This has led many providers to tell women that they do not attend VBAC. They emphasize the risks of VBAC—mainly the risk of uterine rupture, which is very small—in order to scare women into consenting to a repeat cesarean instead. At the same time, they tend to downplay the significant risks associated with repeat cesareans. But the real challenge of the 1999 ACOG VBAC guidelines is not medical or legal—it is organizational. The ACOG guidelines made it more difficult for providers and hospitals to manage organizational and quality-of-life concerns. The fact is that VBAC involves more labor-intensive monitoring than a repeat cesarean or even a vaginal birth for a woman with no previous cesareans. That means that VBAC requires a significant commitment on the part of the provider and ideally an organizational structure with around-the-clock coverage (like a residency program).

But while VBAC was less convenient than a scheduled repeat cesarean for physicians, most of the obstetricians that I interviewed did attend VBACs and had a strong commitment to making this choice available to women—even though their liability insurers discouraged it. Dr. Garcia said,

> There's malpractice and we're obligated to take a course and it's very conservative. It discourages VBACs, for instance. It's very conservative. It's not even in line with ACOG about that. But we all have to take it every two years for our insurance. We all do it. We don't agree with it but we all do it. We don't follow it. Like, our practice does offer VBACs and other offices will not. So we are directly practicing against what they recommend, but we think that is the best thing for our patients. We don't think every woman wants to have a C-section.

It was a commitment to honoring women's preference to avoid repeated cesareans that led most of the obstetricians that I interviewed to permit, and even encourage, VBAC among their patients with a previous cesarean.

The fact that many providers offered VBAC because they believed that it was important for women to have a choice suggests why woman-centered reproductive regimes might increase the odds of VBAC.

Providers are more likely to honor women's wants and needs in legal environments that define pregnant women's right to make choices about childbirth as fundamentally important. Maternity care providers vary in their views of abortion, but most of them have witnessed *reproductive injustice* during their practice, and recognizing that injustice can turn maternity care providers into reproductive justice warriors. For example, when I asked him if he had a lot of young clientele in his rural practice, Dr. Ribeiro said,

> The youngest we've had is 14. And the father was her father, from Mexico. He fled back. Terrible things happen to people. Forty percent of women are sexually assaulted at some point in their life. My daughter is 17 and she thinks I'm an idiot because I give her these books on how to avoid sexual assault. I give her books on the formation of the Women's Movement. She knows nothing about it. She takes all this shit for granted.

Dr. Ribeiro had a strong commitment to RJ, to the point where he taught his teenage daughter about the feminist movement because he did not want her to take her rights for granted. He also acknowledged the ways that economic disadvantage restricted RJ. For example, when I asked him how the clientele that he served influenced his practice, he said,

> Certain people can't afford things. You offer everyone the same thing. But if you need to go to see a perinatologist and you don't have any insurance to cover that and you're looking, even with a reduced rate, at a $200 bill and you barely have enough money to get gas to get to your visit, $200 might as well be $50,000. So for those people, sometimes, I believe their care is compromised. They aren't able to get some of the more technical things done. If they wanted amniocentesis, it would almost be out of the question. That costs thousands of dollars. It is an issue dealing with people who don't have money.

Like many maternity care providers who served low-income clients, Dr. Ribeiro recognized the inequality of access to care that could contribute to reproductive injustice.

But while he might have been unable to provide equal quality of care to everyone, he was strongly committed to RJ and he understood the importance of honoring women's choices about their reproductive health-care. His story about fighting a merger of his more rural hospital with a Catholic hospital network illustrated this:

> [A Catholic hospital network] wanted to buy our system, and actually they signed a contract. What that meant is that you couldn't do tubal ligations anymore in our hospital. We contacted some people back east and we ended up suing the hospital and [the purchase] didn't go through. Part of the issue was that if you're a poor woman, the people on the board felt, "Well, just drive to [the nearest city]." But study after study has shown that when you restrict access to anything, you in effect keep it from people, and the people you keep it from are the poor people because they can't afford it. . . . [So I sued my hospital] that to me has just shit all over women and doesn't give a damn. They say things like, "It's only 80 women who are getting tubal ligations a year." I said, "Does there have to be a count?" They think that I'm being a smart-ass and have no idea that I'm serious. I really asked, "It's 84? How many women does it have to be?" and they said, "Don't be a smart-ass." That conversation didn't go well.

In his case, the recognition that many pregnant women faced serious challenges, especially low-income pregnant women, to obtaining necessary reproductive care, let alone choices, solidified a strong commitment to ensuring access to reproductive choice. He knew that becoming a Catholic hospital would restrict his patients' access to contraception and sterilization procedures, so he fought against it and won.

Reproductive Health Regimes and Other Birth Choices

Of course, not everyone wants a VBAC and some women would choose a medicalized, technological birth. But most women, including those who oppose the legality of abortion, embrace the idea of having a choice. Most women believe that they should be able to make choices about their births and that they make those choices in the best interests of their children—present and future. And while many women might choose a medicalized birth, the impact of woman-centered laws on birth choices is most visible when pregnant women reject medicalization and select non-technological alternatives: VBAC, midwife-attended birth, and out-of-hospital birth.

Women often choose midwifery care and/or out-of-hospital birth to avoid medical interventions for philosophical, religious, or spiritual reasons.[38] They may make these choices with the belief that their choices will benefit them and their babies, even if they are less convenient for doctors and hospitals. Their rejection of the medicalization schema means that they choose options that do not fit the typical obstetric mold. For this reason, I expect that they will be more able to realize their preferences when the legal environment defines women's reproductive autonomy as important. In other words, reproductive health regimes should influence the odds of midwife-attended and out-of-hospital births, which represent an important opportunity for women to exercise choice in birth even though they are much rarer than hospital-based physician-attended births.

I analyzed the effects of reproductive health laws on the odds of a midwife attending a low-risk birth and of a low-risk birth occurring in an out-of-hospital setting. I used a strategy similar to the one I used for VBAC, and I found that the odds of a midwife-attended birth in low-risk pregnancies were 12% lower in states with bans on abortion at a specific pre-viability age, 5% lower in states with mandatory waiting periods before an abortion, and 10% lower in states with parental involvement laws.[39] They were also 8% lower in states that required special reporting from abortion clinics, 4% lower in states that required abortion clinics to meet ambulatory surgery center standards, and, unsurprisingly, 23% lower in states that prohibited direct-entry midwifery. More unusually, the odds of a midwife attending a low-risk birth were 31% *lower* in in states that protected women's health clinics. But overall, the predicted probability of a midwife-attended low-risk birth was much lower in states with fetus-centered reproductive health regimes. Figure 7.5 illustrates the predicted effects for the average state, a hypothetical state with all reproductive health restrictions, and a hypothetical state that protects reproductive rights.[40]

Finally, *out-of-hospital birth* refers to homebirth or birth in a free-standing birth center. Only about 1% of all births in the US occur outside a hospital, but being able to choose the location where one gives birth is an important element of reproductive choice and RJ. Midwives

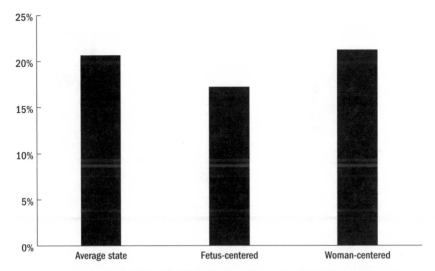

Figure 7.5. Average Probability of a Midwife Attending a Low-Risk Birth by Reproductive Health Regimes, 1995–2015. Source: Natality Detail Files and compiled legal data from Nexis Uni. (See the online Technical Appendix, table 7.4, for the model results.)

attend most out-of-hospital births, and research has shown that home-birth and birth center births have equally good outcomes, with fewer complications, compared with hospital births for women with low-risk pregnancies.[41] Once again, fetus-centered reproductive health laws were associated with lower odds of out-of-hospital birth. The odds of out-of-hospital birth were 8% lower in states with a ban on abortion at a specific gestational age, 15% lower in states with parental involvement laws, 10% lower in states that criminalize substance use during pregnancy, and 23% lower in states that require abortion clinics to meet the standards of ambulatory surgery centers. On the other hand, feticide laws, special reporting requirements for abortion providers, and laws that require hospital admitting privileges were associated with higher odds of out-of-hospital birth. Also, the odds of out-of-hospital birth in low-risk pregnancies were 13% lower in states that protected women's health clinics from violence. While the probability of out-of-hospital birth is very low overall, leading to small absolute differences across regime-types, figure 7.6 illustrates the contrast between the average state, a hypothetical fetus-centered state with all restrictions of reproductive rights, and a hypothetical woman-centered state with

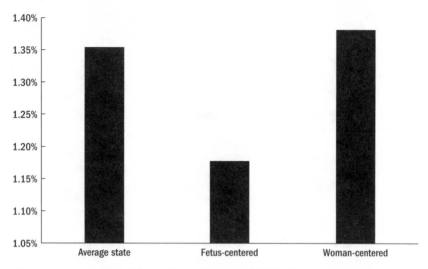

Figure 7.6. Average Probability of Out-of-Hospital Birth for Low-Risk Births by Reproductive Health Regimes, 1995–2015. Source: Natality Detail Files and compiled legal data from Nexis Uni. (See the online Technical Appendix, table 7.4, for the model results.)

no restrictions of reproductive rights. It is clear from figure 7.6 that woman-centered laws are part of an environment that is more hospitable to out-of-hospital birth.

My Body, My Choice

Access to contraception, abortion, sterilization, VBAC, midwifery care, and out-of-hospital birth are all RJ issues, and reproductive health regimes have important effects on them. While abortion opponents often claim that their goal is to protect the life of fetuses and not to limit women's rights, laws that restrict abortion and prioritize fetuses attack women's rights more generally. Based on my analyses in this chapter, I argue that laws that prioritize women's rights over fetal life make it more likely that women will have choices beyond standard obstetric care. On the other hand, limits on women's ability to terminate a pregnancy have unintended consequences for pregnant women when they give birth. They deny many women who have experienced a previous cesarean the right to informed consent or refusal in subsequent pregnancies. VBAC advocates argue that forcing a woman to have major abdominal surgery (or any surgery or procedure) without her consent is a violation of her civil rights. Performing medical procedures against a pregnant woman's wishes violates her rights to informed consent and bodily integrity, even though, theoretically, women do not lose the right to make medical decisions when they are pregnant. Fetus-centered reproductive health regimes also reduce the odds that women with low-risk pregnancies will give birth with alternative providers or outside of high-tech hospitals. As a result, some birth advocates have taken up the causes of VBAC and homebirth as RJ issues.

8

Reproductive Regimes

The Legal Environment and Maternity Care in the United States

This book has examined the (sometimes unexpected) ways the legal environment influences maternity care practices. Laws have small effects on this field on a day-to-day basis, but they amount to different odds of evidence-based versus organizationally expedient practices. Tort laws loom large over physicians and hospitals, especially in obstetrics. Fear of malpractice liability produces ritual practices that exaggerate the legal threat and justify the intensification of the medicalization schema, with its reliance on scienciness and its fetishization of technology. Reproductive health laws have less conscious, but still significant, effects as a legal backdrop for the maternity care field. Tort and reproductive health regimes are important environments for maternity care practices, and they help to shape some of the trade-offs that maternity care providers must make.

Liability Risk, Tort Regimes, and Maternity Care Outcomes

The laws that first come to mind in the maternity care field are tort laws that govern malpractice. Malpractice liability risk is culturally powerful and theoretically drives defensive medicine, leading physicians to order extra tests and perform unnecessary procedures to defend themselves from liability. But practically, the risk of medical liability has declined dramatically over time, dropping far more precipitously than medical error rates and, by many accounts, leaving legitimate victims of negligent care without recourse. In fact, the analyses in chapters 4 and 5 showed that malpractice liability risk can deter risky and scientifically unsound medical practices and promote more evidence-based practices. On the other hand, organizationally convenient practices are more common in states with tort reforms that reduce providers' liability risk. At an aggregate level, provider-friendly tort regimes support organizational expedience and provider convenience, and patient-friendly tort regimes support evidence-based best practices. For example, Florida has a provider-friendly tort regime that caps non-economic damages at $250,000. While preterm and low-birth-weight births are a primary cause of infant mortality, Florida's preterm birth and low-birth-weight rates are near the national average but its infant mortality rates are above average. It also has the fourth-highest cesarean rate in the country. In contrast, Vermont is a patient-friendly state without caps on damages and with very low rates of malpractice litigation. It has below-average infant mortality and one of the nation's lowest cesarean rates, as well as very low preterm and low-birthweight birth rates. Table 8.1 shows the comparison between Florida and Vermont in maternity care outcomes. While the differences in infant mortality rates and low-birthweight birth rates in table 8.1 are not dramatic, these rates are clearly higher in provider-friendly Florida. The differences in cesarean rates are more dramatic—with rates in Florida consistently 5–10% higher than in Vermont.

The fact that tort liability is necessary to deter opportunism does not mean that doctors are villains who unreflexively impose the medical model of care and care only about themselves. In fact, they are neither heroes nor villains. Rather, they are members of organizations with outside lives and they must juggle a variety of constraints from their profession, the practice and/or hospital that they work in, and the norms of the maternity care field. Most obstetricians enter medicine because they care about people and they specialize in obstetrics because they care specifically about women and babies. Some support reproductive rights and others oppose abortion—which is also true of midwives. Most are committed to women's care and to producing healthy birth outcomes for both women and babies. The maternity care providers I talked to were also committed to women's reproductive rights. They wanted women to be able to make choices about their births, but they also faced organizational constraints that limited the choices that they could offer. They faced pressures from their socialization into the medicalization schema, professional norms, and organizational needs, as well as any personal convictions that they might have. Liability insurers and hospital risk managers encouraged them to amplify medicalization to protect themselves from liability, and professional guidelines sometimes did the

TABLE 8.1. Maternity Care Outcomes in Provider-Friendly Florida and Patient-Friendly Vermont, 1995–2015

	Infant mortality rate (per 1,000 live births)		Low-birth-weight birth rate (% of all births)		Cesarean rate (% of all births)	
Year	Florida	Vermont	Florida	Vermont	Florida	Vermont
1995	7.4	6.5	7.7	5.4	21.7	16.7
1996	7.4	7.0	7.9	6.2	21.6	16.5
1997	7.1	6.9	8	6.3	22.2	15.6
1998	7.2	7.5	8.1	6.5	22.4	16.5
1999	7.3	7.5	8.2	5.7	23.8	16.4
2000	7	6.5	8	6.1	25	17.3
2001	7.3	6.4	8.2	5.9	26.4	17.8
2002	7.5	4.2	8.4	6.4	28.5	20.9
2003	7.5	5.2	8.5	7.0	30.8	22.6
2004	7	4.5	8.5	6.4	33.2	24.1
2005	7.2	6.5	8.7	6.2	34.9	25.9
2006	7.2	5.7	8.7	6.9	36.1	26
2007	7.1	5.1	8.7	6.2	37.2	26.8
2008	7.2	4.6	8.8	7.0	37.6	27.2
2009	6.9	6.2	8.7	6.7	38.1	27.8
2010	6.5	4.2	8.7	6.1	37.8	27.5
2011	6.4	4.9	8.7	6.7	38.1	27.8
2012	6	4.3	8.6	6.2	38.1	27.1
2013	6.1	4.4	8.5	6.7	37.7	27.3
2014	6	4.6	8.7	7.1	37.2	25.8
2015	6.2	4.6	8.6	6.6	37.3	25.5
Total	**6.9**	**5.6**	**8.4**	**6.4**	**31.7**	**22.8**

same. While there appears to be more smoke than fire around medical malpractice liability risk, the smoke can be terrifying (and it can affect liability insurance costs, which only increases the terror). For this reason, the culture of fear has serious effects, while the actual tort environment has subtle but real effects—sometimes in the opposite direction. More specifically, higher risk of tort liability appears to encourage more cautious maternity care practices, while lower liability risk may promote what is easiest or more efficient for organizations.

It is important to note that trial lawyers are also not villains in the maternity care field—even though physicians, the profession, and hospital risk managers view them as such. While the tort reform movement was effective in vilifying malpractice lawyers, these attorneys provide an important service to victims of catastrophic errors or negligence. The rate of medical injury is extremely high and most victims never receive compensation. Tort liability is necessary to deter healthcare organizations and individual providers from engaging in opportunistic and efficiency-oriented behavior that contradicts good medical practice. The biggest problem with the medical negligence system is that there are too few plaintiff's attorneys and the costs of litigating are too high to address most of the negligent errors in American healthcare. There are simply far more injuries than there are opportunities to address them through litigation. A second problem, which I highlighted in chapter 5 on EFM, is that lawyers' understandings of medicine, coupled with their tendency to fetishize documentation *on paper*, can reinforce obsolete and unscientific medical practices. The lawyers I talked to seem to understand medicine better than physicians seem to understand law, but they understand it through their own lens and that has some undesirable and unintended consequences for women's choices in giving birth.

In short, defensive medicine is not a significant problem in American obstetrics, despite strong myths about it. Maternity care providers intervene into labor and birth more than is optimal for maternal and infant health, but they do not do so primarily for legal reasons—the medicalization schema and the organizational protocols that it generates are more likely to be the cause. At the same time, liability risk under tort law is necessary to encourage higher-quality care and discourage healthcare providers from taking known medical risks to patient health because it might benefit their organizations or themselves. It is not perfect, but it is better than the alternative: tort reforms that reduce liability risk without motivating providers to improve the quality of care. The main effect of tort reforms is to leave even more victims of malpractice without adequate compensation for their injuries than when states follow common tort laws.

From a policy perspective, my findings suggest that tort reforms that reduce liability are detrimental to patients. What would be beneficial to both injured patients and the emotional security of providers would be public funds to compensate victims of medical errors—especially those who do not suffer catastrophic enough injuries to find remedies through the courts. Also, publicly funded, universal health insurance would make it much easier for victims of medical negligence to obtain the services that they need to care for themselves and their loved ones. It would make it less necessary for victims of medical errors to sue their providers, which would reduce the threat of lawsuits. The US has the highest litigation rates in the world, as well as the only private, for-profit health insurance system in the developed world—and that is no coincidence.

As someone who grew up in Canada and moved to the United States over two decades ago, I have seen firsthand that American healthcare is expensive, unequal, and inhumane—and that there is a better way that costs less, is more equitable, and covers all preexisting conditions. Admittedly, I have lived under both systems and like Canada's much better, so I tend to see single-payer healthcare as a solution to many problems. Many Americans dislike the idea of a single-payer or national healthcare system because they call it "socialism," but the US already has socialized medicine in the form of Medicare, Medicaid, the IHS, and the VA, which cover more than 30% of the population. When I ask my students if they would prefer a capitalist fire department, where firefighters only put out a fire if you have up-to-date private insurance or can pay the bill, they think that a taxpayer-funded "socialist" fire department is a much better idea. It all depends on how you frame it. A single-payer healthcare system would cost much less per person than the current system—people would pay more to the government for single-payer healthcare, but less overall. Single-payer healthcare has the added bonus of reducing liability risk for providers without tort reforms that encourage opportunistic behavior over evidence-based care.

Organizational Expedience: The "Weekend Birth Dearth"

While the key informant interviews and the extant literature both point to important organizational reasons for many unscientific obstetric practices, I was not able to test this directly in my analyses of early-term induction, EFM use, and cesareans. But there is one birth outcome that provides a good proxy for organizational expedience: the "weekend birth dearth." The "weekend birth dearth" refers to the fact that fewer births

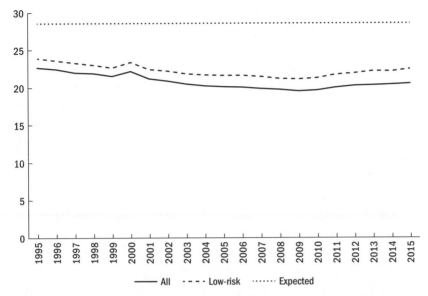

Figure 8.1. Percentage of Births on Saturday or Sunday, 1995–2015. Source: Natality Detail Files.

in the US occur on weekends than one would expect based on random chance. Physicians and hospitals tend to prefer for births to occur on weekdays. Of course, left to their own devices, babies will arrive any time of the day and any day of the week—unless providers schedule, induce, speed up, or surgically intervene in labor. Assuming that the natural distribution of births is equal on each day of the week, two sevenths or 28.6% of births should occur on Saturday or Sunday. But only 20.8% of births occurred on weekends from 1995 to 2015, which is 7.8% fewer than should occur with random chance. Figure 8.1 illustrates the distribution of weekend births over time, and shows that the percentage of births that occurred on weekends is lower than one would expect if births were randomly distributed across the week.

If tort reforms that reduce liability encourage providers to prioritize organizational considerations over medical ones, then they should influence the odds of weekend births. Using the same strategy as in other chapters to examine low-risk births to mothers without a previous cesarean, I did indeed find that the odds of a weekend birth were 2.1% lower in states that cap only punitive damages and 4.5% lower in states that cap non-economic damages (with or without caps on punitive damages). In a model that separated out caps only on punitive damages alone, caps only on non-economic damages, and caps on both, I found that the odds of a weekend birth were 2.6% lower in states with punitive damages, 3.9% lower in states with caps on non-economic damages, and 5.3% lower in states with caps on both. They were also 2.2–2.3% lower in states with expert requirements.[1] In short, tort reforms that reduce liability risk are associated with more weekday births and fewer weekend births than one would expect due to chance.[2]

While a somewhat lower percentage of births occurring on the weekend might not represent a significant threat to maternal or infant health, it implies interventions into labor rather than spontaneous labor and birth. The fact that weekend births are more common when providers face more liability risk also further strengthens the argument that tort liability discourages medical interventions that are unnecessary but are organizationally efficient. Note again that this is the opposite effect of defensive medicine (which I originally expected to find): instead of intervening *more* when they face more liability risk, providers intervene *less*. Research on birth has consistently demonstrated that birth outcomes are better when providers intervene less, so this suggests that maternity care providers give better quality care in states with more liability risk.

Of course, organizational efficiency can also take priority when the main client cannot speak for himself or herself: in fetus-centered reproductive health regimes where the government takes a paternalistic role regarding the fetus (and a punitive approach to pregnant women). In contrast, an emphasis on women's choices in woman-centered reproductive health regimes should reduce the prominence of organizational considerations. While reproductive health regimes play a less conscious role in physician decision-making, I examined the odds of a weekend birth in low-risk births to mothers without a previous cesarean. Using the same strategy as in other chapters, I found that the odds of a weekend birth were 1.9% lower in states with a "partial-birth abortion" procedure ban, 2.4% lower in states with mandatory waiting periods, 1.8% lower in states with feticide laws, and 1.5% lower in states that define prenatal substance use as child abuse. Laws that require parental involvement in minors' abortions and abortion bans had no effect. TRAP laws were also associated with fewer weekend births.

The odds of giving birth on the weekend were 1.9% higher in states with reporting requirements for abortion facilities, but they were 1.1% lower in states that require abortion facilities to meet the standards of ambulatory surgery facilities and 2.3% lower in states that require abortion providers to have hospital admitting privileges or to be located in close proximity to a hospital.[3] While reproductive health laws have very small effects on the odds of a weekend birth, the results suggest that organizational expedience has a higher priority in fetus-centered reproductive health regimes.

Is a Pregnant Woman a Person?

From an RJ perspective, it is tempting to be polemical in the current reproductive rights climate, which seems to become more fetus-centered by the hour. Reproductive rights are under siege in the United States, in ways that inflict cruelty on all women who can get pregnant, including those who give birth. When state legislatures restrict pregnant women's rights, they treat pregnant women and their fetuses as adversaries and they lose sight of the fact that mothers care more than anyone else about their fetuses/babies. Pre-viability abortion bans and procedure bans not only affect access to abortion, they prioritize fetal life over women's basic human rights. Special reporting requirements for abortion providers and facility restrictions deter physicians from providing abortions and lead to clinic closures. In fact, while tort reform advocates often claim that medical liability has reduced the supply of physicians because many potential doctors do not want to deal with malpractice lawsuits, fetus-centered laws and rhetoric have done the same thing with abortion providers—and probably more effectively. Laws that punish pregnant women for prenatal substance use instead of offering them treatment and laws that prohibit direct-entry midwifery for women who want to give birth at home constrain women's choices. These laws are bad for all women who are pregnant or can become pregnant, regardless of how they feel about abortion.

Anti-abortion laws are cruel because they fail to recognize the circumstances under which women get pregnant. Women don't always have power over when they have sex or their partners' willingness to use contraception. This is most obvious in cases involving rape, but many women have unequal power in heterosexual relationships. Sometimes women get pregnant just as they are trying to get out of an abusive relationship, and giving birth will mean being tied to their abusers for life. Even if everyone used contraception perfectly, sometimes it fails. I have known women who have gotten pregnant while taking oral contraceptives, and I had a student once who got pregnant after having her tubes tied. Some women in that position are in a stable relationship and can financially afford a child, so they have a baby (often not their first). Others, for a variety of reasons, will do *anything* to avoid having a baby (or another baby). That is why banning abortions or making them very hard to get does not necessarily reduce the number of abortions. It only makes it harder for women to get safe abortion care, especially poor women (who always have fewer healthcare options). Poor women are both more likely to need abortions, partly because they are less likely to have power in their sexual relationships, and less likely to be able to afford safe ones.

Of course, we know what reduces the need for abortion (around the world). It is not laws that make abortions illegal or harder to get or more expensive in order to punish pregnant women (but not the men who got them pregnant). It is empowering women and girls and providing free and open access to effective contraception and comprehensive sexuality education—things that many abortion opponents also oppose. Restricting legal abortion access only drives it underground, where bad things can happen. Some abortions are simply necessary, and there are many reasons that they may be necessary—so they should be safe and legal (and free).

Of course, this book is not about abortion—it is about maternity care practices surrounding *birth*. But the fetus-centered logic behind anti-abortion laws affects birth as well as abortion, and it affects typical births as well as extreme cases involving prosecutions of pregnant women and forced cesareans. As I showed in chapters 5 and 7, the odds of EFM are higher and the odds of VBAC for mothers with a previous cesarean are lower in states with more restrictive reproductive health laws. EFM is an organizationally expedient, scientifically dubious technology, and pregnant women are more likely to avoid it if they give birth in states that respect women's reproductive rights. VBAC is often a healthier birth choice than repeat cesarean for women with a previous cesarean, but it requires a commitment from the maternity care provider. This commitment is more likely when women give birth in a state that prioritizes women's rights to make their own healthcare decisions. I also found that fetus-centered reproductive health regimes are associated with lower odds of midwife-attended birth and out-of-hospital birth and, in general, with medicalized birth practices that benefit providers.

A Tale of Two Regimes: Oregon and Mississippi

Perhaps a more extended example is in order. The state with the fewest restrictions on reproductive rights and the most legal protections for abortion rights is Oregon. In contrast, Mississippi, Indiana, and Oklahoma have all placed the maximum of restrictions on reproductive rights and offer no protection for abortion rights. I consider the cases of Oregon and Mississippi and their maternal and infant health outcomes to illustrate the importance of pregnant women being able to make decisions about their reproductive healthcare. Notably, these two states have similar tort regimes, with caps on non-economic damages, reform of the JSL rule, and expert requirements. In other words, both are provider-friendly tort regimes.

Woman-centered reproductive health regimes recognize that women are the best advocates for fetuses, and they permit women who want to avoid medical surveillance to do so. In Oregon, there are no legal restrictions on abortion, medical clinics have legal protection from violence, and state laws explicitly protect abortion rights. While 30% of women in Oregon live in counties without an abortion provider, the governor, state senate, and state house all favor reproductive rights. Unlike most states, which require a licensed physician to provide abortions, Oregon legally permits nurse practitioners to provide both surgical and medication abortions. The state of Oregon has no biased counseling requirements, no mandatory waiting periods before an abortion, and no parental involvement requirements for minors seeking abortions. The state protects medical facilities, including abortion clinics, by defining property damage and interference with facility operation as felonies.[4]

Oregon legally requires comprehensive insurance coverage of reproductive health services, including prescription contraceptives and abortions. Prescription benefit plans must provide payment, coverage, or reimbursement for prescription contraceptives.[5] Oregon's Medicaid program also covers abortion services with public funds, and has since 1984.[6] In August 2017, Oregon's governor, Kate Brown, signed the nation's most progressive reproductive health policy into law: the Reproductive Health Equity Act (RHEA). The RHEA requires health insurers to provide contraception and abortion without a co-pay and dedicates state funds to pay for reproductive healthcare for non-citizens. The state also manages substance use during pregnancy by requiring healthcare providers to encourage and facilitate drug counseling, rather than by punishing pregnant addicts.

Oregon's state laws ensure that survivors of sexual assault receive access to emergency contraception (EC). Since 2003, Oregon has had a Sexual Assault Victim's Emergency Medical Response Fund that pays for medical assessments for sexual assault survivors.[7] Since 2007, Oregon law has required that emergency department personnel provide medically accurate information about EC, offer EC, and dispense EC upon request.[8]

Oregon is clearly a woman-centered reproductive health regime, but how does it do on measures of maternal and infant health? The state has above-average maternity care outcomes in terms of infant mortality, preterm birth, and low-birth-weight rates. It also has below-average rates of teen pregnancy, uninsured adults, and preventable hospital admissions, and it receives high rankings for healthcare quality.[9] As table 8.2 illustrates, low-birth-weight rates were lowest in Oregon in the late 1990s, but did not vary dramatically over time. Cesarean rates increased in tandem with national increases, but were below average for the US. Table 8.2 also shows the comparison statistics for Mississippi, which contrast sharply with Oregon's.

Figures 8.2 to 8.4 compare the infant mortality rates, low-birth-weight rates, and cesarean rates of woman-centered Oregon and fetus-centered Mississippi with those of provider-friendly Florida and patient-friendly Vermont.[10] Figures 8.2 and 8.3 clearly show that infant mortality and low-birth-weight rates are highest in fetus-centered Mississippi. But Florida, with its $250,000 cap on non-economic damages, also has higher low-birth-weight rates. Cesarean rates are also much higher in fetus-centered Mississippi and provider-friendly Florida

TABLE 8.2. Maternity Care Outcomes in Woman-centered Oregon and Fetus-centered Mississippi, 1995–2015

	Infant mortality rate (per 1,000 live births)		Low-birth-weight birth rate (% of all births)		Cesarean rate (% of all births)	
Year	Oregon	Mississippi	Oregon	Mississippi	Oregon	Mississippi
1995	6.1	10.4	5.7	9.8	17.0	25.7
1996	5.4	10.9	6.0	9.8	16.4	27.2
1997	5.7	10.6	5.2	10.1	16.9	27.7
1998	5.4	10.1	5.2	10.6	18.0	26.2
1999	5.7	10.1	5.1	9.8	19.0	26.0
2000	5.6	10.6	6.0	10.1	20.0	28.4
2001	5.4	10.5	5.8	10.3	21.0	30.4
2002	5.7	10.2	6.2	11.5	24.3	31.3
2003	5.6	10.9	6.4	8.5	25.5	28.3
2004	5.5	9.9	6.1	8.3	27.2	29.2
2005	6.0	11.5	6.0	11.5	28.5	33.9
2006	5.4	10.5	6.1	12.1	28.4	35.5
2007	5.7	10.0	6.6	12.0	28.7	35.9
2008	5.1	9.9	6.5	11.6	29.9	35.5
2009	4.9	10.1	5.8	10.8	29.8	37.5
2010	5.0	9.6	6.1	12.3	28.5	37.0
2011	4.6	9.2	6.2	11.3	29.1	36.8
2012	5.3	8.9	6.6	11.6	28.5	38.1
2013	4.9	9.6	5.9	11.5	29.3	37.4
2014	5.1	8.2	6.1	10.9	28.4	37.5
2015	5.2	9.5	6.4	10.4	27.4	37.7
Total	5.4	10.1	6.0	10.5	24.9	32.2

than in woman-centered Oregon or patient-friendly Vermont. While tort and reproductive health laws are far from the only differences between these states, figures 8.2 to 8.4 illustrate the contrast between these regime-types.

Mississippi is not just one of the states with the most restrictions on reproductive rights, it also has worst-in-the-nation status for infant and maternal mortality rates, preterm birth rates, and low-birth-weight rates. There are many reasons for Mississippi's worst-in-the-nation

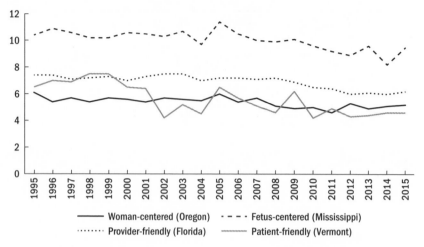

Figure 8.2. Infant Mortality Rates in Florida, Vermont, Oregon, and Mississippi, 1995–2015. Source: *US News and World Report*, 2019.

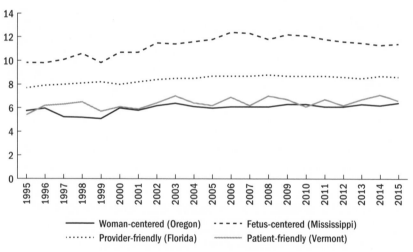

Figure 8.3. Low-Birth-Weight Birth Rates in Florida, Vermont, Oregon, and Mississippi, 1995–2015. Source: *US News and World Report*, 2019.

status, including its high poverty rate, low median income, low scores for education, high incarceration rate, and especially its history of racial segregation and discrimination. In fact, Mississippi did not vote to ratify the 13th Amendment, which abolished slavery, until 1995, and did not notify the federal government of that vote until 2013. Mississippi was

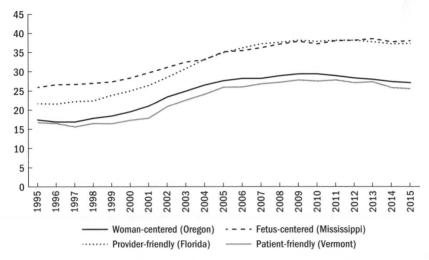

Figure 8.4. Cesarean Rates in Florida, Vermont, Oregon, and Mississippi, 1995–2015. Source: *US News and World Report*, 2019.

one of 17 states that did not adopt the Medicaid expansion under the ACA, and it ranks worst in the nation for health care access and health care quality. According to *US News and World Report*, Mississippi had higher-than-average rates of uninsured adults and preventable hospital admissions.[11] It also has the second-highest teen pregnancy rate in the United States (after Arkansas).[12]

In addition to having poor maternal and infant outcomes, Mississippi is an extreme example of a fetus-centered reproductive regime. There were 8 abortion clinics in Mississippi in 1992 but increased TRAP laws led most of them to close. There is only one remaining clinic in Mississippi that provides abortions: Jackson Women's Health Organization. TRAP laws in Mississippi include the following:

- A unique licensure scheme distinguishes abortion providers from other medical providers and requires that any facility that provides 10 or more abortions per month, or 100 or more per year, be licensed as an "abortion facility."[13]
- Abortion facilities in Mississippi must comply with 35 pages of administrative, professional qualification, medical testing, and physical plant requirements.[14]

- Physicians who provide abortions in Mississippi must be board-certified in obstetrics and gynecology, and must have both admitting and staff privileges at a local hospital.[15]
- The Mississippi state licensing agency has the authority to inspect and investigate abortion clinics, with no guarantee of patient privacy or confidentiality.[16]
- Mississippi state law requires that all abortion services after the first trimester take place in an ambulatory surgical facility or a hospital, which cannot be located within 1,500 feet of a church, school, or kindergarten.[17] It also prohibits licensing of abortion facilities as ambulatory surgical facilities, even though no ambulatory surgical facilities provide abortions. (The courts permanently barred this statute from going into effect in *Jackson Women's Health Organization v. Amy*, No. Civ. A. 3:04CV495LN (S.D. Miss. June 14, 2005).)

In addition to imposing unnecessary regulations on abortion providers, the Mississippi government has worked tirelessly to ban abortions outright. Its government imposes medical surveillance on women in the name of their fetuses, and treats the relationship between a pregnant woman and her fetus as adversarial (with the government as the protector of fetuses). The state never repealed its pre-*Roe* abortion ban, which defined providing an abortion by any means as a felony with a prison term of 1 to 10 years.[18] Mississippi also enacted a near-total ban on abortion in 2007, to become effective if the Supreme Court overturns *Roe v. Wade.* Under this law, anyone who provides an abortion, unless it is necessary to preserve the woman's life or the pregnancy is the result of a rape that has been formally reported to law enforcement, could be imprisoned for up to 10 years.[19] In 2014, Mississippi banned abortions after 20 weeks from the pregnant woman's last menstrual period (approximately 18 weeks after conception), unless an abortion is necessary to prevent permanent impairment of the life or physical health of the woman, or in the case of a "severe fetal abnormality."[20] Then a new 2018 law placed the point of fetal viability at 15 weeks—well ahead of where medical providers place the viability line—and prohibited abortions after 15 weeks from the pregnant woman's last menstrual period.[21] The US District Court for the Southern District of Mississippi temporarily enjoined this law in July 2014.[22]

Despite this setback, the legislature passed a "Heartbeat Bill" in March 2019 that effectively bans abortion as early as six weeks after a woman's last menstrual period (approximately four weeks after conception), when many women do not even know that they are pregnant. This exasperated the US District Judge, Carlton W. Reeves, who had previously enjoined the 15-week ban and noted that six weeks is less than 15.[23] He blocked the "heartbeat" law before it could take effect. Still, state attorneys and the governor claim that the state has an interest in protecting unborn children, and Mississippi's governor, Phil Bryant, has said, "Please rest assured that I also have not abandoned my hope of making Mississippi abortion-free."[24]

In addition to attempting, repeatedly, to ban abortions, Mississippi passed a "partial-birth abortion" ban in 1997 that outlaws the dilation and extraction (D&X) procedure as early as 12 weeks.[25] In 2016, Mississippi also banned the use of a dilation and evacuation (D&E) abortion procedure unless it is necessary to save the woman's life.[26] This effectively bans the most common, and often the safest, procedure for second-trimester abortions.

The state of Mississippi has also created many obstacles for women who want or need an abortion, including one of the longest mandatory waiting periods in the US. Women seeking an abortion in Mississippi must receive counseling from the same physician who will perform the abortion, and then must wait 72 hours between the counseling and the procedure. The physician must inform her of the probable gestational age of the "unborn child," describe medical risks associated with the procedure, and describe the risks of carrying the pregnancy to term. The physician also must provide a state-mandated lecture detailing that medical assistance benefits may be available for prenatal care, childbirth, and neonatal care, and that the father is liable for child support even if he has offered to pay for the abortion. They also must inform abortion patients that they have a right to review state-prepared materials that describe the "unborn child," and offer a list of agencies that offer alternatives to abortion.[27] The list of agencies includes crisis pregnancy centers (CPCs), which often give factually inaccurate information in order to convince a woman not to have an abortion, and it does not differentiate between biased CPCs and legitimate health centers.[28]

Mississippi requires consent from *both* parents for women under age 18 who have never been married or freed from the care, custody, or control of their parents.[29] The state also limits insurance coverage for abortion by prohibiting public funding for abortion under its Medicaid program and explicitly prohibiting insurance plans for public employees as well as private insurance plans on its state exchange from covering abortion services.[30] The state of Mississippi provides no special legal protections to health clinics.

Mississippi has also defined crimes based on the claim that the state has an interest in preserving fetal life. The state defines murder to include the murder of an "unborn child," and permits wrongful death actions related to "the death of any person or of any unborn quick child."[31] The definition of "human being" in Mississippi criminal statutes on murder, homicide, and assault includes "an unborn child at every stage of gestation from conception until live birth."[32] Despite efforts to pass a law that defines chemical endangerment of a child or fetus as a crime, Mississippi does not legally define prenatal substance use as child abuse or require healthcare providers to provide testing or report suspected substance abuse cases.[33] But Mississippi courts have prosecuted women for child abuse based on substance use during pregnancy, using the rationale that Mississippi's felony child abuse law defines poisoning as child abuse.[34] Courts have prosecuted pregnant addicts under this child abuse law, even in the absence of a clear definition of "poisoning." One example, which I described in chapter 2, is the case of Rennie Gibbs, a low-income black teen who was prosecuted for murder after having a stillbirth because she had a cocaine byproduct in her system. (The cause of the baby's death was almost certainly that the umbilical cord was wrapped around her neck.)

As a whole, Mississippi has many laws that express a commitment to the state's interest in fetal life, but the state does a remarkably poor job investing in the health and welfare of mothers and babies after they are born. Its high uninsured population and its high rates of infant mortality and preterm and low-birth-weight births suggest that Mississippi could much better spend the resources that it uses to restrict abortion access to improve the health of its already-born population. In contrast, Oregon provides very open access to abortion (and contraception), and has better healthcare quality and far superior maternal and infant health outcomes. While there is no clear causal relationship—one would not expect that eliminating reproductive rights restrictions in Mississippi would necessarily or immediately produce dramatic improvements in its healthcare outcomes—it seems clear that fetus-centered reproductive health regimes have a misplaced policy emphasis that does not improve the health of their populations.

The lessons to take from this are especially important given the dire reproductive health situation in the United States right now. Alabama recently passed the most restrictive abortion law in the country. In addition to Mississippi, the states of Kentucky, Ohio, Georgia, Missouri, and Louisiana passed heartbeat abortion bans in 2019. The apparent goal of the recent barrage of abortion restrictions is to provoke legal challenges and appeals that will end up in front of the new conservative majority on the US Supreme Court. The religious right's ultimate goal is to force the Supreme Court to reconsider the decision in *Roe v. Wade*. If they succeed, one of the casualties is likely to be pregnant women's right to informed consent and bodily integrity—regardless of whether they intend to terminate their pregnancies or carry them to term.

From a policy perspective, the obvious solution is to legally support women's ability to make decisions for themselves and their fetuses. But true reproductive justice requires that money and health insurance no longer be barriers to reproductive healthcare for anyone who needs it, which means universal insurance coverage with comprehensive coverage of reproductive healthcare, including abortion. The Hyde Amendment, which prohibits the use of public funds to pay for abortions for women on Medicaid, IHS, or VA insurance, represented a legislative strategy to restrict poor women's access to abortions. Unless and until Congress repeals it, there can be no reproductive justice. Poor women would also experience less surveillance under single-payer insurance than with the tiered system of Medicaid compared to private insurance.[35] Single-payer health insurance is not perfect, and countries like Canada and the UK still have inequalities in healthcare, but it would be undoubtedly better than the fragmented health care industry in the United States. Health care should be a right, not a for-profit medical-industrial complex.

ACKNOWLEDGMENTS

This book is the product of an extremely long gestation, and it required a great deal of help and support. When my ideas for the study were starting to form, Lynn Paltrow and the National Advocates for Pregnant Women introduced me to full-spectrum reproductive justice theory at the 2007 National Summit to ensure the Health and Humanity of Pregnant and Birthing Women. My exposure to interdisciplinary scholars and activists at that conference was germinal to my later development of the idea of reproductive health regimes. (If you are wondering what I mean by *germinal*, it replaces the male-dominated term *seminal*.) At the Summit, I learned about some of the cases of forced cesareans and criminalization of substance addiction that I discuss in this book, and I met and made connections with important birth advocates like Henci Goer and Susan Jenkins.

In the early stages of the research, the National Science Foundation funded the project under Grant No. 0958190. Any opinions, findings, and conclusions or recommendations expressed in this material are those of the author and do not necessarily reflect the views of the National Science Foundation. I am eternally grateful to the small community of sociologists of reproduction who have been my colleagues, and provided feedback and inspiration throughout the gestation of this book. They include Theresa Morris, Barbara Katz Rothman, Elizabeth Chiarello, Miranda Waggoner, Shannon Carter, Danielle Bessett, Wendy Simonds, Jeanne Flavin, Susan Markens, and especially Christine Morton. I also owe gratitude to my former graduate students/colleagues who provided valuable research assistance in the early stages of the project: Megan M. Henley and Katrina Running.

My former writing group members, Jane Zavisca, Sandra Way, Alexandra Kalev, and Rochelle Cote, provided valuable feedback along the way. I am indebted to Robin Stryker for helping to coin the term "reproductive regimes." At the University of Arizona, Corey Abramson,

Ronald Breiger, Jennifer Dawn Carlson, Christina Diaz, Jennifer Earl, Jeremy Fiel, Joseph Galaskiewicz, Terrence Hill, and Erin Leahey provided constructive feedback during informal conversations and/or the Hot Mess Potluck. My accountability writing group, Francine Gachupin, Sheila Gephart, and Ashley Langer, also gave me motivation and helped me to stay on track. I owe special thanks to my colleague Jim Shockey, who introduced me to the high-performance computing environment that made it possible to finally complete the analyses and helped me to figure out some of the results.

I extend special thanks to the many people in the maternity care field (obstetricians, CNMS, administrators, and lawyers) who took time out of their busy lives to let me interview them. Without them, this research would not have been possible.

At NYU Press, I am deeply grateful to my editor, Ilene Kalish. She has put together the best book list on reproduction and law, and I appreciated her guidance and support during the long process of completing this manuscript. I am also thankful to Sonia Tsuruoka, the Assistant Editor at NYU Press, who coordinated the review process and assisted me with copyediting challenges. Thank you also to Martin Coleman, the Director of Editing, Design, and Production, for coordinating the production process, and to James Harbeck for careful copyediting. Finally, I extend thanks to the marketing team, Mary Beth Jarrad, Sydney Garcia, Sarah Bode, and Megan Madden.

Last, but definitely not least, I owe thanks to my family. I could not have completed this book manuscript without the support, enthusiasm, encouragement, and love of my husband, Greg Pilling. Of course, I also owe a huge debt of gratitude to my children, without whom I would never have written this book: Troy, Axel, Dash, Cameron, and especially Nutmeg, who started it all.

Appendix A

INTERVIEW METHODS AND DATA

I conducted 26 *key informant interviews* with experts from the maternity care field to understand the relationships between the institutional environment and maternity care practices. *Key informant interviews* are qualitative in-depth interviews with a range of people with specialized, firsthand knowledge about their community.[1] Interviews with key informants provide opportunities to examine specialized systems or processes and to clarify quantitative research results. The key informants that I interviewed were community experts, with insights into important events, problems, and possible solutions in the maternity care field. They included nine obstetricians and three certified nurse midwives (in total 12 maternity care providers), nine medical malpractice attorneys, three hospital administrators, and two health insurance directors. I wanted to interview liability insurers, but the major liability insurance companies in the area declined to participate in the study. I could not use random sampling methods to interview key informants, and the interviews are small in number, took place in a single state, and are not representative. At the same time, key informant interviews provide insights into how different actors within the maternity care field understand the law as well as the benefits and drawbacks of different obstetric procedures.

I selected a targeted, non-representative sample of individuals in positions with important stakes in maternity care in order to understand the *processes* behind the quantitative findings and the culture of the field. A targeted sampling strategy was appropriate because I expected the quantitative analysis to provide generalizable findings, and the purpose of the key informant interviews was to supplement these findings with an understanding of how medical workers understand the legal environment and how legal workers understand medicine.

In contacting potential participants, I attempted to be non-invasive by using intermediaries or requesting participation via email or letter. I assured them that their participation was voluntary and that I would not contact them again if they indicated that they preferred not to participate. I used snowball sampling through my personal networks, and drew on my contacts to make the initial connection and to ask potential respondents to contact me via email or telephone. I also used internet searches to locate maternity care providers, health insurance company offices, medical liability insurers, and malpractice attorneys throughout the local region. I then sent them email and/or formal written letters to make initial contact and to solicit voluntary participation, using a script approved by the Institutional Review Board at the University of Arizona. All participants were in Arizona, both to permit face-to-face interviews and to control for state-level variation in the legal environment. There is no reason to expect Arizona to be an outlier among non–tort reform states and, in fact, it is very average in terms of its malpractice environment—without caps on damages, but with reform of the JSL and with expert requirements. It has fetus-centered reproductive health laws, and has increased restrictions on reproductive rights over time (especially after 2010).

The interviews took place in 2010 and 2011 and I used partially structured interview questions to elicit open-ended responses about the issues that are important in the maternity care field. Interviews lasted an average of one hour and took place at a time and location of each respondent's choice. Locations included their office, my office, their home, and cafes. I conducted all interviews face to face and digitally recorded them for transcription and analysis. Throughout this book, all names are pseudonyms.

Tables A.1 to A.3 display descriptive information for the sample of key informants. I aggregated the data to protect informants' confidentiality. In table A.1, the maternity care providers who acted as key informants were disproportionately female, which overstates their representation in the population of OB/GYNs. (CNMs are almost all women). There was some racial-ethnic variation among maternity care providers, which is probably representative of the population of OB/GYNs and CNMs, but is not representative of the local population (which is approximately 45% non-Hispanic white and 43% Hispanic).

Table A.2 shows the descriptive characteristics of medical malpractice attorneys. Malpractice attorneys were very willing to do interviews and they often wanted me to use their real names, although I did not.

TABLE A.1. Descriptive Statistics for Maternity Care Providers
(OB/GYN, CNM), N = 12

Gender		
Female	11	91.7%
Male	1	8.3%
Racial-ethnic identity		
White	8	66.7%
Hispanic	2	16.7%
African American	1	8.3%
Multi-racial	1	8.3%
Marital status		
Married	9	75.0%
Domestic partner	1	8.3%
Single/divorced	2	16.7%
Parent	10	83.3%
Average # children	1.9	
Years of experience (average)	15.8	
Less than 5	1	8.3%
5 to 10	3	25.0%
11 to 20	5	41.7%
More than 20	3	25.0%
Position/Education		
Obstetrician/gynecologist (MD)	9	75.0%
Certified nurse midwife (CNM)[i]	3	25.0%
Income		
Obstetrician average income (rounded)	$285,000	
CNM average income (rounded)	$81,000	

i A CNM has a Master's degree in nursing.

They were forthcoming partly because they were passionate about
the cause of the people that they represented, especially if they were
plaintiff's attorneys, and also because they felt misunderstood. They
wanted to share their perspective because the tort reform movement
had such a strong impact on public opinion about them—treating them
as pariahs who wage "frivolous" lawsuits on unsuspecting and innocent

TABLE A.2. Descriptive Statistics for Medical Malpractice Attorneys, N = 9

Gender		
Female	4	44.4%
Male	5	55.6%
Racial-ethnic identity		
White	9	100%
Marital status		
Married	7	77.8%
Single/divorced	2	22.2%
Parent	9	100%
Average # children	2.4	
Years of experience (average)	25.1	
Less than 5	0	
5 to 10	1	11.1%
11 to 20	2	22.2%
More than 20	6	66.7%
Average income (rounded)	$439,000	

healthcare providers. The attorney informants were gender-mixed and were all non-Hispanic white, which reflected the population of medical negligence attorneys but not the local population (45% non-Hispanic white). Confirming the observations of the attorneys themselves about the aging of this professional field, a majority (two thirds) had over 20 years of experience.

Table A3 shows descriptive characteristics for hospital administrators and health insurance administrators. I spoke to both female and male administrators, although the two medical insurance directors were both men. Two of the administrators were married, one was single, one was widowed, and one had a same-sex domestic partner.

I analyzed the data with Dedoose software, using an abductive approach that combines inductive and deductive logic to build an explanation for a set of observations.[2] Abductive reasoning aims to uncover cause-and-effect relationships rather than general rules. This approach begins with existing theories and uses the available set of observations to develop understandings of cause and effect. Abductive analysis can

TABLE A.3. Descriptive Statistics for Hospital and Insurance

Gender		
Female	2	40%
Male	3	60%
Racial-ethnic identity		
White	4	80%
Asian/Pacific Islander	1	20%
Marital status		
Married	2	40%
Domestic partner	1	20%
Single/divorced	2	40%
Parent	2	40%
Average # children	1.0	
Years of experience (average)	15.0	
Less than 5	1	20%
5 to 10	1	20%
11 to 20	2	40%
More than 20	1	20%
Position		
Hospital administrator	3	60%
Health insurance administrator	2	40%
Education		
MBA	2	40%
MD	2	40%
JD	1	20%
Average income (rounded)	$216,000	

build on, challenge, or confirm existing theories as the data determine the theoretical concepts that are relevant. As I analyzed the data, I developed codes related to cesarean delivery, defensive medicine, electronic fetal monitoring (EFM), health disparities, health insurance, induction of labor, informed consent, liability insurance, medical risks, a midwifery approach, medicalization, medical malpractice, quality of care, reproductive justice (RJ), the standard of care (SOC), technology, tort laws, and vaginal birth after cesarean (VBAC).

Appendix B

LEGAL DATA AND MEASURES

I collected state-level measures of tort and reproductive health laws from publicly available sources from 1995 to 2015 to examine the effects of the legal environment. Following Currie and MacLeod (2008), I coded the enactment or repeal of state laws by month and year. If a law took effect in the middle of a particular month, then I coded the new law as effective during the following month. Similarly, if a state repealed a law in the middle of a month, I coded the law as in effect for that month. I coded laws that the courts enjoined as unconstitutional but the legislature did not repeal as present among the state's legal statutes because they reflect the fetus-centered intent of the reproductive health regime.

TORT LAWS

For tort variables, I began by obtaining Currie and MacLeod's data for 1985–2005 from Janet Currie.[1] Currie and MacLeod (2008) collected data on caps on damages, JSL rules, and the collateral source rule (CSR) that disallows evidence of payments made by other sources (like insurance companies). I extended their data an additional 10 years to 2015 using the Nexis Uni database (formerly Lexis Nexis) to find statutes that changed state tort laws governing caps on damages, JSL, and expert requirements. I excluded the CSR data from my statistical models to simplify the analysis. The CSR had weak or nonexistent effects in my models, and none of the key informants discussed it as part of their understanding of the malpractice environment.

Caps on Damage Awards

Caps on damage awards are what most people think of when they hear the term "tort reform." The Currie and MacLeod data included measures of state laws capping three variables:

1. the maximum dollar amount of total damages
2. the maximum dollar amount of punitive damages
3. the maximum dollar amount of non-economic damages

I recoded these variables into indicators for whether a state had caps on punitive damages, caps on non-economic damages, or caps on total damages. I also tested the effect of different levels of caps on damages, but model results that included the cap amounts were inconsistent and the specifications became very complex. The models in this book include indicators for caps on punitive damages *only* and caps on non-economic damages (alone or in combination with punitive damages). The tables in the online Technical Appendix also include a second model that tests the effects of indicators for caps on punitive damages only, caps on non-economic damages only, and caps on both (or on total damages). For the sake of simplicity, I focus on the effects of caps on punitive damages alone and the effects of caps on non-economic damages, with or without caps on punitive damages (including caps on total damages) in most of the book. Caps on non-economic damages should have stronger effects on medical liability than caps on punitive damages because courts are much more likely to award non-economic damages. Table B.1 illustrates the descriptions and average values of each of the tort reform variables.

JSL Reform

The tort data measure JSL reform for economic and non-economic damages. In Currie and MacLeod's (2008) data, 0 means that the state follows the JSL rule, and 1 means that the state has abolished JSL and assigns damages to defendants individually in proportion to their fault. They also included decimals that represent the proportion of fault a defendant must have in order to hold that defendant jointly and severally liable (e.g., 0.5 means that a defendant must be at least 50% at fault to liable). For the purposes of the analysis, I coded JSL reform as 0 in states that retained the JSL for either economic or non-economic damages, and I coded all others as 1 (proportionate liability). I tested other specifications and the results changed very little but they became more difficult to interpret. Table B.1 contains the description and average for this variable.

TABLE B.1. Descriptions and Descriptive Statistics for Tort Laws, 1995–2015

Variable	Metric	Mean	(SD)
Punitive damages cap only	Cap on punitive damages only (1 = yes)	0.13	(0.33)
NE damages cap only	Cap on non-economic damages only (1 = yes)	0.28	(0.45)
Caps on both punitive and NE damages	Caps on both punitive and non-economic damages, or on total damages (1 = yes)	0.19	(0.39)
NE damages cap	Cap on non-economic damages, with or without a cap on punitive damages, or cap on total damages (1 = yes)	0.55	(0.50)
JSL reform	0 = joint and several liability; 1 = proportionate liability or defendant must be responsible for > 20% of harm	0.61	(0.49)
Expert requirements	Requirements for expert testimony or certification of merit in medical malpractice cases (1 = yes)	0.54	(0.50)
Suit rate	Rate of OB malpractice suits per 100,000 births	22.8	(18.0)
N	State-months over 21 years	12,600	

Expert Requirements

Interviews with attorneys suggested that expert requirements were a primary cause of declining medical malpractice lawsuits. The exact requirements vary somewhat across states and include laws that require an affidavit or certificate of merit from a medical expert before a medical malpractice case can move forward (28 states) and standards for who can qualify as a medical expert (32 states). I obtained data on these requirements from the National Conference of State Legislatures, which enumerates the language of the expert laws and their statutory citation.[2] I then cross-referenced the statutory citations in Nexis Uni to obtain the effective date of each law. I initially separated out merit certification requirements and expert witness standards, but their intent and effects are similar so I ultimately combined them into a single indicator (1 = expert requirements). The description and average for this measure are in table B.1.

Rate of Obstetric Malpractice Lawsuits

To measure malpractice litigation activity, I used the NPDB Public Use Data File, which contains data on 1,123,266 malpractice claims and 25,054 obstetrics-related claims involving acts committed between January 1, 1994, and December 31, 2015.[3] I calculated the rate of obstetric malpractice suits per 100,000 births for each state and year by dividing the number of obstetric lawsuits from the NPDB by the number of births per state and year. Similarly, I calculated the total rate of malpractice suits per 100,000 population for each state and year by dividing the total number of claims by official population statistics.[4] As indicated in table B.1, the average rate of obstetric-related malpractice claims was 22.8 per 100,000 births, or 0.023%.

REPRODUCTIVE HEALTH LAWS

To obtain data on reproductive health laws, I searched websites and then cross-referenced them with statutes in Nexis Uni to obtain the effective date of the laws (month and year). The NARAL website has details on state laws, including their statute names and numbers.[5] I supplemented this information with data from the Guttmacher Institute, which summarizes current laws governing abortion and contraception.[6] I obtained details on statutes that criminalize substance use among pregnant women as a form of child abuse from Child Welfare Information Gateway, which lists the relevant statutes, and I cross-referenced these statutes in Nexis Uni to find their effective dates for longitudinal analysis.[7] The Midwives Alliance of North America and the North American Registry of Midwives provided data on the legality and regulation of midwifery, with statutory citations that I could cross-reference.[8]

Pre-Viability Abortion Bans

Some states have abortion bans at specific gestational ages or have total abortion bans in their statutory laws. These laws include pre-*Roe* abortion bans that state legislatures never repealed, although they are unconstitutional and unenforceable. They also include recent "heartbeat bills" and total abortion bans that intend to go into effect immediately if *Roe v. Wade* is repealed. Around 2010, when many state governorships and/or legislatures shifted to Republican control, several states enacted second-trimester abortion bans—often at 20 to 24 weeks—based on a scientifically unsound claim that fetuses can feel pain at that point in pregnancy. While I initially separated out pre-*Roe* and second-trimester abortion bans, their effects tend to operate in the same direction and they share the goal of prohibiting abortion. These bans also followed

TABLE B.2. Descriptions and Descriptive Statistics for State-Level Reproductive Laws, 1995–2015

Variable	Metric	1995	2015
Abortion ban	1 = never repealed pre-Roe abortion ban or has second-trimester abortion ban	17 (34%)	25 (50%)
"Partial-birth" abortion ban	1 = ban on intact dilation and extraction (D&X) abortion procedure	0 (0%)	32 (64%)
Waiting period	1 = mandatory waiting period before an abortion	15 (30%)	27 (54%)
Parental involvement	1 = parental notification or parental consent requirement for minors	28 (56%)	39 (78%)
Feticide law	1 = legal recognition of fetuses as possible victims of homicide	9 (18%)	35 (70%)
Drug abuse	1 = prenatal substance use defined as child abuse	3 (6%)	20 (40%)
Reporting requirement	1 = special reporting requirement for abortion providers	30 (60%)	43 (86%)
Facility restrictions	1 = abortion clinics required to meet standards of ambulatory surgery centers and/or physical specifications for room size or corridor width	7 (14%)	26 (52%)
Hospital privileges	1 = abortion providers must have hospital admitting privileges and/or be located within 30 miles of a hospital	3 (6%)	22 (44%)
Mandatory ultrasound	1 = abortion providers must conduct a sonogram and show it to women seeking an abortion	0 (0%)	16 (32%)
Midwifery prohibited	1 = direct-entry midwifery illegal by statute	12 (24%)	7 (14%)
Clinic protection	1 = state protects women's health clinics from violence	12 (24%)	17 (34%)
N	States	50	

distinct temporal trends, with states copying one another in enacting new restrictions around the same time. For these reasons, the analyses in this book combine these types of abortion bans together. Table B.2 illustrates the frequency of pre-viability abortion bans at the beginning and end of the 1995–2015 study period. As table B.2 shows, the number of state-level pre-viability abortion bans increased during this period.

Procedure Bans

Beginning in the late 1990s, many states legislatively prohibited the intact dilation and extraction (D&X) abortion procedure, which the anti-abortion movement calls "partial-birth abortion" (a non-medical term). Intact D&X is a surgical procedure that removes a deceased fetus from the uterus in a second-trimester abortion or after an intrauterine fetal demise. Abortion providers use this procedure in less than 0.5% of all abortions in the United States. Intact D&X is most common in cases involving an intrauterine fetal demise or a fetus with severe congenital anomalies, and it can be safer for the mother in second-trimester abortions.

There were several important dates for legal action regarding "partial-birth abortion" bans. In 1995, the Republican-led US Congress passed a "partial-birth abortion" ban, which President Clinton vetoed in 1996 and 1997. In 2000, the US Supreme Court struck down individual state laws that banned "partial-birth abortion" in *Stenberg v. Carhart*.[9] In response, President George W. Bush signed the Partial-Birth Abortion Ban Act of 2003 into law on November 5, 2003.[10] After that time, few states passed additional bans on the intact D&X procedure, but many of those with previous procedure bans did not repeal them. In the 2007 case of *Gonzales v. Carhart*, the US Supreme Court upheld the 2003 federal Partial-Birth Abortion Ban Act.[11] I coded states with state-level D&X procedure bans as having a "partial-birth abortion" ban after November 2003, even though the federal ban was in effect for all states. As a result, there was very little change in these statutes from 2003 to 2013, when some state legislatures again began to legislate state-specific "partial-birth abortion" bans. Table B.2 illustrates the frequency of "partial-birth abortion" bans in 1995 and 2015. Notably, no states had "partial-birth abortion" bans in 1995, but many states enacted them in 1997 and 1998. By 1999, more than half of states had these laws.

Mandatory Waiting Periods for Abortion

All states require that patients have informed consent before undergoing medical treatment, but abortion counseling requirements often include a mandatory waiting period of at least 24 hours, and up to 72 hours, between counseling and an abortion.[12] Currently, 27 states have mandatory waiting periods, and 14 require that counseling take place in person. I created an indicator for whether a state required a waiting period between counseling and an abortion (1 = yes). Table B.2 shows the frequency of mandatory waiting periods in 1995 and 2015.

Parental Involvement for Minors

A majority of states require parental notification or parental consent before minors can obtain an abortion. There is some variation in parental involvement laws: some require consent or notification of one parent, but four states require the involvement of both parents. Some require government-issued identification (10 states) and/or proof of parenthood (four states). I was unable to conserve all of this variation in the analysis, and instead used an indicator of whether a state had a parental notification or parental consent requirement for minors seeking an abortion (1 = yes). Table B.2 shows the frequency of parental involvement laws in 1995 and 2015.

Feticide Laws

Many states have enacted fetal homicide laws to increase penalties for crimes against pregnant women. These laws often have names like the Fetal Protection Act, the Preborn Victims of Violence Act, and the Unborn Victims of Violence Act. Currently, 38 states have fetal homicide laws and 29 states apply fetal homicide laws to the earliest stage of pregnancy. Table B.2 shows the prevalence of fetal homicide laws in 1995 and 2015.

Criminalization of Prenatal Substance Use

States have increasingly criminalized pregnant women with substance abuse problems for being pregnant while addicted to drugs or alcohol. Several states have convicted women for child abuse because of substance use in pregnancy and others have expanded their child-welfare policies to include prenatal drug exposure as a form of child abuse or neglect. Some also require healthcare providers to report prenatal substance use and others require healthcare providers to test for it. For the purpose of analysis, I use an indicator for whether the state defines prenatal substance use as child abuse or neglect. Table B.2 illustrates the frequency of these laws in 1995 and 2015 and reveals a dramatic rise in these laws over time.

Reporting Requirements

Most US states require abortion providers to submit regular reports to the state. Some require them to indicate the method of payment, and some require information about the woman's reason for seeking the procedure. I use an indicator for abortion reporting requirements in the analysis, and table B.2 shows the prevalence of these laws in 1995 and 2015.

Facility Restrictions

Two of the more common TRAP laws that states have enacted over time are strict laws that apply a state's standards for ambulatory surgical centers to abortion clinics and laws that specify measurements for room size and/or corridor width. Notably, most ambulatory surgical centers offer procedures that are riskier and require higher levels of sedation than first-trimester abortions. Room size and corridor specifications do not improve safety, and their purpose is to force clinics to close. I grouped these laws together to create an indicator for facility restrictions. Table B.2 shows the prevalence of these laws at the beginning and end of the 1995–2015 period, with significant increases across states after 2010.

Hospital Admitting Privileges and Distance to Hospital Laws

Other important TRAP laws include requirements that providers have admitting privileges or transfer agreements with a local hospital, and laws that specify a maximum distance between the clinic and the hospital. These requirements are not necessary for safe transfer to a hospital if there are complications, but they create barriers to abortion services because hospitals do not have to offer privileges to abortion providers. I created an indicator for whether a state requires that abortion providers have hospital privileges, have a transfer agreement with a hospital, and/or be located within a specific proximity to a hospital. Table B.2 illustrates the frequency of these laws in 1995 and 2015, and reveals that few states had these laws in 1995 but over two fifths had them in 2015.

Mandatory Ultrasound Laws

Since 2009, some states have also implemented mandatory ultrasound laws that require abortion providers to perform an ultrasound and show it to the pregnant woman prior to performing an abortion. I collected data on these laws and used them in some analyses of later periods. As

Table B.2 shows, no states had these laws in 1995, but 32% of states had enacted them by 2015.

Prohibitions of Direct-Entry Midwifery

Some states prohibit direct-entry midwives from practicing legally," which severely restricts out-of-hospital birthing options for women. Others permit it but leave it unregulated. More midwifery-friendly states regulate and license midwives. I initially coded midwifery in 5 categories:

5 = regulated: licensure, certification, registration, or permit
4 = unregulated: legal by judicial interpretation or statutory inference
3 = unregulated: not legally defined, but not prohibited
2 = unregulated: legal by statute, but licensure unavailable
1 = unregulated: prohibited by statute, judicial interpretation, or stricture of practice

I later collapsed these categories and tested indicators for both 1 = midwifery is licensed and regulated compared to 0 = all others (unregulated and illegal), and 1 = midwifery is illegal and prohibited by statute compared to 0 = all others (regulated and unregulated). I use the indicator for whether midwifery is illegal in the models in chapters 5 and 7. Table B.2 illustrates the frequency of this indicator in 1995 and 2015. Notably, more states permitted direct-entry midwifery over time.

Clinic Protection

Some states explicitly protect women's clinics against violence by mandating buffer zones or implementing other laws that prohibit interference. Clinic protections guarantee equal protection for women using abortion services and restrict the ability of anti-abortion protestors from engaging in threats or use of force. I used an indicator for whether a state had a law protecting abortion clinics, women's health clinics, or women seeking abortion services. Table B.2 shows the frequency of these laws during the 1995–2015 period, illustrating that the number of states with these protections rose from about one quarter to about one third of states.

Appendix C

BIRTH DATA AND METHODS

For the quantitative analyses, I analyzed the effects of tort and reproductive health laws on birth outcomes using birth certificate data from the Natality Detail Files (1995–2015). The Natality Detail Files contain data on all recorded births in the United States (averaging slightly less than 4 million births per year). Because of the large number of cases, I drew a 10% random sample (nearly 400,000 per year). Throughout this book, I define low-risk births as births between 37 and 42 weeks gestation to women without a previous cesarean, carrying one baby (singleton) that is positioned head-down (vertex), without maternal conditions of diabetes, hypertension, eclampsia, cardiac disease, or lung disease, and without complications of placenta previa, placenta abruptio, premature rupture of membranes, cord prolapse, hydramnios (low amniotic fluid), blood clotting disorders, or uterine bleeding. VBAC-eligible births are otherwise low-risk births to mothers with a previous cesarean. Table C.1 illustrates the total number of births in the sample by year, the number of low-risk births, and the number of VBAC-eligible births.

Health-related research makes extensive use of the Natality Detail Files, but these data have some known data quality problems. Hospitals must collect the data and submit it to state vital records offices, and then the Natality Branch creates a national data set. As a result, data quality depends critically on the training of the hospital staff completing the birth certificate, resulting in inconsistent quality. There is no national standard with follow-up or oversight. Lean budgets have produced lower standards for the timeliness and quality of data since the late 1990s.[1] Birth certificates correspond imperfectly with medical record data, which represent the "gold standard." Agreement between birth certificates and medical records is "almost perfect" for measures of delivery method (vaginal or cesarean), prior obstetrical history, and infant Apgar score. Agreement with medical records is also "substantial" for several

TABLE C.1. Sample Size by Year, Natality Detail Files 1995–2015

Year	All Births		Low-Risk Births		VBAC-Eligible Births	
	N	%	N	%	N	%
1995	387,153	4.6%	231,683	5.2%	26,973	4.1
1996	386,963	4.6%	231,191	5.1%	27,030	4.1
1997	384,483	4.6%	230,274	5.1%	27,045	4.1
1998	391,067	4.6%	235,064	5.2%	27,247	4.2
1999	392,561	4.6%	235,397	5.2%	27,303	4.2
2000	403,999	4.8%	242,530	5.4%	28,737	4.4
2001	401,251	4.8%	240,823	5.4%	30,288	4.6
2002	400,374	4.7%	239,147	5.3%	31,400	4.8
2003	395,186	4.7%	236,753	5.3%	31,687	4.8
2004	397,814	4.7%	239,351	5.3%	32,240	4.9
2005	414,799	4.9%	205,297	4.6%	34,409	5.2
2006	427,416	5.1%	211,613	4.7%	35,843	5.5
2007	432,777	5.1%	242,726	5.4%	38,084	5.8
2008	426,462	5.1%	238,279	5.3%	37,580	5.7
2009	414,019	4.9%	147,022	3.3%	23,075	3.5
2010	400,827	4.7%	197,508	4.4%	34,072	5.2
2011	396,871	4.7%	165,527	3.7%	29,405	4.5
2012	395,833	4.7%	168,285	3.7%	30,646	4.7
2013	394,408	4.7%	171,543	3.8%	31,731	4.8
2014	399,224	4.7%	190,923	4.2%	35,194	5.4
2015	399,552	4.7%	194,897	4.3%	36,312	5.5
Total	8,443,039	100%	4,495,833	100%	656,301	100%

other important variables, including gestational age, but agreement is only moderate for most maternal risk factors and comorbidities and for several complications of pregnancy, labor, and delivery.[2]

These data problems could lead to misestimates of the effects of complications on maternity care outcomes. In most cases, these misestimates are likely to be undercounts of risks and complications, leading to a possibility that some maternity care outcomes, like induction or cesarean delivery, will have medical indications when there appear to be none. Since hospitals influence maternity care practices and hospitals that provide low-quality birth certificate data are likely to be low-quality in other dimensions, worse-than-average hospitals may be especially likely to underestimate complications. Even though these measures are imperfect, they are the best indicators of clinical risk that are available at the population level, and undercounts of complications are unlikely to significantly change the effects of the legal environment that underpin my arguments in this book.

INDIVIDUAL-LEVEL MEASURES

Variables in the dataset include place of delivery, birth attendant, parity, and medical and health data such as the number of prenatal visits, method of delivery, obstetrical procedures, medical risk factors, and infant health characteristics. Demographic variables include the age, race-ethnicity, marital status, and education of the mother. I measured age in years and the best measure of education that was available for all 21 years is a six-level measure (0–8 years, 9–12 years, high school/ GED, some college/associate degree, bachelor's degree, and master's, doctorate, or professional degree). I constructed mutually exclusive indicators for mother's race-ethnicity (Hispanic/Latina, black, Native American, Asian/Pacific Islander, or non-Hispanic white). Marital status is a dichotomous measure (married = 1). Parity is a mother's number of live births, including the current birth. Table C.2 illustrates the measures and descriptive statistics for these measures for all births, low-risk births to mothers without a previous cesarean, and VBAC-eligible births.

During the 1995–2015 period, there was a 2003 revision to the vital statistics birth certificate reporting measures. States adopted the revised birth certificate at different times, so that some states reported measures from the 1989 revision and others used the 2003 revision to report data in the same year.[3] This led to systematically incomplete data for a variety of measures across states and years, including adequacy of prenatal care, gestational weight gain, stimulation of labor, electronic fetal monitoring, prolonged labor, dysfunctional labor, fetal distress, cord prolapse, and premature rupture of membranes. As a result, I could not include these measures in the quantitative models. For risks that I used to exclude births from the low-risk or VBAC-eligible categories, like cord prolapse and premature rupture of membranes, I used the available measures as an exclusion criterion, but they may be undercounts

TABLE C.2. Descriptive Statistics for Maternal and Pregnancy Characteristics, Natality Detail Files 1995–2015

Variable	ALL		Low-risk		VBAC-eligible	
	Mean	(SD)	Mean	(SD)	Mean	(SD)
Maternal age (in years)	27.49	(6.13)	27.02	(6.01)	29.77	(5.57)
Education (1–6 scale)[i]	3.60	(1.32)	3.61	(1.33)	3.67	(1.33)
Parity (# of births)	2.07	(1.23)	1.98	(1.19)	2.67	(0.99)
	N	%	N	%	N	%
Education						
1 = 0–8 years	430,645	5.3%	248,144	5.3%	35,530	5.4%
2 = 9–11 years	1,221,035	15.1%	700,040	15.0%	85,729	13.1%
3 = HS/GED	2,316,571	28.6%	1,327,273	28.5%	184,762	28.2%
4 = Some college/associate degree	2,050,863	25.3%	1,163,615	25.0%	170,422	26.0%
5 = Bachelor's degree	1,305,503	16.1%	768,209	16.5%	112,913	17.2%
6 = Master's, doctorate, professional degree	772,843	9.5%	451,467	9.7%	66,945	10.2%
Race-ethnicity						
Hispanic/Latina	2,252,467	26.7%	1,254,157	26.4%	191,742	28.8%
Black, non-Hispanic	1,300,859	15.4%	677,910	14.3%	99,336	14.9%
Native American	91,170	1.1%	45,767	1.0%	6,164	0.9%
Asian	465,718	5.5%	260,475	5.5%	33,061	5.0%
White, non-Hispanic (ref)	4,262,879	50.5%	2,417,863	51.0%	328,435	49.3%
Married	5,328,869	63.1%	2,957,341	62.4%	468,342	70.3%
Previous cesarean	1,014,742	12.0%	—	—	—	—
Induced labor	1,792,526	21.2%	1,043,026	22.0%	32,532	4.9%
Pre-term	997,386	11.8%	—	—	—	—
Early-term	2,161,848	25.6%	1,368,013	28.8%	248,878	37.4%
Post-term	822,058	9.7%	—	—	—	—
Breech	392,332	4.6%	—	—	—	—
Multiple	274,469	3.3%	—	—	—	—
Diabetes	345,384	4.1%	—	—	—	—
Chronic hypertension	89,756	1.1%	—	—	—	—
Pre-eclampsia	343,160	4.1%	—	—	—	—
Eclampsia	23,829	0.3%	—	—	—	—
Dependent Variables						
Early-term induction	410,793	4.9%	265,870	5.6%	—	—
Early-term repeat cesarean[ii]	291,221	28.7%	—	—	219,524	33.6%
Electronic fetal monitor (EFM)[iii]	2,939,806	83.9%	1,760,449	83.8%	207,277	80.4%
Cesarean[iv]	2,369,977	28.1%				
Primary cesarean	1,435,453	17.4%	638,162	13.5%	—	—
Repeat cesarean	873,957	10.6%	—	—	569,246	85.5%
N	8,443,039		4,742,440		665,913	

i For mother's education, N = 8,097,460 in the full sample because of 345,579 missing cases.

ii Denominator includes births to mothers with a previous cesarean only. For the whole sample, N = 1,014,742 births. For VBAC-eligible births, N = 652,725.

iii Includes 1995–2003 only because some states stopped reporting EFM after 2003. For all births, N = 3,506,193. For low-risk births, N = 2,100,376. For VBAC-eligible births, N = 257,923.

iv There were 187,370 births without information about whether the mother had a previous cesarean. These births included 60,567 cesareans, but there is no way to discern if they were primary or repeat cesareans. As a result, the denominator for primary and repeat cesareans as a proportion of all births is N = 8,255,669.

because of inconsistency in the data. Table C.3 illustrates the patterns in missing data for the dependent variables in chapters 4–7 for the whole sample over time.

As table C.3 shows, the number of missing cases increases dramatically for some measures, like EFM use, after the introduction of the 2003 revision of the birth certificate. This includes some complications, like placenta abruptio (after 2003), placenta previa (after 2004), cord prolapse (after 2004), and premature rupture of membranes (after 2006), that I used to exclude cases from the subsamples of low-risk and VBAC-eligible births. In other words, missing data on these medical complications could mean that a small number of cases in the low-risk and VBAC-eligible subsamples had these complications. These complications are rare: when data were available, placenta previa occurred in 0.33% or less of pregnancies, placenta abruptio occurred in 0.58% or less, and premature rupture of membranes was slightly more common at approximately 3% of valid cases.

For most individual-level variables in the models, the number of missing cases in the full sample was less than 5% and often less than 1% (4.1% for education, 1.0% for Hispanic ethnicity, 0.55% for black ethnicity, 1.1% for Native American ethnicity, 5.5% for Asian ethnicity, 0.3% for parity, 3.7% for previous cesarean, 0.32% for induction). Some pregnancy complications had reliable data for the whole 1995–2015 period (1.17% missing for breech presentation, 0 missing for multiple births, 0.19% missing for diabetes, chronic hypertension, preeclampsia, and eclampsia.) As a result, I used listwise deletion for missing data in the models. For EFM, the dependent variable in chapter 5, the amount of missing data increased from less than 1% before 2003 to 6.11% in 2003 and 19.18% in 2004. No states reported EFM use on their birth certificate form after 2006. As a result, models of EFM include data from 1995 to 2003 only.

STATE-LEVEL CONTROL VARIABLES

While I am primarily interested in the effects of tort and reproductive health laws, a variety of state-level characteristics may influence maternity care practices. All models control for economic indicators from the US Bureau of Economic Analysis and US Census Bureau: per capita income (adjusted for inflation in thousands of 2015 dollars)[4] and percentage of the population living below the federal poverty line. I used

TABLE C.3. Percentage Missing by Year, Natality Detail Files 1995–2015

Year	Induced labor	EFM	Cesarean	VBAC	Midwife-attended birth	Out-of-hospital birth
1995	0.47	0.46	0.00	0.00	0.17	0.00
1996	0.31	0.31	0.00	0.00	0.09	0.00
1997	0.25	0.25	0.00	0.00	0.04	0.00
1998	0.40	0.39	0.00	0.00	0.02	0.00
1999	0.61	0.61	0.00	0.00	0.03	0.00
2000	0.51	0.51	0.00	0.00	0.03	0.00
2001	0.38	0.38	0.00	0.00	0.02	0.00
2002	0.31	0.31	0.00	0.00	0.02	0.00
2003	0.38	6.11	0.00	0.00	0.17	0.00
2004	0.17	19.18	0.00	0.00	0.22	0.00
2005	0.18	30.85	0.37	0.37	0.08	0.00
2006	0.16	48.77	0.34	0.37	0.06	0.00
2007	0.47	100.00	0.37	0.51	0.05	0.00
2008	0.60	100.00	0.34	0.64	0.05	0.00
2009	0.38	100.00	0.31	21.91	0.05	0.00
2010	0.30	100.00	0.23	15.54	0.07	0.00
2011	0.32	100.00	0.21	9.74	0.11	0.00
2012	0.25	100.00	0.14	8.09	0.05	0.00
2013	0.13	100.00	0.13	6.55	0.06	0.00
2014	0.10	100.00	0.09	2.5	0.05	0.00
2015	0.04	100.00	0.06	1.21	0.05	0.00
Total	0.32	48.67	0.13	3.23	0.07	0.00

data for the percentage living below the poverty line by state and year. Models also control for health care indicators from the US Census Bureau, the Department of Health and Human Services, and Centers for Medicare & Medicaid Services (CMS): the percentage enrolled in Medicaid and percentage uninsured, the number of hospital beds per 1,000 population, and healthcare expenditures per capita, adjusted for inflation in thousands of 2015 dollars.[5] Table C.4 shows descriptions and descriptive statistics for these control variables.

I used measures of citizen ideology and state legislative ideology over time, developed by Berry et al.[6] These longitudinal measures

TABLE C.4. Descriptions and Descriptive Statistics for State-Level Controls

Variable	Metric	Mean (SD)	Source
Per capita income (PCI)	In thousands of 2015 dollars	41.38 (7.08)	US Bureau of Economic Analysis
% Poverty	% living below federal poverty line	12.61 (3.43)	US Census Bureau
% Uninsured	% without health insurance	13.63 (4.12)	US Census Bureau, Current Population Surveys
% Medicaid	% on Medicaid	13.42 (4.54)	
Beds	Hospital beds per 1,000 population	2.98 (0.93)	US Dept of Health and Human Services
Health care expenditures per capita	In thousands of 2015 dollars	6.82 (1.46)	Centers for Medicare and Medicaid Services (CMS), Office of the Actuary
Suit rate	Number of OB malpractice suits per 100,000 births	22.75 (18.00)	National Practitioner Data Bank, Public Use Data File
Average payment	Average payment in OB malpractice suits in thousands of 2015 dollars	608.76 (613.63)	
Citizen ideology[i]	Revised 1960–2016 citizen ideology series (0 = extremely conservative to 100 = extremely liberal)	50.12 (15.62)	Citizen and Government Ideology Data, 1960–2017 (https://rcfording.wordpress.com/state-ideology-data/)
State government ideology[ii]	NOMINATE measure of state government ideology (0 = extremely conservative to 100 = extremely liberal)	46.22 (14.88)	
N	State-years over 21 years	1050	

i Berry et al., 2007; Berry et al., 2010.
ii Berry et al., 2013.

use voting records in state legislatures, the outcomes of congressional elections, the interest group ratings of members of congress, the partisan division of state legislatures, and the party of the governor to gauge the political ideology of a state's citizens and of state legislatures over time, on a scale from 0 (extreme conservative) to 100 (extreme liberal). The measures account for changes in citizen and state government ideology over time, with some states experiencing more fluctuations between liberal and conservative views and Democratic versus Republican legislatures.

Citizen ideology refers to the average position of active voters in a state, on a liberal-to-conservative scale. The measure estimates citizen ideology in each congressional district based on an ideology score of the district's incumbent (from a rating organization) and an estimated ideology score for the challenger in the election (based on the average ideology score of all incumbents in the state from the same party), weighted by the election results. The state's citizen ideology score is an unweighted average of citizen ideology scores for the state as a whole. As a longitudinal measure, the citizen ideology measure changes over time. It estimates support for the incumbent and a "hypothetical challenger" during non-election years based on the results of the previous and following elections, with an assumption that voter support changes gradually between elections.

State government ideology is the average position on a liberal-to-conservative scale of state elected officials, weighted according to the power that they have over policy decisions. This measure allows for ideological distinctions within parties, and accounts for parties' share of seats in both state legislatures as well as the governorship. Berry et al. used ideology ratings for the governor and for representatives of the two major parties in both the state house and state senate, producing five separate annual ideology scores. To account for the relative power of each of these political actors, Berry et al. weighted these scores based on the assumption that the governor and the legislative branch are equally powerful (each holds 50% of the power in the state government) and that the two chambers of the legislative branch have equal strength (each has 25% of the power in the state government). They then calculated a score that weights the majority and minority parties based on their representation each chamber of the legislature to measure the state government's ideological midpoint at a specific point in time. Other scholars in political science have used these measures in numerous studies.[7]

STATISTICAL MODEL

I combined the birth data and state-level control variables with the legal data (Appendix B) and constructed multilevel logit models to analyze the effects of the legal environment on the odds of maternity care outcomes including early-term induction, EFM, cesarean delivery, and VBAC. Multilevel modeling (MLM) provides unbiased estimates of state-level and year-specific effects by accounting for the non-random nature of state-level and year-specific error terms.[8] Like a fixed-effects model, MLM controls for differences across states and years, but MLM uses clustered data to analyze all three levels (individual, state and year) and is designed to handle heterogeneity across contexts.[9] The models treat births as nested within states and years while including fixed effects for year. As a robustness check, I ran logistic regression models with fixed effects for state and the results were essentially the same.

The analysis uses three nested levels, assessing the effects of the legal environment on births within years and states. At the individual level are dichotomous (0 = no, 1 = yes) dependent variables measuring the odds of each maternity care outcome in the Natality Detail Files (early-term births in chapter 4; EFM in chapter 5; primary and repeat cesarean in chapter 6; VBAC, midwife-attended birth, and out-of-hospital birth in chapter 7; and weekend births in chapter 8). At the state level, models include economic and healthcare controls, tort or reproductive health laws, and, for tort models, the rate of obstetric malpractice litigation. This leads to the following prediction equation:

$$\log\left[\frac{\text{outcome}}{(1-\text{outcome})}\right]$$

$$= \gamma_0 + \gamma_1 \text{ (year)} + \gamma_2 \text{ (maternal and pregnancy characteristics}_{ij})$$

$$+ \gamma_3 \text{ (state economic and health care environment}_j) + \gamma_4 \text{ (state laws}_j) + u_{oj}$$

$$+ e_{ij}$$

In this equation, γ_0 is the individual-level intercept, γ_1 is the year fixed effect, γ_2–γ_4 are the vectors of fixed-effect coefficients for individual- and state-level variables, i represents the individual case, j represents the state in which the birth occurred, u represents the random (state-level) intercept, and e is the error term. The models account for clustering within states and compute maximum-likelihood standard errors for clustered data. While the slope or magnitude of individual-level variables can vary across states, the best-fitting model is an intercept-only model that treats the direction and magnitude of the fixed effects as similar across states. I used the PROC GLIMMIX procedure in SAS to estimate multilevel logit models.[10]

NOTES

INTRODUCTION

1 Morris, 2013. Cesareans are also called C-sections, but I will use the term *cesarean* throughout this book in order to be consistent.

2 Gourevitch et al., 2017; Plough et al., 2017.

3 Mythen, 2008; Rothman, 2014; Scamell, 2014; Scamell and Alaszewski, 2012.

4 A "birth doula" is a non-medical birth companion who supports a woman in labor by providing continuous care and emotional support.

5 Berk and Macdonald, 2009; Burawoy, 1983; Esping-Andersen, 1990; Williams, 2002. In the most well-known typology of welfare regimes, Esping-Andersen (1990) defined three ideal types of welfare regime in developed countries: liberal, conservative, and social democratic. These welfare state types connect the family to the state and the labor market, which means that they influence reproductive practices as well as gender and race.

6 Edelman, 2001; Edelman, 2016.

7 The 1989 birth certificate revision asked about EFM. After 2003, many states adopted a revised birth certificate form that did not ask about EFM. While not all states adopted the 2003 revision immediately, some states had no valid data after 2003 and could not be included in the analysis. Rather than omit entire states, I examined only the 1995–2003 period in chapter 5.

CHAPTER 1. BIRTH MATTERS

1 Throughout this book, I will use the cisgendered terms *woman* and *mother* to refer to individuals with a uterus, even though some individuals who give birth identify as gender-queer or as transmen. I made this choice for two reasons. First, procreation is perhaps the most quintessentially gendered activity that most individuals will ever experience. Others are likely to treat those who are pregnant as women during pregnancy and birth, and the vast majority self-identify as women, regardless of their sexual identity or partner's gender. Secondly, I find the language of "pregnant persons" to be both awkward and reminiscent of the false gender-neutrality of court cases that argued that discrimination against pregnant women was not gender discrimination.

2 Fenech and Thomson, 2014; Forssén, 2012.

3 Davis-Floyd, 2004; Jordan and Davis-Floyd, 1992; Rothman, 1982.

4 Davis-Floyd et al., 2009; Jordan and Davis-Floyd, 1992; Davis-Floyd and Sargent, 1997.

5 Davis-Floyd, 2004; Kitzinger, 2005; Rothman, 1982; Simonds, Rothman, and Norman, 2007.

6 Following Rothman (1982), I will primarily use the term *medical model* to describe obstetrician-attended hospital birth. It could also be called the *obstetric model* or the *hospital model.*

7 This book uses data from the United States, and therefore the literature review and discussion focus primarily on the United States. Other Anglo-American countries like Canada, the United Kingdom, and Australia have similar histories of medicalization of childbirth, but currently use more midwifery-based care than the US. They also have very different healthcare systems, medical malpractice environments, and reproductive rights laws.

8 Ehrenreich and English, 2010; Leavitt, 1988.

9 Rooks, 1999.

10 Goer and Romano, 2012; WHO, 1985.

11 Davis-Floyd, 2004; Rothman, 1982; Simonds, Rothman, and Norman, 2007; Wagner, 2008.

12 An episiotomy is a surgical incision at the opening of the vagina to enlarge the opening so that the baby can come through.

13 Goer and Romano, 2012; Wagner, 2008.

14 Donnison, 1999; Ehrenreich and English, 2010; Loudon, 1993; Loudon, 2000.

15 Abbott, 1988; Freidson, 1988; 2001; 2006.

16 Ehrenreich and English, 2010; Shaw, 2013.

17 Ehrenreich and English, 2010; Loudon, 2000.

18 Meyer and Rowan, 1977; Powell and DiMaggio, 1991.

19 Davis-Floyd and Sargent, 1997; Jordan and Davis-Floyd, 1992.

20 Jordan and Davis-Floyd, 1992: 56.

21 Davis-Floyd and Sargent, 1997.

22 Conrad, 2007; Davis-Floyd, 2004; Rothman, 1982.

23 Kitzinger, 2005; Morris, 2013; Simonds, Rothman, and Norman, 2007; Wagner, 2008.

24 All names of interviewees are pseudonyms.

25 Goer and Romano, 2012; Wagner, 2008; WHO, 1985.

26 Davis-Floyd, 2004; Tillett, 2005.

27 Conrad, 2007. *Medicalization* is the "process by which nonmedical problems become defined and treated as medical problems."

28 Borst, 1995; McKendry and Langford, 2001; Tjaden, 1987.

29 Cartwright and Thomas, 2001; Lane, 1995; Rothman, 2014; Scamell, 2014; Scamell and Alaszewski, 2012.

30 Axelrod, 1973; Fiske and Taylor, 2013; Mandler, 1984; Strauss, 1997.

31 Powell and Colyvas, 2008.

32 Conrad, 2007.

33 Craig et al., 2018; Freidson, 1988; Michalec, 2012; Michalec and Hafferty, 2013.

34 Conrad, 2007; Turner, 1987.

35 Swidler, 1986.

36 Swidler, 1986: 273.

37 Ehrenreich and English, 1978.

38 Leavitt, 1988: 179.

39 Collins and Bailey, 2012. The *Oxford Living Dictionaries* define "sciency" as "of a somewhat scientific or technical nature" (https://en.oxforddictionaries.com/definition/sciency).

40 Latour, Woolgar, and Salk, 1986; Starr, 2017.

41 Davis-Floyd, 2004; Tillett, 2005.

42 Romney, 1980.

43 Davis-Floyd, 2004.

44 Davis-Floyd, 2004.

45 Romney and Gordon, 1981.

46 Goer, 1995; Klein, 1988; Klein et al., 1994; Klein, 1995.

47 Goer and Romano, 2012; Tillett, 2005.

48 Misoprostol is a synthetic prostaglandin that is FDA approved for treating gastric ulcers. Since the 1990s, obstetricians have used it to ripen the cervix and induce labor, usually cutting the 200 µg pill into quarters and inserting one quarter of a pill into the vagina. It can also induce an abortion or complete a miscarriage that is in progress, often in conjunction with mifepristone (formerly called RU-486). One of its side effects is uterine hyperstimulation, which can cause fetal distress and increases the likelihood of uterine rupture. The studies that led ACOG to restrict VBAC since 1999 showed that the risk of uterine rupture was relatively low in the absence of labor induction, but unacceptably high in pregnancies with misoprostol induction. Instead of banning or restricting the use of misoprostol to induce labor, ACOG restricted the conditions under which obstetricians should attend VBAC.

49 Pitocin is a synthetic form of oxytocin, the hormone that is involved in uterine contractions and labor. Obstetricians use Pitocin to start labor, to increase the speed of labor, and to stop bleeding after birth. It can cause hyperstimulation of the uterus, maternal nausea, fetal distress, and, in extreme cases, uterine rupture.

50 Abrishami, Boer, and Horstman, 2014; Blume, 2013; Warner, 1978.

51 Dant, 1996; Schiermer, 2016.

52 Davis-Floyd, 2004; Rothman, 2000.

53 Alfirevic et al., 2017; Bassett, 1996; Goer and Romano, 2012; Graham et al., 2006; Parer, Ikeda, and King, 2009.

54 Bassett, Iyer, and Kazanjian, 2000.

55 Caronna, 2004; Scott et al., 2000.

56 Scientific management was a theory of management and industrial production developed by Frederick Winslow Taylor (sometimes called "Taylorism"). In the late 19th and early 20th centuries, Taylor used empirical methods to analyze efficient procedures for manufacturing. He studied time and motion patterns for manual labor to improve productivity and efficiency in factory production.

The goal of scientific management was to increase economic efficiency by observing the work process and optimizing work tasks. Many labor scholars criticized scientific management as inhumane and exploitative of workers. By the 1930s, scientific management was no longer a distinct school of thought, although elements of it remain in contemporary management and industrial engineering.

57 Bassett, Iyer, and Kazanjian, 2000; Petrakaki, Klecun, and Cornford, 2016; Warner, 1978.

58 Dant, 1996; Durkheim, 1995; Schiermer, 2016; Wyatt et al., 1993.

59 Amnesty International, 2010; Frisbie et al., 2004; Main et al., 2015; Mayer and Sarin, 2005.

60 Kitzinger, 2005; Kitzinger, 2012.

61 Goer and Romano, 2012.

62 Norsigian, 1992.

63 Simonds, Rothman, and Norman, 2007.

CHAPTER 2. LAW MATTERS

1 Institutions are "stable, valued, recurring patterns of behavior" that govern social behavior (Huntingdon 1968: 9).

2 DiMaggio and Powell, 1983: 148.

3 DiMaggio and Powell 1983; Meyer and Rowan, 1977; Powell and DiMaggio, 1991.

4 DiMaggio and Powell, 1983.

5 Abbott, 1988; Freidson, 2006.

6 Freidson, 2006.

7 DiMaggio and Powell, 1983; Powell and Colyvas, 2008.

8 Scott et al., 2000.

9 Grol, 2001; Mykhalovskiy and Weir, 2004; Timmermans and Kolker, 2004.

10 Powell and DiMaggio, 1991; Thornton, 2012. An *institutional logic* is the set of material and symbolic practices, beliefs, values, and assumptions that provide meanings within an institutional field. Institutional logics inform organizational behavior and decision-making within an institutional field.

11 DiMaggio and Powell, 1983.

12 Edelman, Uggen, and Erlanger, 1999; Edelman, 2002; Edelman, 2016.

13 Edelman, 2016: 12.

14 Bernstein, 2010; Danzon, 1985; Rabin, 1980.

15 Eisenberg et al., 1997; Eisenberg and Wells, 2006.

16 Yang et al., 2009. In statistical analyses, I test the effects of caps on non-economic damages, with or without caps on punitive damages, and of caps on punitive damages alone. Yang et al. 2009 used a similar approach, but distinguished maximum levels for non-economic damages (up to $250,000, $250,001–500,000, $500,001–750,000, and $750,000 or above). I ran models with these measures and the results were inconsistent—sometimes with positive effects of low-dollar caps, negative for mid-dollar caps, and positive again for high-dollar caps. For ease of interpretation, I did not separate out different upper limits for non-economic

damage awards, although I did run models that included caps on damages alone, caps on non-economic damages alone, and caps on both. In most cases, these models had similar results to models with caps on damages alone and caps on non-economic damages, with or without caps on punitive damages.

17 Brennan et al., 1991; Leape et al., 1991; Localio et al., 1991.

18 Ransom et al., 1996.

19 Mello and Brennan, 2001.

20 Mello et al., 2010.

21 Danzon, 1985; Hubbard, 2006.

22 Guirguis-Blake et al., 2006; Metzler and Meara, 2012. A frivolous lawsuit is any lawsuit that has no merit or justification in fact, and/or where the plaintiff knows that they have little chance of winning in court. Frivolous lawsuits may also be a form of harassment against the defendant.

23 Hubbard, 2006.

24 Kelly and Mello, 2005.

25 A *remittitur* is a procedural process that reduces an excessive jury verdict, such as excessively large money damages. A *legislative remittitur* is a process that reduces jury verdicts through legislation that assumes that those verdicts are necessarily excessive, without considering the specifics of any legal cases.

26 Danzon, 1985; Hyman and Silver, 2006; Localio et al., 1991; Mello and Brennan, 2001.

27 Avraham, 2007; Currie and MacLeod, 2008

28 MacCoun, 1996; Vidmar, 1995.

29 Avraham, 2007; Lee, Browne, and Schmit, 1994.

30 Currie and MacLeod, 2008.

31 To analyze the effects of JSL versus PL, statistical analyses throughout this book include an indicator for JSL reform (0 = JSL, 1 = PL).

32 Dranove and Watanabe, 2010.

33 The NPDB cautions that some providers charged in these cases may not specialize in obstetrics.

34 I obtained census population totals from United States Census Bureau, 2019 (www.census.gov/programs-surveys/popest/data/data-sets.All.html).

35 As I discuss in chapter 3, *defensive medicine* is the overuse of tests and procedures in order to reduce liability risk, rather than for legitimate medical reasons. Most maternity care providers and public health scholars view trends such as climbing cesarean rates as symptoms of defensive medicine.

36 I used multilevel models of states nested in years to account for the over-time trend. See Appendix C for details on the methods. Table 2.2 in the online Technical Appendix summarizes the descriptive statistics for state-level control variables. Table 2.3 in the online Technical Appendix displays descriptive statistics for the legal variables, and table 2.4 gives the model results. The intra-class coefficient (ICC) was 0.46, which means that the over-time trend (figure 2.3) explained about 46% of the change in lawsuits per 100,000 births from 1995 to 2015. The suit

rate was higher in wealthier states (higher per capita income and higher health-care expenditures per capita). A higher percentage uninsured or on Medicaid and more hospital beds per 1,000 were associated with fewer obstetric lawsuits. For measures of political ideology (see Appendix C), I used citizen ideology and state government ideology scores that range from 0 to 100, with 0 = extremely conservative and 100 = extremely liberal. These measures are correlated at 0.57, but they did not pose problems of multicollinearity (VIF < 2). State political ideology had mixed effects, so that the rate of lawsuits was higher when citizen ideology was more conservative and when government ideology was more liberal.

37 An average of 10.9 more in a model that included caps on non-economic damages with or without caps on punitive damages, and 11.2 more in a model that included caps on non-economic damages only and caps on both. The effects are all statistically significant in a two-tailed test, so these effects are unlikely to occur due to chance. The effect of 0.8 is statistically significant and positive. While this is small, I have more than 98% confidence, based on the statistical analysis, that these caps on damages are associated with a non-zero *increase* in the rate of lawsuits ($p < 0.02$). Separating out caps on non-economic damages alone and caps on both punitive and non-economic damages, caps on both were associated with 1.7 more lawsuits per 100,000 births. Caps on non-economic damages alone had no significant effect.

38 I created indicators for whether caps on punitive or non-economic damages were implemented within one year, both before and after the legislation, and included them in the model. For the year after implementation, I added the effect of having caps and the effect of caps being enacted within a year before calculating the predicted value.

39 Ross and Solinger, 2017; Shaw, 2013.

40 Luna and Luker, 2013; Ross and Solinger, 2017; Shaw, 2013.

41 Andreassen and Trondsen, 2010; Lazarus, 1994; Link et al., 2008.

42 Race-ethnicity and social class are distinct but related concepts in race-stratified societies like the United States. I try to avoid conflating them throughout this book, although many people of color have low incomes and many low-income people are people of color. People of color cross-cut all social classes but share a history of discrimination that leads race-ethnicity to have effects on health in general, and reproductive health in particular, that are independent of socioeconomic status. Empirically, people of color in the United States are also more likely than non-Hispanic whites to have low incomes because of the legacy of white supremacy. At the same time, people of all race-ethnicities can have low incomes and experience class-related disadvantages.

43 Davis, 1981; Roberts, 1997.

44 Owens, 2017.

45 Berry, 1998; Davis, 1981; Hernandez, 1976; Roberts, 1997.

46 Balsa and McGuire, 2003; Burgess, Fu, and Ryn, 2004; LaVeist, Rolley, and Diala, 2003; Link and Phelan, 1995; Malat, 2001.

47 Jerman, Jones, and Onda, 2016.
48 Dennis, Manski, and Blanchard, 2014; Jones, Upadhyay, and Weitz, 2013; Sable, 1982.
49 Gurr, 2011.
50 Link and Phelan, 1995; Link et al., 2008; Mayer and Sarin, 2005.
51 Cohen, 2008; LaVeist, 2000.
52 Amnesty International, 2010; Creanga et al., 2017; Frisbie et al., 2004; Main et al., 2015.
53 Amnesty International, 2010; Main et al., 2015; WHO et al., 2014.
54 Frisbie et al., 2004; Getahun et al., 2009; Paul et al., 2008.
55 Aron et al., 2000; Dubay, Kaestner, and Waidmann, 1999; Getahun et al., 2009; Morris and Schulman, 2014; Morris et al., 2016.
56 Bridges, 2011.
57 Luna and Luker, 2013; Ross and Solinger, 2017.
58 Ross, 2017; Ross and Solinger, 2017.
59 Morris and Robinson, 2017; Shaw, 2013.
60 NAPW, 2020.
61 Burns, Dennis, and Douglas-Durham, 2014.
62 Bird, 2014; Crist, 2010; Murphy, 2014.
63 Brown, 2014; Murphy, 2014.
64 Bird, 2014; Paltrow, 2012.
65 *People v. Jorgensen*, 2015 NY Slip Op.
66 Fentiman, 2017; Flavin, 2009; Flavin and Paltrow, 2010; Paltrow and Flavin, 2013.
67 Burrows, 2010.
68 Martin, 2014.
69 Driessen, 2006; Minkoff and Paltrow, 2004.
70 Borges, 2017; Kukura, 2017b; Pérez D'Gregorio, 2010; WHO, 2015. The WHO uses the term "disrespectful care." Some Latin American countries like Argentina and Venezuela have implemented laws prohibiting "obstetric violence." Obstetric violence can include verbal humiliation, physical violence, and/or forced or coerced medical interventions, often in conjunction with discrimination based on racial-ethnic or economic background, age, and gender identity.
71 The UN Declaration on the Elimination of Violence against Women defined "Gender-based Violence" as "Any act of gender-based violence that results in, or is likely to result in, physical, sexual or psychological harm or suffering to women, including threats of such acts, coercion or arbitrary deprivations of liberty, whether occurring in public or in private life" (UN 1993). Structural or institutional violence is physical and/or psychological violence perpetrated by a group or institution.
72 Anon., 2015; Laine, Taichman, and LaCombe, 2015: 320.
73 Schiller, 2015.
74 Beck, C., 2004; Kitzinger, 2006.
75 ImprovingBirth.org, 2014.
76 Anon., 2016; Bregel, 2016; Capozzola et al., 2016.

77 Zadrozny, 2015. For information on the initial case, see Grant, 2017. A story on the March 2017 settlement is available in Greenfield, 2017.

78 Anon., n.d. "Birth Video Epidural and Episiotomy."

79 Borges, 2017; Diaz-Tello, 2016; Kukura, 2017b.

80 Cantor, 2012; Draper, 1996; Fentiman, 2017; Morris and Robinson, 2017; Paltrow and Flavin, 2013.

81 Annas, 1990; Daniels, 1993; Draper, 1996; Samuels, 1991; Thornton and Paltrow, 1991. Lynn Paltrow, the Founder and Executive Director of NAPW, was a staff attorney at the ACLU, Reproductive Freedom Project and acted as counsel to the Estate of Angela Carder.

82 *Stoners v. George Washington University Hospital, et al.*, Civil Action No. 88–0M33 (Sup. Ct. D.C.).

83 *In Re A.C.*, 573 A.2d 1235.

84 *Cruzan v. Director, Missouri Dept. of Health*, 497 U.S. 261.

85 *In Re Baby Boy Doe*, 632 N.E.2d 326, 198 Ill. Dec. 267, 260 Ill. App. 3d 392.

86 Kukura, 2017a; Paltrow and Flavin, 2013.

87 Morris, 2013; Morris and Robinson, 2017.

88 Chavkin, 1992; Scott, 2002.

89 *New Jersey Division of Youth and Family Services v. V.M. and B.G. in the matter of J.M.G.*, 408 N.J. Super. 222, 974 A.2d 448.

90 Waters, 2011.

91 Daniels, 1993; Kukura, 2017a; Paltrow, 2012.

92 Burns, Dennis, and Douglas-Durham, 2014; Jones, Ingerick, and Jerman, 2018.

93 See Appendix C. Table 2.5 in the online Technical Appendix gives descriptive data on these laws, showing that states have passed a growing number of abortion restrictions over time.

94 Jones and Weitz, 2009; Medoff, 2012; Nash, 2019.

95 Alabama, Arizona, Arkansas, Delaware, Louisiana, Massachusetts, Michigan, Mississippi, New Mexico, Oklahoma, Washington, and West Virginia.

96 Kansas, North Dakota, and South Dakota. More recent efforts to pass total abortion bans are a moving target: at the moment that I write this, Alabama just passed a total abortion ban, following "heartbeat" laws that ban abortions after six weeks from a woman's last menstrual period in Ohio and Mississippi.

97 Delaware, Kentucky, Massachusetts, Minnesota, North Carolina, and Utah had second-trimester bans in 1995. By 2015, Alabama, Arizona, Arkansas, Georgia, Idaho, Indiana, Kansas, Kentucky, Louisiana, Michigan, Mississippi, Missouri, Nebraska, North Dakota, Ohio, Oklahoma, Texas, West Virginia, and Wisconsin had passed second-trimester abortion bans.

98 Alabama, Arizona, Arkansas, Florida, Indiana, Iowa, Kansas, Louisiana, Mississippi, North Carolina, North Dakota, Oklahoma, South Dakota, Texas, Virginia, and Wisconsin.

99 Title X is the federal Family Planning Program under the US Department of Health and Human Services that provides funding for affordable contraception

and other reproductive health services like cervical and breast cancer screening, and testing and treatment for sexually transmitted infections (STIs).

100 Jerman et al., 2017.

101 Goodwin, 2017; Reingold and Gostin, 2016.

102 Flavin and Paltrow, 2010.

103 Chiarello, 2013; Moore, Ryan, and Stamm, 2019.

104 Berry et al. (1998; 2013) measure the political ideology of citizens in a state and state legislatures over time (see Appendix C). The state legislature scores were considerably higher (or more liberal), on average, in woman-centered and patient-friendly states than in fetus-centered and provider-friendly states. The relationship with citizen political ideology was less clear.

CHAPTER 3. MYTHS OF MALPRACTICE

1 Powell and Colyvas, 2008; Powell and DiMaggio, 1991.

2 Powell and Colyvas, 2008; Swidler, 1986; Weick, 1995. According to Weick, *sensemaking* activities use known patterns, meanings, and understandings to negotiate meaning and construct a coherent account of the world.

3 Michalec, 2012; Michalec and Hafferty, 2013.

4 Heimer, 1999.

5 Edelman, 2016.

6 Hale, 2006; Lumalcuri and Hale, 2010; Reyes and Reyes, 2012; Shwayder, 2010. I searched these journals for review articles, research articles, data articles, discussions, editorials, examinations, mini reviews, news, practice guidelines, and replication studies containing the terms "malpractice" or "liability" from 1995 to 2015. I found 46 articles on this subject in *Obstetrics & Gynecology* and 30 in *AJOG*.

7 Shwayder, 2010. Among the obstetricians who had experienced lawsuits, some were named in a lawsuit that primarily involved another provider and some were named in lawsuits for gynecological procedures or lab errors rather than for bad birth outcomes.

8 Anderson et al., 2005.

9 Peters, 2009.

10 According to research by the Rand Corporation (Jena et al. 2012), obstetrics and gynecology is the seventh most frequent specialty to have a malpractice claim annually, after neurosurgery, thoracic-cardiovascular surgery, general surgery, orthopedic surgery, plastic surgery, and gastroenterology. Obstetrics and gynecology has the highest liability insurance premiums because of the longer statute of limitations for birth injury cases, which leads to the most expensive tail coverage costs.

11 Born and Karl, 2016; Smith, Celis, and Bird, 2015.

12 For the purpose of analysis in this book, I was unable to calculate accurate premium costs by state and over time because of significant within-state variation. I attempted to calculate average premium rates by state and year using reports from *Medical Liability Monitor*, but I was not confident in the accuracy of these

measures. Some states have insurance rates that vary by county or city. Some have multiple liability insurance companies, but no information is available about how much market share each company covered. I ultimately concluded that any use of the calculations that I had would be dubious at best.

13 Most states delay the statute of limitations until a child turns 18, although some have revised their statute of limitations to begin when a child turns six (Warlick, 1996).

14 Cartwright and Thomas, 2001; Lane, 1995; Scamell, 2014.

15 Beck, U.,1992; Heyman, Alaszewski, and Brown, 2013; Mythen, 2008; Power, 2007.

16 Cartwright and Thomas, 2001; Lane, 1995; Rothman, 2014; Scamell, 2014; Scamell and Alaszewski, 2012.

17 Bordalo, Gennaioli, and Shleifer, 2012; Tversky and Kahneman, 1992.

18 Powell and Colyvas, 2008.

19 Shwayder, 2010.

20 See chapter 1.

21 Shoulder dystocia occurs when a baby's head is delivered vaginally but the shoulders get stuck in the mother's pelvis. It is a rare complication that occurs in 0.2–0.3% of vaginal deliveries of babies in a vertex (head-down) position. It is one of the most frightening and unpredictable complications that maternity care providers can experience.

22 Davis-Floyd, 2004; Morris, 2013; Rothman, 1982; Simonds, Rothman, and Norman, 2007.

23 A *false positive* is an incorrect test result or evaluation that indicates that a condition is present when it is not.

24 Meyer and Rowan, 1977; Powell and DiMaggio, 1991.

25 Based on the classification scheme that I developed in chapter 2, Arizona is neither provider-friendly nor patient-friendly. Arizona changed from JSL to PL in 1995, and implemented expert requirements in 2004. In many respects, Arizona was very average among malpractice environments.

26 Approximately 45% of claims never lead to a lawsuit. Among those that do, only 1% of all types of malpractice suits, and 3.4% of obstetric malpractice suits, from 1995 to 2015 led to a judgement at trial. The rest were settled or dismissed. According to Peters (2009), when malpractice cases do end in a jury trial, physicians win 80–90% of cases with weak evidence of medical negligence, approximately 70% of cases with borderline evidence, and 50% of cases with strong evidence against them.

27 The exact requirements for expert testimony vary somewhat across states. The statistical analyses in this book include a single indicator measure that includes credential requirements for witnesses and requirements that plaintiff's lawyers provide a certification of merit from an expert before proceeding with a tort claim (coded as 1 = expert requirements).

28 *Endogenous* means having an internal cause or origin.

29 Abbott, 1988; Freidson, 1988; Freidson, 2006; Timmermans and Oh, 2010.

30 Abbott, 1988; Edelman, 2000z; 2016; Freidson, 2006.

31 Edelman, 2016; Heimer, 1999.

CHAPTER 4. WHAT'S THE RUSH?

1 From here on, I use the term *elective* induction.

2 Moore and Rayburn, 2006; Wing, 2000.

3 For examples, see Brody, 2003; Jarvis, 2010; and Cuda Kroen, 2011.

4 Simpson, 2010; Simpson and Thorman, 2005; Wing, 2000.

5 Here and in other chapters, I define low-risk births as births between 37 and 42 weeks gestation to women without a previous cesarean, carrying one baby (singleton) that is positioned head-down (vertex), without maternal diabetes, hypertension, eclampsia, cardiac disease, or lung disease, and without complications of placenta previa, placenta abruptio, premature rupture of membranes, cord prolapse, hydramnios (low amniotic fluid), blood clotting disorders, or uterine bleeding. I define otherwise low-risk births to mothers with a previous cesarean as VBAC-eligible births, where *VBAC* refers to vaginal birth after cesarean.

6 Dickert-Conlin and Chandra, 1999; LaLumia, Sallee, and Turner, 2015.

7 See also Leonhardt, 2006, or McPhate, 2017.

8 Shim, 2010. Shim defines *cultural health capital* as "the repertoire of cultural skills, verbal and nonverbal competencies, attitudes and behaviors, and interactional styles, cultivated by patients and clinicians alike, that, when deployed, may result in more optimal health care relationships" (1).

9 Gage-Bouchard, 2017; Gengler, 2014; Shim, 2010; Dubbin, Chang, and Shim, 2013.

10 Simpson and Thorman, 2005; Wing, 2000.

11 Clark et al., 2008; Szymczak and Bosk, 2012.

12 Hospitalists are physicians who specialize in hospital inpatient care and do not have a clinical office with scheduled patient appointments. Hospitalists perform many of the same tasks as residents. Obstetric hospitalists work exclusively in the Labor and Delivery department of a hospital, so that there is always a physician available to care for pregnant and laboring women. Hospitals that employ obstetric hospitalists do not always permit them to deliver babies, but research has found that they have lower cesarean delivery rates and better maternal and infant outcomes when they do.

13 ACOG, 2009b; Moore and Rayburn, 2006. Induction can be medically necessary because of maternal diabetes or high blood pressure, premature rupture of membranes (breaking of the amniotic sac without labor), a placenta that detaches from the uterine wall (abruptio placentae), intrauterine growth restriction, or insufficient amniotic fluid.

14 See table 4.1 in the online Technical Appendix for more detail.

15 Simpson, 2010; Simpson and Thorman, 2005.

16 Caughey and AHRQ, 2009; Simpson, 2010.

17 Mercer, 2005; Wagner, 2008. These medications include cervical ripening agents (dinoprostone or misoprostol) and artificial oxytocin to stimulate contractions

(Pitocin). See Wagner (2008) for an extensive discussion of the risks of hyper-stimulation of the uterus due to induction medications.

18 Ehrenthal, Jiang, and Strobino, 2010; Luthy, Malmgren, and Zingheim, 2004; Vahratian et al., 2005; Vrouenraets et al., 2005.

19 Politi et al., 2010.

20 ACOG, 2009b; 2013a; 2013b; 2019a. According to ACOG (2009b), maternal or fetal conditions that may be indications for labor induction include placental abruption, chorioamnionitis, fetal demise, gestational hypertension, preeclampsia, eclampsia, premature rupture of membranes, post-term pregnancy, maternal medical conditions (diabetes, renal disease, chronic pulmonary disease, or chronic hypertension), or fetal compromise (severe fetal growth restriction, isoimmunization, or oligohydramnios). ACOG reaffirmed this in 2013 and 2019.

21 Maternity care providers calculate the expected date of delivery (EDD) as 40 weeks from the woman's last menstrual period (LMP), which is approximately 38 weeks from conception. This is the standard method for calculating pregnant women's due date, even though it means that they are not actually pregnant in the first two weeks of their pregnancy.

22 ACOG, 2009b; Moore and Rayburn, 2006; Murthy et al., 2011.

23 ACOG, 2013a; 2013b.

24 Engle and Kominiarek, 2008; Glantz, 2005; Simpson, 2010; Spong et al., 2011. Apgar is a backronym based on the name of its originator, Dr. Virginia Apgar, and it stands for "appearance, pulse, grimace, activity, and respiration." An Apgar score ranges from 0 to 10, with 10 being the best score. Late prematurity leads to higher morbidity and mortality rates due to physiologic and metabolic immaturity, even when the infant is the size and weight of many term infants.

25 The raw numbers are available in the online Technical Appendix in table 4.2.

26 ACOG, 2004. The risk of stillbirth is small after 42 weeks, but there is also a risk of more difficult labor, birth trauma, growth restriction in the uterus, and meconium aspiration (when a fetus has a bowel movement (meconium) in the amniotic fluid and inhales some of the fluid).

27 Augensen et al., 1987; Bochner et al., 1988; Caughey and Bishop, 2006; Mohide, 1987; Yudkin, Wood, and Redman, 1987.

28 Kirmeyer et al., 2009; Simpson, 2010.

29 ACOG, 2009b.

30 The four measures are Elective Delivery, Cesarean Section, Exclusive Breast Milk Feeding, and Unexpected Complications in Term Newborns. The goal of these PC measures is for hospitals to decrease their rates of elective delivery before 39 weeks, to decrease their rate of cesarean delivery among first-time low-risk mothers, to increase the rate of exclusive breastfeeding, and to decrease the rate of unexpected complications. See Joint Commission, 2020.

31 Fisch et al., 2009; Osterman and Martin, 2014.

32 See Appendix C for details on the methods and measures.

33 Murthy et al. (2011) found the same effect.

34 Dubbin, Chang, and Shim, 2013; Gage-Bouchard, 2017; Shim, 2010.

35 See table 4.5, model 1, in the online Technical Appendix for model results. I calculated predicted probabilities at the mean value of all control variables. Model 2 in table 4.5 separates out caps on punitive damages alone, caps on non-economic damages alone, and caps on both. In model 2, the odds of early-term induction were 2.6% lower in states with caps on punitive damages only than in states with no caps on damages, but they were 14.7% higher in states with caps on non-economic damages only and 5% higher in states with caps on both.

36 Recall from chapter 1 that, under JSL, anyone with any responsibility for harm can be liable for the full damages. Under PL, defendants are liable in proportion to their responsibility.

37 Currie and MacLeod, 2008.

38 This is unsurprising given that none of the allegations in the National Practitioners' Databank (NPDB) were clearly related to scheduled early-term births.

39 This effect represented 7% higher odds for black women than for non-Hispanic white women for the whole 1995–2015 period, but 15% higher odds after 2009. The difference in odds was not significant before 2010. Similarly, Hispanic women had 4% lower odds of an early-term repeat cesarean before 2010, but 6% higher odds than non-Hispanic white women from 2010 to 2015. When normative pressures reinforced 39 weeks as the SOC, providers appear to have especially applied this guideline to non-Hispanic white women, while women of color were more likely to receive procedures outside the SOC. Again, this highlights health disparities that contribute to reproductive injustice.

40 See table 4.6, model 1 in the online Technical Appendix. If I separate out caps on punitive damages alone, caps on non-economic damages alone, and caps on both (model 2 in table 4.6), caps on punitive damages alone had no significant effects but the odds of an early-term repeat cesarean were 9.6% higher in states with caps on non-economic damages only and 6.3% higher in states with caps on both than in states with no caps on damages. I do not include a figure for early-term repeat cesareans because the effects of year are so strong that the predicted probabilities produce a graph that is hard to read.

41 The over-time trend represents the fixed effects of year, after accounting for all individual- and state-level effects.

42 DiMaggio and Powell, 1983.

43 See table 4.7 in the online Technical Appendix for model results for the two periods.

44 When I separated out caps on non-economic damages only and caps on both punitive and non-economic damages for 1995–2009, I found that the odds of early-term induction were 14.8% higher in states with caps on punitive damages alone, 25.6% higher in states with caps on non-economic damages alone, and 25.6% higher in states with caps on both than in states without caps on damages.

45 See table 4.8 in the online Technical Appendix for model results. When I separated out caps on non-economic damages and caps on both, the odds of an

early-term repeat cesarean were 20.1% higher in states with caps on punitive damages only, 14.4% higher in states with caps on non-economic damages only, and 29.2% higher in states with caps on both than in states without caps on damages from 1995 to 2009.

46 JSL reform and expert requirements had no significant effects on early-term repeat cesareans. More obstetric malpractice suits per 100,000 births were connected to a very small decrease in the odds of an early-term repeat cesarean in VBAC-eligible births.

47 Brennan et al., 1991; Leape et al., 1991; Localio et al., 1991; Mello and Brennan, 2001.

48 Grol, 2001; Mykhalovskiy and Weir, 2004; Timmermans and Kolker, 2004.

49 Freidson, 1988; Timmermans and Kolker, 2004.

50 Grol, 2001; Szymczak and Bosk, 2012; Timmermans and Kolker, 2004; Timmermans and Oh, 2010.

CHAPTER 5. THE MACHINE THAT GOES PING!

1 Some hospitals have wireless, waterproof monitors that laboring women can wear in the shower or while moving around the room.

2 A Doppler ultrasound is a sound-generating monitor that uses changes in frequency or wavelength to detect the fetal heartbeat.

3 Leonardi, Nardi, and Kallinikos, 2013; Maller, 2015; Pinch, 2008.

4 Petrakaki, Klecun, and Cornford, 2016.

5 Bridges, 2011.

6 Gordon et al., 1999; Hodnett et al., 2013.

7 Graham et al., 2006; Parer, 1997.

8 As I discussed in chapter 4, *iatrogenic risks* are risks that medical treatment or diagnostic procedures cause during the course of treatment.

9 ACOG, 2019; Mayberry, Clemmens, and De, 2002. Oxytocin is the main hormone that stimulates contractions, and it rises during labor. Epidurals also reduce the natural release of prostaglandin F2 alpha, which helps to thin out and open the cervix, beta-endorphins that help to manage pain, and epinephrine and norepinephrine, which increase the mother's energy and alertness.

10 Alfirevic et al., 2017; Goer, 1995; Wagner, 2008. Pitocin is a synthetic form of oxytocin that stimulates uterine contractions. It can overstimulate contractions, leading to fetal distress. For this reason, many nurses view it as a high-risk medication.

11 ACOG, 2009a; Goer, 1995; Goer and Romano, 2012; Parer, Ikeda, and King, 2009.

12 Abrishami, Boer, and Horstman, 2014; Blume, 2013.

13 Caronna, 2004; DiMaggio and Powell, 1983; Scott et al., 2000.

14 Bassett, 1996; Bassett, Iyer, and Kazanjian, 2000.

15 Bassett, Iyer, and Kazanjian, 2000; Morris, 2013.

16 Parer, Ikeda, and King, 2009.

17 ACOG, 2009a.

18 American Academy of Nursing, 2015.

19 Reports of fetal monitoring on birth certificates represent *reporting* rates and not necessarily use rates. There are limitations to using birth certificate data to measure EFM use, because reporting on birth certificates may not accurately reflect actual practices. Previous research has found that birth certificates are imperfectly correlated with medical record data, which is the "gold standard," but agreement with medical records for EFM is unknown. In the case of EFM, birth certificate data reveal variation in *reporting*, which may underestimate actual use because some clinicians or hospitals may neglect to report EFM on birth certificates. At the same time, *reporting* of EFM is itself a potential response to the legal environment because hospitals with an interest in signaling legal compliance should be especially likely to report EFM to signal compliance with the SOC. As a result, the dependent variable measures *reported* EFM use, which may underestimate actual use. See Appendix C for more details on the measures and methods.

20 As in other chapters, I define low-risk pregnancies as between 37 and 42 weeks gestation to women without a previous cesarean, carrying one baby (singleton) that is positioned head-down (vertex), and without placenta previa, placenta abruptio, premature rupture of membranes, cord prolapse or maternal diabetes, hypertension, or eclampsia. See Appendix B and Appendix C for measures and methods. The online Technical Appendix contains descriptive statistics for 1995–2003 (tables 5.1–5.3) and model results (table 5.4).

21 I discuss the results of model 1 in table 5.4 of the online Technical Appendix. This model uses a measure that combines caps on non-economic damages alone and caps on both non-economic and punitive damages. Model 2 in table 5.4 includes separate measures for non-economic damages alone and caps on both non-economic and punitive damages. In that model, caps on punitive damages alone had the expected negative relationship with EFM use, so that births in states with these caps had 5.0% *lower* odds of EFM (OR = 0.95) than states with no caps on damages. But births in states with caps on non-economic damages alone had 42.9% *higher* odds of EFM (OR = 1.429) and those in states with caps on both had 4.9% *higher* odds of EFM (OR = 1.049) than states without caps.

22 The odds are 25.5% higher in model 1 and 25.4% higher in model 2.

23 In model 1, the odds of EFM are 28.7% lower for births in states with PL than in states with JSL. In model 2, they are 19.1% lower. Hospitals can have *vicarious liability* under JSL, which is based on a third party's responsibility or ability to control another actor's negligent or malicious behavior. *Vicarious liability* occurs when care providers are legally responsible by association for the actions or omissions of others. It is a common concern for healthcare organizations that offer privileges to individual physicians or for care networks with providers who are not technically their employees.

24 The choice of a one-year period is somewhat arbitrary, but no other benchmark for the lead-up period was a better choice.

25 In model 1, the odds of EFM are 17.6% lower in the year before legislation to cap punitive damages than in other states without caps. In model 2, they are 23.5% lower. In the first year after enacting caps on punitive damages, the odds of EFM are only 5.5% lower than in states with no caps in model 1 and 10.6% lower in model 2. In other words, the difference in odds is larger before enacting caps than after. More than one year after enacting caps on punitive damages, the odds of EFM are 11.7% lower in model 1 and 23.0% in model 2 compared to states without any caps on damages. To calculate the odds for the first year after enacting a cap, one must examine the interaction between presence of a cap and its recent adoption (β (PunitiveCap)+β (EnactPunitive)= -0.11+0.06=-0.05; e-0.05=0.948).

26 The odds of EFM were 8.0% higher in the year *before* enacting caps on non-economic damages in model 1, and 11.2% in model 2, compared to other states without caps on damages. The odds of EFM were 12.8% higher in the year *after* enacting caps on non-economic damages in model 1, and 38.5% higher in model 2, compared to states without caps on damages. More than one year after passing caps on non-economic damages, there was no significant effect of these caps on the odds of EFM in model 1, but caps on non-economic damages alone were associated with 26.2% higher odds of EFM in model 2, while caps on both punitive and non-economic damages were associated with 21.4% lower odds of EFM use compared to states with no caps on damages. To calculate the odds for the first year after enacting a cap, one must examine the interaction between presence of a cap and its recent adoption (β(NECap)+β(EnactNEcap)= 0.01+0.11=0.12; e0.12=1.128).

27 Chaiken and Trope, 1999; Fiske and Taylor, 2013; Vaisey, 2009. The dual-process model has a basis in cognitive research that focuses primarily on individual values and motivations, but it can also apply to organizations as cultural actors that operate based on institutional scripts.

28 Schiermer, 2016.

29 Abrishami, Boer, and Horstman, 2014; Blume, 2013; Caronna, 2004; Scott et al., 2000.

30 Bassett, 1996; Simonds, Rothman, and Norman, 2007.

31 Bassett, 1996; Bassett, Iyer, and Kazanjian, 2000; Blume, 2013.

32 All states mandate informed consent, which is an ethical concept that is foundational within the medical profession. Failure to obtain informed consent constitutes malpractice and makes physicians liable for negligence or battery. As a result, tort liability risk may influence variation in informed consent. But there is also tremendous variation in adherence to the doctrine of informed consent: every institution develops its own list of procedures, surgeries, or situations that require full informed consent, and the amount that physicians have to disclose is subject to local norms. The principle of informed consent requires that all patients understand and agree to all medical procedures after receiving information about their diagnosis, the nature and purpose of any proposed treatment or procedure, and the risks and benefits of treatment in comparison to alternatives (including

doing nothing). According to the American Medical Association (1998), informed consent requires that the physician (not a delegated representative) should disclose and discuss:

The diagnosis, if known.

The nature and purpose of a proposed treatment or procedure.

The risks and benefits of proposed treatment or procedures.

Alternatives (regardless of cost or extent covered by insurance).

The risks and benefits of alternatives.

The risks and benefits of not receiving treatments or undergoing procedures.

Most states rely on the standard of what a "reasonable physician" would provide, but this is open to interpretation.

33 Ross and Solinger, 2017; Shaw, 2013.

34 See Appendix B for legal measures.

35 Results are available in table 5.5 of the online Technical Appendix.

36 All other variables are set to their mean values.

CHAPTER 6. IF IN DOUBT, CUT IT OUT

1 Carrier et al., 2013; Dubay, Kaestner, and Waidmann, 1999; Frakes, 2012; Yang et al., 2009.

2 As in other chapters, I define low-risk births as births between 37 and 42 weeks gestation to women without a previous cesarean, carrying one baby (singleton) that is positioned head-down (vertex), without maternal conditions of diabetes, hypertension, eclampsia, cardiac disease, or lung disease, and without complications of placenta previa, placenta abruptio, premature rupture of membranes, cord prolapse, hydramnios (low amniotic fluid), blood clotting disorders, or uterine bleeding. VBAC-eligible births are otherwise low-risk births to mothers with a previous cesarean. Table 6.1 in the online Technical Appendix shows the raw percentages.

3 ACOG, 1999.

4 WHO, 1985; WHO, 2014.

5 These figures are based on data from the National Hospital Discharge Survey (NHDS) for 1970–2004, and from vital records after 1989.

6 Molina et al., 2015.

7 Brink, 2002; Cyr, 2006.

8 Amnesty International, 2010; Main et al., 2015; WHO et al., 2014.

9 WHO, 2014.

10 Amnesty International, 2010; Aron et al., 2000; Creanga et al., 2017; Getahun et al., 2009; Main et al., 2015.

11 Gould, Davey, and Stafford, 1989; Wagner, 2008. In the online Technical Appendix, tables 6.2 to 6.4 show descriptive statistics and table 6.5 shows model coefficients and odds ratios.

12 The predicted probability for non-Hispanic whites and Native Americans is the same, so the line for non-Hispanic whites does not show up in figure 6.3. In

models of repeat cesarean in VBAC-eligible births, there was no difference in the odds of a repeat cesarean between black, Hispanic, and non-Hispanic white women with a previous cesarean but no other risk factors, but Asian women had 28% lower odds than otherwise similar non-Hispanic white women.

13 Burgess, Fu, and Ryn, 2004; LaVeist, 2000; Link et al., 2008.

14 This is not something that I can test directly because the NCHS vital statistics data do not contain information about insurance before 2014.

15 Dubbin, Chang, and Shim, 2013; Shim, 2010.

16 Kozhimannil, Law, and Virnig, 2013; Plough et al., 2017. See also Ariadne Labs, n.d.

17 Brink, 2002; Weaver and Magill-Cuerden, 2013. Sometimes this phrase refers to Victoria Beckham ("Posh Spice"), who had cesarean deliveries with her four children. Victoria Beckham has said that her cesareans were medically indicated and not elective.

18 See Bob Parsons, "Joan Rivers—Go Daddy Girl," www.youtube.com/watch?v=rZ5P1jOTuzI. She actually had a body double in the commercial; see Duboff, 2011.

19 DeVries et al., 2008; Gossman, Joesch, and Tanfer, 2007; Hopkins, 2000.

20 Handa, Harris, and Ostergard, 1996; Handa et al., 2011; Memon and Handa, 2012; Lukacz et al., 2006; Nygaard, 2005; Sze, Sherard, and Dolezal, 2002.

21 ACOG, 2007.

22 Truven Health Analytics, 2013.

23 Lippman, 1999.

24 Aron et al., 2000; Bridges, 2011; Davis, 1983; Frisbie et al., 2004; Getahun et al., 2009; LaVeist, 2000; Morris et al., 2016; Morris and Schulman, 2014; Roth and Henley, 2012.

25 Declercq et al., 2006.

26 ACOG, 2007; Declercq et al., 2014.

27 Daltveit et al., 2008; Gray et al., 2007; Kennare et al., 2007; Lyell et al., 2005; Makoha et al., 2004; Molina et al., 2015; Morales, Gordon, and Bates, 2007; Smith et al., 2006.

28 Knight et al., 2008.

29 DiMatteo et al., 1996.

30 Hansen et al., 2008; MacDorman et al., 2006; Molina et al., 2015.

31 Bordalo, Gennaioli, and Shleifer, 2012; Scamell, 2014.

32 ACOG has ethically permitted primary cesarean delivery on maternal request (CDMR) since 2007. CDMR accounts for an estimated 0.5–2.5% of births and may be more a symptom than a cause of rising cesarean rates.

33 Austin et al., 2013; Morris, 2013; Politi, Han, and Col, 2007.

34 These figures do not include other allegations that might be related to claims that a provider should have performed a cesarean or should have performed one sooner, like "failure to treat fetal distress," "failure to perform procedure," "failure

to recognize a complication," "delay in treatment," "delay in treatment of identified fetal distress," or "improper choice of delivery method."

35 Braun et al., 2016; Johnson, Blair, and Stanley, 2011. The main causes of CP are low birth-weight, premature birth, and maternal infection during pregnancy—none of which a cesarean delivery can resolve. The CDC estimates that *birth hypoxia*, the disruption of the oxygen supply during birth, is responsible for less than 10% of CP cases.

36 Goer, 1995; Wagner, 2008.

37 See Appendix C for more detail on measures and methods.

38 In the online Technical Appendix, table 6.5 shows the results for two models: one that combines caps on non-economic damages and caps on both punitive and non-economic damages, and one that separates out caps on non-economic damages only from caps on both. The intra-class correlation (ICC) in an intercept-only model was 0.037, which suggests that state-level variation accounts for 3.7% of the variation in primary cesareans in low-risk births. In model 1, the odds-ratio (OR) for caps on punitive damages only and for caps on non-economic damages were both 0.97, suggesting that the odds of a cesarean were approximately 3% lower in states with caps (with all else being equal). When I analyzed caps on punitive damages alone, caps on non-economic damages alone, and caps on both in model 2, none of these caps had significant effects on the odds of a low-risk primary cesarean. Based on the −2 log likelihood (lower is better), model 1 improves upon the base model and provides a better fit to the data than model 2. Figure 6.5 shows predicted probabilities based on model 1.

39 Currie and MacLeod, 2008.

40 In the online Technical Appendix, table 6.6 shows the results for two models of the odds of a repeat cesarean in VBAC-eligible births. In model 1, caps on punitive damages only had no significant effect. The OR for caps on non-economic damages or caps on both was 0.95, which suggests approximately 5% higher odds of a repeat cesarean in states with non-economic damage caps. When I analyzed caps on punitive damages alone, caps on non-economic damages alone, and caps on both in model 2, only caps on both had an effect on the odds of a low-risk primary cesarean, and its effect was only statistically significant in a one-tailed test (OR = 0.96).

41 ACOG, 1999.

42 Goer, 1995; Hoffman et al., 2005; Lydon-Rochelle, 2001; Rossi and Prefumo, 2015; Wagner, 2008; Wing, Lovett, and Paul, 1998.

43 The five measures are Elective Delivery, Cesarean Birth, Antenatal Steroids, Health Care–Associated Bloodstream Infections in Newborns, and Exclusive Breast Milk Feeding. These PC measures define quality improvement in terms of lower rates of elective delivery before 39 weeks, lower rates of cesarean delivery among first-time low-risk mothers, higher rates of antenatal steroid use in preterm births, lower rates of infection in newborns, and higher rates of exclusive breastfeeding. See Joint Commission, 2020.

44 ACOG, 2010.
45 In the online Technical Appendix, table 6.7 shows the results for each time period for primary cesareans in low-risk births, and table 6.8 shows the results for repeat cesareans in VBAC-eligible births.
46 Danielian, Wang, and Hall, 1996; Gifford et al., 1995; Hannah et al., 2000.

CHAPTER 7. CHOICE MATTERS
1 Ehrenreich, 2008; Paltrow, 2012.
2 Boucher, 2004; Luker, 1984; Rohlinger, 2002.
3 Daniels, 1993; Fentiman, 2017; Minkoff and Paltrow, 2004; Paltrow, 2012.
4 It is interesting to think about physicians and hospitals "offering" or refusing to "offer" VBAC. Presumably vaginal birth would happen most of the time without physicians needing to do anything—it is something that a woman does, not something that a physician "offers." But the idea that it is something that physicians and hospitals "offer" fits with the idea that physicians "deliver" babies, rather than women giving birth.
5 Rosenstein et al., 2019.
6 Morris and Robinson, 2017.
7 Chalidze, 2009; Heidari, 2015; Miller, 2007; Minkoff and Paltrow, 2004; Stohl, 2017.
8 United Nations, 1948; 1966.
9 Strasser, 1999.
10 There are exceptions for unconscious or mentally incompetent patients.
11 Goldberg, 2009; *Cruzan v. Director, Missouri Dept. of Health*, 497 U.S. 261.
12 Declercq et al., 2006; Goldberg, 2009.
13 Fentiman, 2017; Morris and Robinson, 2017.
14 *In Re AC.*, 573 A.2d 1235; *In Re Baby Boy Doe*, 632 N.E.2d 326, 198 Ill. Dec. 267, 260 Ill. App. 3d 392.
15 *Pemberton v. Tallahassee Memorial Regional Center*, 66 F. Supp. 2d 1247.
16 *In Re A.C.*, 573 A.2d 1235; *In Re Baby Boy Doe*, 632 N.E.2d 326, 198 Ill. Dec. 267, 260 Ill. App. 3d 392.
17 Hartocollis, 2014.
18 *Dray v. Staten Island University Hospital*, 2016 NY Slip Op.
19 *In Re A.C.*, 573 A.2d 1235; *Dray v Staten Is. Univ. Hosp.*, 2018 NY Slip Op.; McClain-Freeney, 2018.
20 Rinat Dray had two previous cesareans and Laura Pemberton had a vertical cesarean scar.
21 Chalidze, 2009; Pratt, 2013.
22 National Institutes of Health, 1981.
23 King, 2010; Mozurkewich and Hutton, 2000; Rossi and D'Addario, 2008.
24 Gregory et al., 1999; Lydon-Rochelle, 2001; Spong et al., 2007.
25 Hoffman et al., 2005; Rossi and Prefumo, 2015; Wagner, 2008; Wing, Lovett, and Paul, 1998.
26 ACOG, 1999.

27 Rossi and Prefumo, 2015; Wagner, 2008; Wing, Lovett, and Paul, 1998.
28 Pratt, 2013; Rosenstein et al., 2019; Stohl, 2017.
29 Daltveit et al., 2008; Gray et al., 2007; Kennare et al., 2007; Makoha et al., 2004; Morales, Gordon, and Bates, 2007.
30 Latendresse, Murphy, and Fullerton, 2005; MacDorman et al., 2012.
31 See Appendix C for the measures and methods. Table 7.2 in the online Technical Appendix shows the models. In the base model, I examined the effects of maternal characteristics on the odds of VBAC, and found that the odds of VBAC decreased by 3.7% for each year of maternal age, and increased by 8% for each additional level of maternal education. Hispanic mothers had 3% higher odds and Asian women had 28% higher odds of VBAC than non-Hispanic white women. The odds of VBAC were 14% higher for married than unmarried women, and they increased by 44% with each subsequent birth. At the state level, the odds of VBAC were slightly lower in states with a higher per capita income and a lower percentage in poverty, lower in states with more hospital beds per 1000, and lower in states with higher per capita healthcare expenditures.
32 See model 1 in table 7.2 of the online Technical Appendix. Based on the log-likelihood (smaller is better), model 1 provides a better fit to the data than model 2, which includes a count of TRAP laws instead of separating out the most common TRAP laws. The results for model 2 are similar, except that bans on abortion in the second trimester have a larger negative effect, and laws that define prenatal substance use as child abuse are not statistically significant. The number of TRAP laws is significant in a one-tailed test only, but is not in the predicted direction.
33 Abortion bans, procedure bans, waiting periods, parental involvement, feticide, drug abuse as child abuse, reporting requirements, facility restrictions, hospital admitting privileges, or proximity requirements, and prohibitions of direct-entry midwifery by statute.
34 No abortion restrictions, waiting periods, parental involvement, feticide, drug abuse as child abuse, reporting requirements, facility restrictions, hospital admitting privileges, or proximity requirements, and protection of health clinics from violence or other damages.
35 These figures hold all other variables at their mean to obtain the predicted probability.
36 ACOG, 1999.
37 The results for the pre- and post-ACOG periods are in table 7.3 of the online Technical Appendix.
38 Klassen, 2001.
39 The results of these models are in table 7.4 of the online Technical Appendix.
40 While the predicted probabilities are higher than one might expect from the raw data, it is important to remember that they are model predictions that hold constant all other characteristics and separate out low-risk pregnancies without a previous cesarean.
41 Janssen et al., 2009.

CHAPTER 8. REPRODUCTIVE REGIMES

1 See table 8.2 in the online Technical Appendix.

2 Non-Hispanic white women were significantly less likely to give birth on weekends than Hispanic, African American, Native American, or Asian women. Older mothers, more educated mothers, married mothers, and mothers with more previous births were less likely to give birth on weekends. These characteristics are all associated with a higher likelihood of induction.

3 See table 8.3 in the online Technical Appendix for the model results.

4 Or. Rev. Stat. § 164.365 (Enacted 1972; Amended 2003).

5 Applicable provisions of Insurance Code. Or. Rev. Stat. §743A.066.

6 Or. Admin. R. 410-130-0562; Or. Dep't of Human Servs., Office of Medical Assistance Programs, Medical-Surgical Servs. Rulebook, 410-130-0562 (Dec. 2012).

7 Or. Rev. Stat. § 147.005 (Enacted 2003); Or. Admin. R. § 137-084-0001, -0010, -0020.

8 Applicable provisions of Insurance Code. Or. Rev. Stat. § 435.252-.256 (Enacted 2007).

9 US News and World Report, 2019b.

10 Florida is neither woman-centered nor fetus-centered, with a combination of anti-abortion and pro-choice reproductive health laws. It has a "partial-birth abortion" procedure ban, requires parental consent for minors seeking an abortion, defines prenatal substance use as child abuse, has special reporting and licensing requirements for abortion providers, does not explicitly protect clinics from violence, and has implemented TRAP laws including requirements that abortion clinics meet ambulatory surgical center standards and that abortion providers have hospital admitting privileges and a transfer agreement with a nearby hospital. On the other hand, it has no abortion ban or waiting period for abortion, does not prohibit public employees from providing information about abortion, had no feticide law until 2014, and has licensing for direct-entry midwifery. Vermont is a woman-friendly state, with very pro-midwifery laws and no anti-abortion laws except a special reporting requirement for abortion providers.

11 US News and World Report, 2019a.

12 US Department of Health and Human Services, 2016.

13 Ambulatory Surgical Facilities. Miss. Code Ann. § 41-75-1(e), (f) (Original Statute Enacted 1983; Relevant Provision Enacted 1991; Last Amended 2012), § 41-75-5 (Enacted 1983); Miss. Code R. §§ 15 301 044.

14 Ambulatory Surgical Facilities. Miss. Code Ann. § 41-75-29(2) (Enacted 1991); Miss. Code R. §15 301 044.

15 Ambulatory Surgical Facilities. Miss. Code Ann. §41-75-1(f) (Enacted 2012). Courts have permanently enjoined this provision as violating the "undue burden" standard (see *Planned Parenthood of Southeastern Pa. v. Casey*, 505 U.S.).

16 Ambulatory Surgical Facilities. Miss. Code Ann. § 41-75-17 (Enacted 1983).

17 Ambulatory Surgical Facilities. Miss. Code Ann. § 41-75-1. Originally enacted in 1983, amended in 1996 and 2006.

18 Miss. Code Ann. § 97-3-3 (Enacted 1952; Last Amended 1997).

19 Miss. Code Ann. § 41-41-45 (Enacted 2007).

20 Miss. Code Ann. §§ 41-41-133, -137, -141 (Enacted 2014).

21 H.B. 1510, 133rd Leg. Sess. (Miss. 2018).

22 *Jackson Women's Health Org., et al. v. Currier, et al.*, 760 F. 3d 448.

23 Thebault, 2019.

24 Arons, 2019.

25 Miss. Code Ann. §§ 41-41-71, 41-41-73 (Enacted 1997). The federal "partial-birth abortion" ban superseded this law in 2006 (*Gonzales v. Carhart*, 550 U.S.).

26 Miss. Code Ann. §§ 41-41-151 to -163 (Enacted 2016), H.B. 519, Reg. Sess. (Miss. 2016).

27 Miss. Code Ann. §§ 41-41-33, -35 (Enacted 1991; Last Amended 1996).

28 Miss. Code Ann. § 41-41-33 (1996).

29 Miss. Code Ann. §§ 41-41-31 (Enacted 1991), 51, -53, -57 (Enacted 1986), -55 (Enacted 1986; Last Amended 2007). When parents are divorced or unmarried, only the custodial parent must consent.

30 Miss. Code Ann. § 41-41-91 (Enacted 2002) and §§ 41-41-97, -99 (Enacted 2010).

31 Miss. Code Ann. § 11-7-13; Miss. Code Ann. § 97-3-19, -37.

32 Miss. Code Ann. § 97-3-37.

33 SB 2797, Jan. 19, 2015. SB 2518, Feb. 8, 2016. SB 2577, Jan. 16, 2017. SB 2426, Jan. 15, 2018. SB 2113, Jan. 11, 2019.

34 Hensley and Liu, 2019.

35 Bridges, 2011.

APPENDIX A. INTERVIEW METHODS AND DATA

1 Lewis-Beck, Bryman, and Liao, 2004; Tremblay, 1957.

2 Tavory and Timmermans, 2014.

APPENDIX B. LEGAL DATA AND MEASURES

1 The data were available at http://econ.columbia.edu/public_data.

2 Morton, 2014.

3 US Department of Health and Human Services (USDHHS), *National Practitioner Data Bank Public Use Data File (NPDB)*. The NPDB cautions that some providers charged in these cases may not specialize in obstetrics.

4 I obtained Census population totals from United States Census Bureau, 2019 (www.census.gov/programs-surveys/popest/data/data-sets.All.html).

5 NARAL Pro-Choice America, n.d.

6 See www.guttmacher.org.

7 Child Welfare Information Gateway, 2019.

8 See http://mana.org/ and http://narm.org/.

9 *Stenberg v. Carhart*, 530 U.S.

10 18 U.S. Code § 1531—Partial-birth abortions prohibited.
11 *Gonzales v. Carhart*, 550 U.S.
12 Missouri, North Carolina, Oklahoma, South Dakota, and Utah currently have 72-hour mandatory waiting periods. Most other states with mandatory waiting periods have 24-hour waits. A few (Alabama, Arkansas, and Tennessee) have 48-hour waiting periods.

APPENDIX C. BIRTH DATA AND METHODS

1 Luke et al., 2006.
2 DiGiuseppe et al., 2002.
3 Luke et al., 2006.
4 US Bureau of Labor Statistics, 2020 (www.bls.gov/data/inflation_calculator.htm).
5 Henry J. Kaiser Family Foundation, 2017.
6 Berry et al., 1998; 2013.
7 Berry et al., 2007; Berry et al., 2013; Enns and Koch, 2013.
8 Raudenbush and Byrk, 2002.
9 Allison, 2009; Ene et al., 2015; Raudenbush and Byrk, 2002.
10 Ene et al., 2015.

BIBLIOGRAPHY

Abbott, Andrew. 1988. *The System of Professions: An Essay on the Division of Expert Labor*. Chicago: University of Chicago Press.

Abrishami, Payam, Albert Boer, and Klasien Horstman. 2014. "Understanding the Adoption Dynamics of Medical Innovations: Affordances of the Da Vinci Robot in the Netherlands." *Social Science & Medicine* 117:125–33.

Alfirevic, Zarko, Declan Devane, Gillian Gyte, and Anna Cuthbert. 2017. "Continuous Cardiotocography (CTG) as a Form of Electronic Fetal Monitoring (EFM) for Fetal Assessment during Labour." *The Cochrane Database of Systematic Reviews* 2(2):CD006066.

Allison, Paul David. 2009. *Fixed Effects Regression Models*. Los Angeles: Sage.

American Academy of Nursing. 2015. "Electronic Fetal Heart Rate Monitoring." Retrieved April 17, 2019 (www.aannet.org/initiatives/choosing-wisely/electronic-fetal-heart-rate-monitoring).

American College of Obstetricians and Gynecologists (ACOG). 1999. "Practice Bulletin No. 5. Vaginal Birth after Previous Cesarean Delivery." *Obstetrics & Gynecology* 94(1).

———. 2004. "Practice Bulletin No. 55. Management of Postterm Pregnancy." *Obstetrics & Gynecology* 104:639–46.

———. 2007. "Committee Opinion, No. 394. Cesarean Delivery on Maternal Request." *Obstetrics & Gynecology* 110(6):1501–5.

———. 2009a. "Practice Bulletin No. 106: Intrapartum Fetal Heart Rate Monitoring: Nomenclature, Interpretation, and General Management Principles." *Obstetrics & Gynecology* 114(1):192–202.

———. 2009b. "Practice Bulletin No. 107: Induction of Labor." *Obstetrics & Gynecology* 114(2, part 1):386–97.

———. 2010. "Practice Bulletin No. 115: Vaginal Birth after Previous Cesarean Delivery." *Obstetrics & Gynecology* 116(2, part 1):450–63.

———. 2013a. "Committee Opinion No. 560: Medically Indicated Late-Preterm and Early-Term Deliveries." *Obstetrics & Gynecology* 121(4):908–10.

———. 2013b. "Committee Opinion No. 561: Nonmedically Indicated Early-Term Deliveries." *Obstetrics & Gynecology* 121(4):911–915.

———. 2019. "Practice Bulletin No. 209: Obstetric Analgesia and Anesthesia." *Obstetrics & Gynecology* 133(3):e208–25.

Amnesty International. 2010. *Deadly Delivery: The Maternal Health Care Crisis in America*. New York: Amnesty International.

Anderson, Gerard F., Peter S. Hussey, Bianca K. Frogner, and Hugh R. Waters. 2005. "Health Spending in the United States and the Rest of the Industrialized World." *Health Affairs* 24(4):903–14.

Andreassen, Hege K., and Marianne Trondsen. 2010. "The Empowered Patient and the Sociologist." *Social Theory & Health* 8(3):280–87.

Annas, George J. 1990. "Foreclosing the Use of Force: A.C. Reversed." *The Hastings Center Report* 20(4):27–29.

Anon. n.d. "Birth Video Epidural and Episiotomy." Retrieved May 20, 2019 (www .youtube.com/watch?v=lCfXxtoAN-I).

Anon. 2015. "Our Family Secrets." *Annals of Internal Medicine* 163(4):321.

Anon. 2016. "Nurse Wrestles Mother into Position—Injury Results." *Healthcare Risk Management* 38(10), October 10, 2016 (www.reliasmedia.com/articles/138752 -nurse-wrestles-mother-into-position-injury-results).

Ariadne Labs. n.d. "Delivery Decisions Initiative." *Ariadne Labs.* Retrieved May 21, 2020 (www.ariadnelabs.org/areas-of-work/delivery-decisions-initiative/).

Aron, David C., Howard S. Gordon, David L. DiGiuseppe, Dwain L. Harper, and Gary E. Rosenthal. 2000. "Variations in Risk-Adjusted Cesarean Delivery Rates According to Race and Health Insurance." *Medical Care* 38(1):35–44.

Arons, Jessica. 2019. "The Last Clinics Standing." *American Civil Liberties Union.* Retrieved June 19, 2019 (www.aclu.org/issues/reproductive-freedom/abortion /last-clinics-standing).

Augensen, Kare, Per Bergsj, Torunn Eikeland, Kjell Askvik, and Johannes Carlsen. 1987. "Randomised Comparison of Early versus Late Induction of Labour in Post-Term Pregnancy." *BMJ* 294:1192–5.

Austin, Laurel C., Susanne Reventlow, Peter Sandøe, and John Brodersen. 2013. "The Structure of Medical Decisions: Uncertainty, Probability and Risk in Five Common Choice Situations." *Health, Risk & Society* 15(1):27–50.

Avraham, Ronen. 2007. "An Empirical Study of the Impact of Tort Reforms on Medical Malpractice Settlement Payments." *Journal of Legal Studies* 36(S2):S183–229.

Axelrod, Robert. 1973. "Schema Theory: An Information Processing Model of Perception and Cognition." *American Political Science Review* 67(4):1248–66.

Balsa, Ana I., and Thomas G. McGuire. 2003. "Prejudice, Clinical Uncertainty and Stereotyping as Sources of Health Disparities." *Journal of Health Economics* 22(1):89–116.

Bassett, Ken. 1996. "Anthropology, Clinical Pathology and the Electronic Fetal Monitor: Lessons from the Heart." *Social Science & Medicine* 42(2):281–92.

Bassett, Ken L., Nitya Iyer, and Arminee Kazanjian. 2000. "Defensive Medicine during Hospital Obstetrical Care: A By-Product of the Technological Age." *Social Science & Medicine* 51(4):523–37.

Beck, Cheryl Tatano. 2004. "Post-Traumatic Stress Disorder Due to Childbirth: The Aftermath." *Nursing Research* 53(4):216–24.

Beck, Ulrich. 1992. *Risk Society: Towards a New Modernity.* Newbury Park, CA: SAGE.

Berk, Richard, and John Macdonald. 2009. "The Dynamics of Crime Regimes." *Criminology* 47(3):971–1008.

Bernstein, Anita. 2010. "Distributive Justice through Tort (and Why Sociolegal Scholars Should Care)." *Law & Social Inquiry* 35(4):1099–1135.

Berry, Roberta M. 1998. "From Involuntary Sterilization to Genetic Enhancement: The Unsettled Legacy of Buck v. Bell." *Notre Dame Journal of Law, Ethics & Public Policy* 12:401–48.

Berry, William D., Evan J. Ringquist, Richard C. Fording, and Russell L. Hanson. 1998. "Measuring Citizen and Government Ideology in the American States, 1960–93." *American Journal of Political Science* 42(1):327–48.

Berry, William D., Evan J. Ringquist, Richard C. Fording, and Russell L. Hanson. 2007. "The Measurement and Stability of State Citizen Ideology." *State Politics & Policy Quarterly* 7(2):111–32.

Berry, William D., Richard C. Fording, Evan J. Ringquist, Russell L. Hanson, and Carl E. Klarner. 2010. "Measuring Citizen and Government Ideology in the U.S. States: A Re-Appraisal." *State Politics & Policy Quarterly* 10(2):117–35.

Berry, William D., Richard C. Fording, Evan J. Ringquist, Russell L. Hanson, and Carl Klarner. 2013. "A New Measure of State Government Ideology, and Evidence that Both the New Measure and an Old Measure Are Valid." *State Politics & Policy Quarterly* 13(2):164–82.

Bird, Bernice. 2014. "Fetal Personhood Laws as Limits to Maternal Personhood at Any Stage of Pregnancy: Balancing Fetal and Maternal Interests at Post-Viability among Fetal Pain and Fetal Homicide Laws." *Hastings Women's Law Journal* 25:39–56.

Blume, Stuart S. 2013. "Medical Innovations: Their Diffusion, Adoption, and Critical Interrogation." *Sociology Compass* 7(9):726–37.

Bochner, Clifford J., John Williams, Lony Castro, Arnold Medearis, Calvin J. Hobel, and Maclyn Wade. 1988. "The Efficacy of Starting Postterm Antenatal Testing at 41 Weeks as Compared with 42 Weeks of Gestational Age." *AJOG* 159(3):550–4.

Bordalo, Pedro, Nicola Gennaioli, and Andrei Shleifer. 2012. "Salience Theory of Choice under Risk." *Quarterly Journal of Economics* 127(3):1243–85.

Borges, Maria. 2017. "A Violent Birth: Reframing Coerced Procedures during Childbirth as Obstetric Violence." *Duke Law Journal* 67:827–62.

Born, Patricia H. and J. Bradley Karl. 2016. "The Effect of Tort Reform on Medical Malpractice Insurance Market Trends: Medical Malpractice Tort Reform and Insurance Markets." *Journal of Empirical Legal Studies* 13(4):718–55.

Borst, Charlotte G. 1995. *Catching Babies: The Professionalization of Childbirth, 1870–1920.* Cambridge, MA: Harvard University Press.

Boucher, Joanne. 2004. "The Politics of Abortion and the Commodification of the Fetus." *Studies in Political Economy* 73:69–88.

Braun, Kim Van Naarden, Nancy Doernberg, Laura Schieve, Deborah Christensen, Alyson Goodman, and Marshalyn Yeargin-Allsopp. 2016. "Birth Prevalence of Cerebral Palsy: A Population-Based Study." *Pediatrics* 137(1):e20152872.

Bregel, Sarah. 2016. "Alabama Mom Finally Gets Justice After Traumatic Birth Left Her Permanently Injured." *Babble*. Retrieved May 20, 2019 (www.babble.com/parenting/caroline-malatesta-alabama-mom-wins-law-suit-after-birth-injury/).

Brennan, Troyen A., Liesi Hebert, A. Russell Localio, and Joseph P. Newhouse. 1991. "Incidence of Adverse Events and Negligence in Hospitalized Patients." *NEJM* 324:370–6.

Bridges, Kiara. 2011. *Reproducing Race*. Berkeley: University of California Press.

Brink, Susan. 2002. "Too Posh to Push? Cesarean Sections Have Spiked Dramatically. Progress or Convenience?" *U.S. News & World Report* 133(5):42–3.

Brody, Jane E. 2003. "As Cases of Induced Labor Rise, So Do Experts' Concerns." *New York Times*, January 14. Retrieved May 21, 2020 (www.nytimes.com/2003/01/14/health/as-cases-of-induced-labor-rise-so-do-experts-concerns.html).

Brown, Geneva. 2014. "Bei Bei Shuai: Pregnancy, Murder, and Mayhem in Indiana." *Journal of Gender, Race, and Justice* 17(2):221–56.

Burawoy, Michael. 1983. "Between the Labor Process and the State: The Changing Face of Factory Regimes under Advanced Capitalism." *American Sociological Review* 48(5):587–605.

Burgess, Diana J., Steven S. Fu, and Michelle Ryn. 2004. "Why Do Providers Contribute to Disparities and What Can Be Done about It?" *Journal of General Internal Medicine* 19(11):1154–9.

Burrows, Cassandra. 2010. "The War on Drugs Coming to a Womb Near You." *National Advocates for Pregnant Women*, June 10. Retrieved July 23, 2020 (advocatesforpregnantwomen.org/blog/2010/06/the_war_on_drugs_coming_to_a_w.php).

Burns, Bridgit, Amanda Dennis, and Ella Douglas-Durham. 2014. *Evaluating Priorities: Measuring Women's and Children's Health and Well-Being against Abortion Restrictions in the States*. Cambridge, MA: Ibis Reproductive Health and the Center for Reproductive Rights.

Cantor, Julie D. 2012. "Court-Ordered Care—A Complication of Pregnancy to Avoid." *NEJM* 366(24): 2237–40.

Capozzola, Damian D., Joshua H. Haffner, Kathleen Juniper, and Jamie Terrence. 2016. "'Bait and Switch' Advertising Brings $16 Million Verdict." *Healthcare Risk Management* 38(10).

Caronna, Carol A. 2004. "The Misalignment of Institutional 'Pillars': Consequences for the U.S. Health Care Field." *Journal of Health and Social Behavior* 45:45–58.

Carrier, Emily R., James D. Reschovsky, David A. Katz, and Michelle M. Mello. 2013. "High Physician Concern About Malpractice Risk Predicts More Aggressive Diagnostic Testing In Office-Based Practice." *Health Affairs* 32(8):1383–91.

Cartwright, Elizabeth, and Jan Thomas. 2001. "Constructing Risk." In *Birth by Design: Pregnancy, Maternity Care and Midwifery in North America and Europe*, edited by R. DeVries, C. Benoit, E. Van Teijlingen, and S. Wrede, 218–229. New York: Routledge.

Caughey, Aaron B., and J. T. Bishop. 2006. "Maternal Complications of Pregnancy Increase beyond 40 Weeks of Gestation in Low-Risk Women." *Journal of Perinatology* 26(9):540–5.

Caughey, Aaron B., and United States Agency for Healthcare Research and Quality (AHRQ). 2009. *Maternal and Neonatal Outcomes of Elective Induction of Labor.* Rockville, MD: United States Agency for Healthcare Research and Quality.

Chaiken, Shelly, and Yaacov Trope. 1999. *Dual-Process Theories in Social Psychology.* New York: Guilford Press.

Chalidze, Lisa L. 2009. "Misinformed Consent: Non-Medical Bases for American Birth Recommendations as a Human Rights Issue." *New York Law School Law Review* 54:59–104.

Chavkin, Wendy. 1992. "Women and Fetus: The Social Construction of Conflict." *Women & Criminal Justice* 3(2):71.

Chiarello, Elizabeth. 2013. "How organizational context affects bioethical decision-making: Pharmacists' management of gatekeeping processes in retail and hospital settings." *Social Science & Medicine* 98:319–29.

Child Welfare Information Gateway. 2019. "State Statutes Search." Retrieved June 5, 2019 (www.childwelfare.gov/topics/systemwide/laws-policies/state/).

Clark, Steven L., Michael A. Belfort, Gary A. Dildy, and Janet A. Meyers. 2008. "Reducing Obstetric Litigation through Alterations in Practice Patterns." *Obstetrics & Gynecology* 112(6):1279–83.

Cohen, Hillel W. 2008. "Getting Political: Racism and Urban Health." *American Journal of Public Health* 98:S17–19.

Collins, Dave, and Richard Bailey. 2012. "'Scienciness' and the Allure of Second-Hand Strategy in Talent Identification and Development." *International Journal of Sport Policy and Politics* 5(2):183–91.

Conrad, Peter. 2007. *The Medicalization of Society: On the Transformation of Human Conditions into Treatable Disorders.* Baltimore: Johns Hopkins University Press.

Craig, Sienna R., Rebekah Scott, and Kristy Blackwood. 2018. "Orienting to Medicine: Scripting Professionalism, Hierarchy, and Social Difference at the Start of Medical School." *Culture, Medicine and Psychiatry* 42(3):654–83.

Creanga, Andreea A., Carla Syverson, Kristi Seed, and William M. Callaghan. 2017. "Pregnancy-Related Mortality in the United States, 2011–2013." *Obstetrics & Gynecology* 130(2):366–73.

Crist, Juliana Vines. 2010. "The Myth of Fetal Personhood: Reconciling Roe and Fetal Homicide Laws." *Case Western Reserve Law Review* 60(3):851–87.

Cuda Kroen, Gretchen. 2011. "Doctors To Pregnant Women: Wait At Least 39 Weeks." *NPR*, July 18. Retrieved May 21, 2020 (www.npr.org/2011/07/18/138473097/doctors-to-pregnant-women-wait-at-least-39-weeks).

Currie, Janet, and W. Bentley MacLeod. 2008. "First Do No Harm? Tort Reform and Birth Outcomes." *Quarterly Journal of Economics* 123(2):795–830.

Cyr, Ronald M. 2006. "Myth of the Ideal Cesarean Section Rate: Commentary and Historic Perspective." *AJOG* 194(4):932–6.

Daltveit, Anne Kjersti, Mette Christophersen Tollanes, Hege Pihlstrom, and Lorentz M. Irgens. 2008. "Cesarean Delivery and Subsequent Pregnancies." *Obstetrics & Gynecology* 111(6):1327–34.

Danielian, P. J., J. Wang, and M. H. Hall. 1996. "Long Term Outcome by Method of Delivery of Fetuses in Breech Presentation at Term: Population Based Follow Up." *BMJ* 312(7044):1451–3.

Daniels, Cynthia R. 1993. *At Women's Expense: State Power and the Politics of Fetal Rights*. Cambridge, MA: Harvard University Press.

Dant, Tim. 1996. "Fetishism and the Social Value of Objects." *Sociological Review* 44(3):495–516.

Danzon, Patricia Munch. 1985. *Medical Malpractice: Theory, Evidence, and Public Policy*. Cambridge, MA: Harvard University Press.

Davis, Angela Y. 1981. *Women, Race, & Class*. New York: Vintage Books.

Davis-Floyd, Robbie E. 2004. *Birth as an American Rite of Passage*. Second Edition. Berkeley, CA: University of California Press.

Davis-Floyd, Robbie E., Lesley Barclay, Betty-Anne Daviss, and Jan Tritten. 2009. *Birth Models That Work*. Berkeley: University of California Press.

Davis-Floyd, Robbie E., and Carolyn Fishel Sargent. 1997. *Childbirth and Authoritative Knowledge*. Berkeley: University of California Press.

Declercq, Eugene R., Carol Sakala, Maureen P. Corry, and Sandra Applebaum. 2006. *Listening to Mothers II: Report of the Second National U.S. Survey of Women's Childbearing Experiences*. New York: Childbirth Connection.

Declercq, Eugene R., Carol Sakala, Maureen P. Corry, Sandra Applebaum, and Ariel Herrlich. 2014. *Listening to Mothers III: Report of the Third National U.S. Survey of Women's Childbearing Experiences*. New York: Childbirth Connection.

Dennis, Amanda, Ruth Manski, and Kelly Blanchard. 2014. "Does Medicaid Coverage Matter? A Qualitative Multi-State Study of Abortion Affordability for Low-Income Women." *Journal of Health Care for the Poor and Underserved* 25(4):1571–85.

DeVries, Raymond, Edwin van Teijlingen, Meredith Vanstone, Eugene Declercq, Ivy Lynn Bourgeault, Cecilia Benoit, Jane Sandall, and Sirpa Wrede. 2008. "Too Posh to Push? Comparative Perspectives on Maternal Request Caesarean Sections in Canada, the US, the UK and Finland." In *Patients, Consumers and Civil Society* (*Advances in Medical Sociology*, vol. 10), edited by S. M. Chambré and M. Goldner, 99–123. Bingley, UK: Emerald Group.

Diaz-Tello, Farah. 2016. "Invisible Wounds: Obstetric Violence in the United States." *Reproductive Health Matters* 24(47):56–64.

Dickert-Conlin, Stacy, and Amitabh Chandra. 1999. "Taxes and the Timing of Births." *Journal of Political Economy* 107(1):161–77.

DiGiuseppe, David L., David C. Aron, Lorin Ranbom, Dwain L. Harper, and Gary E. Rosenthal. 2002. "Reliability of Birth Certificate Data: A Multi-Hospital Comparison to Medical Records Information." *Maternal and Child Health Journal* 6(3):169–79.

DiMaggio, Paul J., and Walter W. Powell. 1983. "The Iron Cage Revisited: Institutional Isomorphism and Collective Rationality in Organizational Fields." *American Sociological Review* 48(2):147–60.

DiMatteo, M. Robin, Sally C. Morton, Heidi S. Lepper, Teresa M. Damush, Maureen F. Carney, Marjorie Pearson, and Katherine L. Kahn. 1996. "Cesarean Childbirth and Psychosocial Outcomes: A Meta-Analysis." *Health Psychology* 15(4):303–14.

Donnison, Jean. 1999. *Midwives and Medical Men.* 2nd edition. New Barnet, UK: Phillimore & Co.

Dranove, David, and Yasutora Watanabe. 2010. "Influence and Deterrence: How Obstetricians Respond to Litigation against Themselves and Their Colleagues." *American Law and Economics Review* 12(1):69–94.

Draper, Heather. 1996. "Women, Forced Caesareans and Antenatal Responsibilities." *Journal of Medical Ethics* 22(6):327–33.

Driessen, Marguerite A. 2006. "Avoiding the Melissa Rowland Dilemma: Why Disobeying a Doctor Should Not Be a Crime." *Michigan State University Journal of Medicine and Law* 10:1–56.

Dubay, Lisa, Robert Kaestner, and Timothy Waidmann. 1999. "The Impact of Malpractice Fears on Cesarean Section Rates." *Journal of Health Economics* 18(4):491–522.

Dubbin, Leslie A., Jamie Suki Chang, and Janet K. Shim. 2013. "Cultural Health Capital and the Interactional Dynamics of Patient-Centered Care." *Social Science & Medicine* 93:113–20.

Duboff, Josh. 2011. "Meet Joan Rivers' GoDaddy Body Double." *Yahoo! Entertainment,* February 8. Retrieved May 21, 2020 (www.yahoo.com/entertainment/blogs/the famous/meet-joan-rivers-godaddy-body-double-133015204.html).

Durkheim, Emile. 1995. *The Elementary Forms of Religious Life.* Reprint edition. New York: Free Press.

Edelman, Lauren B. 2002. "Legality and the Endogeneity of Law." In *Legality and Community: On the Intellectual Legacy of Philip Selznick,* edited by Robert A. Kagan, Martin Krygier, and Kenneth Winston, 187–202. New York: Rowman & Littlefield.

Edelman, Lauren B. 2016. *Working Law: Courts, Corporations, and Symbolic Civil Rights.* Chicago: University of Chicago Press.

Edelman, Lauren B., Christopher Uggen, and Howard S. Erlanger. 1999. "The Endogeneity of Legal Regulation: Grievance Procedures as Rational Myth." *American Journal of Sociology* 105(2):406–54.

Ehrenreich, Barbara, and Deirdre English. 2010. *Witches, Midwives, and Nurses: A History of Women Healers.* 2nd edition. New York: The Feminist Press at CUNY.

Ehrenreich, Nancy, ed. 2008. *The Reproductive Rights Reader.* New York: NYU Press.

Ehrenthal, Deborah B., Xiaozhang Jiang, and Donna M. Strobino. 2010. "Labor Induction and the Risk of a Cesarean Delivery among Nulliparous Women at Term." *Obstetrics & Gynecology* 116(1):35–42.

Eisenberg, Theodore, John Goerdt, Brian Ostrom, David Rottman, and Martin T. Wells. 1997. "The Predictability of Punitive Damages." *Journal of Legal Studies* 26(S2):623–61.

Eisenberg, Theodore, and Martin T. Wells. 2006. "The Significant Association between Punitive and Compensatory Damages in Blockbuster Cases: A Methodological Primer." *Journal of Empirical Legal Studies* 3(1):175–95.

Ene, Mihaela, Elizabeth A. Leighton, Genine L. Blue, and Bethany A. Bell. 2015. *Multilevel Models for Categorical Data Using SAS® PROC GLIMMIX: The Basics.* Paper 3430–2015. Columbia: SAS Institute, University of South Carolina.

Engle, William A., and Michelle A. Kominiarek. 2008. "Late Preterm Infants, Early Term Infants, and Timing of Elective Deliveries." *Clinics in Perinatology* 35(2):325–41.

Enns, Peter K., and Julianna Koch. 2013. "Public Opinion in the U.S. States: 1956 to 2010." *State Politics & Policy Quarterly* 13(3):349–72.

Esping-Andersen, Gøsta. 1990. *The Three Worlds of Welfare Capitalism.* Cambridge, MA: Polity.

Fenech, Giliane, and Gill Thomson. 2014. "'Tormented by Ghosts from Their Past': A Meta-Synthesis to Explore the Psychosocial Implications of a Traumatic Birth on Maternal Well-Being." *Midwifery* 30(2):185–93.

Fentiman, Linda C. 2017. *Blaming Mothers: American Law and the Risks to Children's Health.* New York: NYU Press.

Fisch, John M., Dennis English, Susan Pedaline, Kerri Brooks, and Hyagriv N. Simhan. 2009. "Labor Induction Process Improvement: A Patient Quality-of-Care Initiative." *Obstetrics & Gynecology* 113(4):797–803.

Fiske, Susan T., and Shelley E. Taylor. 2013. *Social Cognition: From Brains to Culture.* Thousand Oaks, CA: SAGE.

Flavin, Jeanne. 2009. *Our Bodies, Our Crimes: The Policing of Women's Reproduction in America.* New York: NYU Press.

Flavin, Jeanne and Lynn M. Paltrow. 2010. "Punishing Pregnant Drug-Using Women: Defying Law, Medicine, and Common Sense." *Journal of Addictive Diseases* 29(2):231–44.

Forssén, Annika S. K. 2012. "Lifelong Significance of Disempowering Experiences in Prenatal and Maternity Care: Interviews with Elderly Swedish Women." *Qualitative Health Research* 22(11):1535–46.

Frakes, Michael. 2012. "Defensive Medicine and Obstetric Practices." *Journal of Empirical Legal Studies* 9(3):457–81.

Freidson, Eliot. 1988. *Profession of Medicine: A Study of the Sociology of Applied Knowledge.* Chicago: University of Chicago Press.

Freidson, Eliot. 2006. *Professional Dominance: The Social Structure of Medical Care.* New Brunswick, NJ: Aldine.

Frisbie, W. Parker, Seung-Eun Song, Daniel A. Powers, and Julie A. Street. 2004. "The Increasing Racial Disparity in Infant Mortality: Respiratory Distress Syndrome and Other Causes." *Demography* 41(4):773–800.

Gage-Bouchard, Elizabeth A. 2017. "Culture, Styles of Institutional Interactions, and Inequalities in Healthcare Experiences." *Journal of Health and Social Behavior* 58(2):147–65.

Gengler, Amanda M. 2014. "'I Want You to Save My Kid!' Illness Management Strategies, Access, and Inequality at an Elite University Research Hospital." *Journal of Health and Social Behavior* 55(3):342–59.

Getahun, Darios, Daniel Strickland, Jean M. Lawrence, Michael J. Fassett, Corinna Koebnick, and Steven J. Jacobsen. 2009. "Racial and Ethnic Disparities in the Trends in Primary Cesarean Delivery Based on Indications." *AJOG* 201(4):422.e1–7.

Gifford, Deidre Spelliscy, Sally C. Morton, Mary Fiske, and Katherine Kahn. 1995. "A Meta-Analysis of Infant Outcomes after Breech Delivery." *Obstetrics & Gynecology* 85(6):1047–54.

Glantz, J. Christopher. 2005. "Elective Induction vs. Spontaneous Labor." *Journal of Reproductive Medicine* 50:235–40.

Goer, Henci. 1995. *Obstetric Myths Versus Research Realities: A Guide to the Medical Literature.* Westport, CT: Praeger.

Goer, Henci, and Amy Romano. 2012. *Optimal Care in Childbirth: The Case for a Physiologic Approach.* Seattle: Classic Day.

Goldberg, Holly. 2009. "Informed Decision Making in Maternity Care." *Journal of Perinatal Education* 18(1):32–40.

Goodwin, Michele. 2017. "Whole Woman's Health v. Hellerstedt: The Empirical Case against Trap Laws." *Medical Law Review* 25(2):340–51.

Gordon, Nancy P., David Walton, Eileen McAdam, Judy Derman, Gina Gallitero, and Lynda Garrett. 1999. "Effects of Providing Hospital-Based Doulas in Health Maintenance Organization Hospitals." *Obstetrics & Gynecology* 93(3):422–6.

Gossman, Ginger L., Jutta Joesch, and Koray Tanfer. 2007. "Trends in Maternal Request Cesarean Delivery from 1991 to 2004." *Obstetrics & Gynecology* 109(3):784–5.

Gould, Jeffrey B., Becky Davey, and Randall S. Stafford. 1989. "Socioeconomic Differences in Rates of Cesarean Section." *NEJM* 321(4):233–9.

Gourevitch, Rebecca A., Ateev Mehrotra, Grace Galvin, Melinda Karp, Avery Plough, and Neel T. Shah. 2017. "How Do Pregnant Women Use Quality Measures When Choosing Their Obstetric Provider?" *Birth* 44(2):120–7.

Graham, Ernest M., Scott M. Petersen, Dana K. Christo, and Harold E. Fox. 2006. "Intrapartum Electronic Fetal Heart Rate Monitoring and the Prevention of Perinatal Brain Injury." *Obstetrics & Gynecology* 108(6):656–66.

Grant, Rebecca. 2017. "Ethics of the Delivery Room: Who's in Control When You're Giving Birth?" *Independent.* Retrieved May 21, 2019 (www.independent.co.uk /news/long_reads/childbirth-delivery-room-ethics-doctor-patient-healthcare -a8085346.html).

Gray, Ron, Maria A. Quigley, C. Hockley, Jennifer J. Kurinczuk, Michael J. Goldacre, and Peter Brocklehurst. 2007. "Caesarean Delivery and Risk of Stillbirth in Subsequent Pregnancy: A Retrospective Cohort Study in an English Population." *BJOG* 114(3):264–70.

Greenfield, Rebecca. 2017. "Woman Forced into Violent Episiotomy Settles with Doctor." *Yahoo! News.* Retrieved May 21, 2019 (www.yahoo.com/news/woman-forced -into-violent-episiotomy-settles-with-doctor-182947205.html).

Gregory, Kimberly D., Lisa M. Korst, Patricia Cane, Lawrence D. Platt, and Katherine Kahn. 1999. "Vaginal Birth After Cesarean and Uterine Rupture Rates in California." *Obstetrics & Gynecology* 94(6):985–9.

Grol, Richard. 2001. "Successes and Failures in the Implementation of Evidence-Based Guidelines for Clinical Practice." *Medical Care* 39(8 Suppl 2):II46–54.

Guirguis-Blake, Janelle, George E. Fryer, Robert L. Phillips, Ronald Szabat, and Larry A. Green. 2006. "The US Medical Liability System: Evidence for Legislative Reform." *Annals of Family Medicine* 4(3):240–6.

Gurr, Barbara. 2011. "Complex Intersections: Reproductive Justice and Native American Women: Complex Intersections." *Sociology Compass* 5(8):721–35.

Guttmacher Institute. 2020. (www.guttmacher.org).

Hale, Ralph W. 2006. "Medical Professional Liability Revisited." *Obstetrics & Gynecology* 107(6):1224–5.

Handa, Victoria L., Joan L. Blomquist, Leise R. Knoepp, Kay A. Hoskey, Kelly C. McDermott, and Alvaro Muñoz. 2011. "Pelvic Floor Disorders 5–10 Years After Vaginal or Cesarean Childbirth." *Obstetrics and Gynecology* 118(4):777–84.

Handa, Victoria L., Toni A. Harris, and Donald R. Ostergard. 1996. "Protecting the Pelvic Floor: Obstetric Management to Prevent Incontinence and Pelvic Organ Prolapse." *Obstetrics & Gynecology* 88(3):470–8.

Hannah, Mary E., Walter J. Hannah, Sheila A. Hewson, Ellen D. Hodnett, Saroj Saigal, and Andrew R. Willan. 2000. "Planned Caesarean Section versus Planned Vaginal Birth for Breech Presentation at Term: A Randomised Multicentre Trial." *Lancet* 356(9239):1375–83.

Hansen, Anne Kirkeby, Kirsten Wisborg, Niels Uldbjerg, and Tine Brink Henriksen. 2008. "Risk of Respiratory Morbidity in Term Infants Delivered by Elective Caesarean Section." *BMJ* 336(7635):85–7.

Hartocollis, Anemona. 2014. "Mother Accuses Doctors of Forcing a C-Section and Files Suit." *New York Times*, May 16.

Heidari, Shirin. 2015. "Sexual Rights and Bodily Integrity as Human Rights." *Reproductive Health Matters* 23(46):1–6.

Heimer, Carol A. 1999. "Competing Institutions: Law, Medicine, and Family in Neonatal Intensive Care." *Law & Society Review* 33(1):17–66.

Henry J. Kaiser Family Foundation. 2017. "Health Care Expenditures per Capita by State of Residence." Retrieved March 20, 2019 (www.kff.org/other/state-indicator/health-spending-per-capita/).

Hensley, Erica, and Michelle Liu. 2019. "Delivering Justice: Why a Mississippi County Is Prosecuting Some Pregnant Women and New Moms." *Mississippi Today*. Retrieved June 19, 2019 (mississippitoday.org/2019/05/11/delivering-justice/).

Hernandez, Antonia. 1976. "Chicanas and the Issue of Involuntary Sterilization: Reforms Needed to Protect Informed Consent." *Chicano Law Review* 3:3–37.

Heyman, Bob, Andy Alaszewski, and Patrick Brown. 2013. "Probabilistic Thinking and Health Risks." *Health, Risk & Society* 15(1):1–11.

Hodnett, Ellen D., Simon Gates, G. Justus Hofmeyr, and Carol Sakala. 2013. "Continuous Support for Women during Childbirth." *The Cochrane Database of Systematic Reviews* 7:CD003766.

Hoffman, Matthew K., Anthony Sciscione, Maha Srinivasana, D. Paul Shackelford, and Lamar Ekbladh. 2005. "Uterine Rupture in Patients with a Prior Cesarean Delivery: The Impact of Cervical Ripening." *Obstetrical & Gynecological Survey* 60(1):22–3.

Hopkins, Kristine. 2000. "Are Brazilian Women Really Choosing to Deliver by Cesarean?" *Social Science & Medicine* 51(5):725–40.

Hubbard, F. Patrick. 2006. "The Nature and Impact of the Tort Reform Movement." *Hofstra Law Review* 35:437–538.

Hyman, David A., and Charles Silver. 2006. "Medical Malpractice Litigation and Tort Reform: It's the Incentives, Stupid." *Vanderbilt Law Review* 59:1086–135.

ImprovingBirth.org. 2014. "Trauma, Traumatic Birth, and Recovery." Retrieved May 17, 2019 (https://improvingbirth.org/2014/07/trauma/).

Janssen, Patricia A., Lee Saxell, Lesley Page, Michael C. Klein, Robert M. Liston, and Shoo K. Lee. 2009. "Outcomes of Planned Home Birth with Registered Midwife versus Planned Hospital Birth with Midwife or Physician." *Canadian Medical Association Journal* 181(6–7):377–83.

Jarvis, Jan. 2010. "More Dallas-Fort Worth Hospitals Saying No to Pregnant Women Who Want to Induce." *Fort Worth Star-Telegram*, March 6. Retrieved May 21, 2019 (www.star-telegram.com/entertainment/living/family/moms/article3825075.html).

Jena, Anupam B., Amitabh Chandra, Darius Lakdawalla, and Seth Seabury. 2012. "Outcomes of Medical Malpractice Litigation against US Physicians." *Archives of Internal Medicine* 172(11):892–4.

Jerman, Jenna, Lori Frohwirth, Megan L. Kavanaugh, and Nakeisha Blades. 2017. "Barriers to Abortion Care and Their Consequences for Patients Traveling for Services: Qualitative Findings from Two States." *Perspectives on Sexual and Reproductive Health* 49(2):95–102.

Jerman, Jenna, Rachel K. Jones, and Tsuyoshi Onda. 2016. *Characteristics of U.S. Abortion Patients in 2014 and Changes since 2008*. New York: Guttmacher Institute.

Johnson, Sandra Lucille, Eve Blair, and Fiona J. Stanley. 2011. "Obstetric Malpractice Litigation and Cerebral Palsy in Term Infants." *Journal of Forensic and Legal Medicine* 18(3):97–100.

Joint Commission. 2020. "Perinatal Care Measures." *The Joint Commission*. Retrieved May 21, 2020 (www.jointcommission.org/measurement/measures/perinatal-care/).

Jones, Bonnie Scott, and Tracy A. Weitz. 2009. "Legal Barriers to Second-Trimester Abortion Provision and Public Health Consequences." *American Journal of Public Health* 99(4):623–30.

Jones, Rachel K., Meghan Ingerick, and Jenna Jerman. 2018. "Differences in Abortion Service Delivery in Hostile, Middle-Ground, and Supportive States in 2014." *Women's Health Issues* 28(3):212–8.

Jones, Rachel K., Ushma D. Upadhyay, and Tracy A. Weitz. 2013. "At What Cost? Payment for Abortion Care by U.S. Women." *Women's Health Issues* 23(3):e173–8.

Jordan, Brigitte, and Robbie Davis-Floyd. 1992. *Birth in Four Cultures: A Crosscultural Investigation of Childbirth in Yucatan, Holland, Sweden, and the United States*. 4th edition. Prospect Heights, IL: Waveland Press.

Kelly, Carly N., and Michelle M. Mello. 2005. "Are Medical Malpractice Damages Caps Constitutional? An Overview of State Litigation." *Journal of Law, Medicine & Ethics* 33(3):515–34.

Kennare, Robyn, Graeme Tucker, Adrian Heard, and Annabelle Chan. 2007. "Risks of Adverse Outcomes in the Next Birth after a First Cesarean Delivery." *Obstetrics & Gynecology* 270–6.

King, Tekoa L. 2010. "First Do No Harm: The Case for Vaginal Birth After Cesarean." *Journal of Midwifery & Women's Health* 55(3):202–5.

Kirmeyer, Sharon, Joyce A. Martin, Michelle J. K. Osterman, and Ruth A. Shepherd. 2009. *Born a Bit Too Early: Recent Trends in Late Preterm Births*. NCHS data brief 24. Hyattsville, MD: National Center for Health Statistics.

Kitzinger, Sheila. 2005. *The Politics of Birth*. London: Elsevier Butterworth Heinemann.

———. 2006. *Birth Crisis*. New York: Routledge.

———. 2012. "Rediscovering the Social Model of Childbirth." *Birth* 39(4):301–4.

Klassen, Pamela E. 2001. *Blessed Events: Religion and Home Birth in America*. Princeton, NJ: Princeton University Press.

Klein, Michael C. 1988. "Episiotomy and the Second Stage of Labour." *Canadian Family Physician* 34:2019–25.

Klein, Michael C. 1995. "Studying Episiotomy: When Beliefs Conflict with Science." *Journal of Family Practice* 41(5):483–8.

Klein, Michael C., Robert J. Gauthier, James M. Robbins, Janusz Kaczorowski, Sally H. Jorgensen, Eliane D. Franco, Barbara Johnson, Kathy Waghorn, Morrie M. Gelfand, Melvin S. Guralnick, Gary W. Luskey, and Arvind K. Joshi. 1994. "Relationship of Episiotomy to Perineal Trauma and Morbidity, Sexual Dysfunction, and Pelvic Floor Relaxation." *AJOG* 171(3):591–8.

Knight, Marian, Jennifer J. Kurinczuk, Patsy Spark, and Peter Brocklehurst. 2008. "Cesarean Delivery and Peripartum Hysterectomy." *Obstetrics & Gynecology* 111(1):97–105.

Kukura, Elizabeth. 2017a. "Birth Conflicts: Leveraging State Power to Coerce Health Care Decision-Making." *University of Baltimore Law Review* 47:247–94.

———. 2017b. "Obstetric Violence." *Georgetown Law Journal* 106:721–802.

Laine, Christine, Darren B. Taichman, and Michael A. LaCombe. 2015. "On Being a Doctor: Shining a Light on the Dark Side." *Annals of Internal Medicine* 163(4):320.

LaLumia, Sara, James M. Sallee, and Nicholas Turner. 2015. "New Evidence on Taxes and the Timing of Birth." *American Economic Journal* 7(2):258–93.

Lane, Karen. 1995. "The Medical Model of the Body as a Site of Risk: Case Study of Childbirth." In *Medicine, Health and Risk: Sociological Approaches*, edited by Jonathan Gabe, 53–72. Oxford: Blackwell.

Latendresse, Gwen, Patricia Aikins Murphy, and Judith T. Fullerton. 2005. "A Description of the Management and Outcomes of Vaginal Birth after Cesarean Birth in the Homebirth Setting." *Journal of Midwifery & Women's Health* 50(5):386–91.

Latour, Bruno, Steve Woolgar, and Jonas Salk. 1986. *Laboratory Life: The Construction of Scientific Facts*. 2nd edition. Princeton, NJ: Princeton University Press.

LaVeist, Thomas A. 2000. "On the Study of Race, Racism, and Health: A Shift from Description to Explanation." *International Journal of Health Services* 30(1):217–9.

LaVeist, Thomas A., Nicole C. Rolley, and Chamberlain Diala. 2003. "Prevalence and Patterns of Discrimination among U.S. Health Care Consumers." *International Journal of Health Services* 33(2):331–44.

Lazarus, Ellen S. 1994. "What Do Women Want? Issues of Choice, Control, and Class in Pregnancy and Childbirth." *Medical Anthropology Quarterly* 8(1):25–46.

Leape, Lucian L., Troyen A. Brennan, Nan Laird, Ann G. Lawthers, A. Russell Localio, Benjamin A. Barnes, Liesi Hebert, Joseph P. Newhouse, Paul C. Weiler, and Howard Hiatt. 1991. "The Nature of Adverse Events in Hospitalized Patients: Results of the Harvard Medical Practice Study II." *NEJM* 324(6):377–84.

Leavitt, Judith Walzer. 1988. *Brought to Bed: Childbearing in America, 1750–1950.* New York: Oxford University Press.

Lee, Han-Duck, Mark J. Browne, and Joan T. Schmit. 1994. "How Does Joint and Several Tort Reform Affect the Rate of Tort Filings? Evidence from the State Courts." *Journal of Risk and Insurance* 61(2):295–316.

Leonardi, Paul, Bonnie Nardi, and Jannis Kallinikos. 2013. *Materiality and Organizing: Social Interaction in a Technological World.* Oxford: Oxford University Press.

Leonhardt, David. 2006. "To-Do List: Wrap Gifts. Have Baby." *New York Times,* December 20. Retrieved May 21, 2020 (www.nytimes.com/2006/12/20/business/20leonhardt.html).

Lewis-Beck, Michael S., Alan Bryman, and Tim Futing Liao. 2004. "Informant Interviewing" in *SAGE Encyclopedia of Social Science Research Methods.* Thousand Oaks, CA: SAGE.

Link, Bruce G., and Jo Phelan. 1995. "Social Conditions as Fundamental Causes of Disease." *Journal of Health and Social Behavior* (Extra):80–94.

Link, Bruce G., Jo C. Phelan, Richard Miech, and Emily Leckman Westin. 2008. "The Resources that Matter: Fundamental Social Causes of Health Disparities and the Challenge of Intelligence." *Journal of Health and Social Behavior* 49(1):72–91.

Lippman, Abby. 1999. "Choice as a Risk to Women's Health." *Health, Risk & Society* 1(3):281–91.

Localio, A. Russell, Ann G. Lawthers, Troyen A. Brennan, Nan M. Laird, Liesi E. Hebert, Lynn M. Peterson, Joseph P. Newhouse, Paul C. Weiler, and Howard H. Hiatt. 1991. "Relation between Malpractice Claims and Adverse Events Due to Negligence." *NEJM* 325(4):245–51.

Loudon, Irvine. 1993. *Death in Childbirth: An International Study of Maternal Care and Maternal Mortality 1800–1950.* New York: Clarendon Press.

Loudon, Irvine. 2000. *The Tragedy of Childbed Fever.* New York: Oxford University Press.

Lukacz, Emily S., Jean M. Lawrence, Richard Contreras, Charles W. Nager, and Karl M. Luber. 2006. "Parity, Mode of Delivery, and Pelvic Floor Disorders." *Obstetrics & Gynecology* 107(6):1253–60.

Luke, Barbara, Michael Cooperstock, Eugene R. Declercq, Joann R. Petrini, Irvin Emanuel, Nancy E. Reichman, Isabelle Horon, and Robert Schoen. 2006. *Review of the National Center for Health Statistics Natality Statistics Program*. Atlanta: Centers for Disease Control.

Luker, Kristin. 1984. *Abortion and the Politics of Motherhood*. Berkeley: University of California Press.

Lumalcuri, James, and Ralph W. Hale. 2010. "Medical Liability: An Ongoing Nemesis." *Obstetrics & Gynecology* 115(2 part 1):223–8.

Luna, Zakiya, and Kristin Luker. 2013. "Reproductive Justice." *Annual Review of Law and Social Science* 9(1):327–52.

Luthy, David A., Judith A. Malmgren, and Rosalee W. Zingheim. 2004. "Cesarean Delivery after Elective Induction in Nulliparous Women: The Physician Effect." *AJOG* 191(5):1511–15.

Lydon-Rochelle, Mona, Victoria L. Holt, Thomas R. Easterling, and Diane P. Martin. 2001. "Risk of Uterine Rupture during Labor among Women with a Prior Cesarean Delivery." *NEJM* 345:3–8.

Lyell, Deirdre J., Aaron B. Caughey, Emily Hu, and Kay Daniels. 2005. "Peritoneal Closure at Primary Cesarean Delivery and Adhesions." *Obstetrics & Gynecology* 106(2):275–80.

MacCoun, Robert J. 1996. "Differential Treatment of Corporate Defendants by Juries: An Examination of the Deep-Pocket Hypothesis." *Law & Society Review* 30:121–62.

MacDorman, Marian F., Eugene Declercq, T. J. Mathews, and Naomi Stotland. 2012. "Trends and Characteristics of Home Vaginal Birth After Cesarean Delivery in the United States and Selected States." *Obstetrics & Gynecology* 119(4):737–44.

MacDorman, Marian F., Eugene Declercq, Fay Menacker, and Michael H. Malloy. 2006. "Infant and Neonatal Mortality for Primary Cesarean and Vaginal Births to Women with 'No Indicated Risk,' United States, 1998–2001 Birth Cohorts." *Birth* 33(3):175–82.

Main, Elliott K., Christy L. McCain, Christine H. Morton, Susan Holtby, and Elizabeth S. Lawton. 2015. "Pregnancy-Related Mortality in California: Causes, Characteristics, and Improvement Opportunities." *Obstetrics & Gynecology* 125(4):938–47.

Makoha, F. W., H. M. Felimban, M. A. Fathuddien, F. Roomi, and T. Ghabra. 2004. "Multiple Cesarean Section Morbidity." *International Journal of Gynecology & Obstetrics* 87(3):227–32.

Malat, Jennifer. 2001. "Social Distance and Patients' Rating of Healthcare Providers." *Journal of Health and Social Behavior* 42(4):360–72.

Maller, Cecily Jane. 2015. "Understanding Health through Social Practices: Performance and Materiality in Everyday Life." *Sociology of Health & Illness* 37(1):52–66.

Mandler, Jean. 1984. *Stories, Scripts, and Scenes: Aspects of Schema Theory*. New York: Taylor & Francis.

Martin, Nina. 2014. "A Stillborn Child, a Charge of Murder and the Disputed Case Law on 'Fetal Harm.'" *ProPublica*. Retrieved May 16, 2019 (www.propublica.org/article/stillborn-child-charge-of-murder-and-disputed-case-law-on-fetal-harm).

Mayberry, Linda J., Donna Clemmens, and Anindya De. 2002. "Epidural Analgesia Side Effects, Co-Interventions, and Care of Women during Childbirth: A Systematic Review." *AJOG* 186(5 Suppl):S81–93.

Mayer, Susan E., and Ankur Sarin. 2005. "Some Mechanisms Linking Economic Inequality and Infant Mortality." *Social Science & Medicine* 60(3):439–55.

McClain-Freeney, Lisa. 2018. "Rinat Dray Decision Proves How Hard It Is for Women Subjected to Forced Surgeries to Get Justice." *National Advocates for Pregnant Women*. Retrieved May 20, 2019 (http://advocatesforpregnantwomen.org/blog /2018/04/rinat_dray_decision_proves_how.php).

McKendry, Rachael, and Tom Langford. 2001. "Legalized, Regulated, but Unfunded: Midwifery's Laborious Professionalization in Alberta, Canada, 1975–99." *Social Science & Medicine* 53(4):531–42.

McPhate, Christian. 2017. "To Hell with Baby New Year, Save Money with a Late December Birth." *Dallas Observer*, December 28. Retrieved May 21, 2020 (www.dallasobserver .com/news/expecting-mothers-seek-late-december-births-to-save-money-10203202).

Medoff, Marshall H. 2012. "State Abortion Politics and TRAP Abortion Laws." *Journal of Women, Politics & Policy* 33(3):239–62.

Mello, Michelle M., and Troyen A. Brennan. 2001. "Deterrence of Medical Errors: Theory and Evidence for Malpractice Reform." *Texas Law Review* 80:1595–638.

Mello, Michelle M., Amitabh Chandra, Atul A. Gawande, and David M. Studdert. 2010. "National Costs of the Medical Liability System." *Health Affairs* 29(9):1569–77.

Memon, Hafsa and Victoria L. Handa. 2012. "Pelvic Floor Disorders Following Vaginal or Cesarean Delivery." *Current Opinion in Obstetrics & Gynecology* 24(5):349–54.

Mercer, Brian M. 2005. "Induction of Labor in the Nulliparous Gravida with an Unfavorable Cervix." *Obstetrics & Gynecology* 105(4):688–9.

Metzler, Ian S., and John G. Meara. 2012. "Medical Liability Reform: Evidence for Legislative and Alternative Approaches." *Bulletin of the American College of Surgeons* 97(1):6–11.

Meyer, John W., and Brian Rowan. 1977. "Institutionalized Organizations: Formal Structure as Myth and Ceremony." *American Journal of Sociology* 83(2):340–63.

Michalec, Barret. 2012. "The Pursuit of Medical Knowledge and the Potential Consequences of the Hidden Curriculum." *Health* 16(3):267–81.

Michalec, Barret, and Frederic W. Hafferty. 2013. "Stunting Professionalism: The Potency and Durability of the Hidden Curriculum within Medical Education." *Social Theory & Health* 11(4):388–406.

Midwives Alliance North America. 2020. (https://mana.org/).

Miller, Ruth Austin. 2007. *The Limits of Bodily Integrity: Abortion, Adultery, and Rape Legislation in Comparative Perspective*. Burlington, VT: Ashgate.

Minkoff, Howard, and Lynn M. Paltrow. 2004. "Melissa Rowland and the Rights of Pregnant Women." *Obstetrics & Gynecology* 104(6):1234–6.

Mohide, Patrick T. 1987. "Randomised Comparison of Early versus Late Induction of Labour in Post-Term Pregnancy." *BMJ* 295(6594):388–9.

Molina, George, Thomas G. Weiser, Stuart R. Lipsitz, Micaela M. Esquivel, Tarsicio Uribe-Leitz, Tej Azad, Neel Shah, Katherine Semrau, William R. Berry, Atul A. Gawande, and Alex B. Haynes. 2015. "Relationship between Cesarean Delivery Rate and Maternal and Neonatal Mortality." *JAMA* 314(21):2263–70.

Moore, Alia, Sarah Ryan, and Carol Stamm. 2019. "Seeking Emergency Contraception in the United States: A Review of Access and Barriers." *Women & Health* 59(4):364–74.

Moore, Lisa E., and William F. Rayburn. 2006. "Elective Induction of Labor." *Clinical Obstetrics and Gynecology* 49(3):698–704.

Morales, Kelly J., Michael C. Gordon, and G. Wright Bates. 2007. "Postcesarean Delivery Adhesions Associated with Delayed Delivery of Infant." *AJOG* 196(5):461.e1–6.

Morris, Theresa. 2013. *Cut It Out: The C-Section Epidemic in America.* New York: NYU Press.

Morris, Theresa, Olivia Meredith, Mia Schulman, and Christine H. Morton. 2016. "Race, Insurance Status, and Nulliparous, Term, Singleton, Vertex Cesarean Indication: A Case Study of a New England Tertiary Hospital." *Women's Health Issues* 26(3):329–35.

Morris, Theresa and Joan H. Robinson. 2017. "Forced and Coerced Cesarean Sections in the United States." *Contexts* 16(2):24–9.

Morris, Theresa and Mia Schulman. 2014. "Race Inequality in Epidural Use and Regional Anesthesia Failure in Labor and Birth: An Examination of Women's Experience." *Sexual & Reproductive Healthcare* 5(4):188–94.

Morton, Heather. 2014. "Medical Liability/Malpractice Merit Affidavits and Expert Witnesses." *National Conference of State Legislatures.* Retrieved June 5, 2019 (www.ncsl.org/research/financial-services-and-commerce/medical-liability-malpractice-merit-affidavits-and-expert-witnesses.aspx).

Mozurkewich, Ellen L., and Eileen K. Hutton. 2000. "Elective Repeat Cesarean Delivery versus Trial of Labor: A Meta-Analysis of the Literature from 1989 to 1999." *AJOG* 183(5):1187–97.

Murphy, Andrew S. 2014. "A Survey of State Fetal Homicide Laws and Their Potential Applicability to Pregnant Women Who Harm Their Own Fetuses." *Indiana Law Journal* 89(2):847–83.

Murthy, Karna, William A. Grobman, Todd A. Lee, and Jane L. Holl. 2011. "Trends in Induction of Labor at Early-Term Gestation." *AJOG* 204(5):435.e1–6.

Mykhalovskiy, Eric and Lorna Weir. 2004. "The Problem of Evidence-Based Medicine: Directions for Social Science." *Social Science & Medicine* 59(5):1059–69.

Mythen, Gabe. 2008. "Sociology and the Art of Risk." *Sociology Compass* 2(1):299–316.

NARAL Pro-Choice America. n.d. "State Governments." (www.prochoiceamerica.org /laws-policy/state-government/).

Nash, Elizabeth. 2019. "A Surge in Bans on Abortion as Early as Six Weeks, Before Most People Know They Are Pregnant." *Guttmacher Institute.* Retrieved May 30, 2019 (www.guttmacher.org/article/2019/03/surge-bans-abortion-early-six-weeks-most-people-know-they-are-pregnant).

National Advocates for Pregnant Women (NAPW). 2020. (www.advocatesforpregnant women.org).

National Institutes of Health (NIH). 1981. "Cesarean Childbirth: An NIH Consensus Development Conference." *Clinical Pediatrics* 20(9):555–60.

Norsigian, Judy. 1992. "The Women's Health Movement in the United States." *Women's Global Network on Reproductive Rights Newsletter* (39):9–12.

North American Registry of Midwives. 2020. (http://narm.org/).

Nygaard, Ingrid. 2005. "Should Women Be Offered Elective Cesarean Section in the Hope of Preserving Pelvic Floor Function?" *International Urogynecology Journal* 16(4):253–4.

Osterman, Michelle J. K., and Joyce A. Martin. 2014. *Recent Declines in Induction of Labor by Gestational Age*. NCHS Data Brief 155. Hyattsville, MD: National Center for Health Statistics.

Owens, Deirdre Cooper. 2017. *Medical Bondage: Race, Gender, and the Origins of American Gynecology*. Athens: University of Georgia Press.

Paltrow, Lynn M. 2012. "Roe v Wade and the New Jane Crow: Reproductive Rights in the Age of Mass Incarceration." *American Journal of Public Health* 103(1):17–21.

Paltrow, Lynn M., and Jeanne Flavin. 2013. "Arrests of and Forced Interventions on Pregnant Women in the United States, 1973–2005: Implications for Women's Legal Status and Public Health." *Journal of Health Politics, Policy and Law* 38(2):299–343.

Parer, Julian T. 1997. "Electronic Fetal Heart Rate Monitoring: Research Guidelines for Interpretation." *Journal of Obstetric, Gynecologic & Neonatal Nursing* 26(6):635–40.

Parer, Julian T., Tomoaki Ikeda, and Tekoa L. King. 2009. "The 2008 National Institute of Child Health and Human Development Report on Fetal Heart Rate Monitoring." *Obstetrics & Gynecology* 114(1):136–8.

Parsons, Bob. 2014. "Joan Rivers—Go Daddy Girl." YouTube video, 1:56. Retrieved May 21, 2020 (www.youtube.com/watch?v=rZ5P1jOTuzI).

Paul, Kathleen, Doris Boutain, Lisa Manhart, and Jane Hitti. 2008. "Racial Disparity in Bacterial Vaginosis: The Role of Socioeconomic Status, Psychosocial Stress, and Neighborhood Characteristics, and Possible Implications for Preterm Birth." *Social Science & Medicine* 67(5):824–33.

Pérez D'Gregorio, Rogelio. 2010. "Obstetric Violence: A New Legal Term Introduced in Venezuela." *International Journal of Gynaecology and Obstetrics* 111(3):201–2.

Peters, Philip G. 2009. "Twenty Years of Evidence on the Outcomes of Malpractice Claims." *Clinical Orthopaedics and Related Research* 467(2):352–7.

Petrakaki, Dimitra, Ela Klecun, and Tony Cornford. 2016. "Changes in Healthcare Professional Work Afforded by Technology: The Introduction of a National Electronic Patient Record in an English Hospital." *Organization* 23(2):206–26.

Pinch, Trevor. 2008. "Technology and Institutions: Living in a Material World." *Theory and Society* 37(5):461–83.

Plough, Avery C., Grace Galvin, Zhonghe Li, Stuart R. Lipsitz, Shehnaz Alidina, Natalie J. Henrich, Lisa R. Hirschhorn, William R. Berry, Atul A. Gawande, Doris Peter, Rory McDonald, Donna L. Caldwell, Janet H. Muri, Debra Bingham, Aaron B.

Caughey, Eugene R. Declercq, and Neel T. Shah. 2017. "Relationship between Labor and Delivery Unit Management Practices and Maternal Outcomes." *Obstetrics & Gynecology* 130(2):358.

Politi, Salvatore, Laura D'Emidio, Pietro Cignini, Maurizio Giorlandino, and Claudio Giorlandino. 2010. "Shoulder Dystocia: An Evidence-Based Approach." *Journal of Prenatal Medicine* 4(3):35–42.

Powell, Walter W., and Jeannette A. Colyvas. 2008. "Microfoundations of Institutional Theory." In *SAGE Handbook of Organizational Institutionalism*, edited by R. Greenwood, C. Oliver, R. Suddaby, and K. Sahlin-Andersson, 276–98. Thousand Oaks, CA: SAGE.

Powell, Walter W., and Paul J. DiMaggio. 1991. *The New Institutionalism in Organizational Analysis*. Chicago: University of Chicago Press.

Power, Michael. 2007. *Organized Uncertainty: Designing a World of Risk Management*. Oxford: Oxford University Press.

Pratt, Lisa. 2013. "Access to Vaginal Birth after Cesarean: Restrictive Policies and the Chilling of Women's Medical Rights during Childbirth." *William & Mary Journal of Women and the Law* 20:105–22.

Rabin, Robert L. 1980. "The Historical Development of the Fault Principle: A Reinterpretation." *Georgia Law Review* 15:925–62.

Ransom, Scott B., Mitchell P. Dombrowski, Raeann Shephard, and Michael Leonardi. 1996. "The Economic Cost of the Medical-Legal Tort System." *AJOG* 174(6):1903–9.

Raudenbush, Stephen W., and Anthony S. Byrk. 2002. *Hierarchical Linear Models: Applications and Data Analysis Methods*. Thousand Oaks, CA: SAGE.

Reingold, Rebecca B., and Lawrence O. Gostin. 2016. "Women's Health and Abortion Rights: Whole Woman's Health v Hellerstedt." *JAMA* 316(9):925–6.

Reyes, Jessica Wolpaw, and Rene Reyes. 2012. "The Effects of Malpractice Liability on Obstetrics and Gynecology: Taking the Measure of a Crisis." *New England Law Review* 47:315–50.

Roberts, Dorothy E. 1997. *Killing the Black Body: Race, Reproduction, and the Meaning of Liberty*. New York: Pantheon Books.

Rohlinger, Deana. 2002. "Framing the Abortion Debate: Organizational Resources, Media Strategies, and Movement-Countermovement Dynamics." *Sociological Quarterly* 43(4):479–507.

Romney, Mona L., and H. Gordon. 1981. "Is Your Enema Really Necessary?" *BMJ* 282(6272):1269–71.

Romney, Mona L. 1980. "Predelivery Shaving: An Unjustified Assault?" *Journal of Obstetrics and Gynaecology* 1(1):33–5.

Rooks, Judith P. 1999. "The Midwifery Model of Care." *Journal of Nurse-Midwifery* 44(4):370–4.

Rosenstein, Melissa, Laura Norrell, Anna Altshuler, William Grobman, Anjali Kaimal, and Miriam Kuppermann. 2019. "Faced with a TOLAC Ban, Do Women Switch to a Different Hospital to Attempt VBAC?" *AJOG* 220(1).

Ross, Loretta and Rickie Solinger. 2017. *Reproductive Justice: An Introduction*. Oakland: University of California Press.

Rossi, A. C., and Federico Prefumo. 2015. "Pregnancy Outcomes of Induced Labor in Women with Previous Cesarean Section: A Systematic Review and Meta-Analysis." *Archives of Gynecology and Obstetrics* 291(2):273–80.

Rossi, A. Cristina, and Vincenzo D'Addario. 2008. "Maternal Morbidity Following a Trial of Labor after Cesarean Section vs Elective Repeat Cesarean Delivery: A Systematic Review with Meta-analysis." *AJOG* 199(3):224–31.

Roth, Louise Marie, and Megan M. Henley. 2012. "Unequal Motherhood: Racial-Ethnic and Socioeconomic Disparities in Cesarean Sections in the United States." *Social Problems* 59(2):207–27.

Rothman, Barbara Katz. 1982. *In Labor: Women and Power in the Birthplace*. New York: W. W. Norton.

Rothman, Barbara Katz. 2000. *Recreating Motherhood*. 2nd edition. New Brunswick, NJ: Rutgers University Press.

Rothman, Barbara Katz. 2014. "Pregnancy, Birth and Risk: An Introduction." *Health, Risk & Society* 16(1):1–6.

Sable, Marjorie R. 1982. "The Hyde Amendment: Its Impact on Low Income Women with Unwanted Pregnancies." *Journal of Sociology and Social Welfare* 9(3):475–84.

Samuels, Sue. 1991. "Informed Consent—The Angela Carder Case." *International Journal of Childbirth Education* 6(3):19–20.

Scamell, Mandie. 2014. "Childbirth Within the Risk Society." *Sociology Compass* 8(7):917–28.

Scamell, Mandie, and Andy Alaszewski. 2012. "Fateful Moments and the Categorisation of Risk: Midwifery Practice and the Ever-Narrowing Window of Normality during Childbirth." *Health, Risk & Society* 14(2):207–21.

Schiermer, Bjørn. 2016. "Fetishes and Factishes: Durkheim and Latour." *British Journal of Sociology* 67(3):497–515.

Schiller, Rebecca. 2015. "Terrible Doctors Are Uploading Selfies Taken Next to Women's Vaginas During Childbirth." *Vice*. Retrieved May 17, 2019 (www.vice.com/en_us/article/wd7nmb/doctors-taking-selfies-of-women-post-labour-shows).

Scott, Rosamund. 2002. *Rights, Duties and the Body: Law and Ethics of the Maternal-Fetal Conflict*. Oxford: Hart.

Scott, W. Richard, Martin Ruef, Peter J. Mendel, and Carol A. Caronna. 2000. *Institutional Change and Healthcare Organizations: From Professional Dominance to Managed Care*. Chicago: University of Chicago Press.

Shaw, Jessica. 2013. "Full-Spectrum Reproductive Justice: The Affinity of Abortion Rights and Birth Activism." *Studies in Social Justice* 7(1):143–59.

Shaw, Jessica. 2013. "The Medicalization of Birth and Midwifery as Resistance." *Health Care for Women International* 34(6):522–36.

Shim, Janet K. 2010. "Cultural Health Capital: A Theoretical Approach to Understanding Health Care Interactions and the Dynamics of Unequal Treatment." *Journal of Health and Social Behavior* 51(1):1–15.

Shwayder, James M. 2010. "Waiting for the Tide to Change: Reducing Risk in the Turbulent Sea of Liability." *Obstetrics & Gynecology* 116(1):8–15.

Simonds, Wendy, Barbara Katz Rothman, and Bari Meltzer Norman. 2007. *Laboring on: Birth in Transition in the United States.* New York: Taylor & Francis.

Simpson, Kathleen Rice. 2010. "Reconsideration of the Costs of Convenience: Quality, Operational, and Fiscal Strategies to Minimize Elective Labor Induction." *Journal of Perinatal Nursing* 24(1):43–52.

Simpson, Kathleen Rice and Kathleen E. Thorman. 2005. "Obstetric 'Conveniences': Elective Induction of Labor, Cesarean Birth on Demand, and Other Potentially Unnecessary Interventions." *Journal of Perinatal Nursing* 19(2):134–44.

Smith, Gordon C. S., Angela M. Wood, Jill P. Pell, and Richard Dobbie. 2006. "First Cesarean Birth and Subsequent Fertility." *Fertility and Sterility* 85(1):90–5.

Smith, William J., Tania A. Celis, and Bruce M. Bird. 2015. "Assessing the Impact of Medical Malpractice Awards, Tort Reform, and Investment Returns upon Medical Malpractice Insurance Premiums." *Journal of Business & Economics Research* 13(4):175.

Spong, Catherine Y., Mark B. Landon, Sharon Gilbert, Dwight J. Rouse, Kenneth J. Leveno, Michael W. Varner, Atef H. Moawad, Hyagriv N. Simhan, Margaret Harper, Ronald J. Wapner, Yoram Sorokin, Menachem Miodovnik, Marshall Carpenter, Alan M. Peaceman, Mary J. O'Sullivan, Baha M. Sibai, Oded Langer, John M. Thorp, Susan M. Ramin, and Brian M. Mercer. 2007. "Risk of Uterine Rupture and Adverse Perinatal Outcome at Term after Cesarean Delivery." *Obstetrics & Gynecology* 110(4):801–7.

Spong, Catherine Y., Brian M. Mercer, Mary D'Alton, Sarah Kilpatrick, Sean Blackwell, and George Saade. 2011. "Timing of Indicated Late-Preterm and Early-Term Birth." *Obstetrics & Gynecology* 323–33.

Starr, Paul. 2017. *The Social Transformation of American Medicine: The Rise of a Sovereign Profession and the Making of a Vast Industry.* 2nd edition. New York: Basic Books.

Stohl, Hindi E. 2017. "When Consent Does Not Help: Challenges to Women's Access to a Vaginal Birth After Cesarean Section and the Limitations of the Informed Consent Doctrine." *American Journal of Law & Medicine* 43(4):388–425.

Strasser, Mark. 1999. "A Jurisprudence in Disarray: On Battery, Wrongful Living, and the Right to Bodily Integrity." *San Diego Law Review* 36:997–1042.

Strauss, Claudia. 1997. *A Cognitive Theory of Cultural Meaning.* Cambridge: Cambridge University Press.

Swidler, Ann. 1986. "Culture in Action: Symbols and Strategies." *American Sociological Review* 51(2):273–86.

Sze, Eddie H. M., Gordon B. Sherard, and Jeanette M. Dolezal. 2002. "Pregnancy, Labor, Delivery, and Pelvic Organ Prolapse." *Obstetrics & Gynecology* 100(5, part 1):981–6.

Szymczak, Julia E., and Charles L. Bosk. 2012. "Training for Efficiency: Work, Time, and Systems-Based Practice in Medical Residency." *Journal of Health and Social Behavior* 53(3):344–58.

Tavory, Iddo, and Stefan Timmermans. 2014. *Abductive Analysis: Theorizing Qualitative Research*. Chicago: University of Chicago Press.

Thebault, Reis. 2019. "This State's Abortion Ban 'Smacks of Defiance,'" Says Federal Judge Who Shot Down Earlier Attempt.'" *Washington Post*, May 22, 2019.

Thornton, Patricia H. 2012. *The Institutional Logics Perspective: A New Approach to Culture, Structure and Process*. Oxford: Oxford University Press.

Thornton, Terry E., and Lynn M. Paltrow. 1991. "The Rights of Pregnant Patients: Carder Case Brings Bold Policy Initiatives." *HealthSpan* 8(5). (www.advocatesfor pregnantwomen.org/articles/angela.htm).

Tillett, Jackie. 2005. "Obstetric Rituals: Is Practice Supported by Evidence?" *Journal of Perinatal Nursing* 19(2):91–3.

Timmermans, Stefan, and Emily S. Kolker. 2004. "Evidence-Based Medicine and the Reconfiguration of Medical Knowledge." *Journal of Health and Social Behavior* 45:177–93.

Timmermans, Stefan, and Hyeyoung Oh. 2010. "The Continued Social Transformation of the Medical Profession." *Journal of Health and Social Behavior* 51(1 Suppl): S94–106.

Tjaden, Patricia G. 1987. "Midwifery in Colorado: A Case Study in the Politics of Professionalization." *Qualitative Sociology* 10(1):29–45.

Tremblay, Marc-Adélard. 1957. "The Key Informant Technique: A Nonethnographic Application." *American Anthropologist* 59(4):688–701.

Truven Health Analytics. 2013. "The Cost of Having a Baby in the United States." Ann Arbor, MI: Truven Health Analytics.

Turner, Bryan S. 1987. *Medical Power and Social Knowledge*. Thousand Oaks, CA: SAGE.

Tversky, Amos, and Daniel Kahneman. 1992. "Advances in Prospect Theory: Cumulative Representation of Uncertainty." *Journal of Risk & Uncertainty* 5(4):297–323.

United Nations. 1948. "Universal Declaration of Human Rights." Retrieved May 22, 2019 (www.un.org/en/universal-declaration-human-rights/).

———. 1966. "International Covenant on Civil and Political Rights." Retrieved May 22, 2019 (www.ohchr.org/en/professionalinterest/pages/ccpr.aspx).

———. 1993. "Declaration on the Elimination of Violence against Women." Retrieved July 13, 2020 (www.ohchr.org/en/professionalinterest/pages/violenceagainstwomen .aspx).

United States Census Bureau. 2019. *Population and Housing Unit Estimates Datasets*. Retrieved June 19, 2019 (www.census.gov/programs-surveys/popest/data/data-sets .All.html).

US Bureau of Labor Statistics. 2020. "CPI Inflation Calculator." US Bureau of Labor Statistics. Retrieved May 22, 2018 (www.bls.gov/data/inflation_calculator.htm).

US Department of Health and Human Services (USDHHS). 2015. *National Practitioner Data Bank Public Use Data File (NPDB)*. Rockville, MD: USDHHS.

———. 2016. "Trends in Teen Pregnancy and Childbearing." *HHS.Gov*. Retrieved June 19, 2019 (www.hhs.gov/ash/oah/adolescent-development/reproductive-health-and -teen-pregnancy/teen-pregnancy-and-childbearing/trends/index.html).

US News and World Report. 2019a. "Where Does Mississippi Place in the U.S. News Best States Rankings?" Retrieved June 19, 2019 (www.usnews.com/news/best-states /mississippi).

———. 2019b. "Where Does Oregon Place in the U.S. News Best States Rankings?" Retrieved June 19, 2019 (www.usnews.com/news/best-states/oregon).

Vahratian, Anjel, Jun Zhang, James F. Troendle, Anthony C. Sciscione, and Matthew K. Hoffman. 2005. "Labor Progression and Risk of Cesarean Delivery in Electively Induced Nulliparas." *Obstetrics & Gynecology* 105(4):698–704.

Vaisey, Stephen. 2009. "Motivation and Justification: A Dual-Process Model of Culture in Action." *American Journal of Sociology* 114(6):1675–715.

Vidmar, Neil. 1995. *Medical Malpractice and the American Jury: Confronting the Myths about Jury Incompetence, Deep Pockets, and Outrageous Damage Awards.* Ann Arbor: University of Michigan Press.

Vrouenraets, Francis P., Frans J. Roumen, Cary J. Dehing, Eline S. van den Akker, Maureen J. Aarts, and Esther J. Scheve. 2005. "Bishop Score and Risk of Cesarean Delivery after Induction of Labor in Nulliparous Women." *Obstetrics & Gynecology* 105(4):690–7.

Wagner, Marsden. 2008. *Born in the USA: How a Broken Maternity System Must Be Fixed to Put Women and Children First.* Berkeley: University of California Press.

Warlick, Diane Trace. 1996. "Not Too Late to Sue." *Journal of Nursing* 96(2):56–7.

Warner, Kenneth E. 1978. "Effects of Hospital Cost Containment on the Development and Use of Medical Technology." *The Milbank Memorial Fund Quarterly* 56(2):187–211.

Waters, Jessica L. 2011. "In Whose Best Interest—New Jersey Division of Youth and Family Services v. V.M. and B.G. and the Next Wave of Court-Controlled Pregnancies." *Harvard Journal of Law & Gender* 34:81–112.

Weaver, Jane and Julia Magill-Cuerden. 2013. "'Too Posh to Push': The Rise and Rise of a Catchphrase." *Birth* 40(4):264–71.

Weick, Karl E. 1995. *Sensemaking in Organizations.* Thousand Oaks, CA: SAGE.

Williams, L. Susan. 2002. "Trying on Gender, Gender Regimes, and the Process of Becoming Women." *Gender & Society* 16(1):29–52.

Wing, Deborah A. 2000. "Elective Induction of Labor in the USA." *Current Opinion in Obstetrics & Gynecology* 12(6):457–462.

Wing, Deborah A., Karla Lovett, and Richard H. Paul. 1998. "Disruption of Prior Uterine Incision Following Misoprostol for Labor Induction in Women with Previous Cesarean Delivery." *Obstetrics & Gynecology* 91(5):828–30.

World Bank. 2019. "Maternal Mortality Ratio (Modeled Estimate, per 100,000 Live Births) | Data." Retrieved February 14, 2019. (https://data.worldbank.org/indicator /SH.STA.MMRT).

World Health Organization (WHO). 1985. "Appropriate Technology for Birth." *Lancet* 326(8452):436–7.

———. 2015. *The Prevention and Elimination of Disrespect and Abuse during Facility-Based Childbirth.* Geneva, Switzerland: World Health Organization.

WHO, UNICEF, UNFPA, The World Bank, and the United Nations Population Division. 2014. *Trends in Maternal Mortality, 1990 to 2013.* Geneva, Switzerland: World Health Organization.

Wyatt, MacGaffey, Michael D. Harris, Sylvia H. Williams, and David C. Driskell. 1993. *Astonishment & Power: The Eyes of Understanding.* Washington, DC: Smithsonian.

Yang, Y. Tony, Michelle M. Mello, S. V. Subramanian, and David M. Studdert. 2009. "Relationship between Malpractice Litigation Pressure and Rates of Cesarean Section and Vaginal Birth After Cesarean Section." *Medical Care* 47(2):234–42.

Yudkin, P. L., L. Wood, and C. W. G. Redman. 1987. "Risk of Unexplained Stillbirth at Different Gestational Ages." *Lancet* 329(8543):1192–4.

Zadrozny, Brandy. 2015. "New Mom Begged Doc: 'No, Don't Cut Me!'" *Daily Beast,* June 5.

LEGAL CASES

Best v. Taylor Mach. Works, 689 N.E.2d 1057 (Ill. 1997).

Cruzan v. Director, Missouri Dept. of Health, (88–1503) 497 U.S. 261 (1990).

Dray v. Staten Island University Hospital, 2016 NY Slip Op. 93011(U) (December 1, 2016).

Dray v. Staten Is. Univ. Hosp., 2018 NY Slip Op. 02314 (April 4, 2018).

Gonzales v. Carhart, 550 U.S. 124 (2007).

In Re A.C., 573 A.2d 1235 (1990).

In Re Baby Boy Doe, 632 N.E.2d 326, 198 Ill. Dec. 267, 260 Ill. App. 3d 392 (Ill. App. Ct. 1994).

Jackson Women's Health Org., et al. v. Currier, et al., No. 13–60599, 760 F.3d 448 (5th Cir. 2014).

New Jersey Division of Youth and Family Services v. V.M. and B.G. in the Matter of J.M.G., 408 N.J. Super. 222, 974 A.2d 448 (2008).

Pemberton v. Tallahassee Memorial Regional Center, 66 F. Supp. 2d 1247 (1999).

People v. Jorgensen, 2015 NY Slip Op. 07699 (October 22, 2015).

Planned Parenthood of Southeastern Pa. v. Casey, 505 U.S. 833 (1992).

Stenberg v. Carhart, 530 U.S. 914 (2000).

Stoners v. George Washington University Hospital, et al., Civil Action No. 88–0M33 (Sup. Ct. D.C. 1990).

LEGISLATION

18 U.S. Code § 1531

H.B. 1510, 133rd Leg. Sess. (Miss. 2018).

H.B. 519, Reg. Sess. (Miss. 2016).

Miss. Code Ann. § 11-7-13.

Miss. Code Ann. §§ 41-41-31 (Enacted 1991).

Miss. Code Ann. §§ 41-41-33, -35 (Enacted 1991; Last Amended 1996).

Miss. Code Ann. § 41-41-45 (Enacted 2007).

Miss. Code Ann. §§ 41-41-51, -53, -57 (Enacted 1986).

Miss. Code Ann. §§ 41-41-55 (Enacted 1986; Last Amended 2007).

Miss. Code Ann. §§ 41-41-71, -73 (Enacted 1997).

Miss. Code Ann. § 41-41-91 (Enacted 2002)

Miss. Code Ann. §§ 41-41-97, -99 (Enacted 2010).

Miss. Code Ann. §§ 41-41-133, -137, -141 (Enacted 2014).

Miss. Code Ann. §§ 41-41-151 to -163 (Enacted 2016).

Miss. Code Ann. § 41-75-1 (Enacted 1983; Amended 1996 and 2006).

Miss. Code Ann. § 41-75-1(e), (f) (Original Statute Enacted 1983; Relevant Provision Enacted 1991; Last Amended 2012)

Miss. Code Ann. § 41-75-17 (Enacted 1983).

Miss. Code Ann. § 41-75-29(2) (Enacted 1991).

Miss. Code Ann. § 97-3-3 (Enacted 1952; Last Amended 1997).

Miss. Code Ann. § 97-3-19.

Miss. Code Ann. § 97-3-37.

Miss. Code R. §15 301 044.

Or. Admin. R. § 137-084-0001, -0010, -0020.

Or. Admin. R. 410-130-0562.

Or. Rev. Stat. § 147.005 (Enacted 2003).

Or. Rev. Stat. § 164.365 (Enacted 1972; Amended 2003).

Or. Rev. Stat. § 435.252-.256 (Enacted 2007).

Or. Rev. Stat. § 743A.066.

SB 2113, Jan. 11, 2019.

SB 2426, Jan. 15, 2018.

SB 2518, Feb. 8, 2016.

SB 2577, Jan. 16, 2017.

SB 2797, Jan. 19, 2015.

INDEX

Page numbers in *italics* indicate figures and tables.

ABOUT THE AUTHOR

Louise Marie Roth is Professor in the School of Sociology at the University of Arizona and author of *Selling Women Short: Gender and Money on Wall Street* and *The Business of Birth: Malpractice and Maternity Care in the United States.* Her research examines how organizational cultures, policies, and responses to the law influence justice and quality of life for women in two primary areas: paid employment and reproduction. Her first book, *Selling Women Short* (2006), analyzed gender inequality on Wall Street, with a focus on the effects of performance-based pay.

- May be my methodological proclivities, but feel > qual data or a detailed ethnography could have been → conclusive.
- Highly specific to the unusual US context historically + their medical system - limits around contribution
- 7/10.